*High Definition
Compact Disc Recordings*

High Definition Compact Disc Recordings

Sound Quality Evaluations of Over 1,400 of the Most Technically Excellent Digital Recordings

by HOWARD FERSTLER

McFarland & Company, Inc., Publishers
Jefferson, North Carolina, and London

British Library Cataloguing-in-Publication data are available

Library of Congress Cataloguing-in-Publication Data

Ferstler, Howard, 1943–
   High definition compact disc recordings : sound quality evaluations of over 1,400 of the most technically excellent digital recordings / by Howard Ferstler.
     p. cm.
   Includes bibliographical references (p.) and index.
   ISBN 0-89950-913-4 (sewn softcover : 50# alk. paper) ∞
   1. Compact discs—Reviews. 2. Music—Discography. I. Title.
ML156.9.F47 1994
016.78026'6—dc20   94-17281
                                                                                                 CIP
                                                                                                 MN

©1994 Howard Ferstler. All rights reserved

Manufactured in the United States of America

McFarland & Company, Inc., Publishers
  Box 611, Jefferson, North Carolina 28640

Contents

Acknowledgments	vi
Introduction	1
An Explanation of the Ratings	
Review Criteria	3
Scoring	4
Categories and Companies	6
Availability	7
A Few Notes on Terminology	8
Additional Aids	9
The Recordings	11
Appendices	
A: Test and Sampler Recordings	197
B: Record-Review and Equipment Journals	202
C: A Short List of Outstanding Discs	207
D: Evaluation Hardware Used	211
E: Microphone Pickup Patterns	213
F: Microphone Placement	215
Bibliography	218
Index	223

Acknowledgments

I take full responsibility for any faux pas in this book. The more accurate information that is contained in the introductory sections is almost certainly the result of input from a number of people, particularly Roy Allison, Mike Silverton, Tom Tyson, and Fred Davis — all of whom offered sage advice and criticism aplenty. (Such advice is made even more valuable when one considers the very high quality of their sound systems.) I should also thank these people for pointing out a number of good compact discs to critique (especially Tom Tyson, who supplied me quite a few to audition) and must thank Ron Rumsey and Eddie Woodward for providing access to their rock music collections.

Thanks are also rendered to the staff at the Warren D. Allen Music Library at Florida State University for tirelessly searching out and delivering the bundles of cataloged classical and jazz compact discs I requested from their collection.

I also thank my wife for putting up with all the track switching, A/B manipulations, and schizophrenic listening habits I perfected while auditioning over 3,000 recordings on our two rather formidable stereo systems (see Appendix D).

Introduction

High-quality compact disc (CD) reviews done by music critics of renown are everyday things in our musically oriented society. Hi-fi magazines have them, newspapers have them, and of course, record-review journals have large numbers of them (see Appendix B). There are many good books that are packed with such reviews. One's local public or college library almost certainly has some of them, as well as bibliographic references that provide any number of other sources, particularly music journals.

The problem with typical digital-recording reviews is that the people who write them often fail to mention if the sound quality of the CD is bad, good, or even decent. They may spend paragraphs discussing the artistic merits (or lack thereof) of the recorded material and at the end of the review only briefly mention that the sound was "dated," "sumptuous," "anemic," or simply "good." In many cases, reviewers will not mention sound quality at all. In others, they may be so captivated by the artistic endeavors of the performers that they pronounce a CD as technically very good when the overall sound quality is substandard.

There may be any number of reasons for this. Some reviewers do not have sound systems good enough to discriminate between a decently engineered digital recording and one that is outstanding, or even between one that is decently engineered and another that is not particularly well done. Many reviewers have been music critics for a long time and have had their systems for an equally long time. A few are positively phobic about audio components (call them "technophobes" if you wish) and do not concern themselves with system quality as long as what they have is adequate to allow them to listen through the electromechanical fog and experience the "spirit" of the music. A number of artistically competent reviewers would be satisfied to do their review listening on a table radio. When they want the concert-hall experience, they go to a live performance.

There is nothing wrong with having a small, decent-quality sound system, but it strikes me as rather odd that critics who are doing record reviews for publication would work with poor equipment. This book is different, because I have not one, but two good systems with which to listen

Introduction

to what I am reviewing (see Appendix D). These annotations deal with only the *engineering quality,* not the artistic merits of the recordings.

It is important to remember that this is not a review list of the total number of good-sounding discs available. This listing, rather, provides a substantial sampling of unusually fine recordings by a variety of performing artists and composers. It gives the reader access to enough different musical types to build a modest collection of good performances that also reflect good engineering quality.

An Explanation of the Ratings

Review Criteria

Several criteria were considered when judging the recordings found in this listing. These include sound-stage width, depth, and envelopment; instrumental articulation and delineation; vocal and instrumental realism, including the proper positioning and sizing of soloists in relation to the suppporting ensemble; dynamic range, which can be important even when the music is not "bombastic"; and wide-band frequency response. The latter may not be of particular importance with small-scale works, but it certainly will be with larger-scale ones or organ or synthesizer recordings or presentations with substantial high-frequency content. In sum, these five criteria determine how realistic a recording sounds.

While a pop-music disc may earn a place in this book by judiciously conforming to only a couple of the above criteria, probably the most important standard for determining the excellence of a *classical* presentation will be the sound stage itself. A recording with a fitting sound stage should give the impression that the performers are in front of you at a live concert. None can fully achieve this, but good ones offer the semblance of a three-dimensional image. (This quality may be highlighted if the playback system has a good surround-sound processor and some outboard-mounted "ambience" speakers—accessories that I highly recommend.) One problem with looking for an impressive sound stage in all recordings is that few examples of any kind of popular music have one. Indeed, very few pop-music recording engineers aspire to creating a viable sound stage of any kind. In addition to aesthetic and philosophical motives, the clarity- and impact-enhancement techniques usually employed in making such recordings (especially of rock music) will not allow for that kind of effect.

Consequently, to include at least a reasonable number of pop discs on the list, the ratings of that material are less likely to depend on sound-stage realism than the other four criteria, especially instrumental articulation, vocal clarity, and dynamic impact. The last category in particular will be

An Explanation of the Ratings [4]

important with any heavy-metal rock recordings. A few such albums made the list primarily because of their ability to deliver punchy sound. However, if a disc is fuzzy and indistinct in imaging qualities, with a bloated, nebulous sound stage, no amount of dynamic impact, clarity, and tonal delineation will gain it a place on the list.

In some cases, jazz recordings may also be exempted from strict sound-stage realism requirements. Some jazz material is given expert "purist" engineering treatment when recorded and is therefore quite realistic in stereo perspective (see Appendix F for further data). However, many jazz recordings are the result of the same multimicrophone, heavily processed studio treatment as rock—minus most of the electronic and synthesizer pyrotechnics. Jazz recordings that are the result of purist techniques will ordinarily receive higher ratings than those given the standard pop-recording treatment at the studio.

Scoring

To aid readers, standard letter ratings of B, B+, A, and A+ will appear at the end of each review. No lower scores appear since this is a book of recordings to buy, not ones to avoid. Note that all reviews are of *compact discs*. No LP records were auditioned, nor were analog cassettes. If any of these works are also available as DCC tapes or MiniDiscs, I would expect their quality to equal that of the CD versions, although the MiniDisc may exhibit subtle imperfections.

Compact discs given a B rating have decent sound and in some respects may be near-demo grade. If performers interest you and they have a B-rated disc in the listing, you should not be disappointed in the sound quality. Most of the so-called well-recorded pop (including country and rock) discs on the market would probably achieve nothing better than a B rating, and the majority fall short of this. *None* of the classical discs in the review got a score as low as a B. The criteria for such music were a bit stiffer than for pop material.

Discs given a B+ are similar in quality to the B-rated discs but have fewer flaws and should offer near-total satisfaction to all but the most equipment-jaded, pop-music–loving guests you invite to hear your playback system. Most of the really good pop recordings are in this category. Very few rated better than a B+. The majority of the superior pop CDs on the list are fully digital (that is, they were made with digital recorders rather than old-style analog models), while the lesser-quality recordings were often made from analog masters. Important exceptions to this rule exist, however. Some of the classical discs also rated B+ scores.

Compact discs given an A rating are outstanding and will clearly show

[5] An Explanation of the Ratings

the difference between a good system and a great one, particularly in such important areas as the realism of the stereo sound stage, deep bass reproduction (at least on material that requires deep bass), and instrumental delineation. A fair number of classical recordings produced with any degree of competence within the last ten years will have achieved at least an A rating, but only a few of the rock albums will. Quite a number of jazz releases also scored this high, and even one or two country-western (C&W) discs made the grade.

Compact discs given an A+ are exceptional, demonstration-grade items—the kind of material you should take to a hi-fi shop to evaluate speakers with or play at home when a serious and knowledgeable audio enthusiast shows up to critique your stereo. Assuming the limitations of the small-room environments in which we must listen to recorded music, sound-stage realism will be a salient feature with classical discs awarded an A+. Note that while not every one of the few rock or jazz albums awarded this score will have an absolutely realistic sound stage, they will all be standouts in clarity, impact, and other attention-getting qualities that are usually important to critical pop-music listeners.

In some cases, a disc's letter score will be preceded by a *Qualified* notation, indicating that it has a problem that may impact the standard rating. Its importance may depend on the caliber of the playback system. The written commentary will explain why the qualification has been attached.

It is impossible for even highly qualified listeners to be consistently robotlike in their evaluations. Consequently, the perceived differences between a B+ and an A may be partially influenced by the mental state of the reviewer and his consultants at the audition. This is unavoidable. These discs were reviewed (and often rereviewed) over a rather lengthy period, and attitudes can change from optimistic to pessimistic and back again over a time span of days or weeks. Hopefully, the "mental states" that existed during the listening sessions will have been the result of the intrinsic quality of the recordings themselves. To clarify some preliminary impressions, problematic discs will in many cases have received a number of listening sessions on more than one sound system and given additional evaluations by a number of individuals.

It should also be pointed out that even golden-eared reviewers might award close or equal letter scores to two recordings that have dissimilar technical virtues. A disc that is merely good in deep bass performance but exceptional in sound staging may earn the same score as one that was excellent in bass reproduction and instrumental delineation but somewhat pinched or flattened in sound-stage perspective and imaging. Since I personally auditioned every disc on the list (with pencil and notepad in hand), I am confident that the grades and comments are indicative of what the disc is able to do when the listener is in the most artistically receptive state. The

An Explanation of the Ratings [6]

descriptive terms and letter scores of every recording are ultimately the result of my considered opinions only.

Note that the letter scores should be taken seriously. The individualized comments that precede them are the objective views that were formulated as the music was being heard and are designed to highlight characteristics that may be important to some listeners. The letter scores are a result of the combination of my intellectual and gut-level reactions to the overall quality of the recordings, however. Neither those scores nor the technical comments should be taken in isolation.

As you scrutinize the listings, you may notice the similarity of many commentaries. Good recordings should always elicit somewhat similar descriptive comments. In this case, monotony is good. When a particular aspect of a recording is important (solo instrumental sound, singing voice, string quality, dynamic range, bass response, etc.), it will be noted.

Categories and Companies

As noted above, many categories of music are represented in the listings, including all kinds of classical (from Middle Ages to modern), rock, pop, easy listening, C&W, jazz, and new age. These are completely interfiled by the type of "main entry" used by libraries, to eliminate any problems with crossover categories or individuals who deal with more than one type of music. There is a comprehensive performer-composer-manufacturer index. Consider it a high-speed search tool.

You will no doubt notice a sizable number of high scores awarded to companies like Chandos, Telarc, Chesky, Digital Music Products, Delos, Dorian, Reference Recordings, Harmonia Mundi, Hungaroton, and Hyperion. These labels have consistently delivered readily accessible material of high or very high quality. Companies such as GRP, Concord, Contemporary, Nimbus, Novalis, Archiv, BIS, London, Virgin, MCA, and Geffen are also known for making fine recordings, and many of their productions appear in the reviews.

Over the past few years, the above companies have produced a small avalanche of technically notable recordings. Unfortunately, space is necessarily limited, and only a small sampling of the works by some of them could be auditioned. Experience has shown that a modern recording (post-1985) made by any of these people should almost certainly be worthy of high marks—although it must also be noted that not every release by them that I have listened to has earned a spot in the listing. Even the best of these companies have occasionally turned out a poor recording and will turn out more such discs in the future. It should also be noted that many fine new companies are appearing and even some of the "old-guard" outfits have

[7] **An Explanation of the Ratings**

begun to turn out some good material (often because they have bought into some of the better new outfits and incorporated their advanced recording techniques). In any case, the possibility of substandard material showing up in the recorded repertoire of even the best companies highlights the importance of using this compendium as well as regularly perusing the better record-review journals (see Appendix B).

Availability

There is little doubt that some of the reviewed titles will go out of production. Indeed, a few of them almost certainly have already. Most, however, will remain available in warehouse stockpiles for years. A surprising number have been—and will continue to be—reissued as long as their manufacturers think it profitable to make additional production runs. A fair selection may also be available, used, at independent record stores that handle such material. This is one of the main advantages of the compact disc since a reasonably unblemished older copy sounds as good as a new one.

It is important to remember that while the book deals mainly with compact discs, the ratings it contains should apply equally well to any DAT or DCC (or even MiniDisc) recordings of the same material. DAT is the prerecorded equal of the CD, and the DCC format is also functionally equal to the CD in sound quality. The MiniDisc, while potentially inferior to the other digital formats under certain conditions, is good enough in subjective sound quality to satisfy the needs of most all music lovers. It is important to remember that in all cases the sound-quality ratings indicated on the list will not apply to any analog-cassette or vinyl-LP versions. The former will only be suitable for automotive use, and the latter format is hopelessly out of date.

The listings to follow contain both domestic and foreign titles. While the former should be readily available, the latter may be difficult to obtain unless the purchaser lives near a large and well-stocked record store. If you frequent a library that has a collection of CD recordings, you might talk with the acquisitions librarian about obtaining some of those titles for their collection. While university music libraries usually have the most to offer, many public libraries also have solid collections. Libraries usually deal with wholesalers who can obtain any disc from a variety of sources.

Note that library-loaned, compact-disc recordings—even those that get heavy use—will usually perform as well as any sample purchased new from a record store. Unlike the LP recordings of old, the CD does not gradually lose its sound quality as it is repeatedly played. While a compact disc can be damaged by careless handling, it cannot be damaged by normal use.

An Explanation of the Ratings [8]

A Few Notes on Terminology

The neophyte buff may wonder what the DDD, ADD or AAD markings printed on some compact discs, MiniDiscs, DCC cassettes, or their storage boxes stand for. This is the "SPARS" (Society of Professional Audio Recording Studios) code and refers to the recording process. A "full digital" recording would be DDD, meaning that it was recorded digitally, mixed digitally, and transferred to a digital playback medium (compact disc, MiniDisc, DAT, or DCC). An AAD recording would have been mastered on an analog recorder, mixed on analog equipment, and transferred to a digital playback medium. Most reissued older recordings are AAD. An ADD recording derives from an analog master but was mixed in the digital domain. The use of a digital processor for mixing from an analog master tape may be a sign of extra conscientiousness by the people who did the final work.

Surround sound is mentioned in this book a number of times. The best-known version is patented by Dolby. Most Dolby recordings are video, but a number of audio-only versions are also available. Telarc, RCA, Concord, and ProArte have a combined catalog of several hundred titles. To get the best from a production of this kind, it is necessary to have a Dolby-surround decoder (outboard mounted or built into a receiver), along with at least two additional "effects" speakers to deliver the required ambience. It is also best to have a good center-channel speaker, working with a properly "steered" center signal (such as that provided by Dolby Pro Logic). The Dolby process is an "extraction" system that sends the left-*minus*-right part of the recorded stereo signal (after suitable delay and frequency-response modifications) to the effects speakers and the left-*plus*-right part of it to the center. Under the correct conditions, the result can be impressive. A number of conventional stereo recordings also respond well to Dolby decoding.

Surround processors designed for audio-only use are of either the extraction or the synthesizing type. Extraction processors are similar to Dolby but may have additional features to make non–Dolby recordings sound better. The popular Hafler circuit (available from both Hafler and Dynaco) is one economically priced version. Without usually altering the sound of the two main-channel signals, synthesizing processors tap into the left-*plus*-right information on a recording (and often the L-R signals), sending the results to the speakers after suitable multiple delays, reverberations, and frequency-response alterations. Most surround processors, even when built in to low-cost receivers, have one or more ambience extraction or synthesizing modes to enhance the sound of movie or audio-only sources. While not suitable for altering the sound of every stereo recording, they can significantly improve the playback quality of many.

Another ambience-enhancing system that is mentioned in this book is the Ambisonic process. This is quite different from Dolby but still uses four playback channels (although six are optional) and is designed to work with material that has been specifically designed for Ambisonic decoding. The recording part of the system uses the four-capsule, Calrec-Soundfield microphone working in conjunction with special encoders. The system is popular in Britain, but a few hardware companies are offering the UHJ-spec decoders for sale in the United States. Two recording companies that have embraced the format are Nimbus (in all of its releases) and Hyperion (in a growing number of releases). Even without a decoder, some Ambisonic recordings are capable of adding substantial depth and spaciousness to your listening experience.

Phasiness is mentioned a number of times in the reviews. The term relates to the overly spacious characteristic that may be imparted to a solo instrument or singer if improperly recorded. On some recordings, the left and right channels will appear to be in phase and solidly imaged, while the center will appear to be slightly out of phase and vaguely defined. To get an idea of extreme phasiness, temporarily reverse the leads of one of your loudspeakers and notice how any centralized images become quite diffuse. (There may also be a loss in bass power.) Under typical small-room listening conditions, some recording engineers believe that a slightly phasey quality may subjectively enhance a recording's sense of space and depth. Nevertheless, some knowledgeable audio enthusiasts are adamantly opposed to phasey-sounding recordings.

Additional Aids

In addition to the index, some useful appendices that will further assist you in your reference work are contained in the back of the book. These include a short list of test and sampler discs, critiques of several of the record-review journals, a short list of high-quality recordings culled from the main listing, a discussion of the playback systems used, a drawing showing three popular microphone pickup patterns, and another drawing showing two popular, "purist" microphone placements. There is also a bibliography of material that pertains to recording techniques and playback systems.

The Recordings

1 Abercrombie, John: *Current Events* (with Marc Johnson and Peter Erskine): ECM 1311. This exceptional release is reverberant, full, and much cleaner and better done than typical jazz-guitar recordings. The sound stage is multi-microphone fabricated but tastefully so. There is impressive bass at times and plenty of hi-fi "punch" for dedicated sound-system buffs. This was a good demo disc in 1986 and is still a good one. It is also an AAD item. (A+)

2 Abercrombie, J.: *Getting There* (with Marc Johnson, Peter Erskine, and Michael Brecker): ECM 1321. Wonderfully smooth, clean, and punchy, although not quite to the extent of the above disc. The stage displays good depth, and a decent electrically synthesized ambience rounds out the effect. This is a nice pop-jazz fusion album. (B+)

3 *D'Abraham a Moïse: Gregorian Responses on Texts from Genesis and Exodus*, Shola Hungarica: Quintana 903038. Very smooth and reverberant with a good choral-solo balance. The speaking parts are well sized in relation to the musical ensemble, and the whole presentation has a good church-sound ambience. If you have a surround-sound processor, you will find that using it will enhance the hall ambience effects of music of this kind immeasurably. Even a basic (nonstering) Dolby film sound-track decoder can often work wonders with recordings of this kind. Pro Logic decoders may not work as well as a basic unit due to the effect of the center-steering circuitry, so temporarily switching such a unit to the center "phantom channel" configuration may be required. (A)

4 Akiyoshi, Toshiko: *Interlude* (with Dennis Irwin and Eddie Marshall): Concord Jazz CCD-4324. There is fine clarity, depth, and detail on this digital jazz recording. The instruments on the sound stage are well positioned, and the only flaw is a slightly too close and somewhat metallic-sounding piano. (B+)

5 Albéniz, Isaac: *Iberia*; *Cantos de España*, Rafael Orozco, piano: Valois V-4663. In this release we have a nice "close-up-in-a-medium-sized-hall" sound, with a well-focused, "unbloated" solo piano image and a recorded ambience that complements playback in a home listening-room environment. (A)

6 Albert, Stephen: *Violin Concerto (In Concordiam)*; *Treestone*, Seattle Symphony Orchestra, Ilkka Talvi, violin (*Concerto*), New York Chamber Symphony, Lucy Shelton, soprano (*Treestone*): Delos DE 3059. There is wonderful quality all around on this one, with the segment by the Seattle group clean, broad-staged, and transparent, including the violin part. Ditto the NYCS segment, with the soprano properly positioned and sized and the instrumental ensemble recorded the way a small group of that size should be. (Note that many of the DE-prefix Delos recordings were previously given a D/CD prefix.) (A+)

7 Alden, Howard: *The Howard Alden Trio* (with Lynn Seaton, Mel Lewis, Ken Peplowski, and Warren Vaché): Concord Jazz CCD-4378. Mellow in texture and blended well, this work displays decent transparency and good imaging. The ambience is small-room and suits this music. The electric guitar is well focused and not bloated out of proportion to the other instruments, a rarity with both jazz and other pop music. (B+)

8 Allen, Geri: *In the Year of the Dragon* (with Charlie Haden and Paul Motian): JMT/Polygram 834 428-2. Fairly smooth and clean, with a decent sense of jazz stage depth and breadth. The drums are too widespread across the front (a typical failing on pop recordings in general), but the piano, although a bit muddy, is well focused (a rarity on pop and even a lot of classical recordings). (B)

9 Allen, G.: *The Nurturer* (with Marcus Belgrave, Kenny Garrett, Robert Hurst, Jeff Watts, and Eli Fountain): Blue Note CDP 7 95139-2. Good clarity and detail on this one, although the sound stage is mostly multi-microphone flat. The drums and piano are both well sized, and the former seems far enough to the rear to add a sense of space to the sound (unusual for this kind of production). (B)

10 Allman Brothers Band: *Shades of the World*: Epic EK 47877. This is an exemplary rock album with fine clarity and imaging. The instrumentation is coupled to a decent rock concert-like sound stage. (B+)

11 *Ambrosian Liturgical Chants*, Schola Hungarica: Hungaroton HCD 12889-2. This digital recording has a well-blended ensemble sound that is both clear and smooth. The good cathedral-like "hall" effect adds a necessary realistic touch to music of this kind. The Schola Hungarica group is doing an important job in presenting assorted medieval works, and Hungaroton is doing a fine job of recording them. (A)

12 *American Tribute* (modern "classical" works by Welcher, Cheetham, Sampson, Stevens, Erb, and Schuller), Summit Brass: Summit DCD 127. Tremendous impact, detail, band width, imaging, and clarity. Top-notch stuff in every way with no discernible defects. (A+)

13 Anderson, Ernestine: *Boogie Down* (with the Clayton-Hamilton Jazz Orchestra): Concord Jazz CCD-4407. Very clean, clear, and quite smooth. The vocal-solo imaging is good, although the voice seems a bit more forward sounding than it could be. The rest of the ensemble is laid out quite well, especially the piano, but as usual with both jazz and pop/rock recordings, the drum set seems diffuse and oversized. (B+)

14 Andress, Tuck: *Dream* (with Patti Cathcart): Windham Hill WD-0130. This release is somewhat more forward and electronically synthesized sounding than *Tears* (see 16). Still, this new age effort is quite clear, smooth, and detailed. Unlike *Tears*, this one was not engineered by the performers. (B+)

15 Andress, T.: *Hymns, Carols, and Songs About Snow*: Windham Hill 10135-2. Very clean, articulate, and close up with a good studiolike ambience. In spite of the DDD rating, there is a small amount of background hiss, possibly the microphone amplifiers. This effect tends to make the higher frequencies sound a bit metallic or well etched, depending on your point of view. (B+)

16 Andress, T.: *Tears of Joy* (with Patti Cathcart): Windham Hill WD-0111. The imaging is quite good on this recording, with the vocal-guitar balance near perfect. The bass is good and punchy, and the clarity of the wide-band mix is notable. Overall, the sound is reverberant and stagelike, although still clearly manipulated by the electronics. This disc was engineered by the performers. When this is done, the sound is often a cut above what happens when they leave the job to technicians. (A)

17 *Animal Logic*: IRS D-8220. Good vocal clarity and a decent, broad sound stage. This interesting piece of music is better than average for a rock album. (B+)

18 *Animal Logic II*: IRS Records X2-13106. Clean and etched with a spacious sound stage. The vocals are a bit reverberant but clear. (B+)

19 *Arie Antiche* (assorted baroque works); Maria Bayo, soprano; Ursula Deutschler, harpsichord: Claves CD 50-9023. Very clear and smooth, with the singer well positioned in a fine small-hall environment. The harpsichord balance in relation to the soloist is ideal. One ordinarily does not think about "surround sound" when listening to performances of this kind, but judiciously applied surround processing adds even more depth and ambience to this fine recording. It puts the singer into a very realistic sounding environment. (A+)

20 *Ars Magic Subtiliter* (secular music of the Chantilly Codex), Ensemble P.A.N.: New Albion NA 021. Clear and close up with excellent hall presence. The slight nasal-sibilance quality to the vocals that is apparent at times (almost certainly a microphone effect) is the only flaw in an otherwise fine recording. (A)

21 *Art Ensemble of Chicago/Soweto* (with Lester Bowie, Joseph Jarman, Roscoe Mitchell, and others): DIW-837. Forward-sounding blended jazz with fairly dry acoustics that highlight the detail. This is a notable achievement, given the relative cacophony of some of the presentations. The sound, though dry, was not improved by surround processing, which tended to muddy the already busy sound field. (B)

22 Art Ensemble of Chicago: *Alternative Express* (with Lester Bowie, Joseph Jarman, Roscoe Mitchell, Malachi Maghostut, and Famoudou Moye): DIW-832. As dry sounding as the above recording and just as resistant to surround enhancement. The sound is still forward and heavily blended (even cluttered sounding at times), although the acoustics do tend to filter out the instrumental hash. Note that this is definitely "progressive" jazz, which may not appeal to everyone, even jazz freaks. (B)

23 Art Ensemble of Chicago and Lester Bowie's Brass Fantasy: *Live at the 6th Tokyo Music Joy '90* (with Joseph Jarman, Roscoe Mitchell, Stanton Davis, Steve Turre, and others): DIW-842E. Recorded live, this combination of progressive jazz overlaid with Asian influences is clear and detailed but surprisingly dry and unreverberant sounding. (This seems to be a characteristic of most DIW recordings.) The imaging and spread are good, however, and the stage depth seems OK. This particular recording, unlike the two above, responds well to the kind of synthesized surround enhancement that processors made by Lexicon, Yamaha, and some others can deliver. (B)

24 *The Art of Flemish Song in the Courts of Europe*; Nancy Knowles, soprano and flute; Frank Wallace, baritone and vihuelas de mano: Centaur CRC 2109. There is a good stage presence here with equally good clarity and detail. The overall sound is somewhat distant, although as is common in such recordings, the hall ambience benefits. The latter is made even better with the assistance of any kind of surround enhancement the listener might apply. (A)

25 *The Art of Maureen Forrester*, contralto (songs by Händel, Mahler, Dvořák, Reger, Paladilhe, R. Strauss, Schubert, Schumann, and others); with Andrew Davis, piano; Ofra Harnoy, cello: Mastersound DFCDI 212. This release is somewhat distant sounding but with a realistic presentation nonetheless. There is good clarity aplenty, and the piano is well integrated into the mix. (The cello is equally well done but appears only on the last track.) (A)

26 Astley, Rick: *Free*: BMG 3004-2-R. Good vocal delineations and dynamics. The electric piano sounds better than some of the acoustic models recorded on classical albums and certainly better than most of the stuff found on other pop albums. Surprisingly deep bass at times. (B+)

27 *At the Beach* (classical works by Ibert, Höhne, Thomson, Mendelssohn, Walteufel, Bernstein, Glazounov, and others); Håkan Hardenberger, trumpet and cornet; Roland Pöntinen, piano: Philips 422 344-2. This digital recording is close up in a small-hall kind of way with wonderful piano and trumpet clarity. Trumpets can sometimes overload microphones, and a piano is hard to record properly with any kind of sound-stage depth without a phasey, oversized image as a by product. This disc has few of those defects and all of the positive attributes one could ask for. (A)

28 *Auf Flügeln des Gesanges* (assorted songs by Mendelssohn, Beethoven, Strauss, Massenet, Schubert, and others); Elly Ameling, soprano; Rudolf Jansen, piano; Michel Dispa, cello: Philips 422 333-2. A notable feature here is the very realistic sound stage. Instead of the singer and the instrumental support right in your face, they are placed in a real-hall environment at some distance from the listener and sound fine. The clarity is what you would experience at a non-electrified concert. (A+)

29 Aurora: *Aurora* (with Peter Erskine, Marty Krystall, and Buell Neidlinger): Denon CJ-73148. Transparent, crisp, and well-blended jazz, with a nice sense of space around the ensemble. The listening perspective is mid-distance, and the sound stage is quite nicely laid out. Even the drums image well. (A)

30 *Azahara: Flamenco Guitar Recital*, Paco Peña, guitar: Nimbus NI 5116. This disc is indicative of the quality of the Ambisonic recording process with solo instruments. The result is great detail and clarity combined with near-perfect hall ambience — something that is often missing in works of this scale. There is a three-dimensional image here, as if heard close up in a small hall. (A+)

31 The B-52's: *Cosmic Thing*: Reprise W2 25854. This is very well-recorded rock (mastered by Bob Ludwig) with a good sound stage, fine imaging, and decent vocal-instrumental clarity. (B+)

32 Bach, Carl Philipp Emanuel: *Cello Concerti*, Orchestra of the Age of Enlightenment; Anner Bylsma, cello: Virgin Classics VC 7 90800-2. This recording makes use of what are commonly called authentic, original, or period instruments from the baroque and classical eras and or modern "built-to-original-specifications" versions of the same thing. Such instruments often have a more brilliant (or cutting or strident, depending on how you feel about it) sound than contemporary versions. The result here is a beautifully clean and clear recording with a very good sound stage. (A+)

33 Bach, C. P. E.: *Six Prussian Sonatas*, Anneke Uittenbosch, harpsichord: Etcetera KTC 1011. Very clear and detailed sound from this 1983 recording, with good focus and fine overall ambience. There is a wonderful presence to the harpsichord. (A+)

34 Bach, Johann Christian: *Three Quintets*; *Sextet*, The English Concert: Archiv 423 385-2. The sound of "original-instrument" recordings like this one is typically bright, clean, and detailed, depending on the effect the producer and or conductor may be after. Many critics do not like the lack of vibrato that is common in some period-instrument performances. This is more a matter of aesthetic taste than recording quality, however. Often, the string sound may have just a touch of unwanted brightness or "steeliness" to it unless the recording job is well handled. This one does not and sets the standard for the rest. (A+)

35 Bach, Johann Sebastian: *Arias for Soprano and Violin*; Kathleen Battle, soprano; Itzhak Perlman, violin; Orchestra of St. Luke's: Deutsche Grammophon 429 737-2. There is a nice balance here between the soloists and the orchestra. Clear and detailed, the violin especialy well recorded. Better depth than typical for a DGG recording, probably due to the necessary use of very few microphones. (A)

36 Bach, J. S.: *The Art of Fugue*, Liszt Ferenc Chamber Orchestra, Budapest: Hungaroton HCD 12810-11-2. Wonderfully clean and clear, with a wide, spacious sound stage. At times, the frontal depth is just a tad two-dimensional. (A)

37 Bach, J. S.: *Assorted Preludes and Fugues*; Buxtehude, Dietrich: *Assorted Works for Organ*, Piet Kee, organ: Chandos CHAN 0501. There is an outstanding hall envelopment on this recording, even when heard through two speakers only. The effect is combined with especially good clarity and tonality. The nuances of the organ are fully captured. (A+)

38 Bach, J. S.: *Bach at Bryn Mawr* (including *Prelude and Fugue in G Major*, *Concerto in A Minor*, and *Trio Sonata Number 5 in C Major*), David Higgs, organ: Delos D/CD 3048. There is a fine baroque-organ sound from this modern instrument that is clean, tight, and solid—with good depth and spread. At times just a bit of extraneous rumble or wind noise intrudes; probably the organ machinery, but it does have an effect. Audio enthusiasts with high-definition sound systems may like the noise since they often enjoy hearing recording glitches (after all, such artifacts "prove" the revelatory qualities of those playback systems) as much as they like listening to the sound of the music. (Qualified A+)

39 Bach, J. S.: *Bekannte Kantaten, BWV 51, 56, 140, 145*, Gächinger Kantorei and Bach-Kollegium, Stuttgart; Wüttembergisches Kammerorchester Heilbronn: Novalis 150 029-2. Although done by more than one group and produced over a period of two years, the abilities of the same conductor and engineer give this recording consistency. There is a nice vocal-orchestral balance with a fine midhall listening position. Notable clarity and a realistic concert-hall space top things off. (A)

40 Bach, J. S.: *Bach at St. Bavo's* (assorted organ pieces), Michael Murray, organ: Telarc 80286. Very clear, with a broad, reverberant sound stage. The Telarc spaced-array-microphone technique does very well with organ, especially in a reverberant hall. (A+)

41 Bach, J. S.: *Brandenburg Concertos*, Orchestra of the Age of the Enlightenment: Virgin Classics 7 90747-2. "Period" instruments make this recording as baroquelike as you are likely to hear. In this case, the result is very clean and forward sounding. The violins seem just a tad bright, which is typical with transcriptions of this kind. (A)

42 Bach, J. S.: *Brandenburgische Konzerte*, Musica Antiqua Köln: Archiv 423 116-2. These are the Brandenburgs recorded about as well as they can be, given the current state of the art. The "original" instruments sound transparent and utterly real, and the sound-stage spread and midhall seating position "ambient" effects come across as nearly ideal. (A+)

43 Bach, J. S.: *Cantata BWV 63*; *Cantata BWV 65*, Bach Choir of Bethlehem and Bach Festival Orchestra: Dorian DOR 90113. Brilliant and clean, with a wonderful midhall listening perspective. The depth and spread of the sound stage are exemplary. Dorian is a small company, but the recordings they produce are usually state-of-the-art. (A+)

44 Bach, J. S.: *Choral Preludes*, Joseph Payne, organ: Harmonia Mundi France HMA 1905158. Somewhat distant and fairly dry sounding but with fine transparency and detail. There is a definite baroque sound to the organ that the engineer captured quite well. I found that running the program through my big surround processor in either its "church" or large-hall modes profoundly improved the sound. Too bad this critique rates discs only according to their two-channel stereo performance. (A)

45 Bach, J. S.: *English Suite Number 5*; Chopin, Frédéric: *Nocturne in E-flat*; Beethoven, Ludwig van: *Sonata Number 6 in F Major*, Mieczyslaw Horszokowski, piano: Elektra-Nonesuch 79232-2. This release is close up and detailed, with the piano just a tad diffuse sounding. There is a front-row, small-room perspective here that delivers sound that is very clean and undistorted. (A)

46 Bach, J. S.: *The Four Orchestral Suites*, The Brandenburg Consort: Hyperion CDA 66701/2. Bright, clean, detailed, and technically impeccable. The sound is very "original instrument" in texture with fine imaging and a good sense of depth and hall space. Just a touch of low-level, outside-the-building traffic noise (truck rumble?) at scattered points but not enough to quibble with or seriously degrade the score. The noise was inaudible on my smaller system. (Qualified A+)

47 Bach, J. S.: *The Goldberg Variations*, Keith Jarrett, harpsichord: ECM 839 622-2. Clean, clear, and close up, with extraordinary detail that highlights the intimacy of the work and obscures the hall ambience just a bit too much to sound really real. The sound is neither "you-are-there" nor "he-is-here." Surround enhancement brought out the best in this disc, however. (A)

48 Bach, J. S.: *The Goldberg Variations*, Joseph Payne, harpsichord: BIS CD 519. Excellent detail and stage presentation combined with a just right hall-ambience feel. The result is a good "you-are-there" sound. This release has a more distant perspective than 47, which highlights its greater sense of realism. (A+)

49 Bach, J. S.: *The Goldberg Variations*, Glenn Gould, piano: Columbia MK 37779. Well recorded, especially considering it was done in 1980—except for the often maddening sound of Gould humming along in the background. There are some great dynamics at times, which should surprise those who think baroque music is always rather bland. The piano sounds big and close and has an "in-your-room" character. When listening to a solo piano piece mastered like this one, it may be best to turn off any surround processing circuitry your system may have. (A)

50 Bach, J. S.: *The Goldberg Variations*, Pierre Reach, piano: Cybella CY 1107. More brilliant sounding and forward then the Columbia-Gould version (see 49). There is good piano focus with little center-image diffuseness. The differences between this version and the one by Gould are mainly due to hall-ambience effects, and the recordings are roughly equal—but different enough that I prefer the Columbia release. Unlike the above recording, this one benefits by the judicious use of surround enhancement to place you close up with a "you-are-there" feel. (A)

51 Bach, J. S.: *Magnificat in D Major*; *Jauchzet Gott in Allen Landen*, Monteverdi Choir, English Baroque Soloists: Philips 411 458-2. Smooth, clean, spacious, and first rate. The clarity here is notable, and the "period" instruments sound just about right. (A)

52 Bach, J. S.: *Magnificat in D Major*; Vivaldi, Antonio: *Gloria, RV 589*, Atlanta Symphony Orchestra and Chamber Chorus: Telarc 80194. Smooth and clean with "glorious" ambience. This is how a choral work should sound. The soloists are well placed and properly sized in relation to the orchestra and chorus. Some extremely low-frequency hall rumble occasionally intrudes, a feature of many Atlanta-Telarc recordings. You might want to shut your subwoofer off if you have one. On the inside last page of the inserts that come with all Telarc recordings is a list of the high-performance equipment used during their recording and editing work. Their mistake was in not including a good subwoofer to monitor the low end. A lot of what is itemized on each Telarc "equipment list" is promotional hype, but most of the recordings have been demo grade over the years. (Qualified A+)

53 Bach, J. S.: *Magnificat in D Major*; Händel, George Frideric: *Utrecht Te Deum*, Concentus Musicus Wien, Arnold Schönberg Choir: Teldec 8.42955. A nice and clean original-instrument recording with good detail from the instruments. The choral clarity is even better, especially from the soloists, who are well positioned and properly sized in relation to the instrumental players. Part of the reason for the transparency involves the rather nonreverberant sound field. "Dry-sounding" recordings like this lend themselves very well to the kind of surround enhancement provided by elaborate seven-channel, synthesizing processors such as those made by outfits like Lexicon, Yamaha, Fosgate, and Onkyo. (A)

54 Bach, J. S.: *Mass in B Minor*, Collegium Musicum 90 (with Nancy Argenta, Catherine Denley, Mark Tucker, and Stephen Varcoe): Chandos CHAN 0533/4. Very well handled orchestral-choral sizing, with a very clean overall sound from this "original-instruments" performance. There is plenty of hall ambience with realistic sound-stage depth. (A)

55 Bach, J. S.: *Mass in B Minor*, La Petite Band (with Isabelle Poulenard, Guillemette Laurens, René Jacobs, John Elwes, Max van Egmond, and Harry van der Kamp): Deutsche Harmonia Mundi 77040-2-RG. This is a clean and detailed recording that has a wonderfully delineated sound stage and a fine sense of space. The singers are well positioned in relation to the instrumental players. (A)

56 Bach, J. S.: *Mass in B Minor*, Chicago Symphony and Chorus (with Felicity Lott, Anne Sofie von Otter, William Shimell, Gwynne Howell, and others): London 430 353-2. This effort displays a good sound-stage balance between the orchestra and chorus. There is a clean and "unstrident" string tone, with the brass also very well handled. The soloists are realistically positioned in relation to the rest of the ensemble. (A)

57 Bach, J. S.: *Mass in B Minor*, Atlanta Symphony Orchestra and Chorus (with Sylvia McNair, Delores Ziegler, Marietta Simpson, and others): Telarc 80233. A rich, full, reverberant, and close-up recording of this difficult-to-record-perfectly work. The overall effect is quite modern in relation to the others reviewed here and will appeal to some listeners more than others. The sound stage is broad and blended but at times seems to lack some front-to-back depth. The soloists also seem a bit forward and too widely spread across the stage, but they certainly come across clearly, and this stand-out characteristic will be preferred by many listeners. (A)

58 Bach, J. S.: *Matthäus Passion*, Ensemble et Orchestre de la Chapelle Royal, Collegium Vocale, Gent: Harmonia Mundi France 901155.57. This transcription is quite clear, with the instruments and voices placed in realistic perspective. Very good handling of the individual soloists. (A)

59 Bach, J. S.: *Motets*, Kammerchor Stuttgart, Barockorchester, Stuttgart: Sony SK 45859. This is a very clean and clear recording, with a well-defined choral/orchestral image. A wonderful sense of hall space highlights the effort. (A+)

60 Bach, J. S.: *Organ Works* (including *Toccata and Fugue in D Minor*, *Trio Sonata Number 5 in C Major*) Robert Noehren, organ: Delos D/CD 3028. As with so many Delos recordings, this effort displays near-perfect clarity combined with a midhall listening perspective and an open and spacious hall envelopment. The recording delivers a realistic baroquelike organ sound with fine bass-to-treble balance that sets it apart from most others of its type. A straightforward, light-handed engineering treatment is what music of this kind demands. This disc, engineered by John Eargle, delivers. (A+)

61 Bach, J. S.: *Organ Works, Volume 1*, Jean Guillou, organ: Dorian DOR 90111. Full, wide, deep, and reverberant sound. It is clear that this was recorded in a church. I found that it does very well when fed through an ambience enhancing device and side and or rear speakers are employed. The result is very clear and realistic, but with just a touch of background-noise hall rumble evident—especially when surround enhancement is employed. The artifact may be the wind noise of the organ itself. Some sound enthusiasts would like the effect. (Qualified A+)

62 Bach, J. S.: *Organ Works, Volume 4*, Jean Guillou, organ: Dorian DOR 90151. Outstanding depth, perspective, and clarity, with a sound that is top grade in every way. On a big wide-band system with surround enhancement thrown in for good measure, this disc is nothing but bold, realistic, and memorable. I detected no background rumble similar to that on disc 61. I can easily assume that the other volumes of this series are equal to the two reviewed here. (A+)

63 Bach, J. S.: *Organ Works, Volume 5*, Ton Koopman, organ: Novalis 150 066-2. This release displays a very clear and brilliant baroque organ sound. However, it lacks the full, more bass-rich impact of 61, 62, 65, 66, and 67. Nevertheless the sound stage is quite nice, and the ambience is well matched to the sound of the organ. Given the bass limitations, you do not need a subwoofer or really huge main speakers to enjoy this disc. Note that this recording is part of a different series from the examples produced by Dorian (see 61 and 62). I have not heard volumes 1–4 of this set, but it is easy to assume that they are similar to this one in quality. (A)

64 Bach, J. S.: *Organ Works* (including *Toccata, Adagio and Fugue in C Major, Prelude and Fugue in G Major*), Gunnar Idenstam, organ: Opus 111 OPS 51-9115. Big, close up, and reverberant with brilliant detail and good rich (and sometimes fairly deep) bass. The church acoustics are supportive and almost have a surround-sound effect. (A)

65 Bach, J. S.: *Organ Works* (including *Fantasia and Fugue in G Minor, Passacaglia and Fugue in C Minor*), Michael Murray, organ: Telarc 80049. Recorded in 1979, this disc holds its own with most of the others done since. Big and robust, with subtle (and sometimes not so subtle) very deep bass. A big woofer system is a must if you want the full low-range bandwidth of this recording. (A)

66 Bach, J. S.: *Organ Works* (including *Toccata and Fugue in D Minor, Concerto Number 2 in A Minor, Prelude and Fugue in B Minor*, and *Prelude and Fugue in D Major*), Michael Murray, organ: Telarc 80088. As with most Telarc organ works, there is a powerful, deep bass range here with a very clear, large-scale, and realistic sound. The strongly reverberant hall ambience may not be to every Bach lover's taste, however. It may be Bach, but it is modern Bach, and the recording does not have that old baroque sound. (A)

67 Bach, J. S.: *Organ Works* (including *Prelude and Fugue in C Minor, Toccata, Adagio and Fugue in C Major*), Michael Murray, organ: Telarc 80127. This effort displays *big* organ sound with great depth. The clarity is good, but the sound this organ makes is anything but baroque in coloration. There is some very deep bass at times. (A)

68 Bach, J. S.: *Partita Number 1 in B Minor*; Bartók, Bela.: *Sonata for Solo Violin*; Paganini, Niccolo: *Nel Cor Piü non Mi sento*, Viktoria Mullova, violin: Philips 420 948-2. This is an excellent example of solo violin sound. Overall, there is a nice stereo sound field and hall ambience with the clearly detailed, close up, and well-focused solo instrument sounding just as it should. (A+)

69 Bach, J. S.: *Preludes and Fugues*, Anthony Newman, organ: Newport NC 60001/4. This series of four discs is stunningly clean, smooth, and detailed with wonderful depth and ambience. The bass is solid, "gutsy," and baroque sounding the way it should be—not overblown at all. (A)

70 Bach, J. S.: *Suites for Cello Solo*, Pieter Wispelwey, baroque cello: Channel Classics CCS 1090. Channel has produced some really fine material, and this one is no exception. Close up, clean, and powerful, with outstanding hall ambience and realistic depth. A must for cello students wanting to hear this kind of instrument. (A+)

71 Bach, J. S.: Händel, George Frideric; Telemann, Georg Philipp: *Sonatas*; Gary Schocker, flute; Ted Hoyle, cello; Dennis Helmrich, harpsichord; Marco Grenados, second flute: Chesky CD-46. Very clean sound from the flute, cello, and harpsichord. This is a very realistic-sounding recording that is made possible not so much by Chesky's self-promoted "128-times oversampling" as the proper use of good microphones and careful attention to the final mix. (A+)

72 Bach, J. S.: *Trio Sonatas for Organ*, John Butt, organ: Harmonia Mundi France HMU 907055. Very clean and clear—and very baroque. The sound is interesting in light of the fact that the instrument is a Berkeley (California) modern reconstruction of a baroque original. The result is a fine overall stage depth combined with an expansive width and enveloping ambience. The organ sounds real with good bass—although not ultradeep, like some of the more modern designs. There is some low-level background noise—most likely the wind sound of the organ itself—that I do not consider a true defect. (A+)

73 Bach, J. S.: *The Well-Tempered Clavier, Book 1*, Edward Aldwell, piano: Elektra-Nonesuch 9 79272-2. Smooth and clear, with little piano-recording phasiness. The instrument is well situated in a small-hall environment. (A)

74 Bach, J. S.: *The Well-Tempered Clavier, Book 2*, Keith Jarratt, harpsichord: ECM 847 936-2. This is an outstanding technical achievement, displaying near-perfect tonality and transparency along with a fine small-hall ambience. The middistance listening perspective is just right for this kind of recording. (A+)

75 Bach, J. S.: *Works for Lute*, Lutz Korchhof, lute: Sony S2K 45858. This one sounds fairly close up—but not in a negative sense, especially with music of this kind. There is a good front-row-seat-in-a-small-hall sound combined with fine clarity and just-right depth. The hall ambience that was captured here supports the use of judiciously applied surround enhancement (if your system has the capability) and should make the semblance of realism even better. (A+)

76 Bach, J. S.: *Works for Violin and Harpsichord*; Joseph Swenson, violin; John Gibbons, harpsichord; Elizabeth

Anderson, cello: RCA 60180-2-RC. This recording has a subjectively close up sound stage with correspondingly fine clarity. There is a fine and proper balance between the harpsichord and the strings. (A)

77 Bach, Wilhelm Friedemann: *Oeuvres Pour Clavecin*, Christophe Rousset, harpsichord: Harmonia Mundi France 1901305. There is a clear, almost etched clarity on this release with a good ambient mix from the hall. The harpsichord sounds just a bit too spread out and diffuse for the kind of mid-distance image that the hall ambience is supporting. The instrument has a very close up size but not a truly close up sound. (A)

78 Baker, Anita: *Compositions*: Elektra 60922-2. The good dynamic contrasts, decent sound stage, and fair instrumental delineation are somewhat negated by the vocals being a little buzzy and indistinct—no doubt because of a poor microphone choice. Rock performers should be more critical of microphone quality. Some microphones are advertised as a bit hot in the upper midrange, supposedly to attract singers who want to stand out from the rest of the ensemble. Recordings of this type may also sound a bit better than usual on typical automotive sound systems. (B)

79 *Balletti* (Sonaten und Serenaden am Hof zu Kremsier: works by Schmelzer, Vejvanovsky, Biber, and others), Trompeten Consort Friedemann Immer, Salzburger Barockensemble: Musikproduktion Dabringhaus und Grimm L-3369. Bold, forward, and very baroque with good detail and a fine sense of hall space. Very good imaging too. (A)

80 Bang Tango: *Dancin' on Coals*: MCA MRSD 10196. This effort displays good rock-concert impact. The vocals are decently clean and free of the usual phase-induced fuzziness. (B)

81 Barber, Billy: *Lighthouse*: Digital Music Products CD-455. Even a bit better than the effort below, with outstanding clarity and depth. Unlike that earlier work, which was somewhat subdued in musical impact, this one displays a substantial bandwidth and often impressive dynamics. A superior recording by a superior company. (A+)

82 Barber, B.: *Shades of Gray*: Digital Music Products CD-445. This disc displays a realistic solo piano combined with a good studio or hall ambience. This is an excellent jazz recording and a good example of what Tom Jung and the other people at Digital Music Products are capable of doing. For the most part, all the recordings made by this company are exemplary in terms of engineering. (A+)

83 Barber, Samuel: *Knoxville: Summer of 1915*; Harbison, John: *Mirabai Songs* (plus shorter works by Menotti and Stravinsky), Orchestra of St. Luke's, Dawn Upshaw, soprano: Elektra-Nonesuch 9 79187-2. Very good vocal quality with the soloist well located and sized in relation to the rest of the ensemble. Some background rumble intrudes at times but should not be of audible consequence with most sound systems. (Qualified A)

84 Barber, S.: *Music of Samuel Barber*, Atlanta Symphony Orchestra: Telarc 80250. This disc displays a typically good broad Telarc sound stage with fine clarity. There is a very good sense of hall envelopment. (A+)

85 Barber, S.: *Music of Samuel Barber*, St. Louis Symphony Orchestra:

EMI 7 49463-2. Smooth and clean with a broad sound stage and a fine sense of hall space. This recording exhibits very good string tonality. For years EMI/Angel recordings have little impressed me with their thin, clinical, and sometimes anemic sound. The current crop is much improved, and the company now produces recordings that can often hold their own with the best. (A)

86 Barber, S.: *Symphony Number 1*; *Piano Concerto*; *Souvenirs* (for two pianos), St. Louis Symphony Orchestra, John Browning, piano (with Leonard Slatkin on the second piano in *Souvenirs*): RCA 60732-2-RC. Clean and smooth with a good left-right spread and good depth. The piano is a bit forward in the concerto, but it is also very clearly recorded without a hint of "bloatedness" or phasiness. The dual-piano piece is smooth, clean, and focused. (A)

87 Barber, S.: *Violin Concerto*; Bernstein, Leonard: *Serenade*, English String Orchestra, Hu Kun, violin: Nimbus NI 5329. Wonderful depth and hall feel with good instrumental articulation. The violin seems ideally sized and positioned in comparison to the supporting ensemble. There is also wonderful percussive detail in the Bernstein piece. (A+)

88 *Baroque Music from the Kraměříž Archives*, Musica Antique Praha: Supraphon 11 1416-2 931. Recorded over a two-year period but always in the same location, this disc is clear, clean, and detailed with good ambience and depth. (A)

89 *Baroque Trumpet Music* (short works by Telemann, Händel, Biber, and others), Trompeten Consort: Deutsche Harmonia Mundi 77027-2-RC. This is a brilliant example of baroque sound on a grand scale. The result is clear, dynamic, and smooth. Very good instrumental delineation. (A+)

90 Bartók, Bela: *Concerto for Orchestra*; Enescu, Georges: *Romanian Rhapsodies Numbers 1 and 2*, Royal Scottish Orchestra: Chandos CHAN 8947. Chandos is one of the very best recording outfits these days, and the material they produce is up there with the best. This release is clear and clean with a good sound stage and good dynamics. The string sound is uniform and not overly bright. (A)

91 Bartók, B.: *Concerto for Orchestra*; Dohnanyi, Ernst: *Konzertstück for Cello and Orchestra*, Seattle Symphony Orchestra, János Starker, cello: Delos DE 3095. There is a marvelous sound stage here with the violins on both the left and right instead of huddled to the left as with a lot of contemporary recordings. This is a trademark of many Seattle-Delos discs recorded by John Eargle, and the result is wonderful to listen to on any fine stereo but comes across even better when heard on a system that has a good surround-ambience extraction or synthesizing processor. This is a smooth, wide-range, and detailed recording that sets the standard for recorded orchestral realism. (A+)

92 Bartók, B.: *Concerto for Orchestra*; *Dance Suite*, Chicago Symphony Orchestra: London 400 052-2. This recording displays the usual robust London sound, with excellent clarity, depth, dynamics, and detail. While not quite as good as the newer Delos release (91), this 1981 recording is still capable of separating the men from the boys when comparing speakers or properly placing them. The defect list is short: a touch of high-range string brittleness combined with an occasional bit

of low-volume, low-frequency hall rumble. The former can be handled by cutting the treble on your preamp a little, and the latter should be no problem unless you have a subwoofer system that delivers in the sub-30 Hz range. It was difficult to not award this disc an A+ rating. (Qualified A)

93 Bartók, B.: *Concerto for Orchestra*; *Music for Strings, Percussion and Celesta*, Orchestre Symphonique de Montréal: London 421 443-2. I thought this one was quite clear and detailed, with a nice sound stage and good impact. The strings are somewhat bright (a characteristic of many London recordings) but not particularly uncomfortable to listen to. The two pieces on this disc were recorded months apart — but in the same hall — and the resulting sound is consistent. (A)

94 Bartók, B.: *Concerto for Orchestra*; *Miraculous Mandarin Suite*, Hungarian State Symphony Orchestra: Nimbus NI 5229. Smooth, clean, clinical, and distant. Very good imaging but with the hall and the dynamics coming across as somewhat small and constricted sounding. The recording of the *Concerto* lacks the punch of the two London releases (see 92, 93) and the Delos version (see 91), but some listeners may prefer the smaller-scaled effect. The Calrec "Soundfield" microphone used for the Nimbus Ambisonic recordings often presents a beautiful hall ambience (especially if the playback system has an Ambisonic decoder and the microphone was properly positioned in a good hall), but the microphone itself often seems incapable of producing full, deep bass. (A)

95 Bartók, B.: *Dance Suite*; *Romanian Folk Dances*; *Hungarian Pictures*; *Two Pictures*, Hungarian State Symphony Orchestra: Nimbus NI 5309. Wonderful depth and ambience with equally good transparency. The stage image is quite good on this release, and the overall sound is well defined, although a bit lacking in richness and body. This was also the case with 94 and seems to be an idiosyncrasy of the Ambisonic recording process and the Calrec microphone ensemble. The orchestral textures here are small scale and almost baroquelike. As noted before, some enthusiasts love this kind of effect. (A)

96 Bartók, B.: *Miraculous Mandarin*; Kodály, Zoltán: *Háry János*; *Dances of Galanta*, Seattle Symphony Orchestra: Delos DE 3083. This disc exhibits a wide and deep sound stage combined with excellent orchestral detail and a fine choral blend. The hall ambience is just right, which is typical for recordings made by the Seattle Symphony. (A+)

97 Bartók, B.: *Miraculous Mandarin*; *Music for Strings, Percussion and Celesta*, Detroit Symphony Orchestra: London 411 894-2. Clean and clear with good dynamics and an impressive bass drum. This is a decently realistic and detailed recording. It's one of the better artistic interpretations too. (A)

98 Bartók, B.: *Music for Strings, Percussion and Celesta*; *Divertimento*; *The Miraculous Mandarin*, Chicago Symphony Orchestra: London 430 352-2. This is a better job than the earlier-recorded Chicago Symphony Bartók *Concerto* on London (see 92). It is also a technically outstanding recording of a major piece of music. Clean, clear, and dynamic with an impressive sound stage. Very rewarding to listen to. (A+)

99 Bartók, B.: *Music for Strings, Percussion and Celesta*; *Divertimento*

Bartók (100)

for Strings, Orchestre de Chambre Ferenc Liszt: Quintana 903052. Clear and clean with a close up and smaller-scale sound than most other recorded versions of these works. The overall effect is somewhat dry sounding, although a bit of home-based surround-sound enhancement can add envelopment, especially if the processor is a synthesizing type that adds additional reverberation instead of merely extracting it. It should be pointed out that many listeners prefer a lighter, more antiseptic sound. Those people will love this disc. (A)

100 Bartók, B.: *Sonata for Two Pianos & Percussion*; Brahms, Johannes: *Variations on a Theme by Joseph Haydn for Two Pianos*, Georg Solti and Murray Perahia, pianos: Columbia MK 42625. There is a nice sense of hall space here with a realistic mid-distance listening perspective. Remember, this is two pianos playing, so the exaggerated piano width is the way it should be. The gain is lower than usual for a Columbia release and can be compensated for by merely turning up your amplifier a bit more than usual. (A)

101 Bartók, B.: *String Quartet Number 6*; *Quintet for String Quartet and Piano*, Chilingirian Quartet, Steven De Groote, piano: Chandos CHAN 8660. This piece has fine depth and a good ensemble blend with the piano well integrated. The sound stage seems rather pinched, however. (A)

102 Bartók, B.: *The Three Piano Concertos*, Hungarian State Orchestra, György Sándor, piano: Sony SK 45835. Here we find a well-focused, well-recorded piano situated where it should be in relation to the technically well-handled orchestra. The midhall listening perspective serves these pieces well. There is a very good feeling of stage depth overall. (A)

103 Bartók, B.: *The Wooden Prince*; *Dance Suite*, Budapest Philharmonic Orchestra (*Prince*), Hungarian State Orchestra (*Suite*): Hungaroton HCD 31048. Marred only by a bit of background hiss, this 1988 ADD recording job shows the value of proper microphone use, even when the tape recorder is an older design. Transparent, detailed, and spacious, with both orchestras displaying a wonderful tone and both renditions having just the right hall ambience and depth. (Qualified A)

104 Basie, Count: *The Count Basie Orchestra: The Legend, the Legacy* (directed by Frank Foster, with Eric Dison, Kenny Hing, Danny Turner, David Glasser, and a number of others): Denon CJ 73790. This effort displays a fine sound stage and excellent clarity. It is a better, less brassy-sounding recording than 106. The Denon people are to be commended for their work in recording the material of this outstanding band. (A)

105 Basie, C.: *The Count Basie Orchestra: Live at El Morocco* (directed by Frank Foster, with Derrick Gardner, Melton Mustafa, Bob Ojeda, Mike Williams, and many others): Telarc 83312. This is an outstanding example of spaced-microphone use supported by well-placed accent units. The result is notably transparent with a good sound-stage image. (A+)

106 Basie, C.: *The Count Basie Orchestra: Long Live the Chief* (directed by Frank Foster, with Byron Stripling, Bob Ojeda, Sonny Cohn, Melton Mustafa, Dennis Wilson, and a number of others): Denon 33CY-1018. This is a bright and brassy sounding recording that has a very close up stage image but is also very clean. You might want to back off the treble a bit with your preamp if you are sitting fairly close to your speakers, particularly if they have a flat top end. In a really big room and on the right system, this recording sounds very good. (B+)

107 Basie, C.: *88 Basie Street* (with his orchestra, including Cleveland Eaton, Dennis Mackrel, Bob Summers, Dale Carley, and Sonny Cohn): Pablo 3112-42. The sound here is a bit subdued but could be judged as the way it would actually be heard in a nightclub, the listener sitting somewhat back from the stage. I found that some surround enhancement, via my big Yamaha processor, let this disc move into the major leagues. (B+)

108 Basie, C.: *Fancy Pants* (with his orchestra, including Dale Carley, Sonny Cohn, Jim Crawford, and Eric Dixon): Pablo 2310-920-2. This 1983 AAD recording is clean, spacious, and detailed with a nice open ambience. Given the microphones available at the time and the way they were employed in this case, there would have been little improvement if the recording had been recorded digitally. (B+)

109 Basie, C.: *Kansas City Shout* (with his orchestra, accompanied by Joe Turner and Eddie Vinson): Pablo 3112-52. Here we have a very realistic, transparent, dynamic sound that is very well defined—especially "Clean-head" Vinson's voice. This is an exciting disc, especially considering that it was recorded in 1980. (A)

110 Basie, C.: *Warm Breeze* (with his orchestra, including Freddie Green, Cleveland Eaton, Gregg Field, Frank Szabo, and Grover Mitchell): Pablo 3112-40. Very clear and articulate with a fine sound stage and excellent imaging. A persistent bass thumping noise (the only word for it) underlies the sound throughout the disc. It appears to be stage rumble. On my smaller playback system with its low-bass equalizer shut off, the effect was not a problem, but it was apparent on the big one I used to audition all the recordings found in this book, even with the Allison ESW in its "bypass" mode. This recording was done in 1981 and still ranks with the best in most other ways. Nearly all the printed material in and on the CD's plastic box was in Japanese. (Qualified A)

111 Bax, Arnold: *Symphony Number 4*; *Tintagel*, Ulster Orchestra: Chandos 8312. This compact disc is clear, clean, dynamic, and very impressive. The close up front-row sound here is revealing of orchestral detail. Made in 1983, this is still a classy recording job by the most modern standards. (A+)

112 The Beach Boys: *Surfin' USA*: Mobile Fidelity UDCD 521. This disc was produced from master tapes that were nearly thirty years old at the time. The result is not state-of-the-art sound, but the new producers have done a decent job, and the vocal clarity in particular is quite good—as is the sound stage. Note that the substrata on this disc is *gold* instead of aluminum, and this nearly doubles the retail price. Gold has no effect on sound quality, but it should ensure an archival disc. The gold substrata notwithstanding, some of the other MFSL "Ultra-Disc" reissues I have heard have had a dated sound. (B)

113 Bebop & Beyond: *Bebop & Beyond Plays Thelonious Monk* (with Mel Martin, Warren Gale, Randy Vincent, and others): Blue Moon R2-79154. A close up, distinct, transparent instrumental jazz sound that lacks ambience and realistic perspective. Surround enhancement, if your home listening system has the ability, comes to the rescue here. My big Yamaha DSP unit made a dramatic improvement. (B)

114 Beck, Jeff: *Flash*: Epic EK 39483. This is resonant, spacious, and synthesized-sounding rock with the vocals more nasal sounding than they should be. This is a common failing with rock recordings. If I deleted every somewhat-nasal-sounding-vocals disc from this list, there would be very few rock albums on it. Good dynamics and deeper-than-typical bass for a rock album. (B)

115 Beethoven, Ludwig van: *Christus am Ölberge*, Choeurs et Orchestre National de Lyon: Harmonia Mundi France HMC 905181. Harmonia Mundi France is noted for producing material of technical excellence. This effort displays wonderful tonality, transparency, and depth and is certainly in the company tradition. The orchestra is clear and detailed and is positioned to occupy realistically the space between the loudspeakers in the playback system. The soloists are marvelously well recorded and are imaged as well as any of the instrumentalists. (A+)

116 Beethoven, L.: *Complete Sonatas for Pianoforte and Cello*; Pieter Wispelwey, cello; Paul Komen, pianoforte: Channel Classics 35921. This release displays wonderful small-room ambience, depth, and clarity. (A photo in the accompanying flier shows what appears to be coincident-cardioid microphones recording the session.) The "original" instruments have a terrific you-are-there presence, and their sizing and positioning are excellent. (A+)

117 Beethoven, L.: *Missa Solemnis*; Mozart. Wolfgang Amadeus: *Mass in C Minor*, Atlanta Symphony Orchestra and Chorus: Telarc 80150. In the large-scale Telarc tradition of excellence, the sound stage and blend between the orchestra and chorus on this release are realistic, as is the spatial placement of the soloists. There is a very good organ sound, impressively deep at times and well integrated. (A+)

118 Beethoven, L.: *Missa Solemnis*, The English Baroque Soloists and the Monteverdi Choir: Archiv 429 779-2. Want the *Missa* to sound as it did in Beethoven's day? This original-instruments version does the job. It should be noted that a number of knowledgeable people consider the original- or authentic-instrument sound that is being promoted by some musical purists counterproductive. They point out the inadequacies of many of the instruments of the early period of Western music and note that the composers of that era, if they were alive today, might prefer the sound of modern equipment. With a work of this magnitude they may be right. In any case, this particular recording is clean and detailed with a fine midhall seating position for the listener. There is also a nice sense depth and sound-stage envelopment, with the soloists well integrated. This recording was *Gramophone* magazine's "record of the year" in 1991. (A)

119 Beethoven, L.: *The Five Piano Concertos*, Boston Symphony Orchestra, Rudolf Serkin, piano: Telarc 80061 (these recordings are also available on five separately sold discs). All five performances have the characteristic early Telarc sound: a slightly unfocused center; a wide, enveloping sound stage; and a slightly phasey three-spaced-omni-microphone ambience that will please some and annoy others. All display the clear sound that Telarc is noted for.

Number 1: This recording displays a smooth, spacious orchestral balance with the piano sounding a bit unfocused. It was made in 1983, and B&K 4004S microphones were used. (A)

Number 2: The orchestral textures and hall feel are similar to those of number 1, but the strings seem a bit more biting and brittle. The piano is still a bit diffuse sounding. This recording was made in 1984 and used B&K microphones. (A)

Number 3: There is very smooth sound in this 1982 recording with just a touch of steeliness in the violins but not as much as in number 2. Interestingly, the piano, although still a bit diffuse in central-image tightness, seems better focused than in either of the two later-produced recordings in this set. The microphones were the Schoeps Colette Series, and they appear to have a somewhat better texture than the B&Ks used later on. Playback speaker quality and monitor-room acoustics will have had some influence on this since the mix will be adjusted depending on how the speakers behave. (A)

Number 4: Produced in 1981, this, along with number 5, is the oldest recording in this group. The result is similar in texture and piano soundstage focus to number 3. The microphones were the same. (A)

Number 5: Pretty much the same as number 4, including the microphones, although the strings seem a bit less cutting on this release. (A)

120 Beethoven, L.: *Piano Concertos Numbers 2 and 4*, Philomusica Antiqua, Anthony Newman, fortepiano: Newport NCD 60081. This period-instrument-sounding recording is refreshingly clear and detailed, although the sound will not be to every hi-fi recording buff's taste. The violins are typically brilliant sounding and a little strident, a characteristic more of the instruments themselves than the recording process. The piano is properly sized and correctly located in relation to the orchestra. (A)

121 Beethoven, L.: *Piano Sonatas, Numbers 30, 31 and 32* (volume 6 of a series), John O'Conor, piano: Telarc 80261. Very realistic close up sound; almost a front-row-in-a-small-hall perspective. The piano is well sized and well positioned. (A)

122 Beethoven, L.: *Piano Sonatas, Numbers 9, 10, 19, 20, 22, 24 and 25* (volume 7 of a series), John O'Conor, piano: Telarc 80293. Close up, well detailed, and smooth. The instrument is as well recorded as the one in 121. (A)

123 Beethoven, L.: *String Quartets, Op. 18, Numbers 1, 2 and 3*, Medici String Quartet: Nimbus NI 5173. This release displays a very good soundstage and hall environment. The instruments are quite clear and display fine detail. The Nimbus Ambisonic recording system is at home with music of this kind. Very realistic. (A+)

124 Beethoven, L.: *String Quartets, Op. 18, Numbers 4, 5 and 6*, Medici String Quartet: Nimbus NI 5186. Similar to 123 but with an occasional and subtle background interference that sounds like distant, heavy traffic noise coming from outside the concert hall. It should be pointed out that surround-sound or hall-ambience processors (and Ambisonic decoders) may aggravate noise problems of this kind. The noise will actually sound quite realistic and surround you. Potent subwoofers may also intensify the problem. When this is the case, the offending processor or subwoofer should probably be shut off, although much of the recorded traffic interference will still come from the main speakers as midbass and lower midrange hash. Then, ironically, it will probably sound less realistic. (Qualified A+)

125 Beethoven, L.: *String Quartets, Op. 18*, Vermeer Quartet: Teldec 2292-46337-2. A bit more distant than some of the competition, but the ensemble is realistically positioned in a good small hall and displays excellent clarity and depth. Small-scale or not, a work of this kind benefits from properly captured hall ambience, and this recording has the effect in just the right amount. Surround enhancement heightens the sense of envelopment. (A+)

126 Beethoven, L.: *String Quartets*, Orford String Quartet: Delos D/CD 3031, 3032, 3033, 3034, 3035. This five-volume set, engineered by Marc Aubort between October 1984 and June 1986 (at two different locations), does not contain all seventeen quartets (Opus 18, numbers 3, 4, and 6, are missing, as are the magnificent opuses 131, 132, 133, and 135.) However, those it does contain are well done and exemplify all the advantages and disadvantages of the spaced-array microphone technique that seems to have been used here. The imaging is somewhat diffuse, but the overall subjective effect is quite good. The clarity is also good. A spaced-array technique often results in a recording that works well when listened to from positions both on and off a speaker pair's central axis. The imaging, however, is not usually appreciated by buffs who demand pinpoint localization of the instruments. (A)

127 Beethoven, L.: *Symphony Number 1*; *Symphony Number 2* (transcriptions for piano by Franz Liszt), Jean-Louis Haguenauer, piano: Harmonia Mundi France HMC 901192. Smooth and close up with a nice small-room ambience and good piano tonality. (More eclectic piano transcriptions by Liszt may be found under that composer's name.) (A)

128 Beethoven, L.: *Symphony Number 1*; *Symphony Number 5*, Gewandhaus-orchester Leipzig: Philips 426 782-2. Dynamic, transparent, well defined, and first-class. There is a wonderful blend to the ensemble that does not detract from the excellent left-right sound-stage spread and imaging. (A)

129 Beethoven, L.: *Symphony Number 1*; *Symphony Number 8*; *Overture to Prometheus*, Los Angeles Chamber Orchestra (*Symph. Number 1* and *Number 8*), London Symphony Orchestra (*Prometheus*): Delos D/CD 3013. Done by two ensembles and engineered by three highly competent engineers (Marc Aubort, *1*; John Eargle, *8*: and Tony Faulkner, *Prometheus*), all three of these pieces are fine technical accomplishments. The symphonies are small-scale renditions and have a good spread and clarity. The violins seem just a bit thin sounding in the *Number 8,* and the recording of *Number 1* comes across just a tad better, being smoother and a little less brittle. The hall acoustics in both symphonies seem a bit dry, although there is palpable depth to the sound stages. The best recording is the *Prometheus*, which is smooth, rich, and detailed with fine ambience. All three are still close enough together in quality to rate the same score. (A)

130 Beethoven, L.: *Symphony Number 5*; *Piano Concerto Number 4*, London Symphony Orchestra, Carol Rosenberger, piano: Delos D/CD 3027. The size-placement-timbre balance between the piano and orchestra is very realistic on this release. It is also unusual since most recording engineers overemphasize the piano to highlight its effect when listened to on a typical playback system. Overall, we have good clarity and transparency with a wide, full, rich, reverberant, and spacious sound field. The playback level on this release is a bit lower than average, giving the result a somewhat distant-sounding character at a normal volume-control setting. The sound takes on real bloom when the volume control of your system is advanced a bit to compensate. (A)

131 Beethoven, L.: *Symphony Number 5*; *Egmont Overture*, Boston Symphony Orchestra: Telarc 80060. This early Telarc is full, reverberant, and rich and a match for any of the others here. There is fine string tonality, but the overall sound has a slightly hollow, overly reverberant feel. Tight imaging and instrumental localization are sacrificed to the orchestral blend. This is not objectionable to a number of knowledgeable audio enthusiasts, and many live-concert attendees would feel right at home with this kind of sound. (A)

132 Beethoven, L.: *Symphony Number 6*, The Y Chamber Symphony of New York: Delos DE 3017. Spacious, smooth, and somewhat distant sounding, which results in plenty of good ambience enveloping the players. Beethoven uses a lot of violin force in his symphonies, and the effect can be a bit on the edgy side if the engineer does not use great care in recording the strings. That was done here and those instruments come across quite well. (As noted previously, the reader should be aware that many of the early D/CD-prefix Delos recordings have been re-released with a DE prefix.) (A)

133 Beethoven, L.:*Symphony Number 6*; *Egmont Overture*, Concertgebouw Orchestra: Philips 420 541-2. This work displays a nice left-right spread and a good, somewhat close listening perspective. Getting the microphones this close helps instrumental transparency but could also deliver a steely-sounding violin section. Fortunately, that is not the case here, and the strings blend in smoothly and do not sound edgy. (A)

134 Beethoven, L.: *Symphony Number 9* (Mahler's 1895 reorchestration), Brno Philharmonic Orchestra and Janáček Opera Choir (with Leah Ann Myers, Hene Sameth, James Clark, and Richard Conant): Bridge BCD 9033. Less overpowering in sonic impact than most other versions with a dry, small-hall ambience—almost original instrument. There is good stage depth, however, and the soloists are front-row close up and terrifically recorded. There is also a fine hall bloom around their voices that is very pleasing and realistic. Indeed, it is the choral parts that make this recording a good one to own. (A)

135 Beethoven, L.: *Symphony Number 9*, Academy and Chorus of St. Martin in the Fields (with Karita Mattila, Ann Sofie von Otter, Francisco Araiza, and Samuel Ramey): Philips 426 252-2. Somewhat distant but still with plenty of sparkle, inner-detail-revealing clarity and depth. The string tone is excellent, especially the cellos in the final movement. Outstanding vocal clarity all around, with notable articulation. In some instances, the voices seem farther forward than they should be, however. An occasional and subtle rumble in the background sounds like traffic noise. (Qualified A)

136 Beethoven, L.: *The 9 Symphonies*, London Classical Players and (in the *Symphony Number 9*) The Schütz Choir of London, with soloists Yvonne Kenny, Sarah Walker, Patrick Powers, and Petteri Salomaa: EMI A26-49852. (As far as I can tell, all but 1 and 6 are also available as single discs.) All of these original-instrument recordings, done between 1987 and 1989, have similar sonic signatures. All are well blended with a good, clean unstrident tonality. The depth and spread are also quite good, although the lack of large-hall ambience adds a bit more dryness than many would like. This *Number 9* is not typical, with a small-scale feel that takes getting used to. However, the vocals are extremely well imaged, well positioned, and properly sized in relation to the rest of the ensemble, and the instrumentalists probably sound more like what the people of Beethoven's time heard than any other modern orchestra. Whether the sound suits the modern listener is another thing. (A)

137 Belafonte, Harry: *Belafonte Returns to Carnegie Hall*: Mobile Fidelity MFCD 782. Made in 1960, this reissued recording still has an astonishing live-hall ambience and great clarity. Some recording-tape hiss can be noticed. State of the art when it first appeared, this cheaper aluminum MFSL reissue is *not* one of their expensive "gold" discs, but it sounds better to my ears than a number of those more extravagant items. (Qualified B)

138 Belden, Bob (The Bob Belden Ensemble): *Treasure Island* (with Craig Handy, Glenn Wilson, Marc Cohen, Jeff Hirshfield, and others): Sunnyside SSC-1041D. This jazz disc was done with both ADD and DDD inputs, although the enclosed insert does not say which tracks use which process. In any case, sound is generally clean with subtle deep bass at times. The overall image is fairly centralized, but there is a good sense of stage depth nonetheless. The drums are at least well sized and well focused. (B)

139 *Bella Domna: The Medieval Woman: Lover, Poet, Patroness and Saint*, Sinfonye: Hyperion CDA 66283. Clear, clean, close up, and powerful, with a wonderful vocal clarity that may sound a bit overwhelming at times when compared to the more subdued sound of the instrumental accompaniment. I believe that this is what both the performers and the engineer intended. The sound-stage spread is marvelous. (A+)

140 *Beneventan Chants*, Schola Hungarica: Hungaroton HCD 31168. Very smooth, clear, realistically open, and reverberant. The sound seems to be subjectively a cut above some of the earlier recordings by this group. Maybe I just like this particular selection of medieval music a bit more. (A+)

141 Bennett, Richard Rodney: *I Never Went Away* (assorted short works): Delos DE 5001. This release is nice and smooth with a close up listening perspective that has Bennett and his piano a bit more separated in front-to-back space than they should be. It sounds like somebody else is playing the instrument. Also, his voice has a slight electrified nasality that must be the result of microphone choice. (B)

142 Bennett, Tony: *Astoria: Portrait of the Artist* (with Ralph Sharon, Joe LaBarbera, Paul Langosch, and the U.K. Orchestra Limited): Columbia CK 45348. I felt that this one had good vocal clarity with a stagelike unforced sound. This recording is a cut above a number of other Columbia pop releases. (B)

143 Bennett, T.: *Bennett/Berlin* (with Dexter Gordon, Dizzy Gillespie, George Benson, Ralph Sharon, Joe LaBarbera, and Paul Longosch): Columbia CK 44029. This disc has decent vocal clarity with good integration of the soloist with the orchestra. Performers of Bennett's caliber should be taken seriously, and it is too bad that a better company than Columbia (say Telarc, Chesky, Delos, GRP, or DMP) was not allowed to do the recording job. (B)

144 Benoit, David: *Waiting for Spring* (with Emily Remler, Luther Hughes, Peter Erskine, and John Patitucci): GRP GRD-9595. Smooth, clean, and well-staged jazz with some excellent, punchy deep bass at times. The piano sounds a bit artificial (or electronic) and too far forward in relation to the rest of the ensemble, but it is certainly clear and fairly well focused. The drums are sized well and fit right in. (B+)

145 Berg, Bob: *Cycles* (with Mike Stern, Jeff Andrews, Dennis Chambers, Don Grolnick, David Kikoski, and Jerry O'Sullivan): Denon CJ 72745. This top-grade jazz effort displays an excellent sound stage and good depth in addition to notable clarity and fine detail. The dynamics are also first rate. (A)

146 Berg, Bob: *Short Stories* (with Don Grolnick, Peter Erskine, Will Lee, Mike Stern, Robby Kilgore, Jeff Andrews, and Dave Sanborn): Denon 33CY-1768. This recording falls short of the *Cycles* disc in every way. The same engineer produced the thing, but the recording studio (and perhaps the microphones) were different, showing how much the environment counts. The result still sounds OK but just does not have the snap, clarity, and depth of the other work. (B)

147 Berio, Luciano: *Formazioni*; *Folk Songs*; *Sinfonia*; Royal Concertgebouw Orchestra; Jard van Nes, mezzo-soprano: London 425 832-2. Realistic vocal-instrument textures with no annoying artificial highlighting of the soloists. Very clean, dynamic, and three-dimensional. (A+)

148 Berio, L.: *Voci*; *Requies*; *Corale*, London Sinfonietta: RCA 7898-2RC. Clear and detailed with a realistic sound stage. This music will appeal only to students of serious modern music. Strictly intellectual content, mainly for music school faculty members and graduate students. (A)

149 Berlioz, Hector: *Harold in Italy*, Orchestre Symphonique de Montréal: London 421193-2. This music requires (and this disc delivers) a big, robust sound with a good size-positioning blend between the viola and the orchestra. The hall ambience is quite supportive. (A)

150 Berlioz, H.: *Requiem*; Boïto, Aristo: *Prologue to Mefistofele*; Verdi, Giuseppe: *Te Deum*, Atlanta Symphony Orchestra and Chorus; John Aler, tenor; John Cheek, bass: Telarc 80109. A state-of-the-art recording of these pieces, this release exhibits a very accurate sound-stage perspective and a near-perfect balance between chorus and orchestra. The Telarc crew are right at home when working with this kind of large-scale material, and the microphone techniques employed work better here than with any other kind of music. (A+)

151 Berlioz, H.: *Romeo et Juliette*, Soloists, Choruses and Radio-Sinfonie-Orchester, Frankfurt: Denon CO-73210-2. Overall, this disc has a very realistic somewhat distant sound-stage perspective with a good vocal-orchestral balance. (A)

Berlioz (152)

152 Berlioz, H.: *Symphonie Fantastique*, Frankfurt Radio Symphony Orchestra: Denon 81757 3208-2. Cleaner than the early Telarc recording (see 155), with a better focused and blended sound stage but in no way comparable to the later Telarc attempt (see 156). Overall, this effort is somewhat distant sounding, but that kind of perspective can work well with this recording, and some listeners will certainly enjoy the effect. (A)

153 Berlioz, H.: *Symphonie Fantastique*, London Classical Players: EMI 49541-2. An original-instrument version of this work may seem out of place in the modern world, given the treatment usually afforded it. However, Berlioz worked during the early romantic era, and the instruments of that period did not match what we are using today in tonality, nor did the playing techniques quite match. This recording lacks the impact we have come to expect from the large-scale versions, but it will certainly appeal to purists, and the recording is clear, clean, and generally quite good. I found that surround-sound processing, via my Yamaha DSP unit, made for a remarkably realistic experience. (A)

154 Berlioz, H.: *Symphonie Fantastique*, Utah Symphony Orchestra: Reference Recordings RR-11CD. This effort is somewhat more distant sounding than any of the other *Fantastiques* reviewed here, resulting in a mellow sound blend that is closer to concert-hall realism than more closely miked recordings—but may not appeal to some listeners. There is good clarity and detail in spite of the withdrawn sound, with fine depth. I found that surround processing, judiciously applied during playback, enhances this recording immensely. The efficacy of such manipulations will depend on the kind of surround processor, but even the budget-grade models will probably improve things if used intelligently. This disc has two versions of the raucous last movement, the second sounding satisfyingly more creepy. Note that although the release date of the CD says 1989, this recording was made in 1982 and is from an analog master. (A)

155 Berlioz, H.: *Symphonie Fantastique*, Cleveland Symphony Orchestra: Telarc 80076. Over a decade old, this is a good clear recording with a broad sound stage that seems somewhat diffuse in the center, a characteristic that is typical for a number of Telarc recordings. (B+)

156 Berlioz, H.: *Symphonie Fantastique*; *Roman Carnival Overture*; *Les Francs-Juges Overture*, Baltimore Symphony Orchestra: Telarc 80271. This magnificent recording features an almost three-dimensional sound stage with great instrumental clarity, detail and impact. The wide-frequency-response range is apparent. This is a state-of-the-art recording if there ever was one and shows how far even Telarc has come in the last decade. One of the best recording jobs I have ever heard. If an A++ rating were available, this one would get it. (A+)

157 Berlioz, H.: *Te Deum*, Sinfonie-Orchester Frankfurt: Denon 81757 6142 2. The distant perspective of this recording favors a blended sound stage instead of tight imaging and precise detail. Some engineers and listeners find this effect more realistic than the clinical, close up detail found in a number of other recordings. A lack of stridency in the strings is one friendly by-product. The vocalist is blended well into the overall texture. (A)

158 Bernart de Ventadorn: *Songs* (The Testament of Tristan), Martin

Best, tenor: Hyperion CDA 66211. This smoothly recorded disc has good focus and ambience combined with excellent clarity and detail. Surround enhancement carefully applied by the listener if his or her system has the option should benefit this disc, even though the music involves only the voice of a solo singer. The overall subjective listening perspective is midhall. (A+)

159 Bernhardt, Warren: *Trio 83* (with Eddie Gomez and Peter Erskine), Digital Music Products CD-441. This jazz album displays a nice sound stage, notable smoothness, and fair clarity. While the drums are diffuse, the piano is well placed and right sized—a difficult feat and one that seems to be seldom attempted in recordings like this one. (B+)

160 Bernstein, Leonard: *Arias and Barcarolles*; Gershwin, George: *An American in Paris*; Barber, Samuel: *Overture to "The School for Scandal,"* Seattle Symphony Orchestra, Jane Bunnell, mezzo-soprano; Dale Duesing, baritone: Delos DE 3078. Transparent and detailed in every way that counts, with the vocals in the Bernstein piece finely outlined, realistically positioned, and properly sized in relation to the orchestra. Another championship job by Delos. (A+)

161 Bernstein, L.: *Arias and Barcarolles*; *Songs and Duets*; Judy Kaye, soprano; William Sharp, baritone (with Michael Barrett, Steven Blier, and Sara Sant'Ambrogio): Koch 3-7000-2. Very transparent and close up with good vocal focus and imaging. The piano is somewhat oversized and diffuse. (A)

162 Bernstein, L.: *Candide* (complete), London Symphony Orchestra and Chorus (with Jerry Hadley, June Anderson, Adolph Green, and others): Deutsche Grammophon 429 734-2. This release is quite bright and clear overall with a close-up sound stage that results in the violins being a little brittle sounding. The dynamic contrasts are very impressive, as is the good choral pickup. The realistic positioning of the soloists in relation to the rest of the ensemble is appreciated. (A)

163 Bernstein, L.: *Chichester Psalms*; Barber, Samuel: *Agnus Dei*; Copland, Aaron: *In the Beginning*; *Three Motets*, The Corydon Singers: Hyperion CDA 66219. Very spacious with a three-dimensional sound stage and a realistic orchestral-choral blend. For audio buffs, there is a realistic-sounding bass drum combined with a very wide dynamic range. (A+)

164 *Bestiarium: Animals in the Music of the Middle Ages*, La Reverie: Nuova Era 6970. This unusual recording is exceptionally clean and transparent with smooth vocal delineation. The imaging is outstanding, and the depth and hall envelopment almost simulate surround sound. (A+)

165 Biber, Heinrich: *Die Rosenkranz-Sonaten*, with Franzjosef Maier, Franz Lehrndorfer, Max Engel, and Konrad Junghänel: Editio Classica/ Deutsche Harmonia Mundi 77102-2-RG. This is a smooth and detailed recording of baroque composer Biber's *Rosary Sonatas*. The period instruments have no hint of harshness. The hall feel is quite good. (A)

166 Biber, H., and Johann Heinrich Schmelzer: *Trumpet Music*, The New London Consort: L'Oiseau-Lyre 425 834-2. Clean, clear, and a bit distant sounding but with a nice hall-orchestral balance in any case. The "original" instruments on this disc appear mostly to be modern copies. The sound is authentic. (A)

167 Biber, H.: *Twelve Sonatas*, The Parley of Instruments: Hyperion CDA 66145. A very clear instrumental detail is a feature here. The sound stage has a realistic depth combined with a midhall listening perspective. (A)

168 *Big Band Hit Parade* (with Ray Brown, Dave Brubeck, Cab Calloway, Eddie Daniels, Buddy Morrow, Gerry Mulligan, Doc Severinsen, and Ed Shaughnessy, along with the Cincinnati Pops Orchestra: Telarc 80177. Big, blended, clean, and dynamic. The sound has the standard Telarc soundstage spread, although the depth appears to be somewhat uneven at times. The piano is also a bit too diffuse. (B+)

169 Billings, William: *Anthems and Fuging Tunes*, His Majestie's Clerkes: Harmonia Mundi France 907048. Exceptional in every positive way: clear, clean, smooth, and genuinely realistic. The realistic hall ambience can be made even more palpable when listener-applied surround enhancement is carefully used. (A+)

170 Bizet, Georges: *Carmen Suites Numbers 1 and 2*; Grieg, Edvard: *Suite from Peer Gynt*, Saint Louis Symphony Orchestra: Telarc 80048. This early (1979) Telarc is more distant sounding than some of that company's later recordings. The clarity, depth, and sound stage are quite realistic, as are the dynamic contrasts. Any phasey-sounding qualities resulting from the spaced three-microphone technique employed here are not subjectively annoying or even clearly apparent—at least when the recording is played back in a normal-sized listening room. Just a touch of very deep hall rumble is evident during quiet passages. (Qualified A)

171 Bizet, G.: *Carmen Suite*; *Symphony Number 1*; *L'Arlésienne Suite Number 1*, Cincinnati Symphony Orchestra: Telarc 80224. Big, robust, and clean, with very good depth, detail, and sound-stage spread. Typical of what the Telarc recording technique can accomplish with certain kinds of music played in the right concert halls. (A+)

172 Blakey, Art, and the Jazz Messengers: *Feeling Good* (with Wallace Roney, Kenny Garrett, Jean Toussaint, Tim Williams, Donald Brown, and Peter Washington): Delos D/CD 4007. This effort displays a very wide and yet oddly distant sound stage. The piano is well recorded, but the drum set seems as wide as the stage (an all too common failing) even though major-league drummer Blakey is the headliner here. A bloated drum set is *not* a good thing if a true, nightclub jazz impression is desired, although more than one engineer thinks it is a good way to make a jazz recording sound impressive on home playback systems. There is nice clarity and detail, however, and the disc comes across better on a smaller playback system than a larger one. If the drums had been recorded better, the disc would have easily earned an A score. (B+)

173 Bley, Paul: *The Life of a Trio: Saturday* (with Jimmy Giuffre and Steve Swallow): Owl R2-79230. Note that this disc has the same stock number as the one below; they are considered parts of a two-disc set, even though they come in separate boxes. This release displays a good close up piano focus with the accompanying instrumentalists well sized and realistically positioned in a well-proportioned, acoustically complementary hall. (A)

174 Bley, P.: *The Life of a Trio: Sunday* (with Jimmy Giuffre and Steve

Swallow): Owl R2-79230. Volume 2 of the set, this disc is identical in sound quality to the other recording. Note that Bley plays some pretty "progressive" jazz. (A)

175 Blues Traveler: *Travelers & Thieves*: A&M 75021 5373 2. This effort has decent vocals and good instrumental clarity. The sound stage is good for a rock album, which is what saves the disc and the main reason it made this list. (B)

176 Boccherini, Luigi: *Six Trios, op. 47*, Trio L'Europa Galante: Opus 111 OPS 41-9105. Very clean and close up sounding (you can hear the sounds of the players shifting about and maybe even breathing at times) with an excellent sound stage and realistic depth. A highlight here is the wonderful you-are-there ambience. (A+)

177 Bolcom, William: *Violin Concerto*; *Fantasia Concertante*; *Fifth Symphony*, American Composers Orchestra: Argo 433 077-2. Very good instrumental delineation combined with a good sound stage. The violin is properly placed in relation to the orchestra—no mean feat, given the proclivity of some engineers to excessively highlight a small instrument that is competing with a full orchestra. (A)

178 Bolling, Claude: *Suite Number 2 for Flute and Jazz Piano Trio*; Claude Bolling, piano; Jean-Piérre Rampal, flute: Columbia MK 42318. In spite of the supposed intellectual nature of this type of material, the music is far more jazz oriented than classical (Rampal is a noted classical flutist, and Columbia reserves its MK prefix for classical works). The recording is clear, punchy, and dynamic with a good left-right sound-stage presentation. The ambience is what is required for music of this kind. (A)

179 Borodin, Alexander: *Prince Igor* (overture); *Polovtsian Dances*; *In the Steps of Central Asia*; *Symphony Number 2*, Moscow Radio Grand Symphony Orchestra: Novalis 150 079-2. This effort is well defined, transparent, and small scale, with an almost baroque-like detail being applied to music that is usually treated in a much more heavy-handed manner. This recording responded well to synthesized surround processing via my larger Yamaha unit. (A)

180 Boston Pops: *Aisle Seat: Great Film Music* (short works by Williams, Kander, Vangelis, Steiner, Arlen, Tiomkin, and others): Philips 411 037-2. This effort displays a good sound stage, depth, and clarity combined with plenty of dynamics. There is just a touch of hall rumble on the disc that is evident during the quiet intervals and is made more audible by the need to set the volume level on your playback amplifier or receiver a bit higher than normal to get loud enough sound. (Qualified A)

181 Boston Pops: *America, the Dream Goes On* (short works by Williams, Guthrie, Copland, Gould, Bernstein, and others): Philips 412 627-2. This is a good all-around, almost demo-grade disc with a decent sound-stage perspective, good depth, and wide frequency response—plus excellent clarity. For some reason, the Boston Pops performances are better handled by Philips than a lot of other material the company records. Maybe it's the hall and the layout of the orchestra. Oddly enough, the Copland *Fanfare* at the beginning lacks the dynamic punch and brilliance of both Telarc versions (see 294 and 296), although the rest of the recorded material here seems dynamic and transparent. (A)

Boston Pops (182)

182 Boston Pops: *By Request* (music by John Williams, conductor): Philips 420 178-2. Maybe this material should be indexed under John Williams, but he is now so closely identified with the Pops that I felt it would be better to put these selections here. As usual, this effort has a nice sound stage with plenty of the dynamic punch people have come to expect from Williams's music. There is plenty of good clarity (which is the norm for Pops recordings) and good deep bass at times. The overall quality is a little better than most of the other Philips-Pops recordings. (A+)

183 Boston Pops: *I Love a Parade* (works by Williams, Arlen, Sousa and others): Sony SK 46747. Most recently Pops recordings have been handled by Philips. This Sony effort is just as good as some of those and better than most: dynamic, smooth, and room filling. The bass drum is what you would expect and want from a parade-band recording: strong (maybe too strong for some bass-heavy systems but just right for those with flat response down deep and even many of those which are bass shy). This record sounded excellent on both of mine. Nice depth and sound-stage spread. (A+)

184 Boston Pops: *Music of the Night* (popular works by Styne, Sondheim, Schönberg, Bernstein, Lloyd Webber, and others): Sony SK 45567. This is another effort by Sony (recorded earlier than the above release, I believe) that is nearly as good. The effect is clean and uniform sounding with a good sense of hall space. (A)

185 Boston Pops: *On Stage* (works by Berlin, Hamlisch, Ellington, Rodgers, and others): Philips 412 132-2. Modern Philips-produced Boston Pops recordings are always at least good in quality, and this one shines in program material and orchestral realism. All of the other John Williams–directed Pops recordings I have heard (and that is a lot of discs) are at least equal to this one. I have found that the oomph of the Philips–Boston Pops recordings is such that they sound good on even moderately potent sound systems. Unfortunately, all the pre–Williams Arthur Fiedler recordings of the Pops that I have heard (many great performances notwithstanding) have dated sound. (A)

186 Boston Pops: *Pops Around the World* (overtures by Kabalevsky, von Suppé, Auber, Glinka, Williams, Rossini, and Bernstein): Philips 400 071-2. This is another Pops recording of more serious classical music. This one has good dynamics (nice bass-drum punch) and clarity with plenty of sound-stage spread and depth. Given the 1981 origin, this is a fine engineering effort. (A)

187 Boston Pops: *Pops in Love* (works by Fauré, Debussy, Saint Saëns, Satie, Pachelbel, and others): Philips 416 361-2. Here we have good clarity and detail with the usual high-quality Philips-Pops sound stage. There is some very deep bass on track 3 for subwoofer nuts. Background hall rumble plagues a few of the Pops efforts, and this one has it a bit stronger than usual. (Qualified A)

188 Boston Pops: *Swing, Swing, Swing* (works by Porter, Carle, Ellington, Prima, Miller, and others): Philips 412 626-2. Here we have a large-orchestra sound (maybe a bit too large for some listeners who like this kind of music) combined with good clarity, a proper hall ambience, a decent sound stage, and correct sizing and positioning of the solo performers in relation to the rest of the orchestra. (A)

189 Boston Pops: *Unforgettable* (assorted pieces by Gordon, Rodgers, Hamlisch, Kern, Ellington, and others, with Bob Winter, piano): Sony SK 53380. This is a typical Pops release with a full, reverberant sound (maybe a bit too boomy and reverberant for some). However, many people play music like this at less than powerhouse sound levels, and the slight bass heaviness will act like a built-in loudness control, compensating for the ear's loss of sensitivity when the gain is turned down. The solo piano is clean and solidly imaged but seems too far in front of the rest of the orchestra at times. The orchestral sound has good depth and plenty of separation, as well as fine clarity. This is another "20-bit recording" by Sony. Good things about the sound of this disc are more the result of the concert hall and proper microphone techniques than advanced digital recording process. An old, properly adjusted 16-bit recorder could have done just as good a job. (A)

190 Boston Pops: *We Wish You a Merry Christmas*, with Tanglewood Festival Chorus: Philips 416 287-2. Good Christmas albums are a joy. This one is very well done with fine clarity, detail, and impact. It is nice to have a Christmas symphonic recording with wide-band response — and with impressive bass punch at times. The hall ambience seems better than ever and envelops the instrumentation perfectly. (A+)

191 Brackeen, Joanne: *Fi Fi Goes to Heaven* (with Terence Blanchard, Branford Marsalis, Cecil McBee, and Al Foster): Concord Jazz CCD-4316. This one is impressively big, broad, and smooth. The image has a good overall focus, with the drums well sized but the piano just a bit overexpanded. (B+)

192 Brahms, Johannes: *Ein Deutsches Requiem*, Atlanta Symphony Orchestra and Chorus: Telarc 80092. An outstanding example of proper choral-orchestral sound stage and clarity. Quite realistic sounding with impressive deep bass at times — although the lack of deep-bass potential in the playback system should not seriously detract from the impact. This disc greatly benefits from surround-sound enhancement from a good home-based processor. (A+)

193 Brahms, J.: *Ein Deutsches Requiem*, Orchestre Rèvolutionnaire et Romantique, Monteverdi Choir: Philips 432 140-2. A period-instrument recording that lacks the large-scale impact of the Telarc release (see 192) but still has wonderful clarity and depth. The placement of solo vocalists in relation to orchestra and choir is quite good. (A)

194 Brahms, J.: *Horn Trio*; Beethoven, Ludwig; *Horn Sonata*; Von Krufft, Nicholas: *Horn Sonata*; Lowell Greer, natural horn; Steven Lubin, piano; Stephanie Chase, violin: Harmonia Mundi France HMU 907037. Clean, clear, and close up. The soundstage imaging seems a tad diffuse, except for the violin. The disc exhibits a nice sense of hall space. (A)

195 Brahms, J.: *Piano Concerto Number One*; *Tragic Overture*, Royal Philharmonic Orchestra: Telarc 80252. Excellent sound stage and clarity, the piano sounding just a bit diffuse in relation to the orchestra. (A)

196 Brahms, J.: *Piano Concerto Number Two*, Vienna Philharmonic Orchestra: London 410 199-2. Very realistic with good balance between piano and orchestra and the former realistically sized and placed properly on the sound stage. The violins are just a bit bright (yet certainly not strident), but that is not unusual in some halls and is probably the case here. (A)

197 Brahms, J.: *Serenade Number Two*; *Variations on a Theme by Joseph Haydn*; *Hungarian Dances*, London Symphony Orchestra: Sony SK 47195. Smooth, close up (maybe too close up), and detailed. The overall sound-stage imaging is a bit diffuse, almost Telarc-like. (A)

198 Brahms, J.: *Sonata Number Three*; *Sixteen Waltzes*; *Three Intermezzi* (piano works, volume 1), Antonin Kubalek, piano: Dorian DOR 90141. Very realistic sound, with an excellent close up hall perspective. There is little doubt that the other Kubalek-Dorian recordings produced (and yet to be produced) in the excellent Troy Savings Bank Music Hall environment are equally good. (A+)

199 Brahms, J.: *Sonatas for Viola and Piano*; Schumann, Robert: *Märcheenbilder*, Nobuko Imai, viola, Roger Vignoles, piano: Chandos CHAN 8550. Excellent you-are-there perspective, with midhall balance. The clarity is similar to what would be encountered in a real-world listening situation. There is no in-your-face sound on this disc. (A+)

200 Brahms, J.: *String Quartet in C Minor*; *String Quartet in A Minor*, New Budapest String Quartet: Hyperion CDA 66651. Close up, smooth, and transparent with notably good imaging and a good small-hall ambience. (A)

201 Brahms, J.: *String Quartet in B Flat Major*; *Piano Quintet in F Minor*, New Budapest String Quartet, Piers Lane, piano: Hyperion CDA 66652. Much the same as 200, at least in the quartet work. The quintet has the piano sounding a bit distant compared to the strings, but the lack of close-microphone artifacts is a plus in this case and preferable to the usual "way out in front of the rest of the ensemble" sound common in many other recordings. As in the disc, 200, the small-hall ambience complements the instrumentation. (A)

202 Brahms, J.: *String Quintet Number 2 in G Major*; *Quintet for Clarinet and Strings in B Minor*, Chamber Music Northwest: Delos DE 3066. Smooth, transparent, and revealing, with a bit more apparent stage width than the reverb-direct sound balance (i.e., the listening distance) dictates. A beautiful string tone is evident, nonetheless, with a nice clarinet sound and good individual instrument focus. (A)

203 Brahms, J.: *Symphony Number 2*; Webern, Anton: *Im Sommerwind*, Royal Concertgebouw Orchestra: London 430 324-2. This effort has a notably good sound stage along with decent ambience and clarity but with the violins just a bit dry and edgy. The multimike techniques used to highlight the strings in some classical recordings (but certainly not all) may be the cause of this. It is necessary to get those microphones fairly close to the violins to keep the sound from the other instruments from intruding. This strong, direct sound is less mellow than the more reflected sound that would exist in a hall full of listeners. Sometimes multimiking works to good advantage; sometimes it does not. (A)

204 Brahms, J.: *Symphony Number 4*; *Academic Festival Overture*, Royal Philharmonic Orchestra: Telarc 80155. Very clean, with the typical Telarc large-scale and somewhat amorphous spaced-microphone-array sound.

In some studio or concert-hall environments, this technique works considerably better than others. (A)

205 Brecker, Michael: *Don't Try This at Home* (with Akai EWI and others): Impulse MCAD 42229. This recording displays a good sound stage, particularly the piano. It has less reverb than 206 and sounds a bit cleaner. Still, this is not enough improvement to upgrade the score. The wide drum set is there in force and it hurts the quality of this recording. As I have noted in other reviews, some engineers and performers seem to like the effect. (B)

206 Brecker, M.: *Michael Brecker* (with Akai EWI, Jack DeJohnette, Charlie Haden, Kenny Kirkland, and Pat Metheny): MCA/Impulse: MCAD 5980. Fairly clean and yet reverberant jazz with good focus on all instruments but the drums, which stretch unrealistically nearly all the way across the sound stage. If this were a subjectively close up recording, this might be fine, but the reverb gives too much of a large-room effect and makes the drums seem positively huge. Barely makes the list. (B)

207 Brignola, Nick: *On a Different Level* (with Kenny Barron, Dave Holland, and Jack DeJohnette): Reservoir RSR CD-112. Penetrating and riveting saxophone detail and impact; the instrument sounds like it is right in your room on the first track. Jazz sax players should get this disc and listen to it. The totality is forward and rich-sounding with decent imaging from all instruments but the piano, which is a bit vague. The drum set is mercifully well focused. (B+)

208 Britten, Benjamin: *Purcell Arrangements* (and other folk songs); Derek Lee Ragin, countertenor; Julius Drake, piano: Etcetera KTC 1092. There is good hall ambience and depth in this live recording with fine vocal clarity and a good balance between the absolutely marvelous voice of the singer and the piano. (A)

209 Britten, B.: *Song Cycles*, Benjamin Luxon, baritone; David Willison, piano: Chandos CHAN 8514. This fine effort delivers front-row-seat sound, with great detail and a good blend between Luxon and the piano. A must for those who want to know what a lifelike voice sounds like. (A+)

210 Britten, B.: *War Requiem*; *Sinfonia da Requiem*; *Ballad of Heroes*, London Symphony Orchestra and Chorus, the Choristers of St. Paul's Cathedral (with Heather Harper, Philip Langridge, Martyn Hill, and John Shirley-Quirk): Chandos CHAN 8983/4. This release sports first-class sound in every way. All you could want: depth, spread, clarity, detail, and spectacle with a very three-dimensional image. The sound field exhibits a wonderful dynamism at times, exemplified by the contrast between the cleanly recorded low- and high-volume parts. (A+)

211 Britten, B.: *War Requiem*, Atlanta Symphony Orchestra and Chorus, Atlanta Boy Choir (with Lorna Haywood, Anthony Rolfe, Benjamon Luxon): Telarc 80157. A large-scale work like this one needs a large-scale treatment, and this recording delivers. Spacious and reverberant, with great impact. The sound stage is just right. The overall effect is marred by just a touch of hall rumble in the background, but this should be apparent only on a system with a really potent subwoofer. I could not hear it at all on my smaller system, even with its electronic subwoofer operating. (Qualified A+)

212 Brock, Jim: *Tropic Affair* (with Ted Howe, John Sharp, Jon Thornton, Glenn Kawamoto, and others): Reference Recordings RR-31CD. This marvelous effort displays a good piano focus with transparent percussion (Brock's specialty) that simply explodes out of the speakers after 55 seconds of relatively subdued lead-in material on the first track. Great dynamics and clarity combined with a realistic sound stage and sometimes very impressive bass make this jazz recording a demo-grade item. (A+)

213 Brooks, Garth: *Ropin' the Wind*: Capitol CDP 7 96330 2. This C&W release displays a wide sound stage with the multimiking and synthetic reverb obvious but under control. There is very good vocal-instrumental clarity, but the recording lacks the kind of wide-band frequency response and dynamic impact that it should have. (B)

214 Bruckner, Anton: *Symphony Number 8*, Sinfonieorchester des Norddeutschen Rundfunks Hamburg: RCA 6034-2. Although presented here on the RCA label, this disc was recorded by Deutsche Harmonia Mundi. It shows. The recording has great depth and breadth, with the kind of ambience and sound stage this work demands. The clarity and detail are fine. (A+)

215 Bruckner, A.: *Symphony Number 9*, Vienna Philharmonic Orchestra: Deutsche Grammophon 435 350-2. One of Bernstein's last conducting-recording jobs, this one is big and sweeping with good smoothness and clarity. Being a live recording put certain constraints on the DGG engineers, and the result is a quite realistic effort, although the sound stage still seems somewhat shallow. (A)

216 Bruckner, A.: *Symphony Number 9*, Cincinnati Symphony Orchestra: Telarc 80299. Clear, spacious, reverberant, and large scale with tremendous dynamic range. Nice sound stage and depth. (A)

217 Buffett, Jimmy: *Two on One*: MCAD 5923. This compilation from two previous pop albums is quite transparent and detailed with a good stage spread and good positioning of Buffett within the ensemble. (B+)

218 Buffett, Peter: *One by One*: Narada ND-62004. This is an excellent example of synthesized electronic music with great dynamics and a wide-bandwidth response, especially the bass. (A)

219 Bullock, Hiram: *Give It What U Got*: Atlantic 81790-2. This rock-and-roll effort has a decent sound stage and tastefully generated depth, with fairly deep bass at times. The vocals are a bit fuzzy on some cuts. (B)

220 Burrell, Kenny: *Generation* (with Rodney Jones, Bobby Broom, Dave Jackson, and Kenny Washington): Blue Note CDP 7 46756-2. This is a competently done recorded-live jazz sound, with the guitar well integrated into ensemble and backed up by a properly sized drum set. (B)

221 Burrell, K.: *Guiding Spirit* (his quartet, including Jay Hoggard, Marcus McLurine, and Yoron Israel): Contemporary 14058-2. There is fine depth detail and clarity in this jazz release, appreciably better than 220, although the drum set is typically a bit too wide. (B+)

222 Burrell, K.: *Pieces of Blue and the Blues* (his jazz guitar band, with Rodney Jones, Bobby Broom, Dave

Jackson, and Kenny Washington): Blue Note CDP 7 90260-2. This jazz album has better guitar clarity than the *Generation* disc, with the drums still well focused. Sound-stage depth, although appearing to be synthesized from a multimicrophone array, is decently faked. (B+)

223 Burton, Gary: *Times Like These* (with Michael Brecker, John Scofield, Mark Johnson, and Peter Erskine): GRP GRD-9569. Dynamic, clean, and vibrant jazz. The imaging is good (especially the sax), but the vibes (Burton's instrument), although clear and detailed, seem vaguely positioned and bloated in size. This overemphasizing of the featured instrument or singer is a common characteristic of pop recordings. Still, a fine overall sound. (B+)

224 Busoni, Ferruccio: *Piano Concerto*, Cleveland Orchestra and Men's Chorus, Garrick Ohlsson, piano: Telarc 80207. It should be hard to record a piece as spatially diverse as this one, but Telarc did a good job on it. The orchestra is a tad diffuse sounding, but the piano is well focused and controlled. As usual, Telarc has achieved a good choral-orchestral blend in the sections requiring it. (A)

225 Buxtehude, Dietrich: *Organ Music*, Robert Noehren, organ: Delos D/CD 3023. A clear, transparent, and wonderfully well-recorded sound, with brilliant detail and excellent church ambience and depth. There is some background hash: partially organ wind noise (OK) combined with what sounds like automotive traffic noise (not OK). (Qualified A+)

226 Buxtehude, D.; Sweelinck, Jan Pieterszoon: *Organ Works*, Piet Kee, organ: Chandos CHAN 0514. Very clean, smooth, and transparent baroque organ sound in a wonderfully reverberant church environment. Very fine ambience and depth. Hard to fault this one. (A+)

227 Buxtehude, D.: *Organ Works*, Ton Koopman, organ: Novalis 150 048-2. Remarkably clean and realistic organ sound. The baroque organ is well focused here (a rarity, since organ recordings often have a diffuse, fuzzy, and overly spacious quality), and the effect gives the listener an excellent middistance church seating position. The hall sound is sumptuous and becomes even better when given a bit of surround enhancement, even with a very basic processor. (A+)

228 Byrd, Donald: *Getting Down to Business* (with Joe Henderson, Donald Brown, Peter Washington, and Al Foster): Landmark LCD-1523-2. This "direct-to-two-track" jazz disc is solid and full sounding with good clarity and good dynamics. The drums, unfortunately, are spread out unrealistically wide across the sound stage. The sound of the muted horn comes across quite well. (B)

229 Cage, John: *Second Construction*; Cowell, Henry: *Pulse*; Lundquist, Tjorbörn: *Sisu*; Taïra, Yoshihisa: *Hiérophonie*, Kroumata Percussion Ensemble: BIS CD-232. For percussion freaks only, this recording represents a nice hall feel, with good depth and clarity. The sound field places the listener about where the camera was located for the album cover photo. Plenty of punch here but also some delicate sounds. (A)

230 Campbell, John: *After Hours* (with Todd Coolman and Gerry Gibbs): Contemporary CCD-14053-2. This jazz effort puts forth a good middistance listening perspective with a decent small-nightclub ambience surrounding the instruments. The piano and drums are both well focused and there is plenty of richness in the overall blend. (B+)

231 Canadian Brass: *Basin Street*: Columbia MK 42367. Smooth, reverberant, and spacious — real spacious. Overall, this recording has a good blend with surprisingly good sound-stage imaging for a Columbia job. (B+)

232 Canadian Brass: *Strike Up the Band* (assorted band medleys): RCA 6490-2-RC. A wide sound stage highlights this effort with the instruments etched clearly all the way from far left to far right and with excellent clarity and detail. Nice hall ambience. (A)

233 *The Cantigas of Santa María of Alfonso X, El Sabio*, The Martin Best Ensemble: Nimbus NI 5081. Very clean, clear, spacious, and detailed with a remarkable hall ambience and sense of acoustic space around the performers. Not every Nimbus recording I have heard is successful in delivering the positive aspects of the Ambisonic process, most likely because of hall acoustic deficiencies, but this one excels. (A+)

234 Caram, Ana: *Amazonia* (with Steve Sacks, David Finck, Leandro Braja, Ted Lo, and Cyro Baptista): Chesky JD-45. This recording delivers vocal quality that will separate the sound of a good system from the rest of the pack. The guitar and other accompanying instruments are equally well recorded. The Chesky discs to follow in this listing, in spite of occasional technical problems, are all in a class apart from run-of-the-mill pop recordings. (A+)

235 Caram, A.: *The Other Side of Jobim*: Chesky JD-73. A very realistic sound stage combined with a proper level of studio ambience highlights this disc. The vocal and guitar clarity are also world class. (A+)

236 Caram, A.: *Rio After Dark* (with Steve Sacks, David Finck, Carlos Oliveira, Antonio Jobim, David Chesky, Paquito D'Rivera, and Bill Washer): Chesky JD-28. The "minimalist" microphone technique produces a realistic sound stage in this disc. Needless to say, the result abounds with articulate vocals and crystal-clear instrument sounds. Some bass rumble (almost earthquakelike) intrudes at times, although smaller, more intimate-sounding speaker systems should have no problems with this. Chesky could prevent this kind of thing by investing in more bass-potent monitor speakers. I cannot believe they wanted such background noise in their recording, and the monitors they used apparently could not reproduce the sound. (Qualified A)

237 Carlton, Larry: *Collection* (with Michael Brecker, B.B. King, Jeff Porcaro, and others): GRP GRD-9611. A good, typical GRP jazz sound, with plenty of impact, clarity, and synthesized (and unfortunately sometimes phasey-sounding) sound-stage depth. The guitar is well focused, a welcome change from many other similar productions. The phase tricks that appear from time to time on this release almost have a surround-sound feel, even with only two front speakers. A switch to Dolby ProLogic decoding on my processor resulted in even more interesting effects, none of which were unsettling. The application of a more synthesized surround enhancement, via my Yamaha DSP unit, usually resulted in sound that was too amorphous. (A)

238 *Carmina Burana, Volume 1* (Twelfth- and thirteenth-century manuscript), New London Consort: L'Oiseau-Lyre 417 373-2. Nice and clean, with good depth, spread, and ambience. (A)

239 *Carmina Burana, Volumes 3 and 4*, New London Consort: L'Oiseau-Lyre 425 117-2. This is a better recording in every way than volume 1, probably due to the different recording location. A different engineer and two years of time also differentiate these recordings. (A+)

240 *Carmina Burana: The Great Mystery of the Passion*, Ensemble Organum: Harmonia Mundi France 901323/24. There is a wonderful cathedral ambience in this rendition of thirteenth-century sound combined with authentic detail, depth, and sound-stage spread. The soloists and chorus all blend into a near-perfect facsimile of realism. (A+)

241 *Carnaval* (assorted orchestral-trumpet works by Arban, Clarke, Levy, Paganini, Rimsky-Korsakov, and Bellstedt), Eastman Wind Ensemble, Wynton Marsalis, cornet: Columbia MK 42137. Big and brassy with very full and spacious sound. The trumpet is well focused and has excellent tonality. Columbia tends to record at higher levels then some other outfits (taking a chance on exceeding the peak limits of the compact-disc medium when they do so), and this recording is in that tradition. The bass drum, although clean, may be a bit overdone on some bass-potent playback systems but should be OK on most smaller ones. This is a case where the budget-system owner may have an edge over the high-end audio enthusiast. The sound of this recording has an easy grace that belies the disc's often dynamic impact. (A)

242 Carter, Benny: *In the Mood for Swing* (with Dizzy Gillespie and others): Musicmasters CIJD 60144T. The instrumental work on this jazz recording yielded a somewhat distant but very clear and realistic sound stage. The guitar seemed a bit too far forward compared to the other instruments. (B+)

243 Carter, Elliott: *Concerto pour Hautbois*; *A Mirror on Which to Dwell*; *Penthode*, Ensemble Inter-Contemporain: Erato 45364-2. A transparent and well-etched sound is apparent here, with fine imaging and equally good sound-stage depth and breadth. Good solo-instrument detail is another highlight of this recording. Elliott Carter's music may not be everyone's cup of tea, but this engineering job is an excellent way to evaluate the sounds of singing voices and orchestral instruments in a concert-hall setting and a good way to see if you like this man's kind of music. A high-quality sound system is a must for doing all of this. (A+)

244 Carter, E.: *The Four String Quartets*, Juilliard String Quartet: Sony S2K 47229. This release accurately reproduces the sounds of a small group of stringed instruments working in a good small-hall envelopment. If you are thinking of purchasing this work because of its score, be forewarned that this music does not sound like Beethoven. (A+)

245 Carter, E.: *Three Occasions for Orchestra*; *Violin Concerto*; *Concerto for Orchestra*, London Sinfonietta, Ole Böhn, violin: Virgin Classics 7592712-2. Very clean and smooth with a notable sense of hall space and depth and remarkably good instrumental delineation and imaging—a characteristic that is important with music like this. (A+)

246 Carter, E.: *Vocal Works (1975–1981)*, Speculum Musicae: Bridge Records BCD 9014. A very clean and close up recording of some distinctly modern serious music. The instrumental delineation is revealing. (A+)

247 *The Castle of Fair Welcome* (courtly songs of the later fifteenth century), The Gothic Voices: Hyperion CDA 66194. Remarkably clean with a close up yet spacious effect that is enhanced by listener-applied and carefully controlled surround-sound processing. Very good imaging with realistic depth. There is just a touch of hall rumble at times, which may be traffic noise or a big heater or air-conditioner blower that should have been shut off during the recording session. (Qualified A+)

248 *Catharine Crozier at Grace Cathedral* (playing works by Mendelssohn, Schumann, Liszt, and Reubke), Catharine Crozier, organ: Delos DE 3090. This is a good disc for subwoofer buffs, with impressive bass pedal notes right down into the 20s. The overall sound is rich, broad staged, and reverberant. The Mendelssohn piece does not have quite the low-end reach of 768, but it is still impressive. This is a big-sounding organ and a big, really fine sound system will come alive with this disc. (A+)

249 Cephas, John, and Phil Wiggins: *Bluesmen*: Chesky JD-89. This release is very clear, articulate, and transparent, with a realistic, up-front sound stage. The vocals are extremely well handled here. This is a textbook example of how to record two guys and their instruments. An absolutely marvelous disc. (A+)

250 *Chamber Music for Trumpet and Winds* (works by Finger, Albinoni, Pezel, Telemann, Molter, and others), Wolfgang Basch, trumpet: Deutsche Harmonia Mundi 7976-2-RC. Remarkably clear, detailed, and spacious sound. The sound stage is particularly good, an important characteristic with works of this kind. (A+)

251 *Changing Colors* (classical works by Debussy, Stevens, Kochan, Schumann, and Rubinstein), Jim Self, tuba: Summit DCD-132. A recording for tuba buffs. If you want to know what one really sounds like (not to mention what a hardworking tuba player sounds like as he repeatedly inhales), get this disc. You will find that you will breathe deeply and in sympathy with the guy as you both struggle through the program. Smooth, clean, and accurate. The subjective sound field mimics a you-are-there perspective. (A)

252 *Chant Cistercien*, Ensemble Organum: Harmonia Mundi France 901392. Very good church ambience with fine choral integration into the recording space. The clarity is realistic in spite of the large-scale hall reverberation. Like all such works, the effect of the recording environment is made even more impressive when the listener makes use of a surround processor, even a Dolby-type decoder. The idea is to spread the sound field around you. (A+)

253 *Chants de L'Eglise de Rome: Période Byzantine*, Ensemble Organum: Harmonia Mundi France 901218. Close up and reverberant at the same time, giving one a front-row perspective. Fine detail from chorus and soloists alike. The overall effect is marred by background traffic noise intruding into the church. In a case like this, surround-sound enhancement may actually exacerbate the intrusive sounds. So may a subwoofer. While noises of this kind may enhance "realism" in the modern age (after all, traffic noise is everywhere these days, and we often hear it at live performances), it certainly did not exist in the Middle Ages when music like this was given the background of silence it deserves. (Qualified A+)

254 *Chants Sacrés* (works by Gounod, Franck, Schubert, Niedermeyer, Mascagni, Mendelssohn, Rossini, and others), Barbara Hendricks, soprano: EMI 754098 2. Very clear vocal sound with a realistic hall ambience and an acceptable sound stage. (A)

255 Chapin, Harry: *Gold Medal Collection*: Elektra 60773-2. Chapin died in 1980 but still managed to turn out some technically high-quality recordings for the era. Done in the late 1970s, this compilation has surprisingly good sound with a well-formed sound stage and decent clarity. The vocal imaging is quite good also with none of the too-far-forward, in-your-face feel of many other pop recordings. (B)

256 Chapin, H.: *The Last Protest Singer*: Dunhill DZS 041. Possibly the last stuff Chapin recorded, this work is clean and unstrident with a good soundstage blend and a well-positioned although somewhat too forward-sounding vocal image. (B)

257 Chapin, H.: *Remember When the Music*: Dunhill DZS 035. Smooth and clean with a good hall feel. The solo vocals are a bit closer than they should be in relation to the rest of the ensemble, a typical pop-music flaw. (B)

258 Charles, Ray: *Friendship* (Charles performing with a number of country-and-western stars such as Hank Williams Jr., The Oak Ridge Boys, George Jones, Chet Atkins, Merle Haggard, Johnny Cash, and Willie Nelson): Columbia CK 39415. There is good vocal clarity on this presentation, along with punchy sound—with the bass just a tad boomy when heard over a really big system having a neutral and extended bass capability. However, the balance is quite nice on a smaller system with more typical and limited bass capabilities, and a slightly heavy bass effect is not out of place on a C&W disc anyway (at times, the bass is fairly deep too). This release displays exceptional quality for either a Columbia or country-music disc and is one that all other engineers who record this kind of music should keep in their monitoring rooms as a reference. A fun recording to listen to. (B+)

259 Charles, R.: *Just Between Us* (with Kenny Carr, Lou Rawls, and Milt Jackson): Columbia CK 40703. Uniformly clean, well blended, and well focused, especially Charles's vocals. This is a later production than 258, but it still does not seem quite as good. Together, these two releases are the best-engineered recordings of Charles's material I have heard. (B)

260 Charpentier, Mark-Antoine: *Le Malade Imaginaire*, Les Arts Florissants: Harmonia Mundi France 901336. Rich, full, and transparent with realistic vocal imaging and texture plus a good orchestral blend. A very deep rumbling sound, most likely traffic noise, underlies parts of the performance. (Qualified A)

261 Charpentier, M.: *Motets à Voix Seule et à Deux Voix*, Concerto vocale: Harmonia Mundi France 901149. Three dimensional, clean, and vibrant with a good sense of hall space. There is a realistic placement of the soloists in that space and equally good vocal tonality and articulation. (A+)

Cherubini (262)

262 Cherubini, Luigi: *Overtures*, Academy of St. Martin in the Fields: EMI 7 54438-2. Smooth, vibrant, and clean with a good wide sound stage and stable imaging. The perceived ambience is made even better by home-based surround processing. One of the better EMI efforts and proof of their new commitment to fine sound quality. (A)

263 Chesky, D.: *Club de Sol* (with Brian Brake, David Finck, Steve Kroon, Bill Washer, and Kenny Landrum): Chesky JD-33. This "audiophile-label" release displays a well-etched, realistic sound stage combined with exceptional instrumental detail. There is plenty of sound-stage depth to this minimalist-microphone jazz-salsa recording. (A)

264 Chesky, David: *The New York Chorinhos* (with Romero Lubambo): Chesky JD-39. Another fine Chesky release, exhibiting excellent piano and guitar imaging in a small-studio environment. There is a very good placement of both instruments in a realistic acoustic space. Very uncolored sound. (A)

265 Chopin, Frédéric: *The Four Ballades*, Bernard d'Ascoli, piano: Nimbus NI 5249. Here we have a somewhat distant you-are-there sound that maintains a solid, nonfuzzy stage image. The hall ambience is marvelous and realistic, even without Ambisonic decoding and is one reason this disc rates high. (A+)

266 Chopin, F.: *The Four Ballades*; *The Four Scherzi*, Earl Wild, piano: Chesky CD-44. A good, open small-hall texture surrounds the well-recorded piano, combined with fine tonality and detail. The listening distance is midhall, and the image is solid, stable, and undiffuse. (A+)

267 Chopin, F.: *The Four Scherzi and Other Works*, Ivan Moravec, piano: Dorian DOR 90140. This demograde effort displays extraordinarily clear and clean sound, with a near-perfect close up listening distance and a well-integrated hall ambience. (A+)

268 Chopin, F.: *Piano Concerto Number 1*; Weber, Carl Maria: *Konzertstück in F Minor*, The Hanvover Band, Christopher Kite, piano: Nimbus NI 5291. An original-instrument recording that certainly sounds authentic. Very clean and well-defined tonality reveals both the strengths and weaknesses of the concept. The hall ambience is near perfect, and the restored pianos are well positioned and sized in relation to the ensemble. Nimbus routinely handles works of this type quite well, much better than they usually deal with more dynamic and large-scale items. This may be because of limitations in the Calrec microphone array or of the finicky hall requirements that coincident microphones tend to require. (A+)

269 Chopin, F.: *Piano Music*, Malcom Frager, piano: Telarc 80040. Although this early digital recording was made in 1978, it offers a very realistic up-close, you-are-there perspective with strong dynamics. (A)

270 *Choral Preludes of Bach Pupils for Trumpet and Organ* (works by Krebs, Homilius, and Tag); Edward Tarr, trumpet; Irmtraud Krüger, organ: Christophorus CD 74524. Smooth, clean, and somewhat distant sounding, with nice trumpet detail and instrumental brilliance. As usual, the distant perspective imparts a nice sense of hall space to the sound. (A)

271 Ciconia, Johannes: *Assorted Works*, The Little Consort: Channel

Classics CCS-0290. These are smooth and clean renditions of music by the fourteenth-century composer Johannes Ciconia. Good overall vocal clarity with the instruments blending into a well-proportioned whole. Good depth. (A+)

272 Clapton, Eric: *Journeyman*: Reprise 9 26074-2. This release by a classic rock guitarist displays good vocals with decent frequency response and an OK sound stage. The recording is less forward sounding and contrived than many other rock albums. (B)

273 *Classical-Romantic Trumpet Concertos* (works by Haydn, Hummel, and others), Franz-Liszt-Kammerorchester, Edward Tarr, trumpet: Christophorus CD 74557. Good and clear with a distant but realistic sound-stage perspective. The trumpet is properly sized in relation to the orchestra, a welcome change from the in-your-face presentation found in some recordings. (A)

274 Cobham, Billy: *Picture This* (with Grover Washington, Sa Davis, Ron Carter, and others): GRP D-9551. A smooth, dynamic and clean jazz album. The drums are quite clear and the focus of the ensemble is controlled. The obviously manufactured reverb is well handled. (A)

275 Cobham, B.: *Power Play* (with Dean Brown, Baron Browne, Gerry Elkins, Sa Davis, and Onaje Gumbs): GRP D-9536. Powerful and clean jazz, with good percussive dynamics and good overall balance. The drums are the main feature here, and they are typically (as is the case with most pop-jazz music) too widely imaged, although part of the effect is no doubt the result of a second percussion player adding his share. (B+)

276 Cobham, B.: *Warning* (with Baron Browne, Gerry Elkins, Sa Davis, and Dean Brown): GRP D-9528. This one has great impact with woofer-busting deep bass, to 29 Hz, although the effect may be a bit strong for some tastes and may be missed completely by people owning smaller hi-fis. Cobham is a powerful drummer, but the clarity of his playing is not as sharp on this disc as it was on 274. Percussion freaks should love this one. As in 275, the drum set is too widely spread across the stage, although there is again a second percussion player partially responsible. (B+)

277 *Codex Chantilly: Airs de Cour du XIV Siècle* (fourteenth-century polyphonic chansons by Cunelier, Guido, Baude Cordier, Goscalch, and others), Ensemble Organum: Harmonia Mundi France 901252. Close up, clean, and very detailed, with good small-hall ambience. Just a bit of background noise occasionally intrudes, which is made more obnoxious if the listener is enhancing things by means of a surround-sound or ambience processor. (Qualified A+)

278 *Codex Engelberg 314* (Music of the late Middle Ages), Choral Ensemble of the Schola Cantorum Basiliensis: Deutsche Harmonia Mundi 77185-2. Intimate in perspective, transparent, and clean, with a wonderful hall presence. An occasional intrusion of what is definitely traffic noise interferes more than it should. Adjust your surround-ambience processor or subwoofer if you happen to have such devices. "Straight" stereo reproduction may be best here. (Qualified A+)

279 *Codex Faenza* (Italy, fifteenth century), Ensemble Organum: Harmonia Mundi France 901354. This release is notably well defined and smooth with a fine balance and blending between the ensemble, the soloists, and the recording environment. (A)

280 Cole, Natalie: *Unforgettable*: Elektra 61049-2. This disc has the famous duet between Ms. Cole and her previously recorded father, and the result is first class and worth the price of the whole disc. The overall quality of this CD is quite good. Nat Cole's voice sounds as modern as any during the synthesized duet, a credit to the engineers who remastered it from the rather poor original. (A)

281 Coleridge-Taylor, Samuel: *Hiawatha*, Welsh National Opera Chorus and Orchestra: Argo 430 356-2. Here we have a first-class choral-orchestral blend and broad left-right spread combined with a realistic front-to-back sound stage. The recording also displays an excellent dynamic range, a wide bandwidth, and a correct balance in size between the orchestra-chorus and the soloists. The latter also sound quite real and unforced. (A+)

282 *Colors of the Baroque* (works by Zelenka, Von Eisenach, Höffner, Molter, Philidor, and others), Nick Norton and Anthony Plog, trumpets: Summit Records DCD-108. This is a good example of a baroque chamber ensemble highlighted by a clear and brilliant trumpet sound. (A)

283 The Connells: *Boylan Heights*: TVT Records 2540 CD. This rock effort displays nice stage depth and instrumental clarity. The vocals are occasionally more phasey and diffuse than they should be. Still, the result is cleaner overall than many other rock recordings. The sound stage reacts well to manipulation by your surround-sound processor. (B)

284 Connick, Harry: *Blue Light* (with Benjamin Wolfe, Shannon Powell, Russell Malone, and others): Columbia CK 48685. There is good vocal quality on this release, although Connick is too far forward in relation to the orchestra. The latter is well recorded: detailed, clean, and, dynamic. (B+)

285 Connick, H.: *Harry Connick, Jr.* (with Ron Carter, Reginald Veal, and Herlin Riley): Columbia CK 40702. Good piano focus on this jazz disc with good tonality. A bit of background thump intrudes when the bass plays (probably microphone feedback). Track 9 has a different sound-stage orientation from the others, more distant. Overall, the sound is quite clean. (B+)

286 Connick, H.: *Lefty's Roach Soufflé* (including his trio, featuring Benjamin Wolfe and Shannon Powell): Columbia CK 46223. Nice and articulate, with good lateral positioning of the three instruments. The sound-stage depth is not what it could be, which is in the Columbia tradition of sound-stage flatness. The piano is well focused and at least not phasey. (B)

287 Conte, Luis: *La Cocina Caliente* (with Roland Vazquez, Jonathan Maffett, Alex Acuña, and others): Denon CJ-2237. Another live-to-two-track recording that is punchy, vibrant, and very clean. The deeper drum beats are pitched the way they should be, and the brass is sharp and sized nicely, although the sound stage is somewhat fake sounding. This is a pretty good disc for percussion nuts. (A)

288 Copland, Aaron: *Appalachian Spring*; *Rodeo*; *Billy the Kid*; *Dance Panels* (a 2-disc set entitled *Great Copland Ballets*), Saint Louis Symphony Orchestra (doing most of the material) and the N.Y. Chamber Symphony (doing *Dance Panels*): Angel 7 64315-2. Smooth and clean but also a bit reticent on some of the more dynamic pieces recorded by the St. Louis group. However, a number of listeners may prefer this somewhat laid-back perspective to the more dynamic, reverberant, and forward sound of productions like that of Telarc (see 294, done 10 years prior to this release, incidentally). A subdued effect like this can be partially compensated for by advancing your amp gain a bit above normal, but that does not fully solve the problem. The N.Y. Chamber Symphony recording of the *Dance Panels* has a better hall ambience and a bit better depth, clarity, and bandwidth. A good example of the effect of different recording milieus. (St. Louis material: A; N.Y. Chamber Symphony section: A+)

289 Copland, A.: *Appalachian Spring Suite*; *Eight Poems of Emily Dickinson*; *An Outdoor Overture*, Pacific Symphony Orchestra, Marni Nixon, soprano: Reference Recordings RR-22CD. These three works were recorded in 1986, 1985, and 1982, respectively. The *Spring* is the original thirteen-instrument version and is very well recorded, with fine detail, depth, and lateral spread. The *Poems* are equally good, the vocalist well positioned and quite clear. The *Overture*, although an older recording, holds its own with the others. Most of the Reference Recordings material I have heard has been excellent. (A+)

290 Copland, A.: *Fanfare for the Common Man*, *Lincoln Portrait*; *Canticle of Freedom*; *An Outdoor Overture*; Harris, Roy: *American Creed* (album title: *Portraits of Freedom: Music of Aaron Copland and Roy Harris*), Seattle Symphony Orchestra, James Earl Jones, speaker (on *Portrait*): Delos DE 3140. Very clean, transparent, and dynamic with a good stage spread and workable depth. Mr. Jones's voice seems a bit closer to the listener than its position at the front of the ensemble would dictate at a live performance, but the articulation, as one would expect, is excellent. A judicious amount of manipulation by the engineer has paid off in this case. (A+)

291 Copland, A.: *Old American Songs*; Ives, Charles: *Songs*; Samuel Ramey, bass; Warren Jones, piano: Argo 433 027-2. This effort displays marvelous vocal depth and clarity. There is a very realistic stage presence combined with the kind of ambience that sets a good recording apart from the others. (A+)

292 Copland, A.: *Orchestral Works* (including *Rodeo*, *Quiet City*, *Nonet for Strings,* and *Appalachian Spring*), English Symphony Orchestra: Nimbus NI 5246. Large scale, distant, reverberant (maybe just a bit too reverberant in this case), and brassy, with plenty of dynamic impact when called for, although considerably less than the Telarc version (see 294). This degree of hall echo is unusual in a Nimbus release. There is good stage depth and remarkably clear instrumental delineation in spite of all the reverb. (A)

293 Copland, A.: *Rodeo*; *Billy the Kid*; Grofé, Ferde: *Grand Canyon Suite* (album title: *Out West!*), Seattle Symphony Orchestra: Delos DE 3104. Fine clarity, dynamics, and sound stage. The imaging on the two Copland pieces seems a bit tighter and more focused than that of the *Suite*. The oomph of the *Rodeo* is not quite up to that of the Telarc version (294), but the fi is still plenty hi enough, particularly the gunfight scene in *Billy*. (A+)

294 Copland, A.: *Rodeo*; *Fanfare for the Common Man*; *Appalachian Spring*, Atlanta Symphony Orchestra: Telarc 80078. You'll get plenty of pin-you-to-the-wall impact from the short "Fanfare" on band 1. The piece jumps right out at you, so watch your initial volume-control setting. There is also a very broad, although a bit diffuse, sound stage, good depth, and excellent clarity throughout the entire recording. This all-digital effort was produced in 1982 and has served as a demo item at more than one audio show and dealer showroom. It still compares with the best current stuff. (A+)

295 Copland, A.: *Rodeo* (solo piano version): *Four Piano Blues*; *Piano Variations*; *Old American Songs*, Alan Marks, piano: Nimbus NI 5267. Somewhat distant but very clear with the kind of concert-hall ambience that Ambisonic encoding is noted for. There is a very well focused piano image. (A+)

296 Copland, A.: *Symphony Number 3*; *Music for the Theater*, Atlanta Symphony Orchestra: Telarc 80201. The usual clean, wide-sound-stage Telarc sound, with great dynamic range and a maybe bit more detail than some other releases by this company. The "Fanfare" finale is as strong as that of (and even better recorded than) 294. The sound, however, is marred by a mysterious but slight low-level hall rumble that should not be audible with smaller, less bass-potent (but still high-quality) speaker systems, even though such systems should still be able to do justice to the musical program. (Qualified A+)

297 Copland, A.: *Symphony Number 3*; *El Salon Mexico*, Dallas Symphony Orchestra: EMI CDC-7 47606-2. This recording has a distant perspective, but it is quite clear with a good near-back-row sound stage that ultimately seems more realistic than one might expect. More subdued than 296, but the bass-drum parts still have reasonable punch. (A)

298 Corea, Chick: *Eye of the Beholder* (featuring his "Elektric" Band, with John Patitucci, Dave Weckl, Scott Henderson, and Carlos Rios): GRP GRD-9564. There are many "electric" tricks to satisfy sound-effects freaks on this pop-jazz release, but the disc also has fine clarity and dynamics combined with a well-done electrically synthesized (and, of course, quite unreal-sounding) sound stage. Corea worked on the final mix himself and his attention to detail shows. Another good percussion nut's choice from GRP. Incidentally, this disc responded quite well to being run through a Dolby Pro-Logic processor and five-speaker playback. (A)

299 Corelli, Archangelo: *Concerti Grossi Numbers 1–6*, Philharmonia Baroque Orchestra: Harmonia Mundi France HMU 907014. Brilliantly recorded and very detailed sound. The sound-stage image presents an accurate spatial rendition of a small-sized baroque orchestra. (A+)

300 Corelli, A.: *Concerti Grossi Numbers 7–12*, Philharmonia Baroque Orchestra: Harmonia Mundi France HMU 907015. A brilliant continuation of the six concerti above. The whole series is an engineering masterpiece. (A+)

301 Corelli, A.: *Concerti Grossi 1–12*, The English Concert: Archiv 423 626-2. This is another original-instruments recording that is full of detail with a clean, clear, and blended sound stage. Do not expect this recording, or any other recording using "original" or "period" instruments, to have quite the orchestral texture commonly found in recordings of modern instruments. A number of knowledgeable musicologists and musicians do not like this kind of instrumentation, by the way. It is quite different. (A)

302 Corelli, A.: *Concerti Grossi 1–12* (title on album: *Twelve Concerti Grossi*), Ensemble 415: Harmonia Mundi France HMC 901406/07. Very smooth, clean, and detailed original-instrument baroque sound. The sound stage is broad and spacious but seems to lack a bit of depth. (A)

303 Corelli, A.: *Sonatas*, with Monica Haggett, Alison Bury, Japp te Linden, Hopkinson Smith, and Ton Koopman: Philips 416 614-2. The effect here is of a close-up sound field that clearly reveals instrumental textures. Some low-level background rumble is apparent. Shut off your subwoofer. (Qualified A)

304 Corelli, A.: *Violin Sonatas, Op. 5*, Trio Sonnerie: Virgin Classics VCD 7 90840-2. Close up, balanced, and very clean, with a fine original-instrument texture that highlights why this kind of sound, when experienced at a live performance, is so admired by many knowledgeable music lovers. The strings are particularly transparent, and the icing on the cake is the realistic depth and small-hall ambience. (A+)

305 Corigliano, John; Diamond, David; Lees, Benjamin and Mennin, Peter: *Sonatas for Violin and Piano*; Fredell Lack, violin; Albert Hirsh, piano; Barry Snyder, piano: Bay Cities BCD-1018. Close up and detailed, with the violin smooth sounding, well sized, and centered. The piano is equally well done and placed realistically to the right of the violin. The sound stage is intimate. (A)

306 Corigliano, J.: *Pied Piper Fantasy*; *Voyage*, Eastman Philharmonia Orchestra, James Galway, flute: RCA 6602-2-RC. Quite clear, with an excellent sound stage and fine dynamic contrasts. The hall reverberation was enveloping and realistic. This is a good example of the current RCA/BMG philosophy. (A+)

307 Corigliano, J.: *Symphony Number 1*; Chicago Symphony Orchestra; Stephen Hough, piano; John Sharp, cello: Erato 45601-2. Impressively clear, vibrant, and transparent, with outstanding depth, spread, and dynamics. Superior handling of the short solo sections. Top notch in every technical way. (A+)

308 Cornelius, Peter: *Stabat Mater*; *Requiem*, Choeur et Orchestre Régional de Cannes-Provence-Alpes-Côte d'Azur: Harmonia Mundi France HMC 905206. This release displays a nice sound stage with OK depth and clarity. (A)

309 Cornysh, William: *Sacred and Secular Choral Works* (including *Stabat Mater*, *Salve Regina*, *Magnificat*, and other pieces), The Tallis Scholars: Gimell GIM-014. Clear and detailed with a good sense of hall space. (A)

310 *Country* (original soundtrack album): Windham Hill WD-1039. Nice and smooth with a well-blended albeit mixer-produced sound stage. The piano image is quite good and has a good tone. There is some very deep synthesizer bass on track 11 that should entertain bass enthusiasts, but only if they have systems that can reproduce such low frequencies. (B+)

311 *The Courts of Love: Music from the Time of Eleanor of Acquitaine*, Sinfonye: Hyperion CDA 66367. Close up, clean, and detailed, with a good smaller-hall ambience. There is just a bit of hall-artifact background noise that could almost be the sound of the wind through the windows, but it is not so intrusive as to be annoying. (A+)

312 Cowell, Stanley: *Back to the Beautiful* (with Joe Chambers, Steve Coleman, and Santi Debriano): Concord Jazz CCD-4398. Good piano tonality on this jazz release, with equally positive focus. The rest of the ensemble blends well, and the fine small-room acoustics are well captured. (B+)

313 Cowell, S.: *Departure #2* (featuring his trio, with Bob Cranshaw and Keith Copeland): SteepleChase SCCD-31275. Danish-made, this jazz disc is clean, dynamic, and well finished. The sound is close up, and consequently the imaging is precise, with the drums and piano well integrated into the rest of the group (a rarity in pop-jazz recordings). (A)

314 Crawford, Michael: *Michael Crawford Performs Andrew Lloyd Webber* (with the Royal Philharmonic Orchestra): Atlantic 82347-2. Big and robust, with Crawford's voice at times a bit too big in relation to the rest of the ensemble and at other times buried under the accompaniment. Still, the vocal clarity and focus is good, and the instrumental bass line is often quite powerful and attention-getting for a recording of this type. Some of the material here is "classical" in nature, but a lot of it is pop music. The disc would not be listed in the book if it were treated as a classical item, so I put it here. My wife likes Michael Crawford. (B)

315 Crawford, M.: *The Phantom Unmasked* (with the London Symphony Orchestra): Quality CDL 15105-2. This recording displays good vocal focus and clarity, with a fine integration between Crawford and the large orchestra. This is the best of the Crawford albums I have heard in terms of engineering. (A)

316 Crawford, M.: *Songs from the Stage and Screen* (with the London Symphony Orchestra): Columbia CK 44321. Very good vocal clarity and smoothness, with the overall blend between the singer and the orchestra well handled. Crawford is a bit forward sounding at times, but this is probably best for a recording of music of this type. (B+)

317 Cray, Robert, and His Band: *Don't Be Afraid of the Dark*: Mercury 834 923-2. There are some clean instrumentals and vocals on this blues disc, although there is also just a touch of midrange emphasis and nasality in the mix at times. This was probably done on purpose to add snap to the sound when the cassette version is played back on automotive or budget-grade home audio systems. The left-right spread is decent, with an acceptable sound stage and simulated depth. (B)

318 *The Criminal Trombone* (works by Rossini, Schumann, Mozart, Schubert, and J. S. Bach transcribed for trombone); Christian Lindberg, trombone; Roland Pöntinen, piano: BIS CD-328. Somewhat distant with a fine hall reverb. The overall effect is quite smooth, with excellent instrumental placement on the stage. A very real-sounding recording that works well with surround enhancement. (A+)

319 The Crusaders: *Healing the Wounds* (with Joe Sample, Wilton Felder, Marcus Miller, and others):

GRP GRD-9638. Punchy, detailed, and obviously the result of seriously expert mixer work. While sometimes even the best mixing job leaves a bit to be desired in creating a sense of realism, this disc displays good imaging and an equally fine sound stage. Nearly all pop music (including jazz) is heavily manipulated by the engineers, but the technique can produce honest results if the people doing the job are technically (and musically) adept. This disc is an example of the best that such efforts can achieve. (A)

320 Culture Club: *This Time: The First Four Years*: Virgin/Epic EK 40913. A compendium of works done between 1982 and 1986, the rock-pop disc is a good mixing-console effort with just a bit of "buzziness" in the vocals. The later effect is designed to appeal to people listening to the cassette version on automotive systems, I suppose. The sound stage is fake sounding, of course, but aurally impressive nonetheless. (B)

321 *Cypriot Advent Antiphons* (Anonymous c. 1390), Huelgas Ensemble: Deutsche Harmonia Mundi 7977-2-RC. Very clean and clear with realistic depth and a satisfying soundstage spread. The midhall listening perspective is just right. (A+)

322 *Däfos* (with Mickey Hart, Airto Moreira, and Flora Purim): Rykodisc RCD 10108. Although basically Mickey Hart's brainchild, I am listing this album under its title because of its fame among audio buffs. This recording (which originally appeared as Reference Recordings RR-12CD and is now a Rykodisc reissue) is most "experimental" percussion with some unusual vocals and will appeal only to a certain kind of listener. There is a wonderful sound-stage ambience here combined with fine clarity. Astonishing dynamics reappear throughout the recording but particularly on track 7. If you run the gain high on this disc, be prepared to exercise fully every driver in your speaker systems to the fullest, and wear a seat belt. There is just a faint but unobjectionable hint of background hiss on this pretty much state-of-the-art AAD(!) recording. (Qualified A+)

323 *Daniel and the Lions* (Ludus Danielis), New York Ensemble for Early Music: Fonè 88 F 09-29. The somewhat distant stage perspective displays decent front-to-back depth and sound-stage realism. The clarity is also quite good, considering the space between the listening position and the performers. (A)

324 Daniels, Eddie, and Gary Burton: *Benny Rides Again* (with Mulgrew Miller, Marc Johnson and Peter Erskine): GRP GRD-9665. Crystal-clear, smooth, and vibrant jazz, with a very good sound stage, expertly synthesized depth, and a palpable ambience. Even the slightly wide drum spread does not get in the way of this disc being a near demo-grade item. Feeding the signal into a Pro Logic decoder stabilized the central image for off-axis listening and made the studio effect even better. It also tightened up the drums. (A)

325 Daniels, E.: *Memos from Paradise* (with Roger Kellaway, Eddie Gomez, Al Foster, and others): GRP GRD-9561. Smooth and well blended, with good clarity and a slightly recessed sound stage. There is good imaging, nonetheless, with a nice drum focus in particular. (A)

326 Daniels, E.: *This Is Now* (with Billy Childs, Tony Dumas, Ralph Penland, Vinnie Colaiuta, and Jimmy Johnson): GRP GRD-9635. There are good definition and detail here with a decent sound-stage spread. The stage depth seemed a bit flat, however, but at least the drums are not overblown. You will not find your usual GRP-jazz sound on this disc—either the bad or the good characteristics. (B)

327 Daniels, E.: *To Bird with Love* (with Fred Hersch, Roger Kellaway, John Patitucci, Al Foster, and Steve Thornton); GRP GRD-9544. Like most Daniels recordings, this one is clean, clear, and dynamic. The clarinet is very well recorded. This effort displays a good stage-depth feel, a difficult trick to pull off with the multimiking job obviously done here using a 32-track Mitsubishi recorder. (A)

328 *Danse Royale* (French, Anglo-Norman, and Latin songs from the thirteenth century), Ensemble Alcatraz: Elektra-Nonesuch 9 79240-2. A bit distant for music of this kind but still clear and smooth with good vocal and instrumental articulation. Sound-stage depth, the listening distance notwithstanding, is also quite good. (A)

329 The Darling Buds: *Crawdaddy*: Columbia CK 46816. Plenty of rock punch on this one, with a good sound-stage spread. Although the vocals are mostly obscured by the instrumentation in the usual rock-and-roll manner, some of the tracks reveal that the singers are quite talented. (B)

330 Davis, Anthony: *X, The Life and Times of Malcolm X* (an opera in three acts), Orchestra of St. Luke's (with Eugene Perry, Thomas Young, Priscilla Baskerville, Hilda Harris, and Herbert Perry): Gramavision R2-79470. Very clean and dynamic with exemplary depth and good studio ambience. There is also very good vocal clarity combined with equally good ensemble placement and sizing. Unfortunately, a subtle very low-frequency rumble underlies the recording. It should not be audible on most sound systems. (Qualified A+)

331 Dean, Billy: *Billy Dean*: Liberty CDP 7 96728-2. Dean's second album, and DDD no less, is prehaps the best-recorded C&W disc I have heard. Good vocal clarity, plenty of punch, great dynamics when required, and a decent sound stage are hallmarks. There is a wonderful and welcome lack of nasality in the voice. Every C&W recording engineer should be forced to listen to this disc. (A)

332 Dean, B.: *Young Man*: Liberty CDP 7 94302-2. Dean's first album, I believe. It is very well done for a C&W disc, with good clarity and a decent sound stage. Not quite up to Dean's second effort, 331. (B+)

333 Debussy, Claude: *Le Boîte à Joujoux*; Ravel, Maurice: *Ma Mère l'Oye*, Ulster Orchestra: Chandos CHAN 8711. Broad staged, close up, rich, and vibrant, with a nice sense of depth and ambience. The string tone is also nice. A notable effort but still maybe not delivering the exalted sensation of realism I have experienced from a number of other Chandos releases. (A)

334 Debussy, C.: *La Mer*; Roussel, Albert: *Symphony Number 4*; *Sinfonietta*; Milhaud, Darius; *Suite Provencal*, Detroit Symphony Orchestra: Chandos CHAN 9072. Spacious, transparent, and near perfect, with the kind of impact, imaging, depth, and realism that make for a demo-grade performance. This is technically the best recorded *La Mer* I have heard. (A+)

335 Debussy, C.: *La Mer*; *Jeux*; *Prélude à l'après-midi d'un faune*, Orchestre Symphonique de Montréal: London 430 240-2. Clear and clean, with good dynamic contrasts. The overall sound is smooth, and there is plenty of space around the instruments combined with a nice sense of envelopment. Another good example of what London is doing these days, especially with this orchestra. (A+)

336 Debussy, C.: *Pelléas et Mélisande*, Vienna Philharmonic (with Maria Ewing, François Le Roux, Christa Ludwig, José van Dam, and others): Deutsche Grammophon 435 344-2. An excellent balance between the orchestra and choral group is a highlight here. Although they sometimes seem just a tad forward, the articulation of the vocalists is particularly well handled, and their left-right positioning is quite good. A good sense of hall space combined with a wonderful dynamic range and frequency-response bandwidth are the proverbial icing on the cake of this recording. This release is a cut above previous DGG efforts. (A+)

337 Debussy, C.: *Prélude à l'Apres-midi d'un Faune*; *La Boîte à Joujoux*; *Jeux*, London Symphony Orchestra: Sony SK 48231. Close up, clean, and rich. All three works were recorded in the same studio, but the *Prélude* and *La Boîte* were done a few months earlier. *Jeux* seems to have even more sound-stage depth and seems further back, so there it seems likely that microphone changes were made during the interim period. Then too, maybe I am just letting the musical material get in the way of his critical faculties. This is a marvelous recording. (A)

338 Debussy, C.: *String Quartets*, Emerson String Quartet: Deutsche Grammophon 427 320-2. Good, distinct, clean sound. There is a notable lack of string harshness on this recording. (A)

339 Debussy, C.: *Images Pour Orchestre*; *Trois Nocturnes*, Orchestre Symphonique de Montréal: London 425 502-2. Very smooth, transparent, and vibrant, with good dynamic range. The ambient effect is small hall in nature but still marvelously effective. An occasional thumping sound intrudes during some of the more energetic passages, probably feed-through from the stage to a microphone stand. (Qualified A+)

340 Def Leppard: *Adrenalize*: Mercury 314 512 185-2. Good clarity for such a busy-sounding and obviously electronically processed rock album. The recording displays decent bass at times, plus impressive impact and spacious sound, courtesy of mastering expert Bob Ludwig. (B)

341 Def Leppard: *Hysteria*: Mercury 830 675-2. This is power-rock recording as it should be done. Music like this is supposed to have a tidal-wave punch to it, and this disc delivers. Great dynamics and powerful bass. The sound stage is big and reverberant and lends itself to surround enhancement. Running this disc through my Yamaha DSP unit put me at a rock concert. (B+)

342 Delius, Frederick: *Cello Sonata*; Walton, William: *Passacaglia for Solo Cello*; Bax, Arnold: *Rhapsodic Ballad for Solo Cello*; Bridge, Frank: *Cello Sonata in D Minor*; Raphael Wallfisch, cello; Peter Wallfisch, piano: Chandos CHAN 8499. This effort has a nice small-hall ambience with the piano and cello well located and, especially in the case of the latter, well recorded in tonality and focus. (A)

Delius (343)

343 Delius, F.: *A Walk to the Paradise Garden; Brigg Fair; In a Summer Garden* (and other, shorter works), London Symphony Orchestra: Collins Classics 13362. Smooth, vibrant, and spacious. The hall envelopment is just right. The strings are particularly clean and smooth, important with any recording of Delius. (A+)

344 Diamond, David: *Symphony Number 2; Symphony Number 4; Concerto for Small Orchestra*, Seattle Symphony Orchestra (symphonies), New York Chamber Symphony (concerto): Delos DE 3093. Marvelously clear, revealing, and realistic with a potent bass-drum boom when the score calls for it. In the Delos tradition, this recording displays an outstanding soundstage spread and fine depth combined with a proper midhall listening perspective. Both Seattle and New York segments are expertly done. (A+)

345 Diamond, D.: *Symphony Number 3; Romeo and Juliet; Psalm; Kaddish*, Seattle Symphony Orchestra, New York Chamber Symphony, János Starker, cello: Delos DE 3103. This one is as revealing as 344, with a wonderful sound stage and fine depth, along with that typically Delos near-perfect midhall listening perspective. (A+)

346 DiMeola, Al: *Kiss My Axe* (with Barny Miles, Anthony Jackson, Tony Scher, Omar Hakim, and others): Tomato Records R2-79751. The quality of this DDD entry equals that of 347. Great name for a recording. (A)

347 DiMeola, A.: *World Sinfonia* (with Dino Saluzzi, Arto Tuncboyaci, Gumbi Ortiz, and Chris Carrington): Tomato Records R2-779750. Although heavily processed electronically, this jazz disc has great clarity, plenty of dynamic range, well-synthesized depth, and a wideband width. It doesn't always sound like a live stage presentation, but it certainly sounds impressive. Great name for a record company. (A)

348 Dire Straits: *Brothers in Arms*: Warner Bros. 25264-2. One of the better rock albums in terms of sound quality and lack of processing overkill. Plenty of punch, clarity, and detail. Perhaps the best technical aspect of this album is the vocals, which are a full magnitude above what is found on most other rock releases. (A)

349 The Dirty Dozen Brass Band: *Open Up: Whatcha Gonna Do for the Rest of Your Life?* (with Gregory Davis, Efrem Towns, Roger Lewis, Keven Harris, and others): Columbia CK 47383. This jazz release displays good clarity and impact, with a decent sound stage and fair front-to-back depth. The frequency bandwidth seems just a bit limited. (B)

350 *La Dolce Vita: Music in Renaissance Naples*, The King's Singers and Tragicomedia: EMI 54191-2. Very clear, with a spacious, realistic sound stage and good imaging. Good hall ambience. This one puts EMI right up there with the best. (A+)

351 Dowland, John: *Lachrimae, or Seaven Teares*, The Dowland Consort: BIS CD-315. An excellent example of good two-microphone usage. Clean and clear with a fine, well-focused sound stage. The instruments used here are reproductions of period types, with all their positive (and negative) characteristics. (A)

352 Dowland, J.: *Songs for Tenor and Lute*; Nigel Rogers, tenor; Paul O'Dette, lute: Virgin Classics VC 7 90726-2. Nice ambience and stage depth with an obviously proper spatial relationship between the performers and the church environment in which this recording was made. Good vocal articulation, the lute well positioned, properly sized, and recorded at a realistic level. (A)

353 Dread Zeppelin: *Un-Led-Ed*: IRS D-82048. This rock release has some forward but distinct-sounding vocals that will endear it to owners of automotive sound systems. There is some good fairly deep bass, and the dynamic range is attention-getting. (B)

354 Drew, Kenny: *Kenny Drew Jr.* (with Christian McBride, George Mraz, Winard Harper, Al Foster, Ralph Moore, and Wallace Roney): Antilles 314 510-2. There is plenty of good bass (bass viol) on this jazz album with a well-focused sound stage, excellent clarity, and a feeling of decent depth. The piano and drum set are properly sized and well positioned, although the snare sometimes seems closer than the rest of the set and the overall drum impact is a bit subdued. (A)

355 Dufay, Guillaume: *Missa "L'Homme Armé"*; *Motets*, The Hilliard Ensemble: EMI 7 47628 2. Clean and clear, with a nice close up perspective. The sound stage has an excellent — and realistic — spread and depth. The pre- and early digital EMI recordings have never impressed me a lot, but this one is first rate. I assume that some serious internal, technological and organizational changes are responsible for the improvement in their sound. (A+)

356 Dunlap, Bruce: *About Home*: Chesky JD-59. This is guitar sound at its clearest and most realistic, with wonderful depth and studio ambience. Unfortunately, a rather high level of deep background rumble mars the performance. Another example of Chesky not employing speaker monitors with sufficient low-frequency extension to reveal such artifacts. Switch to its bypass mode or in some other way reduce the output volume of your subwoofer. This recording will not need its contribution. (Qualified A+)

357 Duparc, Henri: *Songs*, sung by Sarah Walker, Thomas Allen, and Roger Vignoles: Hyperion CDA 66323. Very realistic reproduction of solo vocalists listened to midway in a moderate-sized hall. (A)

358 Dupré, Marcel: *Symphony in G Minor*; Rheinberger, Josef: *Organ Concerto Number 1, in E*, Royal Philharmonic Orchestra, Michael Murray, organ: Telarc 80136. This is a very powerful recording with an excellent sound stage, realistic depth, and stunning *deep* bass — down to below 18 Hz. Unless you have a very potent bass-reproduction system, much of the impact of this disc will be lost. There seems to be a bit of background hiss that is unrelated to the recording technology (digital). I assume that it is either microphone noise or the noise of the organ. (Qualified A+)

359 Duruflé, Maurice: *Organ Music* (complete), Todd Wilson, organ: Delos D/CD 3047. Open, spacious, yet detailed and transparent. There is some impressive bass on this one (needless to say) that is sometimes subtle enough to sneak up on you. (A+)

360 Dvořák, Antonín: *Cello Concerto in B Minor*; Saint-Saëns, Camille: *Cello Concerto Number 1*, London Symphony Orchestra, Alexander Micheljew, cello: Nimbus NI 5127. Nice stage spread and depth with good clarity. The violins are a tad brittle, and the overall perspective is a bit distant. The

Dvořák (361)

cello is well positioned in relation to the ensemble, is properly sized, and sounds quite realistic. The brittle strings almost bump this disc from the list, but the realistic sound stage saves it. (B+)

361 Dvořák, A.: *Dvořák and Friends* (with assorted additional Czech wind pieces by Myslivecek and Krommer), The Harmonie Ensemble: Music & Arts CD-691. Close up, clear, and very well endowed with depth and hall ambience. Very good individual instrument detail. (A+)

362 Dvořák, A.: *Piano Concerto, Op. 33*; Janáček, Leos: *Concertino*, Czech Philharmonic Orchestra, Rudolf Firkušný, piano: RCA 60781-2. Good and clean with a well-presented hall ambience. The piano is just a bit too forward in relation to the orchestra. It's well positioned laterally, however, and not at all diffuse or phasey. (A)

363 Dvořák, A.: *Slavonic Rhapsodie*; *Suite for a Large Orchestra*, Janáček Philharmonic Orchestra: Centaur CRC-2121. Better than average sound-stage depth with a wonderful midhall listening perspective. Notable clarity and transparency throughout. (A+)

364 Dvořák, A.: *Symphony Number 6*; Janáček, Leos: *Rhapsody for Orchestra "Taras Bulba,"* Cleveland Orchestra: London 430 204-2. This release exhibits a fine sound stage and good depth. The clarity is excellent with no more than a hint of the string-sound harshness that is a characteristic of some other London recordings. (A)

365 Dvořák, A.: *Symphony Number 9* (New World); *Carnival Overture*; *Othello Overture*, Academy of St. Martin in the Fields: Capriccio 10 386. Smooth, spacious, and transparent, with better imaging than the London version (366) and a better string sound too. However, it is a bit less dynamic than the latter. The sound stage seems just a bit flat. (A)

366 Dvořák, A.: *Symphony Number 9*, Vienna Philharmonic Orchestra: London 400 047-2. Done in 1979, this disc is indicative of the better Decca recording jobs of that era. Brilliant, detailed, and dynamic, with just a bit of brittleness in the strings. The very spacious and enveloping sound stage is a characteristic of late 1970s London discs. Five years from now, when there are a greater number of state-of-the-art microphone competitors, this effort might not qualify for inclusion in a discography of this kind, but it certainly does right now. (A)

367 Dvořák, A.: *Symphony Number 9*; *Carnival Overture*, Los Angeles Philharmonic Orchestra: Telarc 80238. Reverberant and smooth in the Telarc tradition with a wide, deep, and spacious sound stage. That same sound stage is also a bit diffuse (also in the Telarc tradition), but such an anomaly is of little consequence with music of this genera, particularly when the recording is played back on typical systems in typical living rooms. In impact and subjective realism, this release is superior to either 365 or 366. (A+)

368 *Easter's Herald: Gregorian Chants*, Schola Hungarica: Hungaroton HCD 12558-2. Wonderful depth combined with a broad, realistic sound stage, very good clarity, and a fine sense of realism. If you have a surround-sound processor, you can make the ambience of the church even better. (A+)

369 *École Notre-Dame: Messe du Jour de Noël* (mid-12th century),

Ensemble Organum: Harmonia Mundi France 1901148. Very smooth, close up; but still reverberant sound, with fine clarity. At times, the soloists seem just a bit too close to the listener. This makes them more audible, but it does detract from the realism somewhat. It should be noted that quite a few listeners prefer this effect. The exemplary quiet of the hall is only occasionally punctuated by low-level traffic noise. (A)

370 Egan, Mark: *A Touch of Light* (with Bill Evans, Clifford Carter, Gil Goldstein, and Danny Gottlieb): GRP D-9572. Smooth, punchy, percussive, and clean jazz — and obviously heavily manipulated at the mixing console. Still, the sound stage has adequate breadth, the sound itself is clean, and there is even decent bass at times. (B+)

371 Elgar, Edward: *Pomp and Circumstance Marches*; *Wand of Youth*; *Bavarian Dances*, English String Orchestra: Nimbus NI 5136. Quite distant but clear, clean, and reverberant. The Calrec Soundfield microphone has done its job here; the sound is wonderfully transparent with a three-dimensional sound stage and fine imaging. When one compares this Nimbus production with some of the material the company has recorded in other environments, it is obvious that this complex microphone array is more influenced by hall acoustics than some other configurations. (A)

372 Elgar, E., and Frederick Delius: *Songs*; Benjamin Luxon, baritone; David Willison, piano: Chandos CHAN 8529. Quite close up and detailed, with a good blending between the soloist and the piano. The hall ambience is well integrated, giving a front-row effect. (A+)

373 Elgar, E.: *Symphony Number 1*; *Pomp and Circumstance Marches Numbers One and Two*, Baltimore Symphony Orchestra: Telarc 80310. Very dynamic, with a broad and deep sound stage. The orchestral clarity is superior, and lovers of dynamic contrasts will find that the bass drum on the "Pomp 1" is powerful, not overdone. There is an impressive organ part in that piece with substantial depth. The acoustics in the Meyerrhoff Hall in Baltimore are obviously exemplary and have to be playing a big part in this recording's quality. (A+)

374 Elias, Eliane: *Cross Currents* (with Eddie Gomez, Jack DeJohnette, Peter Erskine, Barry Finnerty, and Café): Denon CJ 2180. This jazz release is uniform, clean, and somewhat distant with the drums spread out as usual. However, two people are playing the things (along with still another individual on "percussion"), so who knows what the effect would be like on a live stage? The piano is well focused, and the sound stage has decent depth and a good spread. The overall recorded sound level is low, so a higher-than-normal playback gain setting will be required from your amp. (A)

375 Elias, E.: *So Far So Close* (with Michael Brecker, Randy Brecker, Will Lee, Peter Erskine, Don Alias, and Café): Blue Note CDP 7 91411-2. Smooth and clean, with a better bass line than 374. The imaging is more diffuse, however, and the sound stage seems a bit flatter and more contrived. There is a good piano focus, and the multiple percussion players spread out the drum sound and the other assorted pyrotechnics. (A)

376 *Elizabethan Music: As I Went to Walsingham* (assorted composers), The Musicians of Swann Alley: Harmonia

Ellington (377)

Mundi USA 905192. Smooth sound, with a broad, diffuse sound stage. Clean instrumental textures. (A)

377 Ellington, Duke: *Digital Duke* (with Lew Soloff, Barry Lee Hall, Ron Tooley, Clark Terry, Eddie Daniels, Branford Marsalis, and many others, along with Mercer Ellington conducting): GRP 9548. This is a modern recording of Ellington's music. The result is unstressed, clean, and detailed, with a good sound stage and a fine instrumental blend. The overall gain on this recording is a bit low, and it definitely benefits from setting the amplifier volume on your system well above normal. (A)

378 Elliot, Chris: *Shuffle Off to Buffalo* (playing the Shea's Buffalo Wurlitzer Pipe Organ): CPE 104CD. If big-theater pipe-organ bass is your bag, this is the disc for you. The bass pedals are impressive at times, but even more arresting (from a system performance angle) is the background sound of the organ machinery and the hall during the relatively quiet sections. Subtle big-room ambience aplenty. Fun listening, but anything but high art. (A)

379 *The Emperor's Trumpet* (assorted works by Richter, Caldara, Sperger, and Reutter), Franz-Liszt-Kammerorchester, Edward Tarr, trumpet: Christophorus CD 74558. Nice and smooth with fine depth, breadth, and clarity. Wonderful trumpet realism. (A+)

380 *An English Ladymass* (medieval chant and polyphony), Anonymous 4: Harmonia Mundi France: 907080. Beautifully done, with a fine sense of depth and ambience. The perceived listening position is a bit far back from the sound stage, but the subjective churchlike positioning enhances the effect here. The lack of background rumble found in most recordings of this kind was unusual, a result of the job being done in a recording studio instead of a church. (A+)

381 *The English Lute Song* (works by Johnson, Morley, Lanier, Ferrabosco, Campion, Brewer, and others); Julianne Baird, soprano; Ron McFarlane, lute: Dorian DOR 90109. Nice and realistic in clarity, depth, and hall ambience. The singer and the lute are well placed and well sized. Some low-level hall rumble that almost sounds like traffic noise intrudes occasionally. (Qualified A+)

382 *Enya*: Atlantic 81842-2. This is mellow music by an Irish "New Age" group that comes across as big, smooth, electrically synthesized, and powerful, with a reverberant but well-controlled sound field. The vocals are notably smooth and refined, and the bass is surprisingly strong for a New Age disc. I found that this is good music to write books by. If you have a surround-sound decoder or processor of some kind, you may find that the sound field benefits from its use. (B+)

383 Enya: *Shepherd Moons*: Reprise 9 26775-2. More smooth, obviously electronically processed New Age sound with remarkable ambience and depth. On some tracks, the powerful reverberation slightly obscures what should be excellent vocals. (B+)

384 Enya: *Watermark*: Geffen 24233-2. This New Age release is very clean and liquid, with a good fabricated sound stage, very articulate (and beautiful) vocals, and sometimes surprisingly deep and strong bass — dipping into the low 30s. Just a tad better overall than the two above efforts. This is a good demo album. (A)

385 Erb, Donald: *Concerto for Brass and Orchestra*; *Concerto for Violincello and Orchestra*; *Ritual Observances*, Saint Louis Symphony Orchestra, Lynn Harrell, cello: New World 80415-2. Good clarity, depth, and dynamics, with a midhall listening perspective that is quite right for music of this kind. The solo cello in the second work is well located and realistically sized. (A)

386 *The Essence* (with Billy Higgins, Ray Drummond, and Hank Jones): Digital Music Products CD-480. This is an outstanding technical effort by a company that specialized in state-of-the-art jazz recordings. It displays a very realistic sound stage and an outstanding you-are-there envelopment. Needless to say, the sound is stunningly clear. This is a "DD" recording: direct to two-track, with no console mixing or manipulation. While this will guarantee it no better sound in inherent distortion, the use of this kind of *non*mix forces the engineer to use minimalist microphone techniques intelligently. That almost certainly will result in better sound. (A+)

387 *An Evening with Victoria De Los Angeles* (singing works by Scarlatti, Pergolesi, Paisiello, Brahms, Granados, and others), with Geoffrey Parsons, piano: Collins 12472. A live concert with the usual audience applause and background noise, this recording sports a realistic sound stage. The piano and vocalist are properly placed in a real-world hall. (A)

388 Extreme II: *Pornografitti*: A&M 75021 5313 2. This is punchy, room-filling rock that is better recorded than the first Extreme album, which did not rate a spot on the list. (B)

389 Fagen, Donald: *The Nightfly*: Warner 23696-2. Done in 1982, this is a very clean studio recording, fully justifying its traditional popularity as a salon and hi-fi demo record. Excellent vocal clarity. Has pop-rock music recording technology progressed since this disc appeared? No. (A+)

390 Falla, Manuel de: *Siete Canciones Populares Españolas*; *Concerto* (and other, shorter works), Orquestra de Cambra Teatre Lliure, Victoria De Los Angeles, soprano: Harmonia Mundi France 901432. Very clean and smooth, with a fine orchestral sound stage, particularly the depth. The vocal parts are outstandingly well recorded, the positioning and sizing perfect. There is nothing better than a good performer treated right by her technicians. (A+)

391 Falla, M.: *Three Cornered Hat*, *El Amor Brujo* (complete ballets), Orchestre Symphonique de Montréal: London 410 008-2. The sound is detailed, brilliant, and transparent, with a good sound stage and a nice sense of depth. The recorded pyrotechnics (a characteristic of this music) are also very gripping at times. The orchestral brilliance sometimes results in a slightly edgy but not all that offensive violin sound. This recording was made in 1983 but is still quite up to date. (A)

392 Falla, M.: *Three Cornered Hat*, *Nights in the Gardens of Spain*, London Symphony Orchestra (with Della Jones and Carol Rosenberger): Delos D/CD 3060. Excellent detail, presence, dynamics, and clarity with a fine orchestral spread and depth. This version of the *Hat* has a slight edge in all respects over 391. Very good hall sound. The piano is well integrated in the *Nights*, although some might think it was a bit too close to the audience. (A+)

393 Falla, M.: *La Vida Breve*, Cincinnati Symphony Orchestra (with Alicia Nafé, Antonia Ordóñez, Karen Notare, Catherine Keen, and others): Telarc 80317. Very broad staged, deep, and smooth, with an excellent integration of the solo singers into the overall mix. The choral sound is especially well handled and blends impressively with the instrumentalists. The overall acoustic sound field is a bit dry for a Telarc job, but it still suits this kind of music quite well. (A+)

394 Farrell, Eileen: *Eileen Farrell Sings Johnny Mercer* (with Loonis McGlohon, Doug Buens, Bill Stowe, Jim Pugh, Joo Negri, Phil Thompson, Doug Henry, and Jan Thornton): Reference Recordings RR-44CD. There is nice vocal clarity here with the supporting instrumental ensemble well positioned in relation to the soloist. A good sound stage and a realistic sense of recording space is a hallmark of Reference Recordings. (B+)

395 Fauré, Gabriel: *Quartet Number One in C Minor*; *Piano Trio in D Minor*, Beaux Arts Trio: Philips 422 350-2. Smooth and clean, with good depth and a fairly close-up perspective that enhances material of this kind. The piano is the weak item here. It is sized OK but seems just a tad phasey and diffuse. (A)

396 Fauré, G.: *Requiem*; *Masques et Bergamasques*, Choeurs & Orchestre National de Lyon: Denon 81757 9527-2. Smooth and clean with a good sense of depth and hall space. This recording exemplifies what I consider a fine blend between the orchestra, chorus, and soloists. (A)

397 Fauré, G.: *Requiem*; Duruflé, Maurice: *Requiem*, Atlanta Symphony Orchestra and Chorus: Telarc 80135. Fine depth, spread, and choral-orchestral blending, along with good clarity. The Telarc recording techniques work well with this kind of material. To some listeners it may be a toss-up between this one and 396. (A+)

398 Feinstein, Michael: *Michael Feinstein Sings Burton Lane*: Elektra-Nonesuch 79243-2. Perhaps the best sound to be found on a Feinstein recording. The vocals are clean, and the sound stage is pretty well laid out. Maybe I am just old-fashioned, but in musical content, all of Mr. Feinstein's discs are worth a listen, even if the sound is not always top grade. (B+)

399 Feldman, Morton: *Rothko Chapel*; *Why Patterns?*, University of California Berkeley Chamber Chorus and California EAR Unit: New Albion NA 039CD. There is an excellent sound-stage depth and subjective impression of clarity on this recording. The hall envelopment is what is required for music of this kind. (A)

400 Ferguson, Maynard: *Body and Soul* (with Wayne Bergeron, Alan Wise, Alex Iles, Tim Ries, and others): Black Hawk 501-2. Clean and close up jazz with the mixed drum-percussion section stretched across the sound stage. There are some nice dynamic contrasts on this recording, but the effort still does not match 401. (B)

401 Ferguson, M.: *High Voltage* (with Denis DiBlasio, Todd Carlton, Ray Brinker, Rich Shaw, Michael Higgins, and Steve Fisher): Intima CDI-73279. This effort exhibits a good, albeit synthesized stage spread, with the solo trumpet well positioned in relation to the rest of the ensemble. The clarity is muted by the distant perspective but is still manageable. The usual multiple-performer percussion section probably accounts for the subjectively wide drum spread. (B+)

402 Ferguson, M.: *High Voltage 2* (with John Toomey, Dave Tull, Michael Lufkin, Tom Bevan, Billy Hulting, and Matt Wallace): Intima 7 73360-2. This release is similar in sound quality to the above disc, even though that one was ADD and this one is DDD. Digital does not always guarantee a winner. The hardware employed does not completely control the final result, particularly if the analog recorder is a good one. The intelligent use of the quality equipment on hand is what often counts the most. (B+)

403 Ferguson, M.: *Storm* (with Nelson Hill, Dan Jordan, Denis DiBlasio, Steve Wiest, and quite a few others): Nautilus NR 57 DIDZ 10011. Mastered by Doug Sax, this disc is quite advanced over 401 and 402; which I believe were produced after it. This recording is very clean with plenty of jazz punch, good bass, and a properly piercing trumpet. I also felt it had a notably realistic sound stage. The playback level here is quite low, so it is necessary to turn up the volume control substantially to hear this disc the way it should be. Better than most and made in 1982. (A)

404 *Festa Veneziana* (works by Gabrieli, Riccio, Grillo, Costello, and Picchi), Musica Fiata: FSM FCD-97705. Very clean, clear, and brilliant with a fine sense of ambience and depth. (A)

405 Field, John: *Four Piano Sonatas*, Míceàl O'Rourke, piano: Chandos CHAN 8787. Clean and clear, with the piano well sized, solidly focused, and properly positioned at a fairly close listening position in a moderate-sized hall. The hall reverb on the recording of this early nineteenth-century composer's piano music is just right. (A+)

406 Field, J.: *Nocturnes*, John O'Conor, piano: Telarc 80199. This is a very realistic and clean piano-sound recording of the fifteen nocturnes. The piano is decently focused and the hall feel is complimentary. (A)

407 Field, J: *Sonatas and Nocturnes*, John O'Conor, piano: Telarc 80290. Clear piano sound with just a touch of spaced-microphone diffuseness. (A)

408 *Finnish Trumpet Concertos* (works by Wessman, Linkola, Hauta-Aho, and Segerstam), Finnish Radio Symphony Orchestra, Jouko Harjanne, trumpet: Finlandia RACD 388. Smooth, clean, and vibrant. Here we have a fine sound stage and orchestral-trumpet tonal blend combined with a nice sense of hall space and depth. The trumpet is well sized and properly positioned in relation to the orchestra. (A+)

409 Finzi, Gerald: *Five Bagatelles*; *Clarinet Concerto*; Ashmore, Lawrence: *Four Seasons*; *Greensleeves*, Guildhall String Ensemble, Richard Stoltzman, clarinet: RCA 60437-2-RC. Smooth, clean, and well balanced. The clarinet is well placed, and the orchestra has good depth and lateral spread. Nice hall feel. (A+)

410 Fischer, Clare: *Lembranças* (with Brent Fischer, Dick Mitchell, Tris Imboden, Michitos Sanchez, and Luis Conte): Concord Picante CCD-4404. Good and punchy, with solid and deep (but subtle) bass at times. There is nice clarity overall with a somewhat forward but not overwhelming sound stage. The

Flanagan (411) [64]

electrically added studio ambience is tastefully applied (B+)

411 Flanagan, Tommy: *Nights at the Vanguard* (with George Mraz and Al Foster): Uptown UPCD-27.29. This direct-to-two-track live jazz recording is unstrident and clean with a nice feeling of depth. The sound seems somewhat withdrawn, but the resultant image has a good nightclub perspective. (B+)

412 Flanagan, T.: *Thelonica* (with George Mraz and Art Taylor): Enja R2-79615. This 1982 AAD recording is nice and clean, with better depth than most recordings of this kind. The overall effect seems just a touch thin and lacking in body at times. (B)

413 Fleck, Bela: *Drive* (with Sam Bush, Jerry Douglas, Stuart Duncan, Mark O'Connor, Tony Rice, Mark Schatz, and Peter Rowan): Rounder CD-0255. This jazz release is very clean, transparent, and vibrant. The sound stage is close up with the kind of small-hall ambience that almost produces a they-are-here effect on a large playback system in a large room. Surround manipulation via my larger Yamaha unit really moved this disc into the front ranks. (A)

414 Flim and the BB's: *Big Notes* (with Billy Barber, Bill Berg, Flim Johnson, and Dick Oatts): Digital Music Products CD-454. This jazz technical masterpiece has great clarity, detail, and impact with the final track displaying impressive dynamic range and strong bass down to 22 Hz. What we have here is a real showpiece for impressing your friends or selling good loudspeakers. If your woofers can survive the last track of this disc when it's played at an ambitious listening level, they are tough suckers indeed. (A+)

415 Flim and the BB's: *The Further Adventures of Flim and the BB's* (with Flim Johnson, Billy Barber, Bill Berg, Jimmy Johnson, Luis Conte, Charlie Davis, Rick Baptist, Bruce Paulson, and Dick Oatts): Digital Music Products CD-462. This is a "DD" (direct-to-digital) disc with no intervening mixing work or console manipulations (analog or digital). Digital (as opposed to analog) mixers will not electrically degrade the sound of a recording, but not using one to adjust things after the fact forces the engineer to choose and place his microphones very carefully. The result here is a spectacularly clean, smooth, and realistic effort, right up there with the best. Quite a few DMP discs are recorded this way. (A+)

416 Flim and the BB's: *Neon* (with Billy Barber, Bill Berg, Flim Johnson, Dick Oatts, Bill Barber Senior, Cliff Johnson, and Jack Oatts): Digital Music Products CD-458. This one matches the other DMP recordings by this jazz group in clarity, detail, and general overall realism of sound. (A+)

417 Flim and the BB's: *This Is a Recording* (with Billy Barber, Bill Berg, Jimmy Johnson, Dick Oatts' and others): Warner 26655-2. Every bit as good as the DMP-produced discs by this group. The sound is clean and unobstructed with plenty of depth and punch combined with a wide frequency bandwidth. A credit to the Warner engineers. (A+)

418 Flim and the BB's: *Tricycle* (with Billy Barber, Bill Berg, Flim Johnson, and Dick Oatts): Digital Music Products CD-443. I believe this was the first digital recording by this group. It is jazz at its most dynamic— detailed and clear with very little distortion of any kind. A credit to engineer Tom Jung, who handles all or at least most all the DMP recording jobs. (A+)

419 Flim and the BB's: *Tunnel* (with Billy Barber, Bill Berg, Jimmy Johnson, and Dick Oatts): Digital Music Products CD-447. Same qualities as 418. (A+)

420 *La Flûte Enchantée* (assorted works by Jolivet, Chaminade, Martin, Godard, Saint-Saëns, and Ibert), City of London Sinfonia, Susan Milan, flute: Chandos CHAN 8840. Good clarity, depth, and sound-stage spread, with the flute laterally well positioned but maybe just a tad too forward in relation to the rest of the ensemble. (A)

421 Ford, Ricky: *Manhattan Blues* (with Jaki Byard, Milt Hinton and Ben Riley): Candid CCD-79036. This jazz release is a bit subdued but still clean and well focused. Ford's sax is well delineated, although it is somewhat distant, and the drum set is positioned realistically and is not overly large. The dry acoustics can be helped by means of your surround processor and its careful use. Barely makes the list, however. (B)

422 Ford, R.: *Saxotic Stomp* (with James Spaulding, Charles Davis, Kirk Lightsey, Ray Drummond, and Jimmy Cobb): Muse MDC 5349. This one has decent clarity and detail, with better studio ambience than 421. The improvement is still slight and not enough to up the score. (B)

423 Ford, Robben: *Talk to Your Daughter* (with Vince Denham, Brandon Fields, Mark Ford, and others): Warner 25647-2. The recording-locale listing on the enclosed flyer lists quite a few studios. Consequently, the sound is not consistent throughout, some tracks better than others. The good sections are punchy, clean, and *very* electrically synthesized. This jazz is more like rock than anything else—true crossover stuff. The vocals are clean and well focused. (B to B+)

424 The Four Horsemen: *Nobody Said It Was Easy*: Def American 26561-2. This is heavily "electrically" processed rock, but with decently lucid vocals and good impact. The music and the sound were both improved by using either of the rock modes on my Yamaha DSP unit. (B)

425 *Fourplay* (with Bob James, Lee Ritenour, Hathan East, and Harvey Mason): Warner 26656-2. This is an AAD jazz disc that surpasses a lot of DDD efforts, with good clarity, good dynamics, and solid individual instrument imaging. The bass line is pleasing, especially that produced by the drums, which unfortunately are stretched across the space between the speakers, much too wide in relation to the rest of the combo to imitate a live performance. The minor faults of this disc have nothing to do with its analog origins. (B+)

426 Franck, César: *Complete Masterworks for Organ*, Michael Murray, organ: Telarc 80234. Spacious, powerful, and reverberant. The brilliant organ sound is only slightly marred by instrument's internal wind noise (not an engineering flaw by Telarc, please note). Recordings of this kind respond beautifully to manipulation by your surround processor. (A+)

427 *French Art Songs* (works by Chabrier, Fauré, Hahn, Ravel, Saint Saëns, and Weckerlin), Yolanda Marcoulescou-Stern, soprano: Gasparo GSCD-293. Wonderful vocal clarity and detail, with a close up sound stage and a fine hall feel. The piano accompaniment is well positioned, nonfuzzy, and stable. (A+)

428 *Frese Nouvele!* (Gothic polyphony in the thirteenth to fifteenth centuries), Musica Mensurata: FSM FCD 97736. Reverberant, transparent, and forward, with good detail and good vocal imagery. There is a nice churchlike ambience backing up the work of the performers. (A)

429 Frisell, Bill: *Before We Were Born* (with Arto Lindsay, Joey Baron, and others): Elektra/Musician 9 60843-2. There is a wonderful ambience surrounding the instruments on some but not all of the tracks on this jazz release. The recording was made at a variety of locations, and the sound is variable because of this. The clarity is as variable as the obviously synthesized studio ambience. The fusion-of-rock-and-jazz sound on this release may take some getting used to. I thought it was pretty entertaining. (B to B+, depending)

430 Frishberg, Dave: *Let's Eat Home* (with Jeff Hamilton, Jim Hughard, Rob McConnell, and Snooky Young): Concord Jazz CCD-4402. I felt this one had pretty fine clarity and detail, although the ensemble is obviously multimiked and therefore a bit one-dimensional and lacking in sound-stage depth. This is especially noticeable with the too-far-forward solo vocalist. The drum set also sounds much too wide at times; a typical failing with many recordings of this type. (B)

431 *From Evening to Evening with Gregorian Chant*, Schola Hungarica: Hungaroton HCD 31086. The usual wonderful hall ambience produced by this group is apparent here, with good clarity and depth. Note that these recordings benefit, like most other recordings of medieval music, from judiciously applied surround enhancement, assuming your home system has the capability. Even Dolby decoding can aid the effect immensely, although disabling the steering logic on your Pro Logic decoder might be in order. (A)

432 Fulbert de Chartres: *Stirps Jesse*, Ensemble Venance Fortunat: Quantum QM 6899. Reverberant and spacious, yet articulate and transparent. A fine blend of close-up choral work by a small ensemble and a wonderful cathedral ambience. Quite realistic. (A+)

433 G., Kenny: *Duotones* (with Tony Gable, Kenny McDougald, Randy Jackson, Joe Plass, Alan Glass, Cory Lerios, and others): Arista 8496. This is punchy, clean, and spacious jazz. The sax is well defined and sounds like a saxophone should, although the electrically synthesized and console-manipulated nature of this disc is plainly evident. (I have no idea why this man, Kenny Gorelick, has given up most of his last name to headline this recording and several others.) (B+)

434 Gabriel, Peter: *Security*: Geffen 2011-2. Great impact and clarity for a rock disc recorded in 1982. This is an early DDD item and one of the earliest for a rock production, I believe. The first cut knocks you out of your chair if you advance the gain to realistic levels. I liked the way it came across, however. Not an "easy-listening" rock album by any means, but one of the best. (A+)

435 Gabriel, P.: *Shaking the Tree*: Geffen 9 24326-2. I felt that this release was not up to *Security* in clarity, tonal accuracy, and impact. Interestingly, this disc was done 8 years after the first one, yet it is still AAD! What happened to their digital recorder? Even more disconcerting was the sound quality, variable from track to track. Interestingly, "San Jacinto" is on both discs and seems a bit clearer on the early release. The title song, "Shaking the Tree," seems better recorded than some of the other material and rates an A by itself, but it cannot carry the whole load. (B+ overall)

436 Gabrieli, Giovanni: *Music of Gabrieli and His Contemporaries* (including Isaac, Banchieri, and Diaz), Empire Brass and Friends: Telarc 80204. Smooth, close up, and vibrant, with a broad and deep sound stage. The horns are notably free of the kind of microphone overload that often plagues recordings of massed brass. (A)

437 Galper, Hal: *Invitation to a Concert* (his trio, with Todd Coolman and Steve Ellington): Concord Jazz CCD-4455. Marred mainly by the usual oversized drum-set image, this disc still has good clarity, and the piano at least is well recorded, as is the bass viol. (B)

438 Galper, H.: *Portrait* (his trio, with Ray Drummond and Billy Hart): Concord Jazz CCD-4383. Good and clean, with the piano well focused and properly sized. The bass (viol) is subdued but properly positioned and clean. The drums lack punch, even though they extend clear across the sound stage. Other than that, the listening perspective is middistance, or halfway back to the rear wall in a typical jazz-club environment. (B)

439 *The Garden of Zephirus* (courtly songs of the early fifteenth century), The Gothic Voices: Hyperion CDA 66144. Fine clarity and detail, with a close up listening perspective combined with good hall ambience. The nice overall effect is made even better with surround enhancement. (A)

440 *Gargoyles and Chimera* (exotic works for organ, including works by Dupré, J. S. Bach, Sowerby, and others), David Britton, organ: Delos D/CD 3077. Very clean and detailed, with a fine balance between the instrument and the hall. Some interesting (and sometimes odd) sound effects are possible with this organ. (A+)

441 Garrett, Kenny: *African Exchange Student* (with Mulgrew Miller, Charnett Moffett, Tony Reedus, Tito Ocasio, Ron Carter, and others): Atlantic 82156-2. This jazz release has an excellent sound stage with good front-to-back depth and ambience and good imaging. The saxophone is cleanly handled and is decently imaged. (B+)

442 Garson, Michael: *Serendipity* (with Gary Herbig, Peter Sprague, Jim Lacefield, Billy Mintz, and others): Reference Recordings RR-20CD. This effort displays a wonderful sound stage and depth with detailed and exact imaging. The jazz clarity is exemplary, the only flaw an occasional low-frequency bass rumble (the only word to describe it), which should be audible only on a system having a very potent subwoofer. (Qualified A)

443 Geminiani, Francesco: *La Folia* (and other concertos and sonatas), Purcell Quartet and Purcell Band: Hyperion CDA 66264. Very clean, with just a touch of typical string overbrightness on this original-instruments disc. As noted previously, this effect is as much a part of the actual instrumental sound as a specific recording technique. (A)

444 Geminiani, F.: *Six Concerti Grossi*, Tafelmusik: Sony SK 48043.

Genesis (445)

Forward and brilliant in the original-instrument tradition, but quite powerful with a wonderful depth and soundstage spread. Needless to say, the sound is exceptionally clear. A credit to the Sony recording team. (A+)

445 Genesis: *Invisible Touch*: Atlantic 81641-2. This is a heavily "electronically" manipulated rock album that is a bit buzzy in the vocals but still comes across as an impressive item. There is some subtle deep bass at times, and the dynamic impact is often good. (B)

446 Gershwin, George, and Ira Gershwin: *Crazy for You*, Deadrock Symphony Orchestra (with Beth Leavel, Stacy Logan, Harry Groener, Bruce Adler and others): Angel CDC 7 54618-2. This more serious pop music displays a good orchestral sound stage and excellent choral-solo imaging. The dance-noise effects are also convincing, adding to the realism. The vocals seem to be a bit close up at times, but their clarity is exemplary, and the effect is not really all that negative. (A)

447 Gershwin, G., and I. Gershwin: *Girl Crazy* (with Lorna Luft, David Carroll, Judy Blazer, David Garrison, Frank Gorshin, and others): Elektra-Nonesuch 9 79250-2. Articulate, dynamic, close up, and punchy. However, this recording is also a bit dry and clinical sounding (home-based surround enhancement can mostly correct this, particularly when it is done by a synthesizer-type unit such as those made by Lexicon and Yamaha). I should note that some engineers and many listeners like this kind of well-etched sound. The vocal detail and clarity are excellent. (A)

448 Gershwin, G.: *Lady Be Good: First Recordings of the Unknown George Gershwin*, Kevin Cole, piano: ProArte CDD-365. Here we have a close-up sound that is clear and dynamic. Although there is a fair amount of reverb, the stage image still has the piano-in-your-listening-room kind of perspective. The impression is of a room a bit larger than what you are probably sitting in. If you run the program through a surround-enhancement device, the effect becomes even more pronounced, and the listening room has a more you-are-there feel. (B+)

449 Gershwin, G., and I. Gershwin: *Lady Be Good* (with Lara Teeter, Ann Morrison, Jason Alexander, Ivy Austin, and others): Elektra-Nonesuch 79308-2. Similar in quality to *Girl Crazy* (see 447). The use of surround processing to open things up is still recommended. (A)

450 Gershwin, G.: *Marni Nixon Sings Gershwin* (assorted songs, with Lincoln Mayorga, piano): Reference Recordings RR-19CD. Another winner from RR with a realistic sound stage, believable hall envelopment, fine clarity, and a proper singer-to-piano balance. The sound picture imposes a midhall listening perspective. (A+)

451 Gershwin, G., and I. Gershwin: *Of Thee I Sing*; *Let Them Eat Cake*, Orchestra of St. Lukes, New York Choral Artists (with Maureen McGovern, Paige O'Hara, Larry Keri, Jack Gilford, David Garrison, and others): Columbia M2K-42522. Very good orchestral sound stage, with fine clarity. The chorus is very intelligible and well handled and blends in a near-perfect way with the orchestra. The soloists are equally well recorded with notable (read tight) imaging, although on some occasions they seem a bit oversized. (A)

452 Gershwin, G.: *Piano Improvisations*, Paul Posnak, piano: Special Music SCD 6039. This is a marvelously real-sounding recording of reconstructed modern renditions of Gershwin at the piano. Unlike most piano recordings, the instrument is well imaged and not diffuse or oversized. In this recording, Posnak actually mimics the piano techniques found on several early recordings made by Gershwin. (A+)

453 Gershwin, G.: *Rhapsody in Blue*; *Preludes for Piano*; *Second Rhapsody for Orchestra, with Piano* (with other short works for keyboard): Los Angeles Philharmonic, Michael Tilson Thomas, piano: Columbia MK 39699. While I have never been a big fan of the Columbia "classical" recorded sound, this original jazz-band-orchestrated compact disc conducted by Michael Tilson Thomas is an exceptional well-defined recording of the original Gershwin adaptation. The effect is clean, smooth, and brilliant. The piano is well imaged, and this is probably as close to the "true" George Gershwin jazz-orchestra sound as you will get. (A)

454 Gershwin, G.: *Rhapsody in Blue*; *An American in Paris*; *Concerto in F*, Pittsburgh Symphony Orchestra, Andre Previn, piano: Philips 412 611-2. This one is quite a contrast to 453. Big and robust in a way that many listeners will like, with a bass drum that may be a bit too boomy when the disc is played on a large stereo that has an authoritative deep bass potential. The drum comes across quite nicely when played on a smaller system. The piano is well focused, and the overall sound stage has a nice spread and nice clarity. There is a continual rumble sound floating in the background that demands that any subwoofer be shut down or at least turned down. Again, it is no problem on smaller sound systems. This unfortunate bass heaviness is the one sour note on an otherwise fine release, although I am sure some enthusiasts will like the effect. (Qualified A)

455 Gershwin, G.: *Rhapsody in Blue*; *An American in Paris*, Cincinnati Symphony Orchestra, Eugene List, piano: Telarc 80058. This 1981 all-digital release is dynamic, clean, and brilliant with a wide and deep sound stage in the best spaced-omni-microphone tradition. The piano is a bit diffuse (also in the spaced-omni tradition) but not obnoxiously so. (A)

456 Gershwin, G., and I. Gershwin: *Strike Up the Band* (with Brent Barrett, Don Chastain, Rebecca Luker, Jason Graae, Beth Fowler, and others): Elektra-Nonesuch 9 79273-2. Overall, this is smooth, clear, and detailed orchestral sound. The chorus is well recorded in focus and clarity, but the soloists are just a smidgeon too forward in relation to the rest of the ensemble. (A)

457 Gesualdo, Carlo: *Madrigaux à 5 Voix*, Les Arts Florissants: Harmonia Mundi France 901268. Excellent transparency and detail combined with a realistic sound stage. There is very good vocal articulation, with the ensemble placed in a complementary and pleasant-sounding hall setting. (A+)

458 Gesualdo, C.: *Tenebrae Responsories for Holy Saturday*, The Tallis Scholars: Gimell CDGIM-015. Close up, detailed, and quite smooth, with wonderful hall ambience and realistic stage depth. The stuff I have heard by the Scholars on the Gimell label has been uniformly excellent. (A+)

459 Gibbs, Terry, and Buddy DeFranco: *Chicago Fire* (with John Campbell, Todd Coolman, and Gerry Gibbs): Contemporary CCD-14036-2. This live jazz recording is smooth and detailed, with mostly good focus and a decent sound stage. The drums are sized well, the bass sounds OK, but (as usual and unfortunately) the piano is oversized. The vibes and clarinet are the featured instruments here, and they both sound fine. (B+)

460 Gilbert, William, and Arthur Sullivan: *The Mikado*, Orchestra and Chorus of the Welsh National Opera: Telarc 80284. Clean sound with remarkable clarity and detail. The wide, Telarc sound stage is here as usual, and the soloists are well positioned on that stage and sound quite real. (A+)

461 Gillespie, Dizzy: *Endlessly* (with Barry Eastmond, John Lee, Buddy Williams, Victor Jones, and others): MCA Impulse MCAD 42153. Punchy, clean, and vibrant. The sound stage displays a good spread, and the drums are well focused and not spread too wide. The kick drum is a bit overpowerful, but the effect will come across in a positive manner on many smaller stereo systems. On some tracks, there is some stage-induced rumble. Turn your subwoofer off, or at least turn it down a bit. (Qualified B+)

462 Gillespie, D.: *New Faces* (with Kenny Kirkland, Branford Marsalis, Lonnie Plaxico, and others): GRP D-9512. Smooth, wide band, and clean. The instrumental parts are very distinct and delineated, with remarkable trumpet clarity. There is an excellent stage presence and depth, along with a wonderfully powerful bass line. (A)

463 Gillespie, D.: *To Bird with Love* (with Paquito D'Rivera, Benny Golson, Antonio Hart, Bobby McFerrin, and others): Telarc 83316. This Telarc jazz release is smooth and transparent with a broad sound stage and yet well-imaged instruments, particularly the drums. The hall ambience tends toward dryness, but I found that a bit of manipulation via a synthesizing-type surround processor opens things up and really lets this recording take off. This is a live performance, so there is some audience noise. (A)

464 Gillespie, D.: *To Diz with Love* (with Doc Cheatham, Jon Faddis, Wynton Marsalis, Claudio Roditi, Red Rodney and others): Telarc 83307. Recorded live, this disc exhibits a somewhat distant perspective, with a fine, clearly delinated sound stage. This effort has tighter imaging than typical for Telarc due to the use of an MS array (a variant of the figure-8 coincident technique) for the main microphones, plus some accent mikes. (A)

465 *The Girl with the Orange Lips* (assorted vocal works by Falla, Ravel, Stravinsky, Kim, and Delage), Dawn Upshaw, soprano: Elektra-Nonesuch 9 79262-2. This one displays a good subjective midhall listening position with quite passable clarity and a realistic balance between the singer and her instrumental support. Interestingly, the title song, by Earl Kim, is only 1 minute, 45 seconds long. (A)

466 Glazunov, Alexander: *Orchestral Works*, Hong Kong Philharmonic Orchestra: Marco Polo 8.220309. Smooth and transparent with good depth and stage spread. The sound is a bit dry, but the effect may be preferred by some, particularly if they have a surround-sound or ambience extraction device to open things up. The string tone is quite good, given the fairly close-up sound. (A)

467 Gliere, Reinhold: *Symphony Number 3*, BBC Philharmonic Orchestra: Chandos CHAN 9041. Here we have a wonderful sound-stage blend and overall depth combined with a bright, forward, clean, and front-row sound. The violins are a touch brittle, but the effect may appeal to listeners who prefer sitting close to those instruments at live performances. (A)

468 Golson, Benny, featuring the Freddie Hubbard Quintet: *Stardust* (with Ron Carter, Marvin Smith, and Mulgrew Miller): Denon 81757 1838-2. Very clean and right-there jazz with a wonderful sound stage and notable depth. There is very good imaging overall, with the exception of the too broadly spaced drum set. The piano is well sized, and the sax has a very fine and realistic tonal balance. (B+)

469 Goodrick, Mick: *Biorhythms* (with Harvie Schwartz and Gary Chaffee): CMP CD-46. This one is nice and mellow with a good full sound. A good feature here is the nice bass line, which occasionally has substantial low-range extension. The drums are well sized, but the electric guitar seems to be spread all the way across the stage at times, a characteristic that I can overlook in light of the often very fine "percussive" impact of this jazz disc and the fact that an electric guitar can be set to image any way its operator wants it to at a live concert. (A)

470 Gottlieb, Danny: *Whirlwind* (with Doug Hall, John Abercrombie, Bill Evans, Marc Egan, and others): Atlantic 81958-2. Very transparent and smooth jazz with a good stage image. The drums are appropriately sized, and the other instruments are equally well handled. (B+)

471 Gottschalk, Louis: *Piano Music*, Richard Burnett, playing 19th century pianos: Amon-Ra CD SAR 32. (Also available on Musical Heritage Society 512951T.) The crossed-axis hypercardioid microphone technique probably used here gives the piano a distinct in-hall sound. This technique may be the best way to handle the piano, but it does require that the recording environment be suitable, and the microphones must be of high quality and carefully distanced from the instrument. (A)

472 Gould, Morton: *Dance Variations for Two Pianos and Orchestra*; Piston, Walter: *Concerto for Two Pianos and Orchestra*; Copland, Aaron: *Dance Cubana*, Royal Philharmonic Orchestra, Joshua Pierce and Dorothy Jonas, pianos: Koch 3-7002-2. Remarkably clean, smooth, and reverberant with a close up sound stage and realistic hall depth and ambience. Top-notch sound in every way. (A+)

473 Grant, Amy: *Heart in Motion*: A&M 75201 5321 2. This album displays good vocal clarity along with good pop-music dynamics and clean—often fairly deep—bass. (B)

474 *Great Baroque Arias*, The King's Consort (with Gillian Fisher, James Bowman, John Ainsley, and Michael George), IMP PCD-894. Smooth, close up, spacious, and reverberant. There is a good sense of stage realism. (A)

475 Great White: *Hooked*: Capitol CDP 595330. There is good impact and a decent sound-stage spread on this release. The clarity is good for a rock album. (B)

476 Green, Bunky: *Healing the Pain* (with Billy Childs, Ralph Penland, and

Gregorian Chant (477)

Art Davis): Delos DE 4020. Just about state-of-the-art in every way. Clear, clean, and transparent with a near-perfect blend of everything required to make a fine jazz recording. The sax sounds on the stage instead of in your face, and the depth and width of the ensemble are right on the money. (A+)

477 *Gregorian Chant*, Schola of the Hofburgkapelle, Vienna: Philips 416 808-2 (also available as Musical Heritage Society 512147W). This is a very clear recording. The sound has a front-row perspective, but the big-room ambience is still impressive. (A)

478 *Gregorian Chant from Aquitaine*, Schola Hungarica: Quintana 903031. Very smooth and balanced with an excellent church-hall ambience, realistic clarity, and a fine choral blend. An interesting aside is that this disc features the same musical ensemble and was recorded by the same engineer as in the Hungaroton release below (see 479). The major difference (assuming that the same microphones were employed) was that the churches were different—another case for the importance of the recording environment. (A)

479 *Gregorian Chants in a Village Church*, Schola Hungarica: Hungaroton 12742-2. This disc has a marvelous ambience and sound-stage realism. The environment is very churchlike, and the detail, clarity, and balance are just about state-of-the-art. The soloists are sized and positioned exactly as they should be in relation to the rest of the performing ensemble. (A+)

480 *Gregorian Chants from Austria*, Schola Hungarica: Hungaroton 12950. The vocals in this recording are smoothly recorded and combined into a fine hall-ensemble blend with good clarity. There is possibly a little less depth than in 479 certainly due to environmental differences, although microphone types and their placement will have also affected the result. (A)

481 Grieg, Edvard: *Piano Concerto in A Minor*; *Holberg Suite*; *Lyric Suite*, Seattle Symphony Orchestra: Delos DE 3091. The piano sound is a touch less tightly focused than I normally like, but this disc is still an excellent example of piano-orchestral tonal blending and clarity. Overall it is smooth, spacious, and vibrant, with a fine orchestral sound stage and a rich and dynamic piano sound in the concerto. (A)

482 Grofé, Ferde: *Grand Canyon Suite*; Gershwin, George: *Porgy and Bess* (suite), Detroit Symphony Orchestra: London 410 110-2. I felt that this recording had excellent clarity and good control of the dynamic contrasts coupled to an equally good sound stage. There is plenty of impact in the storm scene in the *Suite*. (A)

483 Grolnick, Don: *Weaver of Dreams* (with Michael Brecker, Randy Brecker, Bob Mintzer, and others): Blue Note CDP 7 94591-2. Clean, punchy, and well-defined jazz with a good nightclub ambience. The sound stage is flat, typical with multimicrophone work, but the drums, piano, and other instruments are well imaged laterally, although the piano sounds a bit too far forward in relation to the other players. (B+)

484 Grusin, Dave: *Dave Grusin and the N.Y./L.A. Dream Band* (with Rubens Bassini, Lee Ritenour, Tiger Okoshi, and others): GRP-D-9501. This is a nice clean live jazz-concert presentation with some impressive

dynamics and a good but not great mixer-generated sound stage. (B)

485 Grusin, D.: *The Gershwin Connection* (with Chick Corea, Lee Ritenour, Gary Burton, Eddie Daniels, John Patitucci, Dave Weckl, Don Grusin, Eric Marienthal, and Sal Marquez): GRP GRD-2005. This is a very articulate recording. The first minute is a piano-roll reproduction of Gershwin playing. After that, Grusin takes over and does his interpretations. One of the best GRP recording jobs. Very clean, transparent, and real. The synthesized sound stage is expertly done. (A+)

486 Grusin, D.: *Migration* (with Branford Marsalis, Omar Hakim, Carlos Rios, and others): GRP GRD-9592. Punchy, clear, and impressive, with subtle and deep bass at times. The well-defined sound stage, although probably electrically synthesized from a multimicrophone grouping, is solid enough to pass for a minimalist job. (A+)

487 Grusin, D.: *Nightlines* (with Phoebe Snow, Randy Goodrum, David Sanborn, and others): GRP 9504. Very crystalline and detailed, with substantial impact and an occasional hint of subtle deep bass that sets recent GRP jazz efforts apart from a lot of the competition. (A)

488 Grusin, D., and Don Grusin: *Sticks and Stones*: GRP GRD-9562. Just two guys here working with mostly electronic instruments, but it sounds like half a dozen. Punchy, liquid, and clear, with a finely honed albeit synthesized sound stage that obviously works just like the players wanted it to. Very impressive bass at times and plenty of percussive impact. Records like this are used by hi-fi salesmen to sell equipment. (A+)

489 Guy, Buddy: *Damn Right, I've Got the Blues*: Silvertone 1462-2-J. The vocal parts are very clean (important in a blues recording) with plenty of rock-caliber punch when called for. There is also a good vocal-instrumental blend. The bass is punchy and fairly deep at times. (B)

490 Hadley, Jerry: *Standing Room Only* (Broadway Favorites, with the American Theater Orchestra): RCA 61370-2. This Dolby Surround recording is clean and smooth, with a wonderful feeling of depth and clarity and with a good balance between the soloist and the supporting ensemble. Designed to sound its best when run through a home–Dolby decoder before going to four or five properly sited speakers, this transcription still sounds fine when played back on a standard two-speaker stereo system. A brief comparison between standard-stereo playback and a "steered" Dolby-processed playback (utilizing five speakers) easily gave the edge to the latter, particularly if the listener is sitting somewhat off the central axis between the speakers. In the latter case, the steering, combined with the center speaker, keeps the soloist centered, while standard-stereo playback allows him to collapse into the nearer "main" speaker. However, standard-stereo playback gave tonal and spacial results that were a close match for the Dolby version, even though it did not include "surround speakers." (A)

491 Hairston, Jester: *Spirituals*, Belmont Chorale: Gasparo GSCD-269. These works are certainly "classical" in nature and deliver a wonderful stage spread and sense of hall envelopment. However, there is a slight lack of front-to-back depth. The clarity, however, is exceptional, considering that thirty people are often singing at the same time. (A)

492 Hall, Jim: *Jim Hall's Three* (with Steve LaSpina and Akira Tana): Concord Jazz CCD-4298. Finely etched and clean jazz, with good dynamics, good bass, and a decent sound stage. The guitar sounds a bit muted, but the drums are good, and the bass viol is appropriately room-filling. (B+)

493 Hall, J.: *These Rooms* (his trio, with Steve LaSpina, Joey Baron, and Tom Harrell): Denon CJ-2297. This jazz release has a close up feel and is reasonably clear with a good sense of hall space. Odd as it seems, the sound stage seems a bit laterally constricted for a recording with such intimate sound. If things had been spread out better, it would have rated a more impressive score. (B)

494 Hamilton, Scott: *The Right Time* (his quintet, with Chris Flory, John Bunch, Phil Flanigan, and Chuck Riggs): Concord Jazz CCD-4311. Nice and smooth, with good imaging for the most part, except for the piano, which is too diffuse. The jazz sax, however, sounds quite good, and the drums are properly sized and sound OK. (B)

495 Hampton, Lionel: *Just Jazz* (with Harry Edison, James Moody, Buddy Tate, Al Grey, Clark Terry, Hank Jones, Milt Hinton, and Grady Tate): Telarc 83313. Smooth and clean and a bit distant and dry, unless the amplifier gain is advanced considerably. When this is done, the ambience blooms out, and the sound comes to life. There is notable individual instrument detail here that is quite impressive at times. There is also much better than average drum focus for a recording of this kind. The "jazz" settings on my Yamaha DSP unit made this well-recorded effort sound even better. (A)

496 Hampton, L.: *Lionel Hampton and the Golden Men of Jazz, Live at the Blue Note* (with Clark Terry, Harry Edison, James Moody, Buddy Tate, Al Grey, Hank Jones, Milt Hinton, and Grady Tate): Telarc 83308. This multimiking job by Telarc is remarkably well defined and detailed, with an excellent sound-stage spread and a good nightclub-stage aural perspective. Multimiking may not always give us the depth we want, but it certainly gives the engineers control when it is needed, particularly if the recording environment is less than optimal. (A)

497 Händel, George Frideric: *Aci, Galatea e Polifemo*; *Sonatas pour Flûte à Bec et Basse Continue*, London Baroque Ensemble (with Emma Kirby, Carolyn Watkinson, and David Thomas): Harmonia Mundi U.K. 901253/54. Smooth and transparent, with exceptional blending of the instruments. I thought the vocal renditions were quite realistic with fine detail, precise imaging, and a proper integration into the sound stage. The three sonatas are smaller in scale, but the instrumental soloists easily equal the larger ensemble in sound quality. (A+)

498 Händel, G. F.: *Arias for Montagnana*, Philharmonia Baroque Orchestra, David Thomas, bass: Harmonia Mundi France HMU 907016. The subjective image here is nice and clear with a close up listening perspective. There is good vocal reproduction in particular with a nice sense of hall space and ambience. (A+)

499 Händel, G. F.: *Cantatas*; *Sonatas*, Ensemble Divitia Cologne: Channel Classics CCS 0890. Wonderfully well recorded with an excellent reproduction of Derek Ragin's marvelous countertenor voice. The period harpsichord, oboe, and cello are also well recorded. (A)

500 Händel, G. F.: *Cantatas and Trio Sonatas* (Kantaten und Triosonaten), Musica Alta Ripa, Johanna Koslowsky, soprano: Musikproduktion Dabringhaus und Grimm L-3399. Nice hall perspective and sound stage with good clarity. The vocals are quite spacious but still clear. (A)

501 Händel, G. F.: *Concerti a Due Cori*, Academy of Ancient Music: Archiv 411 721-2. Over 10 years old, this original-instrument recording still shines. Nice clarity, spread, and depth, with no overbearing string harshness. The sound is marred by some hall rumble that will not be noticeable with most speaker systems. (Qualified A)

502 Händel, G. F.: *Concerti Grossi, Op. 3*, Händel and Haydn Society players: L'Oiseau-Lyre 421 729-2. This is another original-instruments presentation, which in this case has none of the usual string-tone brittleness that seems to plague such recordings. The sound stage is proper, the depth realistic, and the reproduced instruments transparent. (A+)

503 Händel, G. F.: *Concerto Grosso, "Alexander's Feast,"* The English Concert: Archiv 415 291-2. I felt this one was polished and close up sounding with fine clarity and detail. The violins are just a tad overbright, almost certainly due to the nature of these "original" instruments. (A)

504 Händel, G. F.: *Concerti Grossi (12), op. 6*, I Musici de Montréal: Chandos CHAN 9004/5/6. Very smooth, clean, and baroque-sounding, with a wonderful hall spaciousness and realistic sound-stage depth. The only flaw is a low-level, low-frequency stage noise feeding through the flooring to the microphones. This was not audible on my large or small systems with their respective subwoofer equalizers in their "filter-only" modes. This limited their full-output lower ranges to frequencies above 35 and 40 Hz, respectively, rolling off the bass sharply at 12 dB per octave below those points and steeper still below 20 Hz. (Qualified A+)

505 Händel, G. F.: *Concerti Grossi (12), op. 6*, I Solisti Italiani: Denon 81757 6305 2. This effort displays a notably superior sound stage with the presence and clarity maybe a tad better than 506. Overall, this disc is also just a smidgeon better than 504. (A+)

506 Händel, G. F.: *Concerti Grossi (1–6), op. 6*, The Boston Baroque: Telarc 80253. Clear, spacious, warm, and realistic. It would be hard to choose between this recording and 504 and 505, except that the Denon and Chandos recordings have all twelve concerti. (A+)

507 Händel, G. F.: *Giulio Cesare* (Julius Caesar), Concerto Köln (with Jennifer Larmore, Barbara Schlick, Bernada Fink, Derek Lee Ragin, and others): Harmonia Mundi France 901385/87. Brilliant, clear, detailed, and vibrant. The stage spread and depth are outstanding, as is the recorded hall ambience and the sense of envelopment it imparts. The vocals are realistic and blend beautifully. (A+)

508 Händel, G. F.: *Italian Cantatas*, Academy of Ancient Music, Emma Kirkby, soprano: L'Oiseau-Lyre 414 473-2. This is very clean and balanced orchestral sound with a fine blending of the vocalist and the orchestra. The soloist is right where she should be and is recorded with a first-class microphone.

Händel (509)

This transcription is outstanding in every technical way that matters. (A+)

509 Händel, G. F.: *Judas Maccabaeus*, The King's Consort, Choir of New College Oxford (with Emma Kirkby, Catherine Denley, James Bowman, Jamie MacDougall, and Michael George): Hyperion CDA 66641/2. Broad staged, smooth, and crystalline, with fine orchestral detail and a realistic hall ambience. The chorus is properly imaged behind the instrumental ensemble, where it should be, and the soloists appear to be positioned farther in front, also where they should be (a notable accomplishment), and they are all accurately recorded. (A+)

510 Händel, G. F.: *Messiah*, University of California Berkeley Chamber Chorus, Philharmonia Baroque Orchestra (with Loraine Hunt, Janet Williams, Patricia Spence, and others): Harmonia Mundi France 907050/52. A very clean, detailed, somewhat dry and small-scaled sound, befitting the original-instrument orientation. The solo vocalists are very well handled and realistic. The intimacy here is quite different from what many have come to expect listening to more modern orchestral versions of this work. When the program was run through my rather elaborate surround processor, the dryness tended to disappear, and the work became more large scale. (A+)

511 Händel, G. F.: *Messiah*, The Boston Baroque (with Karen Clift, Catherine Robbin, Bruce Fowler, and Victor Ledbetter): Telarc 80322. Telarc has not done a lot of original-instruments work, but they did a top-grade job here. Very clean and well-detailed sound, with good depth and spread. Excellent hall ambience along with very good overall imaging and particularly good vocal focus and clarity. The result, needless to say, is very realistic. (A+)

512 Händel, G. F.: *Oboe Concertos*; *Sonatas*, St. James Baroque Players, Paul Goodwin, oboe: Meridian ECD 84106. There is good blending of the oboe and the ensemble on this analog-mastered recording. The period instruments, particularly the solo oboe, sound natural. The ensemble has a somewhat distant perspective, and the sound stage is not really wide, but it does have depth and fine imaging. A bit of left-minus-right "extraction-type" surround processing, by means of my smaller Yamaha unit (also possible with any basic noncenter-steering Dolby or Hafler-type device) should help to extract additional hall ambience from this recording. "Synthesizing-type" surround processing, via my Yamaha DSP unit, also had a positive effect. (A)

513 Händel, G. F.: *Ottone*, Freiburger Barockorchester (with Drew Minter, Lisa Saffer, Michael Dean, Juliana Gondek, Ralf Popken, and Patricia Spence): Harmonia Mundi France HMU 907073/75. Done at the 1992 Göttingen Festival but not in front of an audience, this effort has a very clean orchestral texture and a marvelous sense of depth and ambience, combined with a wide, uniform stage spread. The vocalists are expertly recorded with a good sense of stage positioning and marvelous tonality. (A+)

514 Händel, G. F.: *Overtures*, The English Concert: Archiv 419 219-2. Another period-instruments recording with the usual bright, clean sound typical of the good ones. I was struck by the accurate stereo sound stage. There is just a slight amount of hall rumble. Cut off your subwoofer. (Qualified A)

515 Händel, G. F.: *Saul*, Concentus Musicus Wien, Konzertvereinugung Wiener Staatsoperchor (with Dietrich Fischer-Dieskau, Anthony Rolfe Johnson, Julia Varady, Elizabeth Gale, and others): Teldec 8.35686. Overall, this disc has a somewhat distant orchestral perspective with a clean, smooth, transparent sound. There is a very good orchestral-choral blend in particular. The soloists are meticulously recorded and have outstanding stage positioning. I found that this recording responded well to even rudimentary surround processing. (A+)

516 Händel, G. F.: *Susanna*, Philharmonia Baroque Orchestra, University of California Berkeley Chamber Chorus (with Lorraine Hunt, Drew Minter, and others): Harmonia Mundi France 907030/32. A very transparent close up sound with a fine sense of depth and ambience. Smooth choral blending, with good articulation. The solo vocals are realistically placed and sized properly in relation to the instrumental ensemble. There is a low-level background rumble throughout, probably an air conditioner or heater system. (Qualified A+)

517 Händel, G. F.: *Theodora*, Philharmonia Baroque Orchestra, The University of California Berkeley Chamber Chorus (with Lorraine Hunt, Drew Minter, Jennifer Lane, Jeffrey Thomas, David Thomas, and others): Harmonia Mundi France HMU 907060/62. Very smooth, clean, spacious, and baroque, much like 516. This disc has an exemplary sound stage with outstanding placement of the vocals in relation to the original-instrument orchestra. I did not notice the motor rumble that was apparent on 516, which was recorded at a different location on a different date. (A+)

518 Händel, G. F.: *Trio Sonatas*, The English Concert: Archiv 415 497-2. Bright, clean, and close up. The authentic instruments have a they-are-here presence that may or may not appeal to the listener. An occasional bit of background noise appears to be traffic sound, but the effect is not distracting. (A)

519 Händel, G. F.: *Water Music*, Orchestra of St. Luke's: Telarc 80279. Exceptionally good, even for a Telarc. There is a remarkable sound-stage depth and spread; a result of the wide-spaced Schoeps microphone array favored by engineer Jack Renner. (Here he used two capsules instead of his usual three.) The hall ambience here is quite good. There are times when the spaced-omni technique works to perfection, and this is one of those. (A+)

520 Händel, G. F.: *Water Music*, Los Angeles Chamber Orchestra: Delos D/CD 3010. Although over a dozen years old, this (apparently) two-microphone spaced-array recording is clean and clear with excellent placement of first violins on the left and the second violins on the right for a more blended (although maybe a tad diffuse) sound. In some listening rooms, the subtle phasey effect may be a plus factor with music of this type. (A)

521 Händel, G. F.: *Water Music*, The English Consert: Archiv 410 525-2. Here we have a typical Archiv recording job of period instruments with a wide, deep sound stage, realistic ambience, and excellent clarity. Archiv "typical" means first class in this case. (A+)

522 Hanson, Howard: *Concerto for Organ, Harp and Strings*; *Nymphs and*

Hanson (523)

Satyr Ballet Suite; *Concerto da Camera in C Minor*, Rochester Chamber Orchestra (first two works), Meliora Quartet, Brian Preston, piano (third work): Bay Cities BCD-1005. Very spacious and clean on the chamber selections with excellent hall ambience. The sound is close up and clear on the quartet selections, although there is some stage noise at times and the piano seems a bit too far back. (A)

523 Hanson, H.: *Symphonies Number 1 and 2*; *Elegy in Memory of Serge Koussevitsky*, Seattle Symphony Orchestra: Delos D/CD 3073. Simply marvelous: clean, smooth, and transparent with the broad-stage sound that Delos is noted for. Excellent imaging too. The three works here were done at the Seattle Opera House, but the three were also done at different dates, indicating that the engineer has his technique down pat. The whole Delos-Seattle series of Hanson's work is very well handled. (A+)

524 Hanson, H.: *Symphony Number 2*; Barber, Samuel: *Violin Concerto*, Saint Louis Symphony Orchestra, Elmar Oliveira, violin: EMI CDC 7 47850-2. Produced by Angel/EMI by Capitol Records and engineered by Marc Aubort, this effort is very smooth and is easily the equal of 523. There is a wonderful sound stage here; the spread and depth are notable and real. The solo violin in the concerto is well focused and sized just right in relation to the rest of the performers — a sign that EMI is now producing material with the best. (A)

525 Hanson, H.: *Symphonies Number 3 and 6*; *Fantasy Variations On a Theme of Youth*, Seattle Symphony Orchestra (Symphonies), New York Chamber Symphony, Carol Rosenberger, piano (*Fantasy*): Delos DE 3092. The symphonies by the Seattle-based group match the sound quality of the other recordings of Hanson's work below and the earlier one above. The Chamber Symphony recording of the *Fantasy* is equally well done, the piano is well sized and properly focused. (A+)

526 Hanson, H.: *Symphony Number 4*; *Serenade for Flute, Harp and Strings*; *Lament for Beowulf*; *Pastorale for Oboe, Harp and Strings*; *Suite From the Opera "Merry Mount,"* Seattle Symphony Orchestra and Chorale (first, third, and fifth works), New York Chamber Symphony (second and fourth works): Delos DE 3105. Fine clarity, spread, and depth on the material recorded in New York and in Seattle. There are some nice dynamic contrasts and plenty of impact in the *Beowulf*, combined with a marvelous integration between the choir and the orchestra. Delos just keeps producing one winner after another, thanks to master recording engineer John Eargle. (A+)

527 Hanson, H.: *Symphony Number 5*; *Symphony Number 7*; *Mosaics*; *Piano Concerto in G Magor*, Seattle Symphony Orchestra, Carol Rosenberger, piano (on the *Concerto*): Delos DE 3130. Smooth, vibrant, and realistic with a wonderfully broad and deep sound stage. The clarity is notable, and the piano in the concerto is recorded expertly by the engineer. (A+)

528 *Harp Music of the Italian Renaissance*, Andrew Lawrence-King, arpa doppia: Hyperion CDA 66229. This pleasant musical material is clear and clean with a good small-hall ambience. The harp is recorded with fine articulation and is easy to listen to. (A)

529 The Harper Brothers: *Remembrance* (with Justin Robinson, Stephen

Scott and Kiyoshi Kitagawa): Verve 841 723-2. This jazz release displays a nice sound stage and good depth. There is good clarity also with wide-band frequency response. This is a direct-to-two-track nightclub live recording job, and surround processing of nearly any kind makes it sound even better. (B+)

530 *The Harpsichord in the Netherlands* (works by Bustijn, Sweelinck, van Noordt, Reincken, and others), Bob van Asperen, harpsichord: Sony SK 46349. Clear and close up, with an in-your-living-room kind of sound stage. The effect will be loved by some and rather disliked by others. (A)

531 Harrell, Tom: *Form* (with Joe Lovano, Daniel Perez, Charles Haden, and Paul Motian): Contemporary CCD-14059-2. This jazz release is full, rich, and clear, with good "spatiality" and depth from a middistance perspective. The drums and the piano are well recorded. (B+)

532 Harrell, T.: *Passages* (with Joe Lovano, Daniel Perez, Peter Washington, Paul Motian, and Cheryl Pyle): Chesky JD-64. This is clean and well-defined "modern" jazz sound with a wide and balanced sound stage that highlights the minimalist microphone techniques employed by this recording company. The stage spread and depth are good, and the trumpet sound is well positioned and very realistic. (A+)

533 Harrell, T.: *Sail Away* (with Joe Lovano, Dave Liebman, James Williams, John Abercrombie, and Ray Drummond): Contemporary CCD-14054-2. As with *Form* (531), this is a rich-sounding recording with good spatial presence. The drums and piano are as tight and controlled here as they were in that release. (B+)

534 Harrell, T.: *Stories* (with Bob Berg, Niels Lan Doky, John Scofield, Ray Drummond, and Bill Hart): Contemporary CCD-14043-2. As with the two previous Contemporary recordings, this one has plenty of richness and space around it. However, the piano is not as well recorded as in those two releases, and it takes on a diffuse and overly large character when it is highlighted. None of the three recordings of Harrell by Contemporary can equal Chesky JD-64 (see 532). (B)

535 Harris, Gene: *Tribute to Count Basie* (with "The Gene Harris All-Star Big Band," including Jon Faddis, Snooky Young, Garnett Brown, Bill Green, Herb Ellis, Ray Brown, and others): Concord Jazz CCD-4337. Here we have a wonderful stage spread and nice clarity, the ensemble enveloped by a small nightclub ambience. The sound field is just a bit lacking in front-to-back stage depth, a characteristic that is mostly apparent because of its contrast with the other, more positive attributes. (B+)

536 Harris, G.: *Black and Blue* (with his quartet, including Ron Eschete, Luther Hughes, and Harold Jones): Concord Jazz CCD-4482. Very clear in every way, particularly the well-proportioned drum set. There is also a good clublike ambience that fits material of this kind. The piano is typically vague in positioning and a bit oversized. (B+)

537 Harris, G.: *Listen Here!* (with his quartet, including Ron Eschete, Ray Brown, and Jeff Hamilton): Concord Jazz CCD-4385. Very nice in clarity, depth of sound stage, and impact. The piano is solid and sized well. However, the drums do not fit the sound stage as they should, although at times their focus seems OK. The cymbals seem to wander about and are just too diffuse. (B+)

538 Harris, G.: *The Gene Harris Trio Plus One* (with Ray Brown and Mickey Roker): Concord Jazz CCD-4303. This recording displays a good live performance pickup with a decent stage presence and good studio ambience. The depth of the sound stage is also OK, and the clarity is quite nice, especially the sax. The drum set is well focused, and the piano is where it should be and properly sized. (B+)

539 Hart, Mickey: *Planet Drums* (with Airto Moreira, Flora Purim, and others): Rycodisc RCD 10206. This is pretty much the same kind of material as featured in Hart's other album, *Däfos* (see 322). In this case, it is listed under Hart's name instead of the title because that is how it is headlined on the CD box. The disc is dynamic in the extreme, with tremendous percussive punch at times and a wide band width. This is the kind of stuff that hi-fi shops love to wow customers with. Even more than the other album, there are some wildly synthesized and electronically modified vocal manipulations. This is not a particularly realistic recording, but it is very impressive nonetheless. Like *Däfos*, this is from an analog master. If they had knocked over the drums (you will have to listen to the other disc to catch the meaning of this), I might have given the disc a still higher score. (A)

540 Havens, Richie: *Sings Beatles and Dylan*: Ryko RCD 20035. This release offers studiolike sound with Havens's voice displaying a somewhat electrically "processed" characteristic. The recording has deeper bass at times—into the high 30s—than any original Beatles or Dylan disc I have heard. (B)

541 Haydn, Joseph: *Complete Works for Lute and Strings*, Jakob Lindberg, lute: BIS CD-360. There is a nice instrumental blend on this simple two-microphone recording with a fine small-room ambience and close up sound. Good clarity with the lute and good focus too, with none of the slightly phasey quality that has shown up on a few other BIS releases. (A)

542 Haydn, J.: *Concerto for Trumpet and Orchestra*; Mozart, Wolfgang Amadeus: *Concerto for Trumpet and Orchestra*; Hummel, Johann: *Concerto for Trumpet and Orchestra*, National Philharmonic Orchestra, Wynton Marsalis, trumpet: Columbia MK 37846. Smooth, clean, and clear with the trumpet very well handled in tonality, although a bit closer in relation to the support ensemble than it should be. (A)

543 Haydn, J.: *The Creation* (*Die Schöpfung*), Wiener Philharmoniker, Wiener Singverein (with Edith Mathis, Francisco Araiza, and José van Dam): Deutsche Grammophon DGG 410 718-2. A realistic yet somewhat distant perspective that will come across on some systems better than others. This recording was made live at the Salzburg Festival, and as such it is not plagued with some of the multimicrophone recording artifacts that show up on a number of other DGG efforts. However, because of this, the sound stage is not really broad, and that may seem odd to listeners who are used to the wide-stage presentation of spaced-omni microphones. Overall, the recording has a reasonably wide frequency response combined with fine clarity and a somewhat dry ambience. The vocals are especially clear, however, and are pretty much stage centered, as they would be at a live concert when heard from a fairly distant seat. Interestingly, I found that this recording responded positively to surround enhancement of any kind and that it was made still more impressive by running the outputs through a Carver "Hologram" processor. A similar effect can be generated by devices made by Lexicon and Polk. (A)

544 Haydn, J. *The Creation*, Atlanta Symphony Orchestra and Chorus (with Dawn Upshaw, Jon Humphrey, John Cheek, Heidi Murphy, and James McGuire): Telarc 80298. Sung in English, this effort is technically magnificent. The sound stage is much broader here than on the DGG version, 543, and the soloists are spread across that stage, giving the effect of being quite close up. The orchestral blend is outstanding, the ambience is rich and reverberant, yet the detail and clarity are first class. While technically superior to the German effort, I will leave it to the listener to judge the relative artistic merits. (A+)

545 Haydn, J.: *Missa in Angustiis (Nelson Mass)*, Symphonie-Orchester und Chor des Bayerischen Rundfunks: Philips 416 358-2. Here we have a somewhat distant sound stage, the listener placed well back in the hall and enjoying soloists who are established in a proper spatial relationship with the chorus, the orchestra, and the recording environment. The result is quite realistic to anyone who sits in a normal seat in a normal hall. However, the rendition does lack the ultraclear close up detail cherished by audio critics who like a front-row perspective and listen to their speakers from six feet away. (A)

546 Haydn, J.: *String Quartets, Op. 54, numbers 1 and 2*, Smithson String Quartet: Deutsche Harmonia Mundi 77028-2-RC. Very clean, clear, and real. The usual superlatives apply: the sound stage is correct, the depth palpable, and the hall ambience just what music like this needs. Another triumph by the Harmonia Mundi group. (A+)

547 Haydn, J.: *String Quartets in G Major, F Major, and D Minor*, Salomon String Quartet: Hyperion CDA 66348. Very clean and clear with an excellent small-hall sense of space. This recording uses modern-built copies of original instruments, except for the cello, which is a true original. (A)

548 Haydn, J.: *Symphonies Numbers 6, 7, 8 (Le Matin, Le Midi, Le Soir)*, The English Concert: Archiv 423 098-2. This is a clean, transparent, and spacious period-instrument disc with an excellent sound stage and realistic hall ambience. (A+)

549 Haydn, J.: *Symphony Number 21; Cello Concerto Number 1; Symphony Number 96*, Scottish Chamber Orchestra, János Starker, cello: Delos D/CD 3062. This effort is highlighted by a wide, deep, and spacious sound stage that occasionally seems a tad diffuse. However, the cello is fairly well focused and placed quite well in relation to the rest of the orchestra. (A)

550 Haydn, J.: *Symphony Number 22; Piano Concerto in D Major; Symphony Number 104*, Scottish Chamber Orchestra, Carol Rosenberger, piano: Delos D/CD 3061. Very clean and spacious—and somewhat diffuse—as with 549. Also as in that recording, the violins seem a tad bright. The piano in the concerto is the weak point, being too large and diffuse for the size of the orchestra. This is a good example of what a simple spaced-array technique can do to compromise the sound of a piano concerto. Still, the effort rates a place on our list because of the other

Haydn (551)

well-recorded material. (A for the symphonies; B+ for the concerto)

551 Haydn, J.: *Symphonies Numbers 35, 38, 39, and 59* ("Sturm & Drang" symphonies, volume 1), The English Concert: Archiv 427 661-2. A clean and clear original-instrument recording with the usual Archiv spacious sound stage. Maybe modern instruments would sound fuller and more up to date, but there is no denying that in some cases going back to the basics does pay off. It surely does here. (A+)

552 Haydn, J.: *Symphonies Numbers 45, 47, and 50* ("Sturm and Drang" symphonies, volume 6), The English Concert: Archiv 429 757-2. Bright, clear, and vibrant in the original-instrument tradition—in much the same way as volume 1 (551). I have not heard them, but I think it can be assumed that volumes 2 through 5 of this series are similar in quality. (A+)

553 Haydn, J.: *Symphony Number 51; Piano Concerto in G Major; Symphony Number 100*, Scottish Chamber Orchestra, Carol Rosenberger, piano: Delos DE 3064. Spacious, clean, and clear with excellent depth. Both the string sound and the focus are better in this recording than in the earlier Delos recordings (see 549, 550). The piano is properly placed and sized and is much better recorded than in D/CD 3061. No fuzzy middle here. This is another triumph by engineer John Eargle, who expertly matches his microphone models and their placement to the hall. Contrast this job (which probably made use of the ORTF technique combined with additional accent microphones at the sides of the orchestra) with the spaced-array technique of Telarc (556, 559) and the coincident (Ambisonic) technique of Nimbus (555). It's worth obtaining (or at least borrowing) all of them just to educate yourself. (A+)

554 Haydn, J.: *Symphonies Numbers 82, 83, and 84: The Paris Symphonies*, Orchestra of the Age of Enlightenment: Virgin Classics VC 7 90793-2. There is an up-close, clean, and detailed sound from this period-instruments recording. Very smooth string texture for this type of instrumentation. (A)

555 Haydn, J.: *Symphonies Numbers 96 and 102*; Austro-Hungarian Haydn Orchestra: Nimbus NI 5135. This release is beautifully imaged with remarkable sound-stage depth. It also has the kind of left-right spread and sense of distance that faithfully mimic a midhall listening position. Very good clarity and detail top off this excellent effort. This recording makes a case for the Ambisonic recording technique with music of this kind when it is transcribed in a proper setting. (A+)

556 Haydn, J.: *Symphonies Numbers 100 and 103*, Orchestra of St. Luke's: Telarc 80282. Fine clarity combined with a wide, deep, and close up sound stage. There is a wonderful overall blend here that is less tightly focused than 555 but with a more close up and richer sound. Each recording has its strong points. Concert-music buffs should educate themselves by having copies of at least one Nimbus and one Telarc recording of a Haydn symphony to see which microphone technique they prefer. (A+)

557 Haydn, J.: *Symphonies Numbers 100 and 104*, Academy of Ancient Music: L'Oiseau-Lyre 411 833-2. Detailed and clear in the period-instrument tradition. There is a fine small-hall sense of space here with a complete lack of string-tone harshness. The recording may be a bit thin for some listeners but the "true" Haydn sound for others. (A)

558 Haydn, J.: *Symphonies Numbers 101 and 102*, The Hanover Band: Hyperion CDA 66528. Music like this is suited to period instruments, and this recording does justice to the performance. Smooth, clean, and vibrant with a nice hall bloom to the sound. The somewhat distant subjective listening position only slightly detracts from the overall impact. (A)

559 Haydn, J.: *Symphonies Numbers 101 and 104*, Orchestra of St. Lukes: Telarc 80311. Smooth and reverberant with good detail and clarity. There is a somewhat amorphous stage image on this release, but that doesn't hurt with this music, provided one is happy with a seat fairly far from the orchestra where blending is more important than pinpoint imaging. In a living-room environment, when one is listening by means of a typical good stereo system, the spaced-array technique does a good job of faking the concert-hall experience. The spaced-omni recording technique is anathema to some and the producer of sonic correctness to others. (A+)

560 Haydn, J.: *Trios for Baryton, Viola and Cello*, Balázs Kakuk, baryton; Péter Lukács, viola; Tibor Párkáyi, cello: Hungaroton HCD 31174. Excellent, somewhat distant spatial rendition. The instrumental clarity is realistic in this original-instrument recording as is the stage depth, the left-right spread, and the hall ambience. Very satisfactory. (A+)

561 Haydn, J.; Johann Hummel; Giuseppe Torelli; Giuseppi Tartini; and Vincenzo Bellini: *Trumpet Concertos*, Scottish Chamber Orchestra, Rolf Smedvig, trumpet: Telarc 80232. Clean and spacious, with the solo trumpet well focused and properly sized in relation to the supporting ensemble (contrast with 542). Smooth sound all around. (A+)

562 Henderson, Joe: *The State of the Tenor: Live at the Village Vanguard, Volume 1* (with Ron Carter and Al Foster): Blue Note CDP 7 46296-2. Very smooth, clean, lucid, and intimate. There is a wonderful live jazz-club acoustic atmosphere on this disc, complete with audience noises (coughing, shuffling, etc.). There is also a good sense of stage depth and an overall realistic feel. (A)

563 Henderson, J.: *The State of the Tenor: Live at the Village Vanguard Volume 2* (with Ron Carter and Al Foster): Blue Note CDP 7 46426-2. This is a continuation of the above recording session, with all the positive attributes intact. Both of these jazz discs feature good stage imaging and proper instrumental sizing. (A)

564 Hersch, Fred: *Forward Motion* (with Rich Perry, Erik Friedlander, Scott Colley, and Tom Rainey): Chesky JD-55. A highlight here is the very good imaging combined with a realistic sound-stage blend. The piano is particularly well recorded, and the whole group displays a wonderful overall clarity. Another Chesky jazz success story. (A+)

565 Hersch, Fred: *Heartsongs* (with Mike Formanek and Jeff Hirschfield): Sunnyside SSC-10470. There is good piano focus here with a nice feeling of depth to the whole ensemble. The overall sound is quite smooth with fine clarity. (B+)

566 Hersch, F.: *Sarabande* (with Charlie Haden and Joey Baron): Sunnyside SSC 1024-D. This release is nice clean jazz with a well-formed mid-distance sound stage and good imaging as well as a nice placement of the piano and drums. Both this and the 565 disc are not bad recordings of Hersch by any means, but it is suggestive to note that we again have an example of Chesky (see the review of *Forward Motion*, 564) handling a performer better than their competitors. (B+)

567 Hicks, John: *Power Trio* (with Cecil McBee and Elvin Jones): Novus 3115-2-N. This jazz release is smooth at times as well as punchy, close up, and well imaged. The drums are focused well and not overbearing (a nice change). The bass sounds like a bass and goes quite deep, although the piano sounds a bit metallic. The sound stage is slightly skewed to the right. (B+)

568 Hicks, J., and Ray Drummond: *Two of a Kind*: Evidence ECD 22017-2. This presentation is unstrident and clean, although the piano is a touch diffuse. There is good tonality from both instruments. (B+)

569 Hildegard of Bingen: *A Feather on the Breath of God*, The Gothic Voices: Hyperion CDA 66039. Excellent vocal clarity combined with outstanding sound-stage realism highlight this recording of the music of the twelfth-century abbess. The hall ambience is well reproduced, and it surrounds the voices with just the right amount of churchlike realism. (A+)

570 Hillier, Paul: *Proensa* (assorted players in a small ensemble): ECM 837 360-2. This is a very clear and detailed "modern classical" work with a proper hall ambience that adds to the required effect, especially the spoken parts. (A)

571 Hindemith, Paul: *Complete Brass Works*, Summit Brass: Summit DCD 115-2. A highlight here is the good delineation of brass instruments (and piano) in a medium-sized hall setting. The piano image is as good as the brass tonality. The listening position is comfortably midhall. (A)

572 Hindemith, P.: *Mathis de Maler*; *Trauermusik*; *Symphonic Metamorphosis*, San Francisco Symphony Orchestra: London 421 523-2. This release has a very clean string tone, excellent hall envelopment, and a solidly refined sound stage. This recording typifies London recording techniques at their best. (A)

573 Hindemith, P.: *Organ Works*; Distler, Hugo: *Spielstücke*; Kropfreiter, Augustinus: *Toccata Francese*, Peter Hurford, organ: Argo 417 159-2. This remarkable recording displays a realistic hall perspective with ultradeep and *strong* bass, down to nearly 18 Hz at times. This is a clear and unstrained organ sound, one of the best engineering jobs of its kind. The playback levels of the deepest notes reproduced here could cause problems with smaller bass-reproduction systems, especially reflex or drone-cone models. The latter types "unload" their woofers below the low-frequency resonance point (acoustic-suspension woofers do not do this), which can cause runaway driver damage at high playback levels. Small woofers of any kind that are equalized for flat bass below their cutoff points may also have trouble with parts of this disc unless the volume is kept low. A particularly strong bass tone is present near the end of track 5. Watch it. (A+)

574 Hindemith, P.: *Sonatas for Viola/Piano and Viola Alone*; Kim Kashkashian, viola; Robert Levin, piano: ECM 833 311-2. Close up (you can sometimes hear Kashkashian breathing) and powerful. Very good viola detail and realism. While the piano is also big and close, it matches the viola well in balance, space, and placement. (A+)

575 Hindemith, P.: *When Lilacs Last in the Dooryard Bloom'd*, Atlanta Symphony Orchestra and Chorus: Telarc 80132. Big (in spite of the often intimate nature of the music), smooth, and spacious in the Telarc tradition. A diffuse sound stage is no problem with a work of this kind, provided the individual soloists are well treated. That is the case here, and the vocals are clear, well focused, and properly located. (A+)

576 Hohner, Robert: *Different Strokes* (his percussion ensemble, with James Armstrong, Carla Becker, Douglas Corella, and many others): Digital Music Products CD-485. This is a remarkably clear and dynamic recording of percussion instruments. The clarity is excellent, and the sound stage is enveloping. Many listeners feel that this kind of sound can become monotonous in short order, but the fidelity is certainly demo grade. (A+)

577 Holland, Dave: *The Razor's Edge* (his quintet, with Steve Coleman, Kenny Wheeler, Robin Eubanks, and Marvin Smith): ECM 1353/833 048-2. A very smooth, open, spacious jazz sound with fine clarity and a very good hall ambience. The drums are well sized and not unreal sounding. Some instruments move too close to the listener when they are doing solo work, an obvious case of excessive instrument highlighting zeal by the engineer. (A)

578 Holland, D.: *Triplicate* (his trio, with Steve Coleman and Jack DeJohnette): ECM 1373/837 113-2. This jazz release is nicely detailed and clean, with excellent depth. As usual, the drums are wider than they would be at any live concert, but the overall sound of this disc in clarity, tonality, and listenability is truly fine. (A)

579 *Hollywood's Greatest Hits* (works by Newman, Korngold, Steiner, Rozsa, Gold, Williams, Jarre, and many others), Cincinnati Pops Orchestra: Telarc 80168. Vibrant, full, dynamic, and rich, as you expect movie music to sound, and clearly in the Telarc tradition. The sound stage is an example of what is produced by a wide spaced-microphone array, but the ambient effect and depth are just right for this kind of music. (A)

580 Holman, Bill: *The Bill Holman Band* (with Lanny Morgan, Bob Militello, Dick Mitchell, Jeff Hamilton, and others): JVC-3308. This jazz transcription is nice and detailed with a good sound stage and decent small-studio ambience. The listening perspective is middistance, and the overall image is good, including the drums. (B+)

581 Holst, Gustav: *The Planets*, Orchestra Symphonique de Montréal: London 417 553-2. Open, detailed, and transparent, with plenty of impact, although not quite a match for 583. Maybe just a bit more revealing of inner detail than the latter, however, along the lines of 584. More dynamic impact than the latter. (A+)

582 Holst, G.: *The Planets*, Philharmonia Orchestra: Nimbus NI 5117. Clean and clear but somewhat thin and distant for a work of this kind, which ordinarily demands great dynamic range, abundant orchestral richness,

Holst (583)

and realistic impact. However, the result here is OK if you like a small-orchestra, small-hall effect. The playback level on this recording is somewhat higher than typical for Nimbus, which usually provides us with a more reticent sound. It is outpointed by all the other Holst entries. (B+)

583 Holst, G.: *The Planets*, Royal Philharmonic Orchestra: Telarc 80133. Big, powerful, and dynamic. There is some impressively deep bass at just the right places. The clarity is good, but certain listeners may find the violin sound just a tad bright compared to some other Telarc-RPO releases. However, this recording really fills the listening room with sound when the gain is advanced a bit above normal, and it certainly does justice to the music. The imaging is typically Telarc: somewhat diffuse but suited to music of this kind, especially on the heavy parts. (A+)

584 Holst, G.: *The Planets*, New York Philharmonic Orchestra: Teldec 46316-2. Less grand, vibrant, and spacious than 583, and with a somewhat more distant orchestral perspective. Central images are a bit better defined than on that recording, however. Quite transparent in texture with a better violin sound than 583, yet oddly enough, not quite as mellow overall. Still, it does not quite deliver the dynamic goods that the latter does. (A)

585 Holst, G.: *Suite Number 1 in E-Flat*; *Suite Number 2 in F*; Händel, George Frideric: *Music for the Royal Fireworks*; Bach, Johann Sebastian: *Fantasia in G Major*, Cleveland Symphonic Winds: Telarc 80038. Made in 1978, this early all-digital recording helped put Telarc on the map. The sound is still clean, clear, and dynamic by modern standards. The bass drum was a revelation when the disc first appeared and made the recording popular at hi-fi salons and shows. These days, drum whacks of this quality are old hat. (A)

586 Holst, G.: *Suite Number 1 in E-Flat*; *Suite Number 2 in F*; *A Moorside Suite*; *Hammersmith*, Dallas Wind Symphony: Reference Recordings RR-39CD. This sonic masterpiece is state-of-the-art in nearly every way: clean, clear, dynamic, and just plain impressive. The bass drum gave my big woofers a decent bit of exercise. This is a powerful recording. (A+)

587 Honegger, Arthur: *Symphony Number 2*; *Concerto da Camera*, I Musici de Montreal: Chandos CHAN 8632. This jewel displays a wonderful hall presence and depth combined with detail and clarity, although the solosits seem a bit too close up. (A)

588 *Horizons: Traditional Music from Around the World*, Helicon (with Chris Norman, Ken Kolodner, and Robin Bullock): Dorian DIS-80103. This is another one of those small-ensemble recordings by Dorian that simply blow you away. The articulation and imaging here is exceptional, and the way the instruments are blended into the sound field is amazing. (A+)

589 Hornsby, B., and the Range: *A Night on the Town*: BMG 2041-2-R. There are some decent vocals on this rock album, with good impact and clarity. The sound stage is contrived, but it is not overmanipulated, and the imaging is stable. (B)

590 Hornsby, B., and the Range: *Scenes from the Southside*: RCA 6686-2-R. This release is a bit better than 589, with fine vocals and a good orchestral blend. The bass is not always ultrastrong, but it is solid and sometimes reasonably deep. The piano that shows up occasionally is well integrated, almost like a live concert. This disc offers smooth tonality with good midrange clarity. (B+)

591 Hornsby, B., and the Range: *The Way It Is*: RCA PCD1-5904. This one has decent vocal and instrumental clarity with a good sound stage. It is technically similar to 589. (B)

592 Howells, Herbert: *Hymnus Paradisi*; *An English Mass*, Royal Liverpool Philharmonic Orchestra and Choir, John Disley, organ (with Julie Kennard and John Ainsley): Hyperion CDA 66488. Recorded 8 months apart, both pieces are smooth, clean, and transparent with a wonderful sense of depth and space. The bass response and dynamic range are quite impressive at times, and the chorus and orchestra blend together quite well. The soloists are positioned precisely the way they would be at a live performance, and their tonality is near perfect. (A+)

593 Hummel, Johann: *Grand Serenades, Numbers 1 and 2*; Gragnani, Filippo: *Quartet for Two Guitars, Clarinet and Viola*, Consortium Classicum: Koch Schwann CD-310-006 F1. This is a wonderful and unusual combination of guitar, violin, viola, clarinet, bassoon, and piano, with a beautiful sound stage, good hall ambience, and clear instrumental delineation. (A)

594 Hummel, J.: *Piano Concerto in A Minor*; *Piano Concerto in B Minor*, English Chamber Orchestra, Stephen Hough, piano: Chandos CHAN 8507. Well defined and clear, but the strings are just a tad brittle. There is a nice sense of hall space and depth. (A)

595 *If There Were Dreams to Sell* (English orchestral songs by Quilter, Butterworth, Elgar, Finzi, Vaughan Williams, and Ireland), City of London Sinfonia, Stephen Varcoe, bass-baritone: Chandos CHAN 8743. The soloist is a bit too far forward on this release, but he is still beautifully clear and pure in tone. A good sense of hall envelopment and depth round out the program. (A)

596 Indian Classical Masters (Budhaditya Mukherjee, sitar): *Rāg Ramkali*; *Rāg Jhiñjoti*; Nimbus NI 5221. This is another fine example of the Ambisonic technique, with remarkable hall ambience and good clarity. There is excellent imaging—typically the case with this microphone configuration. (A)

597 INXS: *X*: Atlantic A2 82140. This rock album offers good dynamics, with spacious wide-band sound and good instrumental delineation. The vocals are a little phasey, a characteristic of many albums of this kind. (B)

598 Ireland, John: *A London Overture*; *These Things Shall Be* (plus assorted shorter works), London Symphony Orchestra and Chorus, Bryn Terfel, baritone: Chandos CHAN 8879. This recording has a wonderfully full and clear sound with a realistic hall envelopment. The stage depth of this St. Jude's-on-the-hill recording is palpable. There is an excellent choral-orchestral blend, and the soloists are perfectly sized and properly integrated into the mix. The organ is impressively massive when called for, yet it blends well too. This is an outstanding disc in every way. (A+)

599 Ireland, J.: *Piano Concerto in E Flat Major*; *Legend*; *Mai-Dun*, London Philharmonic Orchestra, Eric Parker, piano: Chandos CHAN 8461.

Quite good in nearly every way, with nice piano sizing and tight imaging. The orchestral ensemble is well done. There is fine clarity overall, with only a hint of string edginess. (A)

600 Ireland, J.: *Songs*; Rachael Morgan, mezzo-soprano; Tan Crone, piano: Etcetera KTC 1128. There is excellent stage realism here with the piano and the vocalist properly positioned and correctly sized in a small-hall setting. The subjective listening position is reasonably close up but not so much that the performers overwhelm. (A)

601 *The Island of St. Hylarion* (music of Cyprus, 1413-1422), Ensemble Project Ars Nova: New Albion NA-038. This is a wonderfully transparent recording with near-perfect blending of the performers and the hall. There is very good ambience and depth as well. The disc is a fine example of the intelligent use of a good recording environment. (A+)

602 *Italian Baroque Trumpet Music* (works by Stradella, Albrici, Fantini, Bononcini, Corelli, and others), Parley of Instruments, with Stephen Keavy, Crispan Steele-Perkins, and Peter Holman: Hyperion CDA 66255. Overall, a nice sense of hall space, with a good solid stage image and a good "brassy" clarity to the ensemble. One gets the impression that the solo trumpets are placed within the group rather than in front of it. (A)

603 Ives, Charles: *Orchestral Works*, The Gulbenkian Orchestra: Nimbus NI 5316. Very clean and clear, with excellent instrumental delineation and imaging. As expected, the Ambisonic technique enhances the sound; even if you do not have the dedicated decoder to reproduce the recorded ambient field in three dimensions. (A)

604 Ives, C.: Edward MacDowell; Charles Griffes: *Songs*; Thomas Hampson, baritone; Armen Guzelimian, piano: Teldec 9031-72168-2. Very clean, with good hall reverberation and an excellent size-position relationship between the performers. The voice reproduction is quite revealing. The listening perspective puts the listener about halfway back in a small hall. (A+)

605 Jackson, Joe: *Laughter & Lust*: Virgin 2-91628. Cleaner vocals than typical for rock. The orchestral clarity is OK, with the contrived sound stage generally stable and the imaging tight enough. (B)

606 Jamal, Ahmad: *Digital Works* (with Iraj Lashkary, Herlin Riley, and Larry Ball): Atlantic 81258-2. Good jazz piano focus most of the time but with the instrument sounding just a bit diffuse on some tracks. The overall sound is quite clean, and there is otherwise good instrumental separation and articulation. (B+)

607 James, Bob, and Earl Klugh: *Cool* (with Harvey Mason, Gary King, Leonard Gibbs, Ron Carter, and Paul Pesco): Warner 26939-2. This recording is smooth, clean, unclouded, and generally well done. There is a nice sound stage here with an OK feeling of depth for a pop-jazz disc. (B+)

608 James, B,, and E. Klugh: *One on One* (with Ron Carter, Harvey Mason, Ralph MacDonald, Gary King, and Neil Jason): Columbia CK 36241. Although not quite in a class with 607, this one is still nice and clean, with surprisingly fine sound for a Columbia disc recorded in 1979. The guitar is cleanly done and sounds better than the one on a pricey gold "ultra-disc" reissue of a similar production by Mobile

Fidelity that was originally recorded at about the same time. The overall instrumental ensemble is presented on a mixer-created multimicrophone sound stage, but it is handled well, and the blend is OK. (B)

609 James, B., and David Sanborn: *Double Vision* (with Marcus Miller, Steve Gadd, Paul Milton Jackson, and others): Warner 25393-2. The electrically synthesized sound stage on this effort is wide, reverberant, and clean with good articulation and not too much in overdone effects. The drums and bongos are all over the place. This recording works very well with surround enhancement, even Dolby, including Pro Logic. (B+)

610 James, Harry: *Comin' from a Good Place* (with Nick Buono, Gino Bozzacco, William Hicks, Tom Padveen, Tommy Dodd, Dave Stone, and others): Sheffield Labs CD-6. Done originally as an analog-tape backup for the 1976 direct-to-disc LP, this CD version still stands out for its dynamism, clarity, and brilliance. The very realistic sound stage is the result of intelligent microphone use. It is quite unusual to find a disc of this era that is this good. It was and is a credit to the Sheffield recording team. (A)

611 James, H.: *The King James Version* (with Nick Buono, Les DeMerle, Dave Stone, Quin Davis, Pat Largo, and others): Sheffield Labs CD-3. Also done in 1976, and essentially the same quality as CD-6 (610). (A)

612 James, H.: *Still Harry after All These Years* (with Nick Buono, Clay Jenkins, Bill Hicks, Norm Smith, and many others): Sheffield Labs CD-11. Done in 1979, this disc is dynamic, powerful, brassy, and real. The wonderful sound-stage spread is the result of well-thought-out microphone techniques that bring out the depth of the ensemble. This disc can hold its own with some of the best newer jazz recordings. It's refreshing to know that at least a few of the older engineering efforts were so top grade. (A)

613 Janáček, Leos: *Sinfonietta*; *Violin Concerto*; *Taras Bulba*, Philharmonia Orchestra, Christian Tetzlaff, violin: Virgin Classics VC 7 91506-2. Smooth and clear with a good sound stage and good depth. The violin sound in the concerto is a tad close up compared to the rest of the ensemble. There is good overall dynamics and orchestral tonality, nonetheless. (A)

614 Janáček, L.: *Taras Bulba*; *The Fiddler's Child*; *Suite: The Cunning Little Vixen*, Czech Philharmonic Orchestra: Chandos CHAN 9080. Smooth, clean, and dynamic with good hall depth. The organ is well integrated into the ensemble and has a subtle yet sometimes impressive frequency range. This recording job displays a very smooth string tone that contrasts with the harshness on many discs. The lack of a higher score probably has more to do with the recording environment than anything else. (A)

615 *Japanese Orchestral Music*: Malmö Symphony Orchestra: BIS CD 490. The stage reproduced here presents a distant perspective with a spacious and deep sound field. I felt that the disc delivered fine overall clarity with just a touch of low-frequency hall noise in the background that should be inaudible unless the playback system has a big subwoofer. (Qualified A+)

616 Jarrett, Keith: *Tribute* (his trio, with Gary Peacock and Jack DeJohnette): ECM 1420/21. Good piano sound, with the bass and drum set very well blended into the mix. There is also a solidly focused jazz stage image on this presentation. The sound level is low, requiring a higher setting of your volume control than usual to benefit from the quality of this recording. (B+)

617 Jarvis, John: *Something Constructive*: MCAD-5963. This is a wonderful example of a solo-piano recording combined with an electronic synthesizer backup (Jarvis does the whole performance on this disc). The result is very clean, dynamic, rich, and impressive — and obviously exactly what the performer intended. (A+)

618 *The Jazz Album* (assorted jazz-inspired works by Milhaud, Stravinsky and others, including, as one would expect, Gershwin), London Sinfonietta: EMI CDC 7 47991-2. In spite of its title and some of the recorded material, I consider this a classical album. The close up sound stage is clear and detailed, the depth quite good, and the piano is well positioned in relation to the ensemble. The jazz-inspired Gershwin work is *Rhapsody in Blue*, and it is not quite as well engineered as the Columbia version (see 453). (A)

619 The Jazztet: *Real Time* (with Art Farmer, Benny Golson, Curtis Fuller, Mickey Tucker, Ray Drummond, and Marvin Smith): Contemporary CCD-14034-2. Wide sounding, spacious, and clean. There is precise imaging of the assorted instruments (even the drum set) with reasonable sound-stage depth. (B+)

620 *Le Jeu des Pèlerins d'Emmaüs* (A Liturgical Drama of the Twelfth Century), Ensemble Organum: Harmonia Mundi France 901347. Close up and very articulate with the kind of hall ambience and ensemble spaciousness that a recording of this kind demands. Unfortunately, the audiophile-quality result is colored by the usual traffic noise that seems to plague cathedral recording sessions everywhere. If you are using a surround-sound processor to enhance this work, cutting it off will eliminate the traffic sound from seeming to surround you. Unfortunately, it also eliminates some of the cathedral ambience, and the noise is still there, coming from the main speakers up front. If the producers of music like this are going to go for an authentic sound, they should do their recording late at night or on holidays — or blockade the streets in front of the cathedrals during the recording sessions. The traffic noise at least makes this an authentic-sounding "modern" twelfth-century sound performance. (Qualified A+)

621 Joel, Billy: *The Bridge*: Columbia CK 40402. Punchy, clean, and impressive. The heavily processed sound still has a well-focused vocal image and better instrumental sound-staging than one might expect. This is a good recording of a talented performer in action. (B+)

622 John, Elton: *Live in Australia*: MCA 8022. Concert-produced live recordings are often technically compromised due to microphone placement limitations and environmental conditions, but this piece stands out and exhibits very good clarity and ambience. The sound is often punchy, well imaged, full, and spacious, with an excellent voice pickup. (B+)

623 Johnson, Eric: *Ah Via Musicom*: Capitol CDP 7 90517-2. This is heavily processed rock that often has surprisingly good vocals and instrumental clarity as well as some fairly deep bass at times. Overall, there is good mixer-fabricated depth, the guitar powerful, dynamic, and well placed in relation to the accompaniment. (B)

624 Johnson, Frances: *The Music of Frances Johnson and His Contemporaries: Early 19th Century Black Composers*, The Chestnut Brass Company: Music Masters 7029-2-C. Played on nineteenth century instruments, this disc has a close-up sound with fine instrumental detail. The disc responded quite well to both simple and complex surround processing. (A)

625 Johnson, J. J.: *Quintergy* (Live at the Village Vanguard with Ralph Moore, Stanley Cowell, Rufus Reid, and Victor Lewis): Antilles 422-848 214-2. As noted previously, live recordings sometimes compromise sound quality. This disc is an exception, but the perspective is still somewhat distant and subdued. The clarity, although decent, is other than razor sharp and akin to what would be experienced sitting somewhat farther from the stage than one might like at a live performance. The bass seemed a tad heavy at times when the disc was listened to on my larger system but was OK when rechecked on my smaller one. (B)

626 Johnson, Marc: *Two by Four* (with Gary Burton, Lacy Crane, Makoto Ozone, and Toots Thielmans): Emarcy 842 233-2. Nice bass clarity is the first impression—forward, tight, focused, and rich. This is good, since jazz bassist Johnson is the featured player here. The accompanying instruments and the vocalist are well positioned, properly sized, and realistic. (A)

627 Jolivet, André: *Concertino for Trumpet, String Orchestra and Piano*; *Concerto Number 2 for Trumpet*; Tomasi, Henri: *Concerto for Trumpet and Orchestra*, Philharmonia Orchestra, Wynton Marsalis, trumpet: Columbia MK 42096. This is a clear, transparent, and well-defined example of modern trumpet works. The sound is reverberant and full, in the Columbia tradition. (A)

628 Jolivet, A.: *Suite for Flute and Percussion*; Sandström, Sven-David: *Drums*; Cage, John: *Amores*; Harrison, Lou: *First Concerto for Flute and Percussion*, Kroumata Percussion Ensemble, with Manuela Wiesler, flute: BIS CD-272. Strictly for percussion nuts, the overall sound of this release is quite clear with wide dynamics at times and a very good flute tone. Track 12 is a percussion powerhouse that will fully exercise even the biggest speaker systems. The disc is also a good test item for CD player low-level clarity since there are some revealing quiet passages. (A+)

629 Jones, Hank: *Lazy Afternoon* (with Keith Copeland, Dave Holland, and Ken Peplowski): Concord Jazz CCD-4391. Very detailed, clean, and quality-jazz smooth. The drums are well sized and focused, and the piano is OK too. If you listen to this recording closely, you can hear one of the players humming along in the background at times. The sound stage is typically multimicrophone flat. (B+)

630 Jongen, Joseph: *Symphonie Concertante for Organ and Orchestra*; Franck, César: *Fantasie in A*; *Pastorale*, San Francisco Symphony Orchestra, Michael Murray, organ, Telarc 80096. This is a very powerful, clear, and large-scale recording with woofer-torturing bass down to below 19 Hz (be careful here). If you do not have a subwoofer or a very big pair of main speakers, you will not be able to hear what this recording can do for bass-pedal notes. This material was

Joplin (631)

recorded some time back and still holds its own with the best. (A+)

631 Joplin, Scott: *Euphonic Sounds: The Scott Joplin Album*: William Bolcom, piano: Omega OCD 3001. As is always important in a piano recording, this effort displays a good sound stage with just the right studio ambience. The instrument reflects an up-close perspective with a well-controlled and properly focused piano image. (A)

632 Josquin des Prez: *Missa Pange Lingua*; *Missa La Sol Fa Re Mi*, The Tallis Scholars: Gimell GIM 009. This effort displays a nice orchestra-hall balance and a realistic sound-stage presentation. The vocals are very well positioned and clear. (A)

633 Josquin des Prez: *Motets*, La Chapelle Royale: Harmonia Mundi France 901243. Clean, clear sound with very good vocal blending and fine articulation. The sound stage is realistic, and the effort is a first-class example of well-engineered depth and hall ambience adding what is necessary to make recorded musical art seem real. (A+)

634 K., Sara: *Closer Than They Appear*: Chesky JD-67. This effort displays very well positioned and properly focused vocals, with the instrumental support clear and realistically done. The intimate small-hall sound stage is just right for material of this kind, and there is notable depth within that sound stage — quite unusual. (Does this lady have a last name?) (A+)

635 Kabalevsky, Dmitri: *Cello Concerto Number 2*; Glazunov, Alexander: *Chant du Ménestrel*; Khachaturian, Aram: *Cello Concerto*, London Philharmonic Orchestra, Raphael Wallfisch, cello: Chandos CHAN 8579. There is nice clarity and hall feel on this release, the solo cello well sized and well positioned. There are some very smooth orchestral textures and good depth. Another fine Chandos effort. (A+)

636 Kallinikov, Vasily: *Symphony Number 1*; Glazunov, Alexander: *The Sea*; *Spring*, Scottish National Orchestra: Chandos CHAN 8611. The usual Chandos–Scottish National sound: smooth, clean, dynamic, and impressive. The recording has an ear-pleasing string tone, especially the cellos, as well as wonderful depth and a broad, enveloping stage spread. (A+)

637 *Kathleen Battle at Carnegie Hall* (singing works by Händel, Mozart, Liszt, Strauss, Rachmaninoff, Gershwin, and others), with Margo Garrett, piano: Deutsche Grammophon 435 440-2. Wonderfully clear and smooth with a fine front-row listening position. A recording like this demands a simple microphone job, and the DGG engineers resisted the urge to overdo things. The restraint paid off. (A+)

638 *Katmandü*: Epic EK 46064. This is typically heavily processed electrical stuff, but with a decent sound stage, OK clarity, and good rock-and-roll punch. (B)

639 Keezer, G.: *Curveball* (with Steve Nelson, Victor Lewis, and Charnett Moffett): Sunnyside SSC-1045D. Clean and well blended with a good drum image and a well-focused piano. The vibes are clear but a bit too close to the audience for my taste, and the sound field seems a tad lacking in live jazz punch. (B)

640 Keezer, G.: *Waiting in the Wings* (with Rufus Reid, Anthony Reedus, Billy Pierce, Bill Mobley, and Steve Nelson): Sunnyside SSC-1035D.

This effort is a bit superior to 639, being very clean, forward, and bright with a wonderful sound-stage feel. The drums are well sized, and the piano has a stable, unfuzzy image. (B+)

641 Khachaturian, Aram: *Symphony Number 2* (original version); *Gayaneh* (Four Movements from Ballet Suite No. 1, including the *Sabre Dance*), Royal Scottish Orchestra: Chandos CHAN 8945. Clean, brilliant, and filled with realistic depth and ambience. There is notably good imaging throughout the ensemble. While the brightness here may be a bit too concentrated for some, I think the effect works well with this kind of music. This is more proof that Chandos is a major player in the sound-engineering sweepstakes. (A+)

642 King, B. B.: *Live at the Regal*: Mobile Fidelity UDCD 548. Originally mastered in 1971, this expensive reissue still has good clarity with a wide, close up, realistic sound stage — and just a bit of background hiss. This is a significantly better effort than some of the other MFSL "ultra-disc" releases. Note that these "gold-substrata" recordings (most CDs use aluminum) typically retail for about $25 each. Since aluminum should last long enough, what is the point of using gold? Gold will offer *no* improvement in sound quality, by the way. (Qualified B)

643 King, B. B.: *There Is Always One More Time*: MCA MCAD 10295. This release displays excellent vocal clarity and dynamics, although the sound stage on some tracks has the usual flat-stage artificiality. (B)

644 Kings X: *Faith Hope Love*: Atlantic 82145-2. Decent vocal clarity with a passable sound stage and good dynamics raise this effort above the run-of-the-mill rock recording. (B)

645 Kirkland, Kenny: *Kenny Kirkland* (with Branford Marsalis, Jeff Watts, Charnett Moffett, and others): GRP GRD-9657. This jazz release exhibits fine overall sound with wonderful imaging, finely etched detail, and satisfying transparency. The piano is very well done, the drums are pinpointed properly, and the horns are right up front and sound alive. (A)

646 Klugh, Earl: *Whispers and Promises* (with Ronnie Foster, Paul Jackson, Freddie Washington, Gary Schunk, and others): Warner 25902-2. Punchy and full-sounding jazz with a solid (but clearly and obviously electrically synthesized) sound stage. There is good overall detail and transparency. (B+)

647 Kodály, Zoltán: *Dances of Galánta*; *Háry János Suite*; *Peacock Variations*, Chicago Symphony Orchestra: Chandos CHAN 8877. Excellent depth, clarity, and sound-stage spread. I felt that there was very good hall ambience on this recording and that it should respond well to home-based surround-sound enhancement. The drumrolls in the "Napoleon" section were particularly realistic. (A+)

648 Koechlin, Charles: *Sonata for Horn*; *Fifteen Pieces, Op. 180* (and other, shorter works); Barry Tuckwell, horn; Daniel Blumenthal, piano: ASV DCA 716. This effort has a good but somewhat distant hall feel combined with balanced clarity and depth. The piano and horn are both well focused and properly sized (and necessarily small, given the listening-distance factor) in relation to each other. (A)

649 Korngold, Erich: *String Sextet in D Major*; Schoenberg, Arnold:

Krenek (650)

Verklärte Nacht, The Raphael Ensemble: Hyperion CDA 66425. This recording of a pair of modern works displays outstanding depth and soundstage realism. Overall, very clear sound, the hall ambience and sense of envelopment just right for music of this kind. (A+)

650 Krenek, Ernst: *Complete String Quartets*, Sonare-Quartett: Musikproduktion Dabringhaus und Grimm L-4280. This release is nicely done with a smooth, unforced sound that has none of the stridency so commonplace with string quartet recordings. The sound stage is intimate, the instruments maybe just a bit wider apart than they should be; the hall ambience nicely captured. (A)

651 Lacy, Steve: *More Monk*: Soul Note 12110-2. This release displays an uncanny in-your-room detail and presence — certainly one of the best solo-saxophone jazz recordings around. In spite of the intimate and quite small single-instrument environment, this disc responded very well to surround-sound enhancement by a number of techniques. (A)

652 Lambert, Constant: *The Rio Grande*; *Aubade Héroïque*; *Summers Last Will and Testament*, Chorus of Opera North, Leeds Festival Chorus, English Northern Philharmonia (with Sally Burgess and William Shimell): Hyperion CDA 66565. Like so many Hyperion discs, this release has a very realistic sound stage with a fine blend of the chorus and the orchestra. The soloists are positioned and sized as they should be. Overall, the sound has a distant quality that works with music of this kind. (A+)

653 *Lancaster and Valois: French and English Music, 1350–1420*, The Gothic Voices: Hyperion CDA 66588. Very clean, close up, and smooth with a fine sound stage, depth, and imaging. It is important to have a good hall ambience underlying music of this type, and this album delivers. (A+)

654 Lang, David: *Are You Experienced?*, Nouvel Ensemble Moderne and other players: CRI/Emergency Music CD 625. These "modern" classical pieces by David Lang are very well treated here with a recording of great depth, clarity, and impact. The hall pickup was just right for this kind of sound. (A+)

655 Lecuona, Ernesto: *Always in My Heart* (this is the album title, not the name of any Lecuona work; the material here consists of a number of his songs), Placido Domingo with the Royal Philharmonic Orchestra: Columbia MK 38828. Domingo and his guitar support appear to be subjectively positioned a bit too far in front of the orchestra. However, he and all the instruments involved are clearly recorded, a positive by-product of this kind of pan-pot manipulation. The orchestral sound stage behind the singer and guitar is also quite good. This effort makes this list primarily because of the fine tonal quality of the vocal track. (B+)

656 Lee, Peggy: *Moments Like This* (with Mike Renzi, Gerry Niewood, Tony Monte, Jay Leonhart, Steve LaSpina, Jay Berliner, and Peter Grant): Chesky JD-84. This engineering effort is nice and clean with revealing vocal clarity. As is typical for Chesky, there is realistic sound staging with plenty of depth and a good club-like ambience. (A)

657 Lejeune, Claude: *Meslanges*, Ensemble Clement Janequin: Harmonia

Mundi France HMC 901182. I find these to be mostly very realistic, well-blended, clear vocals that are well integrated into the stereo sound stage. The environmental ambience is very supportive. At times, there appeared to be just a hint of midrange roughness. (A)

658 Lennox, Annie: *Diva*; Arista 18704-2. This little pop-music jewel displays excellent clarity, a wide frequency range (especially the bass), and impressive dynamics. The electrically synthesized sound stage is well formed and does not detract from the effect. This is pop music as it should be engineered. (A)

659 Lewis, Mel: *The Definitive Thad Jones: Live from the Village Vanguard: Volume 1* (his jazz orchestra, with Glenn Drewes, Kenny Werner, John Mosca, Gary Smulyan, and others): Musicmasters 5024-2-C. This big-band live recording has a realistic but somewhat distant sound stage. The sound is also just a bit dry and nonreverberant (in spite of the sense of distance), and the overall gain is a bit low and requires more volume from your level control than usual. Surround-sound processing, judiciously applied by the listener, should correct the dry effect to some extent. My Yamaha DSP unit worked wonders. (B)

660 Lewis, M.: *The Definitive Thad Jones: Live from the Village Vanguard: Volume 2* (his jazz orchestra, with Glenn Drewes, Kenny Werner, John Mosca, Gary Smulyan, Dennis Irwin, Jim Powell, Tad Nash, and others): Musicmasters 5046-2-C. This is a continuation of 659, and the sound is the same. The piano on both recordings is well sized and well placed, as are the drums. There are plenty of audience noises for those who like that sort of thing. (B)

661 Lewis, M.: *The Lost Art* (his sextet, with Kenny Werner, Dennis Irwin, Gary Smulyan, Dick Oatts, John Mosca, and Jim Powell): Musicmasters 5023-2-C. It is nice to have a nice drum-set image along with its proper integration into the rest of the ensemble. The clarity of the group as a whole is also good, and the sound stage is spread out nicely. (B)

662 Lewis, M.: *Soft Lights and Hot Music* (with Kenny Werner, Dennis Irwin, Dick Oatts, Ted Nash, and others): Musicmasters 5012-2-C. This release is pretty much in the same league as the two Thad Jones albums above (659, 660), which were recorded at the same time. (B)

663 *Liber Sapientiae* (Gregorian antiphons, psalms, lectures, and responsories in medieval codices from Hungary), Schola Hungarica: Hungaroton HCD 12534-2. A well-blended ensemble effect that is clear and smooth. There is also a good sense of hall space, a characteristic typical with material produced by Hungaroton and Schola Hungarica. I could detect none of the background rumble that seems to plague other such recordings done in cathedrals and churches. (A)

664 Liebman, David, and Richard Bierach: *Chant*: CMP CD-40. This is very progressive jazz (indeed, the material could qualify as modern classical) with the recording quite smooth, transparent, somewhat dry sounding, and finely detailed. The sax and the piano are realistically handled by the engineer, their sound well focused. The transcription responded *very* well to surround enhancement, via my Yamaha sound-field synthesizer set at its jazz "Cellar-Club" setting. (B+)

665 *Lieder aus "Des Knaben Wunderhorn"* (songs by Mendelssohn, Mahler, Schumann, Brahms, and others), Thomas Hampson, baritone; Geoffrey Parsons, piano: Teldec 44923-2. This is an exemplary recording of vocal material, with the stage image well presented. The piano image is considerably better than average for a recording of this type. (A+)

666 *Light in Darkness* (works by Rosauro, Abe, McLeod, Edwards, Miki, Glennie, and Tanaka), with Evelyn Glennie, Philip Smith, Gregory Knowles, Steve Henderson, and Gary Kettel: RCA 60557-2. This release is punchy and dynamic, to say the least. The sound was very spacious and fabricated in perspective, but the disc is certainly a good choice for percussion nuts and performers interested in these instruments. Although not quite state-of-the-art compared to some of the competition, this recording is still a good candidate for hi-fi system transient-response demos. Hi-fi salesmen should like this disc, especially if they are selling gear to hipster music students. (A)

667 Lightsey, Kirk: *From Kirk to Nat* (his trio, with Kevin Eubanks and Rufus Reid): Criss Cross Jazz 1050. This effort is technically nice and clean with an unforced, nicely balanced, and well-managed sound stage. (B+)

668 Lindley, David: *El Rayo-X*: Asylum 524-2. Nice vocals are a highlight here with the supporting instruments spread wide across the stage. This disc displays a light and detailed sound with tight bass that is controlled but not really as deep as it could be. The perspective is fairly intimate (almost baroquelike) with little artificial reverberation. As such, it responds well to surround enhancement. (B)

669 Liszt, Franz: *Années de Pèlerinage: Duexième Année-Italie*, Alan Marks, piano: Nimbus NI 5226. This recording presented a beautiful positioning of the piano in a good hall with proper focus and a sense of size that puts the listener at a good midhall seat. The well-recorded ambience is highlighted by the excellent clarity. The Calrec microphone array is very much at home with solo piano music. (A+)

670 Liszt, F.: *Christus*, Hungarian Radio and Television Chorus, Hungarian State Orchestra: Hungaroton 12831-33-2. A wonderful sense of space and ambience highlights this presentation. The instrumental textures are positively transparent and realistic, as are the sounds of the soloists. This is a first-rate job, another example of the expertise and commitment of the Hungaroton engineers. (A+)

671 Liszt, F.: *Don Sanche*, Hungarian State Opera Orchestra, Hungarian Radio and Television Chorus (with Gérard Garino, Júlia Hamari, Istvan Gáti, and others): Hungaroton HCD 12744-45-2. Highly detailed and transparent with a fine sense of depth and ambience. There was good choral blending and clarity overall with the solo vocals forward a bit, but not excessively so. The front-row perspective of this recording is quite realistic, those well-done solo vocals a real treat. (A)

672 Liszt, F.: *A Faust Symphony in Three Character Portrayals* (arranged for two pianos by the composer), Thomas Hitzlberger and Georg Schütz, pianos: CPO 999 056-2. Smooth, full, and well imaged, with good small-hall ambience surrounding the two instruments. The listening position is midhall, a good choice for a recording of this kind, although some listeners might like to feel a bit closer to the performers. (A)

673 Liszt, F.: *Liszt at the Opera II* (operatic Fantasies, Paraphrases and Transcriptions), Leslie Howard, piano: Hyperion CDA 66571/2. A nice solid piano image is the feature here with the instrument not in the least diffuse or phasey. The perspective is midhall, and this fits in quite well with the typical small-room audio-playback environment most of us live with. (A)

674 Liszt, F.: *Mazeppa*; *Orpheus*; *Tasso: Lamento and Trionfo* (transcribed for organ and piano); François Vaucher, organ; Christian Favre, piano: Preludio PHC-2112. This effort is broad scale, reverberant, and rich with a good contrast between the well-focused, centrally located piano and the more broadly imaged organ. The clarity is good, especially considering the complexity of the works. (A)

675 Liszt, F.: *Missa Choralis*, Hungarian Youth Ensemble Choir: Hungaroton HCD 12747-2. This classy job displays a delightful choral blend with fine detail, clarity, and transparency. A very realistic hall ambience tops off the effect. (A+)

676 Liszt, F.: *Piano Music* (assorted piano works, including the *Mephisto Waltz Number 1* and *Sonata in B Minor*; album title: *Nojima Plays Liszt*), Minoru Nojima, piano: Reference Recordings RR-25CD. This is a close up, powerful, realistic recording job by RR's Keith Johnson. Johnson is a master at accurately picking up hall reverb, using it to enhance a small-room playback situation. In addition to the recording of the "direct" sound of the instrument itself, the secondary hall ambience fills out the sound field and makes for a front-row experience of the first order. (A+)

677 Liszt, F.: *Piano Music* (including the *Mephisto Waltz* and *Three Transcendental Etudes*), Janina Fialkowska, piano: Musica Viva 2-1035. A sense of hall space is important in piano-solo recordings, and this effort mimics a real hall nicely, with a fine you-are-there ambience. There is also a good sense of proper instrumental size in relation to the perceived listening distance. (A)

678 Liszt, F.: *Piano Works* (including *Variationen über das Motiv von Bach Liebesträume*, and *Bénédiction de Dieu dans la Solitude*), Michel Dalberto, piano: Denon 81757 9289-2. This one is close up, vibrant, and quite impressive, with realistic tonality and instrumental dynamics. An excellent small-hall (almost in-your-room) ambience tops off this classy recording job. (A+)

679 Liszt, F.: *Sonata in B Minor* (and other, shorter pieces), John Browning, piano: Delos D/CD 3022. There is good clarity here and good dynamic contrast, with a somewhat distant sound stage. The piano is well focused, and the tonality is fine. (A)

680 Liszt, F.: *Sonata in B Minor* (and other, shorter pieces), Earl Wild, piano: Etcetera KTC 2010. Very good piano clarity and detail, with impressive dynamics and a rock-solid focus. This close-up recording has you in a front-row seat in a small hall. Actually, the hall is *really* small because the overall texture is going to be a bit too dry for some tastes, but I feel that is a big plus here and heightens the intimate nature of this performance. This is hard-to-beat sound reproduction in both engineering and presentation. I found that the dry acoustics responded well to a variety of surround-enhancement techniques. (A+)

681 Liszt, F.: *Sonata in B Minor*; *Funérailles* (and other, shorter works), Alfred Brendel, piano: Philips 434 078-2. This effort displays a well-imaged close-up sound that has excellent textures and equally good tonality as well as very good dynamic range. There is a complete lack of the annoying diffuse or phasey artifacts that tend to mar many solo-piano recordings. (A+)

682 Liszt, F.: *Songs* (volume 1); Nicolai Gedda, tenor; Lars Roos, piano: Bluebell ABCD 021. This is somewhat distant for a solo vocal recording, with the rather unusual situation of the piano appearing to be closer to the listener than the singer. However, the slightly forward piano notwithstanding, the blend of hall ambience, articulation, and sound-stage depth is quite attractive. There are times when this kind of vocal-piano positioning will be found at a live performance. (A)

683 Liszt, F.: *Songs* (volume 2); Nicolai Gedda, tenor; Lars Roos, piano: Bluebell ABCD 022. Similar in quality to 682. (A)

684 Liszt, F.: *Transcriptions and Paraphrases* (piano renditions of works by Bach, Beethoven, Schubert, Weber, Schumann, Chopin, Paganini, Verdi, and Wagner), Earl Wild, piano: Etcetera KTC-2011. This effort displays a fairly close-up small-hall ambience. It is certainly not an in-your-room feel but is definitely not the large-room acoustics of the Musica Viva–Fialkowska recording discussed above. The clarity and tonality are excellent. (A+)

685 *Little Caesar*: Geffen 24288-D2. This is loud, raucous stuff that rates a place here because of decent vocal clarity (for rock) combined with intelligently applied reverberation, a good stereo spread, and potent dynamics. If you want decent rock sound, this disc has it. (B)

686 Little Feat: *Representing the Mambo*: Warner W2 26163. This is much better recorded than your average "funky blues" rock album, with wide dynamics, good clarity, and even a passable (albeit clearly fabricated) sound stage. The vocals in particular are not oversized in relation to the instrumental players, a welcome relief. (B+)

687 Little Feat: *Shake Me Up*: Morgan Creek 2959-20005-2. Nice vocal clarity, the blend between the voice and instruments handled well. There is some subtle deep bass at times combined with the clear and well-etched sound-stage image. (B+)

688 *Little Village*: Reprise 26713-2. This is certainly highly electrified and mixer-manipulated rock, but the clarity is OK, and the left-right spread is good. (B)

689 Lloyd Webber, Andrew: *Highlights from the Phantom of the Opera*: Polydor 831 563-2. See the review of the full-length recording (690) for details. (B+)

690 Lloyd Webber, A.: *The Phantom of the Opera* (original cast recording, with Michael Crawford, Sarah Brightman, Steve Barton, and others): Polydor 831 273-2. While the sound stage of this release is heavily edited by the engineers, the resulting clarity and detail are quite good. The vocals occasionally have more sibilance than they should, almost certainly the result of a poor microphone choice (it would be hard to believe that the sound was edited to sound this way). The bass is pretty good, although the opening sequence with the organ is overblown and sounds like Virgil Fox running wild. The performance deserved better engineering than delivered by this AAD effort by Polydor. They should do it over with the same cast and shoot for an A+. (B+)

691 Lloyd Webber, A.: *Requiem*, English Chamber Orchestra, Winchester Cathedral Choir: EMI 7 47146 2. Surprising dynamics, a nice sense of hall space, good clarity, and an excellent placement of the choir and soloists highlight this disc. Audio buffs will appreciate the occasional decent deep bass. I thought the sound was just a tad strident during the louder parts. (A)

692 Lock Up: *Something Different This Way Comes*: Geffen M2G-24279. There is lots of rock punch on this one, with a full and rich sound. The clarity is quite good for an album of this type. (B+)

693 Los Lobos: *Kiko*: Slash/Warner 26786-2. Punchy and clean, with a wide and obviously mixer-dominated sound stage. Unlike many rock albums, this one displays good deep bass at times. Although engineered by a variety of people and mastered by technical whiz Bob Ludwig, the sound stage is consistently flat sounding. (B+)

694 *The Lost Spindle* (Theatrical Music from the Courts of Ferdinand and Isabella, Fifteenth Century), Live Oak and Company: Titanic Ti-178. Very reverberant (almost empty-auditorium) and spacious. The work was obviously recorded in a very reflective hall. The resulting effect will clearly appeal to some more than others. The sound is otherwise clean and transparent with good depth. (A)

695 Lovano, Joe: *Landmarks* (with John Abercrombie, Ken Werner, Marc Johnson, and Bill Stewart): Blue Note CDP 7 96108-2. This jazz recording exhibits a good detailed sound field with a decent left-right spread and a good sense of imaging. The drums are a bit oversized, but I have heard a lot worse. Good saxophone tonality. (B)

696 *Love Songs* (songs by Copland, Obradors, Ovalle, Strauss, and many others); Arleen Auger, soprano; Dalton Baldwin, piano: Delos D/CD 3029. There is very fine vocal quality on this recording, the singer well positioned in a nice small-hall setting. The piano is a tad diffuse (a common problem, as I have noted countless times), but the effect is not all that bad, and the instrument's tonality is reproduced quite well. (A)

697 Lubambo, Romero, and Raphael Rabello: *Shades of Rio*: Chesky JD-85. Reverberant, spacious, and vibrant, rare in recordings of music like this. There is excellent guitar detail, although the space between the two instruments often seems a bit excessive, as if the engineer felt that spread was more important than intimacy. (A)

698 *Lucille Field Sings Songs by American Women Composers* (works by Patsy Rogers, Ruth Crawford Seeger, Nancy van de Vate, Miriam Gideon, and others): Cambria CD 1037. This effort displays a distant but well-recorded sound stage. There is good vocal realism, with the piano-vocal balance quite good. (A)

699 Lully, Jean Baptiste: *Atys* (excerpts), Les Arts Florissants: Harmonia

Mundi France 901249. I felt that this one was very transparent sounding and bright, typical with period-instrument ensembles. The very slight edginess one hears will be a characteristic of the musical ensemble and not a recording deficiency. The vocal reproduction here is outstanding: clear, properly sized, well placed, and vibrant. (A+)

700 Lynch, Brian: *In Process* (with Jim Snidero, Javon Jackson, Benny Green, Dennis Irwin, and Tony Reedus): Ken Music O11. This is a somewhat distant jazz effort but with good detail and clarity. The ensemble imaging is not too bad. (B)

701 Lynch, Ray: *Deep Breakfast* (with Tom Canning, Beverly O'Mahony, and Ron Strauss): Music West MWCD-102. This is punchy, open, and smooth "mostly electronic" music with a very well synthesized sound stage. It may not sound "real," but this recording is well engineered and vibrant. There is some decent deep bass at times. (A)

702 Mabern, Harold: *Straight Street* (his trio, with Ron Carter and Jack DeJohnette): DIW/Columbia CK 48961. This jazz release is transparent and smooth with good tonality, clarity, and focus from the piano and the bass. As is typical with music of this kind, the drums are bigger than life. (B+)

703 Machaut, Guillaume: *Messe de Notre Dame*; *Le Lai de la Fonteinne*, The Hilliard Ensemble: Hyperion CDA 66358. Very clean vocals, with few direct-sound phase effects. The slightly constricted left-to-right sound stage imparts a distant perspective. There is still a very good hall ambience, however, especially to the *Lai*, which was recorded in a different place from the Mass. (A)

704 Machaut, G.: *Songs* (The Mirror of Narcissus), The Gothic Voices, with Emma Kirkby, soprano: Hyperion CDA 66087. Very close up and clear, with fine detail and spacious, exact imaging. A troublesome traffic noise frequently intrudes, audible even on my smaller sound system. An effect like this is "realistic" only if you are used to the sounds of the big city clattering away outside the concert hall or cathedral you frequent. This disc has some of the worst background clutter I have yet to hear on a high-quality disc. Nevertheless, the overall engineering is exemplary, and I am going to include it with the usual warning. (Qualified A)

705 Madonna: *The Immaculate Collection*: Sire/Warner 26440-2. Not all of Madonna's discs have been examples of topflight engineering. As a matter of fact, most are pretty bad, although her "videos" certainly entertain. However, this CD is an exception. Encoded with a matrixing technique called Q-Sound (the Roland RSS system is similar), the disc sounds like it is being played back through a Carver "sonic hologram" or Sound Concepts enhancement device or a pair of Polk SDA speakers. The vocal quality is pretty good, well centered and well focused. Needless to say, the disc exhibits impressive dynamic impact. Although I would not recommend its use by classical-music recording engineers, the Q-Sound process creates an impressive rock sound stage. (B)

706 Mahler, Gustav: *Songs of a Wayfarer*; *Kindertotenlieder*; *Rückert Lieder*, Cincinnati Symphony Orchestra, Andreas Schmidt, baritone: Telarc 80269. This is an exemplary vocal recording, the soloist sounding smooth, clear, and well focused in relation to the equally well-engineered orchestral accompaniment. Perhaps the most important thing in a recording like this is the microphone that handles the voice, and Telarc is second to none in making use of such equipment. (A+)

707 Mahler, G.: *Symphony Number 1*, London Symphony Orchestra: Collins EC 1029-2. There is nice clarity and depth on this recording with a good midhall listening position. However, the overall sound seemed just a tad dry for a work of this magnitude. I find that this can be an advantage if one is willing to add a little surround enhancement, and my Yamaha DSP unit worked wonders with this presentation. The rating refers to the stereo-only performance, of course, but the disc would be top-scoring if we were rating its adaptability to such processing. (A)

708 Mahler, G.: *Symphony Number 1*, Chicago Symphony Orchestra: London 411 731-2. Big, dynamic, and spacious. There is good detail overall, with the massed strings just a bit brittle on my system—the only characteristic that disqualified the disc for an A+. A subtle, very deep background rumble is evident during the quieter passages, especially with an extraction-type surround processor engaged and particularly if the surround speakers have decent woofers (most do not have them). The rumble is no problem with most standard-sized "main" speaker systems, but subwoofer owners may wish to back off on the "deep-bass" boost a bit. (Qualified A)

709 Mahler, G.: *Symphony Number 1*, Bavarian Radio Symphony Orchestra: Novalis 150 033-2. Very detailed and clean, with excellent front-to-back depth and spread. This release is a little smaller in scale than many recorded versions, but it certainly will appeal to those who are turned off by the more monumental-sounding versions. As with 707, my surround processor got along well with it. (A)

710 Mahler, G.: *Symphony Number 1*, Berlin Philharmonic Orchestra: Philips 420 936-2. This effort has a nice sound-stage spread with fine clarity. The violins are smooth and not overly bright, even though the listening perspective is just a bit too close for my taste. Mahler's symphonies tend to respond well to surround processing, and a close-up sound stage like this one was aided considerably by using either of my units. (A)

711 Mahler, G.: *Symphony Number 2*, Saint Louis Symphony Orchestra: Telarc 80081. This is a large-scale recording of a large-scale work with a broad, spacious sound stage that is in the Telarc tradition—and with pretty good depth. The somewhat diffuse central image may put off some listeners, but it may actually work to advantage in some listening rooms. A very smooth string sound and good clarity top off the recording. (A)

712 Mahler, G.: *Symphony Number 3*, Danish National Radio Symphony and choir, with the Copenhagen Boys Choir and Anne Gjevang, contralto: Chandos CHAN 8970/1. This effort by Chandos is reverberant and powerful with satisfactory stage depth. The soloist is well positioned, and her efforts are properly blended with the fine orchestra and chorus. The hall ambience is decently supportive of the ensemble. This recording company is noted for producing even better sound than what we have here, and I assume that the few deficiencies must be the result of hall acoustics. (A)

713 Mahler, G.: *Symphony Number 4*, London Symphony Orchestra,

Mahler (714)

Patricia Rozario, soprano: Collins Classics 10442. Smooth and clear, with good depth and a marvelous sound-stage spread. The soloist was well integrated, and the vocal textures were quite believable. Like a number of Collins releases, I felt that this one was just a touch dry. If this bothers you as much as it does me, a subtle bit of surround processing (if your system has the capability) may fabricate the missing ambience. The recording did very well when manipulated with either of my processors. (A)

714 Mahler, G.: *Symphony Number 4*, Orchestre de la Suisse Romande, Edith Weins, soprano: Erato 45628-2. Smooth, close up, and clear, with just a touch of brittleness to the violins, but the cellos sound great. There was a very good sound stage and depth on this release, with good hall reverberation. The soloist seems a bit forward, but she is certainly clearly recorded. (A)

715 Mahler, G.: *Symphony Number 4*, Los Angeles Philharmonic Orchestra, Barbara Hendricks, soprano: Sony SK 48380. Nice and smooth with a somewhat distant perspective. The sound stage seemed a bit flat, some small-sized instruments sounding too large and too close in relation to the rest of the ensemble. There were good dynamic contrasts, however, and Ms. Hendricks is well treated by the engineers, properly sized in relation to the orchestra. She sounds great. (A)

716 Mahler, G.: *Symphony Number 5*, Scottish National Orchestra: Chandos CHAN 8829. Chandos is in its element here, and this release is dynamic, supremely clear, and reverberant with a wonderful sound-stage presentation. The recording is quite bright and brassy at times but lacking any brittleness or distortion. This is about as good as a recording gets if you like a front-row seat. If you have been paying attention as you read through these reviews, you will note that the combination of the Scottish National Orchestra and Chandos nearly always produces a top score. (A+)

717 Mahler, G.: *Symphony Number 5*, Philharmonia Orchestra: Deutsche Grammophon 415 476-2. This recording sounds quite clear, with fine instrumental delineation but also with a wide yet subjectively somewhat flat sound stage. As required for this symphony, the sound has a nice dynamic range. This is not the best recording of this work, but it's not chopped liver either. (A)

718 Mahler, G.: *Symphony Number 5*, Cleveland Orchestra: London 425 438-2. This is a bright (but not strident) recording with wide frequency response and tremendous dynamic range. There is an excellent reproduction of cellos and bass as well as a good sound stage and realistic depth. Music like this allows the London engineers to pull out the stops, and they certainly did that here. (A+)

719 Mahler, G.: *Symphony Number 5*, Berlin Philharmonic Orchestra: Philips 422 355-2. This release has dynamics and clarity to match 718 but with somewhat less down-deep bass. However, given the music, really deep bass response is not a problem, and the sound-stage spread and depth comes across as a bit better than the fine London effort. Both recordings will satisfy those in need of first-class sound. (A+)

720 Mahler, G.: *Symphony Number 5*, New York Philharmonia Orchestra: Teldec 46152-2. This release is state-of-the-art in every way and fit to demonstrate the best sound system you can buy. I felt that it was slightly superior to 716, 718, and 719 — all exemplary recordings. It would be a candidate for an A++ rating if I were awarding them. (A+)

721 Mahler, G.: *Symphony Number 6*; Zemlinsky, Alexander: *Six Maeterlinck Songs*, Royal Concertgebouw Orchestra, Jard van Nes, mezzo-soprano: London 430 165-2. This transcription has great impact and plenty of dynamic range combined with an excellent sound stage and superior hall envelopment. There is some very large-scale sound on the Mahler piece. The vocal blending on the Zemlinsky material is realistic. This recording may make use of some multimiking, but it is done as it should be. (A+)

722 Mahler, G.: *Symphony Number 7*, Chicago Symphony Orchestra: RCA RCD-4581. An early RCA/Soundstream recording made in 1980, this release has a nice perspective that is just a tad distant. The great power and depth of this work is amply handled, and the clarity of the complex passages was first rate. I felt there was just a touch of brittleness in the treble at times. (B+)

723 Mahler, G.: *Symphony Number 8*, Atlanta Symphony Orchestra and Chorus (assisted by several other choirs): Telarc 80267. This 80-minute symphony has been shoehorned on a single disc, making it a bargain compared to the double-LP sets of old. It is a magnificent recording of this large-scale work, with soloists, choir, organ, and orchestra very well integrated. Detail is also well maintained, and the organ is impressively large sounding. The soloists used in this performance are spread across the stage (men on the right, women on the left) and have a close-up perspective. Because of this, some may feel the recording lacks a degree of ambience, but in this case the technique enhances the result. (A+)

724 Mahler, G.: *Symphony Number 9*, Chicago Symphony Orchestra: London 410 012-2. Over a decade old, this disc still has decent clarity and a good if not altogether realistic and deep sound stage. There are occasional low-bass thumping sounds in the background that will be a problem only on the most bass-potent speakers. The recording is also just a tad dry, as if it were made in a smaller hall than it should have been. The presentation was helped considerably by the surround processors of both of my playback systems. (Qualified A)

725 Makowicz, Adam: *My Name Is Makowicz* (with Phil Woods, Marc Johnson, Bill Goodwin, and Gene Estes): Sheffield CD-21. Sheffield pioneered direct-to-disc LP recording some years back, and their expertise carries over to this originally analog-recorded jazz piece that was meant to be used as a backup to the D-to-D effort. The low playback level will require a somewhat higher than usual setting of your volume control, but the disc is very detailed, cleanly recorded, well imaged, and displays an excellent sound stage. (A)

726 *Man with the Wooden Flute* (traditional flute music of the British Isles, America, Quebec, and Cape Breton), Chris Norman, flute (with Robin Bullock, Ann Morgan, and Pete Sutherland): Dorian DOR 90166. The sound on this release was very close up, detailed, and articulate, yet blessed with fine hall ambience. Oddly enough, while the ensemble imaging is pretty good, the featured instrument seems a bit diffuse and phasey at times. (A)

727 Mancini, Henry: *Mancini Rocks the Pops*, Royal Philharmonic Pops Orchestra: Denon CD-73078. This orchestral recording of pop music is spacious, lucid, and dynamic. The sound stage displays good depth and is spread out nicely but is a tad too diffuse on some material. (A)

728 *Manhattan Mambo* (with Hilton Ruiz, piano; and others): Telarc 83322. This Telarc pop-music release displays good clarity and dynamic impact with a wide but somewhat flat sound stage. Perhaps that is too critical since the overall sound is quite good and worked very well when run through either of my surround processors. (A)

729 Manhattan Transfer: *Vocalese*: Atlantic 81266-2. This effort has decent vocal-orchestral clarity with good bass-to-treble balance. The vocals are clear, unbuzzy, and not overwhelming in relation to the orchestra, which is unusual for a recording from this group. Although the sound is typically pop album in balance as well as technically one-dimensional and clearly multi-miked, the slightly elevated vocal levels present a semblance of depth. The overall sound quality is considerably better than any of the other Manhattan Transfer recordings I have heard. (B)

730 Mantooth, Frank: *Per-se-vere* (with Clark Terry, Pete Christlieb, Bobby Shew, and others): Optimism CD-3229. Here we have a decent, large-scale (for jazz) sound stage with good clarity and dynamics. This is a "straight" jazz recording that is a mite rough at times. (B)

731 Margitza, Rick: *Hope* (with Steve Masakowski, Marc Johnson, Phil Perry, Airto Moreira, and others): Blue Note CDP 7 94858-2. This jazz recording has a wide sound stage with a forward, somewhat synthesized feel to it. The result displays good detail and transparency with a bit too much in-your-face highlighting of solo instruments. The disc did respond well to surround processing at my end, even Pro Logic. (B)

732 Margitza, Rick: *This Is New* (with Joey Calderazzo, Robert Hurst, Jeff Watts, and Tim Hagans): Blue Note CDP 7 97196-2. This release is punchy, well defined, and blessed with a good sound stage and good imaging, although the drums seem to come from the whole stage area at times. (B)

733 *The Marriage of Heaven and Hell* (motets and songs from thirteenth-century France), The Gothic Voices: Hyperion CDA 66423. Close up, clear, and detailed, with a good small-hall ambience. As usual for recordings made in church or cathedral environment, there is some traffic or machine noise. (Qualified A)

734 Marsalis, Branford: *Crazy People Music* (with Jeff Watts, Robert Hurst, and Kenny Kirkland): Columbia CK 46072. There is good clarity on this one (particularly the sax) with decent imaging—especially the drums, which are mercifully kept the correct size in relation to the rest of the combo. However, the overall sound is a bit thin and dry and lacking in wide-band frequency response. The thin, dry characteristic made this jazz recording quite responsive to manipulations by my big Yamaha DSP unit. Indeed, it would have earned a higher score had such adaptability counted. (B)

735 Marsalis, B.: *Random Abstract* (with Kenny Kirkland, Delbert Felix, and Lewis Nash): Columbia CK 44055. Columbia has traditionally had trouble turning out really good recordings of any music. The series of fine performances by Branford Marsalis is a case in point: good jazz and only fair sound. This disc is one of the better recordings of Mr. Marsalis I have yet heard, but even it sounds somewhat dry and shortchanges the listener in sound-stage depth. (A liberal dose of processing by nearly any kind of surround-sound decoder should help things here, particularly if it is a synthesizing device that adds digitally generated echoes to the ambience speakers.) The clarity is quite good. Interestingly, Marsalis had to go to Japan to get at least decent engineering from Columbia. Even so, it barely makes the list. (B)

736 Marsalis, B.: *Trio Jeepy* (with Milton Hinton, Delbert Felix, and Jeff Watts): Columbia CK 44199. Easily the best Branford Marsalis album in sound quality, surpassing the two above (see 734 and 735). The disc displays a fine clarity combined with a well-done sound stage. The solo sax sound is Marsalis's best yet, and the drums are well focused and articulate. (B+)

737 Marsalis, Ellis: *Ellis Marsalis Trio* (with Bob Hurst and Jeff Watts): Blue Note CDP 7 96107-2. This jazz album by still another member of the highly talented Marsalis family is good and clean with a well-focused piano (rare) and drum set (also rare). There is a nice sound stage and nightclub-acoustics atmostphere that lends itself to surround enhancement. Branford should talk to Ellis about borrowing his engineers. (A)

738 Marsalis, Wynton: *Crescent City Christmas Card*: Columbia CK 45287. Smooth and clear with a good instrumental spread. It's nice to hear instruments like this realistically positioned, especially the drums, which are not ballooned out of proportion. Incidentally, this is not your usual Christmas-music recording. (B+)

739 Marsalis, W.: *Levee Low Moan* (Soul Gestures in Southern Blue, Volume 3, with Marcus Roberts, Wessell Anderson, Todd Williams, Reginald Veal, and Herlin Riley): Columbia CK 47975. Very transparent and uniform. The instruments, particularly the trumpet, are very well placed and sized as they should be. (B+)

740 Marsalis, W.: *Standard Time* (with Marcus Roberts, Robert Hurst, and Jeff Watts): Columbia CK 40461. Clean, dynamic, and very realistic classic-jazz sound. Marsalis's trumpet is right where it is supposed to be and sounds terrific. Although this disc does not quite have the sound-stage depth and hall ambience of a two-microphone "purist" job, it is obvious that Columbia has at least partially reformed many of its old recording practices. (A)

741 Marsalis, W.: *Standard Time, Volume 2: Intimacy Calling* (with Marcus Roberts, Reginald Veal, Herlin Riley, Robert Hurst, and Todd Williams): Columbia CK 47346. Although an artistic continuation of 740 for some reason this one lacks the sonic sparkle. Still good jazz, however. (B+)

742 Marsalis, W.: *Standard Time, Volume 3: The Resolution of Romance* (with Ellis Marsalis, Reginald Veal, and Herlin Riley): Columbia CK 46143. Although this is volume 3, the lower Columbia stock number makes me think that this disc was recorded before volume 2. The sound is more like that heard on volume 1, with possibly a still better sound stage. (A)

743 Marsalis, W.: *Thick in the South* (Soul Gestures in Southern Blue, Volume 1, with Marcus Roberts, Joe Henderson, Bob Hurst, Jeff Watts, and Elvin Jones): Columbia CK 47977. This effort is technically very clear with a good sound-stage spread. The drums are particularly well positioned and not overblown. (B+)

744 Marsalis, W.: *Uptown Ruler* (Soul Gestures in Southern Blue, Volume 2, with Marcus Roberts, Todd Williams, Reginald Veal, and Herlin Riley): Columbia CK 47976. Recorded at the same time as 743, the overall sound is the same. (B+)

745 Martinů, Bohuslav: *Symphonies Number 1 and 2*: Bamberger Symphoniker: BIS CD-362. This effort has fine orchestral balance, ensemble imaging, and dynamic contrasts. The clarity is what one would experience at a mid-hall seating position — realistic. The hall ambience is just right. (A+)

746 Martinů, B.: *Symphonies Number 3 and 4*, Bamberger Symphoniker: BIS CD-363. Essentially the same qualities as 745. (A+)

747 *Masters of Reality*: Delicious Vinyl Records 422-842-2. Here we have a typically mixer-synthesized rock sound stage with little front-to-back depth. However, the disc displays decent instrumental and vocal clarity for this genera. Fake or not, the sound-stage synthesis gives the impression of envelopment. (B)

748 *Masterpieces of the Spanish Golden Age for Organ and Trumpet* (short works by Lully, Cabezón, Durón, Aguilera de Heredia, Soler, and others); Edward Tarr, trumpet; Irmtraud Krüger, organ: Christophorus CHR 74511. This recording is large sounding and reverberant with plenty of depth and hall envelopment. The transparency, detail, and clarity are quite good. (A)

749 Maxwell-Davies, Peter: *Strathclyde Concerto Number 3*; *Strathclyde Concerto Number 4*, Scottish Chamber Orchestra: Collins Classics 12392. Very clean, clear, and dynamic with good hall feel, accurate imaging, and palpable depth. The ambience is what is required for music of this kind. The SCO has made recordings for Telarc, Nimbus, and Delos, and all have been quite good. A fine ensemble. (A+)

750 Mays, B., and R. Drummond: *One to One*: Digital Music Products CD-473. Here we have a delightfully clear and detailed sound image from both the piano and acoustic bass. The close-up positioning puts these guys right in your living room. Because of this, this jazz recording was very responsive to surround manipulation by both of my Yamaha processors. (A+)

751 Mays, Bill, and Ray Drummond: *One to One 2*: Digital Music Products CD-482. This is an excellent piano–acoustic bass recording that is possibly just a tad better in sound-stage realism than the earlier release (see 750). (A+)

752 Mays, Lyle: *Lyle Mays* (with Alejandro Acuña, Billy Drewes, Bill Frisell, Marc Johnson, and Nana Vasconcelos): Geffen 2409-2. This effort is big, full, and smooth, the piano well forward (and maybe just a mite overly large) and backed by an ensemble that is mixer manipulated and supposed to be that way. The jazz sound stage is well spread out, and the result is dynamic and technically entertaining. There are lots of fake effects, but they are expertly done. (A)

753 Mays, L.: *Street Dreams* (with Bill Frisell, Marc Johnson, Steve Rodby, Peter Erskine, Steve Gadd, and others): Geffen 24204-2. This release is smooth, wide band in frequency response, and clean with a good overall balance and a well-controlled albeit electrically synthesized sound stage. It is nice to have well-focused unbloated drums on such a heavily processed disc. (A)

754 McCartney, Paul: *Liverpool Oratorio*, Royal Liverpool Philharmonic Orchestra and Chorus, Choristers of Liverpool Cathedral (with Kiri Te Kanawa, Sally Burgess, Jerry Hadley, and Willard White): EMI CDS 7 54371-2. Yes, this is *the* Paul McCartney, and this is not a pop selection. This is a very good orchestral reproduction of a live performance in a cathedral with very impressive choral integration and a formidable organ pedal at times. The soloists vary in technical work, some well sized and placed properly and some a bit too far forward for my taste. (A)

755 McClure, Ron: *McJeff* (his quartet, with John Abercrombie, Richie Beirach, and Adam Nussbaum): SteepleChase SCCD-31262. Forward, bright jazz that is also a bit one-dimensional. However, the piano is not too large, and its sound is quite good. The drums are spread out too wide. (B)

756 McConnell, Rob, and the Boss Brass: *Boss Brass and Woods* (with Moe Koffman, Jerry Toth, Eugene Araro, Rick Wilkins, and others): MAC/Impulse MCAD 5982. This jazz release is bright, brassy, and clean with a good sound stage. There is very good imaging from every instrument in the ensemble. (A)

757 McEntire, Reba: *For My Broken Heart*: MCA 10400. This is an example of the way C&W recordings can be done if the engineers are competent. The vocal-instrumental clarity is good, and the sound stage still has a balanced and blended sound. (B+)

758 McFerrin, Bobby: *Spontaneous Inventions* (with Robin Williams, Herbie Hancock, Wayne Shorter, Jon Hendricks, and the Manhattan Transfer): Blue Note CDP 7 46298 2. This is very close-up jazz sound with a high level of clarity as a consequence. The sound stage is obviously electronically manipulated in the extreme with sometimes subtle, sometimes powerful deep bass. There is a well-defined piano backup sound. (B)

759 McGovern, Maureen: *Baby I'm Yours* (with Jeff Harris, Mike Renzi, Jeff Mironov, Jay Leonhardt, and others): RCA 60943-2. This one is blemished only by vocals that are sometimes more reverberant in relation to the rest of the ensemble than they should be. The bass is quite strong (and sometimes deep) on this recording, but the vocal-instrumental clarity is not buried under it (heavy bass can be the downfall of some recordings since it tends to muddy the overall sound). The nature of the mix makes this recording come across quite well on a typical automotive playback system. (B)

760 McKenna, Dave: *Shadows 'n' Dreams*: Concord Jazz CCD-4467. The solo piano is a tad oversized, but its sound is reasonably unobstructed and clean and not phasey, and the dynamic contrasts are good. The close-up presentation may be linked by some astute listeners. (B)

761 McNeely, Jim: *Winds of Change* (his trio, with Mike Richmond and Kenny Washington): SteepleChase SCCD 31256. Very good presence and smoothness on this jazz release with plenty of left-to-right spread. Unfortunately, the drums are widely spread out too, extending well beyond the dimensions of the well-centered and well-proportioned piano. (B)

762 *Medieval English Music* (fourteenth and fifteenth centuries), The Hilliard Ensemble: Harmonia Mundi France 1901106. The overall sound here is smooth, clean, and balanced with a good close up listening perspective. This ADD disc is mercifully free of the background noise that seems to plague cathedral-recorded music, indicating that the bass-range, band width limitations of the analog recorder may have automatically corrected for the deficiency. Digital recorders capture even the deepest frequencies, and most low-level recorded "artifact" noise is bass-heavy. Engineers who record with digital gear and are faced with problems of this nature would do well to employ very-low-frequency filters to handle the problem, or they should contract with the local authorities to keep the outside noise under control during recording sessions. (A)

763 *The Medieval Romantics: French Songs and Motets, 1340–1440*, The Gothic Voices: Hyperion CDA 66463. Clean and close up with fine detail and a good ensemble blend. The ambience is small hall in nature and enveloping as it should be. The usual background noise is there, but it is not as intrusive as what I have heard in many other digitally produced medieval-music recordings. (A+)

764 Medtner, Nikolai: *Piano Concerto Number 2*; *Piano Concerto Number 3*, London Philharmonic Orchestra, Geoffrey Tozer, piano: Chandos CHAN 9038. This disc has marvelous clarity, depth, and impact. The piano is done very well, with accurate tonality, although some might consider its subjective stage width in relation to the full orchestra a bit excessive. (B+)

765 Medtner, N.: *Piano Music*, Earl Wild, piano: Chesky AD-1. There is a nice sense of hall space in this subjectively you-are-there recording. The piano is well focused and has fine tonality. Unlike some piano recordings, this one responds well to certain kinds of surround enhancement. (A+)

766 *The Memory of Thomas Beckett*, Schola Hungarica: Hungaroton HCD 12458-2. I have yet to see a bad or even a "just OK" recording by this group when working with the Hungaroton engineers. Very smooth, well blended, and clear with plenty of the kind of cathedral-church ambience that makes music of this kind so enjoyable. The spirit of music, as well as that of audio engineering, is alive and well in Hungary. (A)

767 Mendelssohn, Felix: *Motets*, La Chapelle Royal de Paris, Collegium Vocale de Gand: Harmonia Mundi France HMA 1901142. Smooth and blended, with a good sound stage and fine midhall clarity and ambience. There is a good placement of the soloists within the ensemble. (A)

768 Mendelssohn, F.: *Organ Works*, Peter Hurford, organ: Argo 414 420-2. This is a beautiful organ recording with a wonderful sense of hall envelopment and a three-dimensional sound stage. The comments concerning the highly praised Hindemith organ recording (573) apply here also. Be on your guard for woofer-damaging deep-bass overload, especially on track 8. This recording isn't kid stuff, and cranking the gain up on this and some other tracks may rattle all but the most robust bass-speaker drivers. If you have bass-reflex or "drone-cone" speakers (even fairly large ones), you will be wise to watch the amplifier gain during your first play-through. I have seen drone cones rattle when confronted with this recording, and vented enclosures may emit obnoxious wind-noise sounds at times. Oddly enough, good small acoustic-suspension woofers will not distort with the lowest pedal notes but will simply reproduce them at a reduced level. I consider this a reference standard for organ recordings. (A+)

769 Mendelssohn, F.: *Piano Trio Number 1*; *Piano Trio Number 2*; David Golub, piano: Mark Kaplan, violin; Colin Carr, cello; Arabesque Z-6599. Smooth and clean with a good sound-stage blend, good depth, and OK imaging. There is an excellent string tone from the violin and the cello. At times the piano seemed just a bit diffuse. (A)

770 Mendelssohn, F.: *Quartet Number 2, in A Minor*; *Octet, in E♭ Major*, The Cleveland Quartet: Telarc 80142. This effort displays a wonderful blend and richness, with good clarity. The overall sound is close up and maybe a bit too big with a wide but slightly diffuse sound stage. (A)

771 Mendelssohn, F.: *String Quartets*, The Coull String Quartet: Hyperion CDA 66579. This little jewel displayed good depth, clarity, and detail, with the kind of small-hall ambience that material of this kind requires. The middistance listening perspective is balanced, and the imaging is particularly good. (A+)

772 Mendelssohn, F.: *Symphonies Number 3 and 4*, London Classical Players: EMI/Angel 7 54000-2. This is an original-instruments version of these symphonies that is clean and clear but somewhat distant. The recording lacks the usual original-instrument string brightness—a definite relief. (A)

773 Mendelssohn, F.: *Symphonies Number 3 and 4*, Academy of St. Martin in the Fields: Argo 411 931-2. Very clean with a good listening perspective and a larger-scaled sound than 772. The sound stage is wide but appears to lack some depth. There is just a touch of string harshness. I heard some minor background noise that resembles traffic rumble. Background artifacts like these are hard to shake in the modern world where a concert hall may be in a downtown area. Maybe orchestras should start recording in the middle of the night or have their halls built in the country. (Qualified A)

774 Mendelssohn, F.: *Symphonies Number 3 and 4*, Scottish Chamber of Orchestra: Nimbus NI 5067. Clean, smooth, and somewhat distant. The imaging here is realistic, but the listener who likes this kind of effect will ordinarily enjoy sitting more toward the rear of the hall at live concerts. The recording lacks the dynamics of 773. (B+)

775 Mendelssohn, F.: *Symphony Number 3*; *Hebrides Overture*; *Calm Sea and Prosperous Voyage*, The Hanover Band: Nimbus NI 5318. This is a smooth and clean original-instrument recording with excellent detail and a good sense of hall space. The result seems somewhat distant in perspective but not so much as a number of other Nimbus recordings I have heard. (A)

776 Mendelssohn, F.: *Symphony Number 4*; *Piano Concerto Number One*; *Violin Concerto*; Hanover Band; Benjamin Hudson, violin; Christopher Kite, fortepiano: Nimbus NI 5158.

Clean, clear, dynamic, and a cut above the usual Nimbus sound. There is a nice hall feel to this presentation, and the sound is not a bit dry. The piano is well positioned and sized, as is the violin. I felt this release was recorded better than 775, possibly because the solo instruments were so well integrated. This original-instrument transcription works better than most such experiments, and the anti-original-instrument faction certainly owes it a listen. A recording like this demonstrates how the Calrec microphone can handle small-scale concerto-type music. (A+)

777 Mendelssohn, F.: *Symphony Number 4*; *Overtures and Incidental Music to "A Midsummer Night's Dream,"* Atlanta Symphony Orchestra: Telarc 80318. Smooth, broad staged, and blended, with a good transparent sound and a fine string tone. The Telarc engineering techniques work well with music of this kind. (A+)

778 Mendelssohn, F.: *Violin Sonatas*; Shlomo Minz, violin; Paul Ostrovsky, piano: Deutsche Grammophon 419 244-2. In the past, Deutsche Grammophon has turned out some below-par recordings because of its indiscriminate use of multiple microphones and its obsession with microscopic detail. However, it's pretty hard to do a multimicrophone screwup when recording only two instruments, and this fact has allowed DGG to do a fine job with these works. The middistance sound is clean and clear with a fine small-hall ambience surrounding the players. The focus is also good, especially that of the violin. (A)

779 Mendes, Sergio: *Brasileiro*: Elektra 61315-2. There is a "subtle" clarity here combined with impression impact (you'll have to listen to see what I mean). The vocal and instrumental delineation is remarkable, and the sound stage has depth as well as a good lateral spread. Percussion freaks should love this disc. (A)

780 Mendoza, Vince: *Start Here* (with Bob Mintzer, John Scofield, Joe Lovano, and others): World Pacific CDP 7 94592-2. Clean, spacious, and well-balanced jazz. Two pianos (and not bad engineering) ensure a wide piano sound stage but the one-man drum set is still ridiculously wide. (B)

781 Menotti, Gian Carlo: *Violin Concerto*; Barber, Samuel: *Violin Concerto*, Pacific Symphony Orchestra, Ruggiero Ricci, violin: Reference Recordings RR-45CD. This release shows excellent depth, sound-stage spread, and detail. The solo violin is realistically placed in relation to the rest of the ensemble. This engineering job is a fine example of careful microphone use. (A+)

782 *Messe de Tournai*, Ensemble Organum: Harmonia Mundi France 901353. This wonderful rendition of fourteenth-century mass is clear, detailed, and reverberant in just the right way, with a good blend between the hall and the performers. I found that adding a bit of surround reinforcement, via a good processor (or even a Dolby surround unit) opened up the ambient effect even more. Unfortunately, there is some hall-induced background rumble on this recording that may also be enhanced by such manipulations. Speaker systems with good deep bass potential could also adversely highlight the effect. (Qualified A+)

783 Messiaen, Olivier: *Complete Organ Music*, Hans-Ola Ericsson, organ: BIS CD-409, CD-410, CD-441 and CD-442 (a four-volume set, each disc also available separately). Clean, clear, and big with good deep bass when the material calls for it (although that does not happen a great deal here). The hall ambience encoded into this recording lends itself to any surround processing your home system might be able to add (indeed, any organ recording will benefit from enhancement via a home-based surround processor — judiciously applied, of course). If you are new to classical music and looking for your first organ showpiece, remember that modern stuff like this does not sound like J. S. Bach. (A)

784 Messiaen, O.: *Klavierwerke*, Günter Reinhold, piano: Thorofon CTH 2114. There is a nice sound stage here with a small-hall fairly close-up perspective. The piano sounds clean, focused, and real. (A)

785 Messiaen, O.: *Turangalila-Symphonie*, Orchestra de la Bastille, Yvonne Loriod, piano: Deutsche Grammophon 431 781-2. Dynamic and clear, with a wide, deep sound stage. The hall envelopment is adequate. (A)

786 Metheny, Pat, Dave Holland, and Roy Haynes: *Question and Answer*: Geffen 24293-2. Smooth and clean with good imaging and depth. The electric guitar could have a bit more "bite," but the mellow flavor is no doubt what the artists were after in this jazz DDD recording. The sound is close, and that makes the drum set seem a bit oversized, but still tolerable. (A)

787 Metheny, P.: *Song X* (with Ornett Coleman, Charlie Haden, Jack DeJohnette, and Denardo Colman): Geffen 24096-2. "Advanced" jazz not for the faint of heart, this disc is very clean and clear with good depth and spread. A nice, realistic studio ambience adds flavor. The drums sound wide because two guys are playing the things. (A)

788 Metheny, P.: *Still Life (Talking)* (his "Group," with Lyle Mays, Steve Rodby, Paul Wertico, Armando Marcal, David Blamires, and Mark Ledford): Geffen 9 24145-2. There is a nice sound stage on this release, although the obviously synthesized effect lacks depth and seems to lack the kind of "body" required to sound fully realistic. There is good clarity with decent smoothness, though. My big Yamaha DSP unit brought this recording to life. (B)

789 Miaskovskii, Nicolai: *Symphony Number 6*, Symphony Orchestra of Russia, The "Anima" Moscow Chamber Choir: Olympia OCD 510. This recording exhibits an excellent soundstage spread with good clarity, outstanding imaging, and first-rate orchestral detail. There is realistic depth here and a proper small-hall ambience. At first listening, the work may seem a bit thin, but that is the nature of the music and not a deficiency in the engineering. I found that surround enhancement made this marvelous recording even more impressive. (A)

790 Milhaud, Darius: *Symphony Number 1*; *Symphony Number 2*, Orchestre du Capitole de Toulouse: Deutsche Grammophon 435 437-2. I thought this one showed nice clarity and detail. The listening perspective is midhall, and the sound stage is broad and fairly deep. The sense of recorded space is well blended into the sound from the ensemble. This is another example of the best work from DGG. (A)

791 Miller, Mulgrew: *The Countdown* (with Joe Henderson, Ron Carter, and Tony Williams): Landmark LCD-1519-2. Nice and clean jazz, with the piano well sized and well positioned—important, since that is Miller's instrument. When it is called to do a solo, the sax seems just a bit too forward in relation to the other instruments. (B)

792 Miller, M.: *From Day to Day* (his trio, with Robert Hurst and Kenny Washington): Landmark LCD-1525-2. Clean and sharp with a wide, well-laid-out sound stage. This effort is more forward sounding than *Countdown* with better imaging and better tonality. The solo-piano track on this disc is very well sized and well imaged with good small-room acoustics. (B+)

793 Mingus, Charlie: *Mingus Plays Piano*: Mobile Fidelity MFCD-783. Done in 1963 and reissued by Mobile Fidelity, this disc has lots of pre–Dolby noise-reduction background hiss, but the piano itself is remarkably well recorded: tightly focused, clear, and very close up. Note that this is not one of MFSL's "gold" discs and is therefore sanely priced. It sounds better than a number of those more expensive items. (Qualified B+)

794 Minnelli, Liza: *Liza Minnelli at Carnegie Hall* (with Russell Kassoff, Gerald Tarack, and many others): Telarc 85502. As expected with this label producing it, there is a very good stage image and depth on this release with good hall ambience filling out the bill. The orchestral clarity is not just good but quite realistic. The vocals are sometimes just a bit "amplified sounding," but they are still better than on most other live recordings. Remember, the recording is supposed to mimic a live performance, and most singers in such performances use loudspeaker assistance and amplified sound. I found that this disc responded very well to a variety of surround-sound enhancements from my large and small systems. (A)

795 Mintzer, Bob: *Art of the Big Band* (his band, with Randy Brecker, Peter Erskine, Lincoln Goines, and numerous other players): Digital Music Products CD-479. This is a very realistic and clear nightclub-grade, big-band jazz sound. The comments relating to other Mintzer discs apply here, with the inner detail and clarity even better—if that's possible. This is another candidate for the hypothetical A++ category. (A+)

796 Mintzer, B.: *Big Band* (with Marvin Stamm, Randy Brecker, Bob Smith, Don Grolnick, and others): Digital Music Products CD-451. Wide, spacious, and articulate big-band jazz, especially the trumpets, which cut right through you. The low average playback level on this disc encourages turning up the amplifier gain quite a lot above normal, and this lets the really loud, punchy sections sneak up on you and knock you flat when they happen. This disc responded well to surround enhancement and even to Dolby Pro Logic decoding. (A)

797 Mintzer, B.: *Camouflage* (his band, with Randy Brecker, Peter Erskine, Lawrence Feldman, Laurie Frink, and others): Digital Music Products CD-456. This is very well recorded big-band sound. Crystalline and detailed with a magnificent sound stage. The Mintzer-DMP mix is a winner in every case, and I can easily assume that future presentations will be as good as or even better. (A+)

798 *Misa Flamenca*, Paco Peña, guitar, supported by the Academy of St. Martin in the Fields Chorus: Nimbus NI 5288. As usual with Nimbus, there is a very good stage image with palpable depth. The clarity is quite realistic, given the midhall listening perspective. A recording like this benefits from any kind of surround enhancement you can apply, although playback via the Ambisonic system it was encoded for will probably do an exceptional job. Unfortunately, Ambisonic decoders are not widely available in the United States, although the system is popular in England. (A+)

799 *Mr. Big*: Atlantic 81990-2. There is plenty of impact on this rock release, with decent clarity. Good left-to-right stage spread. (B)

800 Mitchell, Joni, *Night Ride Home*: Geffen GEFD-24302. This one is pleasantly clean and clear with considerable stage depth and a decent sense of envelopment. Mitchell's voice seems spatially detached from the instrumental support on some cuts. Plenty of deep bass at times for you subwoofer people. (B+)

801 *Modern Portraits* (short works by Stravinsky, Prokofiev, Penderecki, Hartmann, and Schnittke), the Moscow Virtuosi: RCA 60370-2. This release displays good small-ensemble clarity with a decent sense of hall space. The sound stage has good depth and breadth. (A)

802 Moeran, Ernest: *Symphony in G Minor*; *Overture for a Masque*, Ulster Orchestra: Chandos CHAN 8577. This one is nice and smooth, the sound stage a bit distant, but with sufficient clarity and detail to satisfy even the most discriminating front-row enthusiast. There was also very good depth and a proper feeling of envelopment. A very real orchestral sound indeed, and another Chandos triumph. (A+)

803 Monteverdi, Claudio: *Il Ottavo Libro de Madrigali 1638:* Balli, the Consort Musicke: Virgin Classics VC 7 91158-2. This is a clean and detailed original-instruments choral work with a fine sound stage and realistic hall space and depth. The singers are particularly well recorded. (A+)

804 Monteverdi, C.: *Ghirlande Sacre*; *Ghirlande Profane*, Accademia Claudio Monteverdi: Europa 350-237. A remarkable hall ambience is a highlight here with great clarity and a you-are-there perspective much better than average. Very clean vocals. Although not specifically designed for such, this recording works even better when played back with surround-sound enhancement. Go get a processor or surround-sound receiver and give it a try. (A+)

805 Monteverdi, C.: *Soprano Duets and Solos*, The Consort Musicke, Emma Kirkby and Evelyn Tubb, sopranos: MCA Classics 25189. These are very clear vocals, well positioned in relation to the instrumental support. The sense of hall depth and ambience are well preserved. (A)

806 Moody, James: *Honey* (with Kenny Barron, Todd Coolman, and Akira Tana): Novus/RCA 3111-2-N. This is obviously multimiked jazz with less than appreciable stage depth but plenty of the kind of detail the technique can deliver. There is also decent ensemble transparency and ample left-to-right spread. The recording has a slightly too forward-sounding solo sax. This is probably as good as a multimicrophone recording can get unless the engineers really spend a lot of time tweaking the results. Most hi-fi sound systems will not clearly outline the differences between this disc and an A-rated job. (B+)

Moody (807)

807 Moody, J.: *Sweet and Lovely* (with Marc Cohen, Todd Coolman, Akira Tana, and Dizzy Gillespie): Novus 3063-2-N. This release has less close up detail and clarity than 806, which imparts a somewhat more distant and realistic sound stage with some playback systems. Unlike a lot of jazz recordings, the drums here are decently sized and focused in relation to the rest of the combo. Most listeners will prefer the other disc because of the better detail. (B)

808 Moranelli, Mark, and the Jazz Forum All Stars: *Speak Low* (with Kenny Barron, Ron Carter, and Jimmy Cobb): Candid CCD 79054. This recording has a somewhat distant live perspective (it was recorded live at Birdland) with good depth and clarity. The club ambience is pretty good. (B)

809 Morgan, Frank: *Bebop Lives!* (his quintet, with Johnny Coles, Cedar Walton, Buster Williams, and Billy Higgins): Contemporary CCD-14-26-2. This is a live recording, complete with audience noise, that has good clarity and fine jazz-stage imaging. The sound seems fairly dry and nonreverberant. Played at high volume, the combo almost seems to be in your room rather than you being at the nightclub. With discrete surround-sound enhancement (via a Lexicon, Yamaha, or similar device), adequate ambient effects can be added, and the disc comes alive. (B+)

810 Morgan, F., and George Cables: *Double Image*: Contemporary CCD-14035-2. There is a nice "bite" to the jazz saxophone on this recording and good focus, the piano properly sized and solid. Both performers are placed in a dry but intimate small-club environment with the listener some distance back. As with the other Frank Morgan recordings, I found that some surround enhancement allowed this performance to deliver sound that was technically and subjectively big league. (B+)

811 Morgan, F.: *Lament* (with Cedar Walton, Buster Williams, and Billy Higgins): Contemporary CCD-14021-2. Nice and smooth with very good detail, particularly the sax and the drums. The latter are well sized, as is the piano. The sound stage is "multi-microphone-flat" but is also pleasantly wide, and the pan-potted highlighting works well in this case. (B+)

812 Morgan, F.: *A Lovesome Thing* (with George Cables, David Williams, Lewis Nash, Roy Hargrove, and Abby Lincoln): Antilles 422-848-213-2. Excellent saxophone detail and bite are the highlight here, with that instrument and the rest of the ensemble well focused and properly positioned in a realistic-sounding studio environment. The drums, as usual, are spread out a bit much, but the effect is not too unsettling. (A)

813 Morgan, F., and the McCoy Tyner Trio: *Major Changes* (with Avery Sharpe and Louis Hayes): Contemporary CCD-14039-2. Very clear, with a fine sound stage. This is very real-sounding jazz. The saxophone sounds authentic, and the piano sounds like a piano. (A)

814 Morgan, F.: *Mood Indigo* (with Wynton Marsalis, George Cables, Ronnie Matthews, Buster Williams, and Al Foster): Antilles 91320-2. Detailed and a bit dry with a comfortable mid-distance listening perspective. There is good clarity, typical with dry recordings, and the piano and drums are well handled. If desired, the dry quality can be corrected by careful use of a good surround-sound device. (B+)

815 Morgan, F.: *Reflections* (his "All Stars," with Joe Henderson, Bobby Hutcherson, Mulgrew Miller, Ron Carter, and Al Foster): Contemporary CCD 14052-2. This effort replicates a decent middistance listening position with acceptable imaging and good, but not great, clarity. (B)

816 Morris, Gary: *Hits*: Warner 25581-2. This disc is nice and punchy with decent clarity and a fairly good sound-stage presentation. The usual buzzy-microphone sound that plagues most C&W and rock albums is subdued here, although there is still more nasality than I would like. This singer's voice does not produce such an effect naturally. (B)

817 Morris, G.: *Plain Brown Wrapper*: Warner 25438-2. This release is decently smooth with a good sound stage, acceptable vocal imaging, and better than typical vocal tone quality for a C&W disc. Morris does not have a typical nasal-sounding country-singer voice, and his engineers should not try to make him into what he is not. Technically, this is probably his best country-music recording. (B+)

818 Morris, G.: *Stones*: MCA UVLD-76005. Morris's excellent voice is fairly well engineered here and only a bit country-style buzzy on this moderately overprocessed disc. There is plenty of reverb and sound-stage manipulation, but this sounds good on some systems, even fairly good ones. There is also decent instrumental tonality, plenty of dynamic impact, and deep-bass extension. On some tracks (particularly the first), the voice seems a bit too large and forward in relation to the rest of the ensemble, an obvious ploy by the engineers to get the listener's attention and enhance the sound when heard on lo-fi home and cheaper automotive systems. (B)

819 Morris, G.: *Why Lady Why?*: Warner 23738-2. This release is decently clean with plenty of the kind of left-right spread that makes a recording get your attention. Morris's fine voice is well focused, but like most of his other C&W releases, it has a slightly microphonelike sound. (B)

820 Morrison, Van: *No Guru, No Method, No Teacher*: Mercury 830 077-2. There is some really good vocal reproduction here that blends very well with the instrumental support. This one has a much better than average sound stage for a rock recording. The result is nice and clean. (B+)

821 Morse, Steve: *High Tension Wires*: MCA 6275. This recording is heavily processed with a "synthesized" unrealistic sound stage that is lacking in depth but is also fairly clear with good dynamic contrasts. Although done in 1989 and obviously a labor of love by Morse, this rock disc still uses AAD technology. (B)

822 Mötley Crüe: *Decade of Decadence*: Elektra 61204-2. If heavy-metal rock is your acoustic fancy, you can hardly top this disc, which features reissued material recorded over several years. This release has fairly good sound staging in spite of the abundant mixing-console processing. Of course, it also has near-thermal meltdown levels at times. (B at the beginning; B+ near the end)

823 Mötley Crüe: *Dr. Feelgood*: Elektra E2 60829. Heavy-metal rock at its best. This piece of dynamite has great impact, spacious effects, and a wide-band frequency response. The vocals are a tad diffuse and phasey. (B+)

824 Mötley Crüe: *Girls Girls Girls*: Elektra 9 60725-2. There are some good dynamics on this presentation with a well-controlled sound stage. The ensemble is more distant and less punchy than the *Dr. Feelgood* album (see 823). (B)

825 Mozart, Leopold: *Seven Symphonies*, Slovak Chamber Orchestra: CPO 999 144-2. This set of obscure works by the father of Mozart is smooth, clean, and well imaged with a good midhall listening position and a fine small-hall ambience. (A)

826 Mozart, Wolfgang Amadeus: *Arias*, Wiener Kammerorchester, Cecilia Bartoli, mezzo-soprano: London 430 513-2. This effort is very cleanly recorded with the orchestra nicely sized and the vocalist properly positioned and correctly sized in relation to the instrumentalists. The voice is marvelously captured. The hall ambience is just what the music requires. (A+)

827 Mozart, W. A.: *Arias*, Academy of Ancient Music, Emma Kirkby, soprano: L'Oiseau-Lyre 425 835-2. There is an excellent balance between the period-instrument orchestra and the vocalist. In addition, there is good tonality in the vocals combined with an equally good midhall listening perspective. (A)

828 Mozart, W. A.: *Clarinet Concerto in A Major*; *Oboe Concerto in C Major*; Academy of Ancient Music; Antony Pay, basset clarinet; Michel Puquet, oboe: L'Oiseau-Lyre 414 339-2. Here we have a spacious and smooth original-instrument orchestral sound with plenty of depth and space around the players. In each concerto the solo instrument is extremely well sized and realistically positioned. (A+)

829 Mozart, W. A.: *Clarinet Concerto, K.622*; *Clarinet Quintet, K.581*, Tokyo String Quartet, Richard Stoltzman, clarinet: RCA 60723-2-RC. There is a good hall space on this one with a rich, reverberant orchestral sound. The clarinet is well sized and well positioned in relation to the ensemble. I felt there was just a touch of roughness in the sound of the high strings at times. (A)

830 Mozart, W. A.: *Clarinet Concerto*; *Horn Concerto Number 3*; *Horn Concerto Number 4*; English Chamber Orchestra; Joaquin Valdepeñas, basset clarinet; Fred Rizner, horn: Summit DCD-131. Smooth, clean, and vibrant with very good depth. The violins are just a bit bright, but the effect adds to the small-hall feel these works require. (A)

831 Mozart, W. A.: *Don Giovanni*, Berlin Philharmonic, Chor der Deutschen Oper Berlin (with Samuel Ramey, Paata Burchuladze, Anna Tomowa-Sintow, and others): Deutsche Grammophon 419 179-2. DGG has not always turned out the best in opera sound, but this release is quite good. The vocals are the strong suit here, with good articulation and imaginative stage positioning that is not unrealistically wide. (It is not uncommon for some recordings to have two, three, or four performers singing intimately to each other while spread clear across the sound stage from speaker to speaker, as wide apart as the whole orchestra. This may work during a live presentation, but it sounds odd on a home sound system.) The orchestral textures are quite good, although the string section sometimes seems a bit pinched.

The ambience and depth are well presented. (A)

832 Mozart, W. A.: *Eine Kleine Nachtmusik*; *Posthorn Serenade*, Prague Chamber Orchestra: Telarc 80108. This release is smooth and clean, with the somewhat diffuse sound field that Telarc is noted for — which some critics do not like, and others praise to the skies. The string sound is clean and unstrident. (A)

833 Mozart, W. A.: *Die Entführung Aus dem Serail*, Vienna Philharmonic Orchestra, Vienna State Opera Choir (with Edita Gruberova, Kathleen Battle, Gösta Winbergh, and others): London 417 402-2. This exciting opera recording shows brilliant and clear orchestral tonality with a wonderful sense of space and depth. The vocalists are uniformly and expertly recorded with fine clarity and stage positioning, a notable achievement. London has turned out some fine opera material, and this is one of them. (A+)

834 Mozart, W. A.: *Idomeneo*, the Monteverdi Choir, The English Baroque Soloists (with Anthony Rolfe Johnson, Anne Sofie von Otter, Sylvia McNair, and others): Archiv 431 674-2. This live-recording, original-instruments rendition is clear and vibrant with an excellent sound stage, good ensemble depth, and plenty of breadth. The vocalists are perfectly blended into the overall ensemble sound. Only an occasional bit of hall rumble-thumping mars the sonics. Back off a bit with your subwoofer and enjoy. (Qualified A+)

835 Mozart, W. A.: *Kathleen Battle Sings Mozart* (assorted arias), with the Royal Philharmonic Orchestra: EMI/Angel 47355-2. The engineer did an excellent job of positioning of Ms. Battle in relation to the orchestra. The vocal clarity is very good, and the orchestra sounds OK too. (A)

836 Mozart, W. A.: *Mass in C Minor*, Boston Early Music Festival Orchestra, Handel and Haydn Society Chorus (with Nancy Armstrong, Dominique Labelle, Jeffrey Thomas, Richard Morrison, and James Christie): Denon 81757 9573-2. This recording displays well-blended orchestral and choral parts, with the soloists very realistically positioned in relation to the rest of the ensemble. There is also a nice sense of hall space combined with transparent clarity. (A)

837 Mozart, W. A.: *Opera Arias*, Kiri Te Kanawa, London Symphony Orchestra: Philips 411 148-2. Although over a decade old, this recording is still marvelous. The solo voice is realistically positioned on stage and in relation to the orchestra. The clarity is fine, and the sense of hall envelopment is quite good. (A)

838 Mozart, W. A.: *Piano Concertos Numbers 6 and 17*, Orchestra Anima Eterna, Jos van Immerseel, piano: Channel Classics CCS 1891. Period-instrument sound isn't always to everyone's taste but this is a clear, crystalline recording, a good example of what appears to be refined multi-microphone use. (A)

839 Mozart, W. A.: *Piano Concertos Numbers 8, 12, and 28*, Orchestra Anima Eterna, Jos van Immerseel, piano: Channel CCS 0690. This is another recording for those who want to sample the sound of this material as it was heard in Mozart's day. The effort is clean and bright but not strident. There is good balance between the piano and the orchestra. (A)

Mozart (840)

840 Mozart, W. A.: *Piano Concertos Numbers 16 and 17*, English Baroque Soloists, Malcolm Bilson, fortepiano: Archiv 415 525-2. The small-scale size of an original-instrument recording is clearly evident here. Those who have cut their teeth on the sound of large modern orchestras may be put off by what this disc offers, but thoughtful listeners should be willing to accept this item for what it is. The recording has very clear sound with a realistic sound stage and fine depth. The fortepiano is well positioned and properly sized in relation to the ensemble. (A)

841 Mozart, W. A.: *Piano Concertos Numbers 17 and 24*, Scottish Chamber Orchestra, John O'Conor, piano: Telarc 80306. As we have come to expect from Telarc, this effort has a good orchestral spread combined with good clarity, the piano clearly miked but just a tad forward and a bit diffuse. The slightly bloated nature of the sound may tighten up somewhat on systems that have a more narrowly focused sound stage. (A)

842 Mozart, W. A.: *Piano Concertos Numbers 18 and 19*, English Baroque Soloists, Malcom Bilson, fortepiano: Archiv 415 111-2. As noted previously, not everyone—and this includes both some professional musicians and knowledgeable music critics—is enamored of this kind of authentic- or original-instruments sound with its sometimes thin and overly bright textures. Nevertheless, this recording has marvelous clarity and a good spatial balance between the piano and the orchestra. There is just a touch of violin harshness that may have as much to do with the instruments as the engineering technique. (A)

843 Mozart, W. A.: *Piano Concertos Numbers 20 and 21*, Orchestra Anima Eterna, Jos van Immerseel, piano: Channel Classics CCS 2391. Similar in sound quality to the other Channel Classics Mozart piano-concerto discs reviewed above (see 838 and 839). (A)

844 Mozart, W. A.: *Piano Concertos Numbers 22 and 23*, Orchestra Anima Eterna, Jos van Immerseel, piano: Channel Classics CCS 2491. Sound similar to 838, 839 and 843. (A)

845 Mozart, W. A.: *Piano Concertos Numbers 24 and 27*, English Baroque Soloists, Malcom Bilson, fortepiano: Archiv 427 652-2. Similar to 840. The piano in both recordings is well integrated into the ensemble, but remember that this is not a "modern" piano and it has its own distinctive sound. Do not expect a Baldwin or Steinway tone. Bilson is recording all the Mozart piano concertos with the English Baroque. A great collection. (A)

846 Mozart, W. A.: *Piano Concertos Numbers 25 and 26*, English Baroque Soloists, Malcolm Bilson, piano: Archiv 423 119-2. This release has the same essential qualities as the Bilson-Archiv recordings listed previously. It can be assumed that all of this collaboration's recordings are in the same class. (A)

847 Mozart, W. A.: *Piano Quartets K.478 and K.493*, Richard Burnett, fortepiano; Salomon String Quartet: Amon Ra CD-SAR-31 (also available as Musical Heritage Society MHS 11232F). This is a typical intelligently recorded original-instruments item, with fine detail and transparency. The overall sound is a bit on the distant side, but for me the result is a wonderful feeling of stage depth, clarity, and ambience. (A)

848 Mozart, W. A.: *Requiem*, Amsterdam Baroque Orchestra, Koor van de Nederlandse Bachvereniging: Erato 45472-2. This original-instrument recording is smooth, clean, spacious, and pretty "lightweight" in excecution. The period sound may not suit everyone since it lacks the body and impact of more modern versions. Of course, the voice parts have all the body found in any modern rendition, and they sound fine. (A)

849 Mozart, W. A.: *Requiem*, Chorus and Orchestra of the Academy of Ancient Music: L'Oiseau-Lyre 411 712-2. Nice balance between the chorus and the orchestra on this original-instrument recording. The solo vocals are well positioned across the stage, and their clarity and that of the instrumental ensemble is good. Some low-level hall rumble intrudes at times. (Qualified A)

850 Mozart, W. A.: *Sinfonia Concertante in E-flat Major for Violin, Viola and Orchestra; Concertante in C Major for Two Violins and Orchestra,* English Chamber Orchestra; Cho-Liang Lin, violin; Jaime Laredo, violin, viola: Sony SK 47693. Very smooth, clean, expansive, and vibrant. The rich overall sound field is marred only by a somewhat flat-appearing sound stage. The solo instruments are very well integrated and are properly sized in relation to the rest of the ensemble. (A)

851 Mozart, W. A.: *Songs from the Operas*, Ferruccio Furlanetto, bass-baritone; Vienna Philharmonic Orchestra: Sony Sk 47192. Here we have a very good stage image, with the orchestra and singer well matched in size and positioning. The overall sound is heard from a midhall distance with good ambience. Sony can deliver the goods on occasion. (A+)

852 Mozart, W. A.: *String Quartets Numbers 14 and 15*, Cleveland Quartet: Telarc 80297. This release is clear and clean with a spacious and subjectively deep sound stage. This presentation is quite a contrast to some of the co-incident-source-microphone recordings of similar works. (A+)

853 Mozart, W. A.: *String Quartets Numbers 14 and 17*, The Classical Quartet: Titanic Ti-154. Done on period instruments, this recording is clean and close up, yet smooth and unstrained. It also lacks the often strident sound of other period-instrument recordings. There is a very good small-hall sound stage with a fine rendition of depth. The instrumental detail is excellent, so much so that one can hear the players moving (and maybe even breathing hard) at times. Under most conditions, the latter is not desirable, but this kind of close-up imaging, the effect heightens realism. (A+)

854 Mozart, W. A.: *String Quartets Numbers 20 and 21*, Kocian Quartet: Denon 33C37-7954. This is volume 4 of the complete Mozart string quartets by this group. The recording has a very close-up sound, although not quite so much as 852. The sound is relatively bright, but a positive result of this is the amazing detail. There is little doubt that the front-row presence may not appeal to everyone, however. Rounding things out is a nice sound-stage spread with decent hall ambience. (A)

855 Mozart, W. A.: *String Quartets Numbers 22 and 23*, Kocian Quartet: Denon 33CO-1522. Volume 5 of the complete quartets by this group. The same close-up bright sound with the same remarkable detail as 854. The same small flaws, also. (A)

Mozart (856)

856 Mozart, W. A.: *Symphonies Numbers 25 and 40*, Philharmonia Orchestra: Denon 81757 6103-2. This release displays a smooth, spacious, transparent sound stage with acceptable depth and a realistic midhall listening perspective. (A)

857 Mozart, W. A.: *Symphonies Numbers 26, 29, and 39*, Sinfonia Varsovia: Denon 81757 9202-2. I felt that this release delivered very clean and detailed sound combined with a realistic small-hall ambience and sense of space. The violins are very well recorded and notably smooth. (A+)

858 Mozart, W. A.: *Symphonies Numbers 32, 33, and 41*, Philharmonia Orchestra: Denon 81757 6579-2. Just as good as 856 with the same quality sound stage and clarity. (A)

859 Mozart, W. A.: *Symphonies Numbers 38 and 39*, English Baroque Soloists: Philips 426 283-2. This release is very well recorded, with the most modern large-scale sound I have ever heard from a period-instruments ensemble. This indicates that playing techniques, no matter what kind of instruments are employed, are often the primary factor in developing the original-instrument sound. There is an excellent sound stage here with notable clarity and envelopment. (A+)

860 Mozart, W. A.: *Symphonies Numbers 40 and 41*, Los Angeles Chamber Orchestra: Delos D/CD 3012. Smooth, spacious, and clean. Almost certainly a spaced-array job, this recording has no problems with the supposedly annoying phasey quality said to plague noncoincident-microphone techniques. A triumph by engineer Marc Aubort, and it was produced in 1981. (Note that any rerelease of this recording may make use of the DE prefix instead of the D/CD code listed here.) (A)

861 Mozart, W. A.: *Violin Concerto Number 3*; *Violin Concerto Number 4*, Camerata Academica des Mozarteums Salzburg, Yuzuko Horigome, violin: Sony SK 48031. Here we have a nice orchestral-violin balance with notable and realistic transparency and detail. The overall depth is good, and the sound stage has a broad, close up, spacious sound. (A)

862 Mozart, W. A.: *Die Zauberflöte*, London Classical Players, Schütz Choir of London (with Anthony Johnson, Andreas Schmidt, Beverly Hoch, Dawn Upshaw, and others): EMI CDS 7 54287-2. A small-scale but very original-instrument–clean recording with a classical small-hall sense of comfort that many will consider an antidote to the large-scale transcriptions produced in the name of modern orchestra sound and engineering technology. In spite of the small ensemble and modestly reverberant room acoustics, the presentation has a somewhat distant perspective, the soloists appearing far enough away to approximate a listening position well back into our hypothetical small hall. Oddly enough, in spite of the subjective distance, the instrumental textures are detailed enough at times to indicate a fair amount of multimicrophone highlighting. The set comes with a diagram of the orchestral-choral floor layout, a nice touch. (A)

863 Mozart, W. A.: *Die Zauberflöte*, Vienna Philharmonic Orchestra (with Uwe Heilmann, Ruth Ziesak, Michael Kraus, Sumi Jo, and Kurt Moll): London 433 210-2. Bright, forward, and detailed. The soloists are very well handled in positioning and movement, but the tonality of their voices could be better (microphone limitations, probably). Still, the sound stage is quite good, as is the hall balance, and together they allow this recording to make it on the list. (A)

864 Mozart, W. A.: *Die Zauberflöte*, Scottish Chamber Orchestra and Chorus (with Barbara Hendricks, June Anderson, Ulrike Steinsky, and others): Telarc 80302. Lifelike, with wonderful depth and spread, although the very realism of the sound, as is sometimes the case at a live presentation, often cuts into the detail of the individual instruments. The soloists are realistically handled. There are some interesting sound effects at times, almost like the stuff found in action movies. Nonetheless, this is a state-of-the-art opera recording. The best of the three *Magic Flute* recordings reviewed here in terms of engineering. (A+)

865 Mozart, W. A.: *Die Zauberflöte* (excerpts), Scottish Chamber Orchestra and Chorus (with Barbara Hendricks, June Anderson, Ulrike Steinsky, and others): Telarc 80345. Essentially most of the musical parts of 864 minus the talking parts. The sound quality is equal. (A+)

866 Mulligan, Gerry, and Scott Hamilton: *Soft Lights and Sweet Music* (with Mike Renzi, Jay Leonhart, and Grady Tate): Concord Jazz CCD-4300. Good clarity and detail. The horns are right up front and have a good jazz-style bite, and the piano is well sized and mercifully well focused. For once in a jazz recording, the drums do not seem twenty-feet wide. (B+)

867 *Music for Holy Week* (Gregorian Chant), Schola Antiqua: L'Oiseau-Lyre 417 324-2. There is fine depth and clarity here with a very realistic perspective in these renditions of the Western liturgical chant. The hall ambience is subdued, adding to the fine clarity but subtracting from the sense of you-are-there involvement. (A)

868 *Music for Holy Week II*, Schola Antiqua: L'Oiseau-Lyre 425 114-2. This effort has a somewhat better sound stage than the earlier production (see 867) with equally good clarity. However, the hall is still somewhat dry. There is some background rumble that I did not notice on the earlier recording. (Qualified A)

869 *Music from the Spanish Kingdoms* (circa 1500), with Nancy Hadden, Emily van Evera, Erwin Headley, Paula Chateauneuf, and Andrew Lawrence-King: CRD-3447. This disc exhibits nice detail with good soundstage depth and hall reverberation. The vocal clarity and articulation are quite good with just a touch of microphone-induced sibilance at times. (A)

870 *Musica al Tempo del Guido Reni* (short works by Frescobaldi, Marini, Selma y Salaverde, and others), Ensemble "Aurora": Tactus TC56012001. Very clean, smooth, and revealing with fine imaging and realistic articulation. A nice small-hall ambience tops things off. (A)

871 *Musica Dolce* (short works by Cavalli, Caccini, Monteverdi, Rossi, D'India, and others); Julianne Baird, soprano; Colin Tilney, harpsichord: Dorian DOR-90123. Smooth and transparent with marvelous vocal clarity, harpsichord detail, and overall depth. The listening perspective has a small-hall middistance feel. While the harpsichord is well focused, the solo vocalist has a somewhat diffuse and vague image. (A)

872 *Musical Heralds from South India* (with Sheik Chinna Moulana and others): Welt Musik SM 1507-2. Very clean and smooth percussion sounds with fine articulation and detail in the sound of the *nadhaswaram*. There is notable ambience and depth, the listening distance somewhat greater than typical for such a small ensemble. The playback level is a bit lower than normal, so advancing the amplifier gain is advised. However, music such as this, like that of the harpsichord, is not designed to be heard at high playback levels. (A)

873 Mussorgsky, Modest: *Boris Godounov*; National Symphony Orchestra; Choral Arts Society; Oratorio Society of Washington; Chevy Chase Elementary School Chorus (with Ruggero Raimondi, Galina Vichnievskaia, Nicolai Gedda, Paul Plishka, Vyacheslav Polozov, Kenneth Riegel, and Romuald Tesarowicz): Erato 45418-2. The sound here is open, spacious, and broad staged with good clarity and a realistic blend between the chorus groups and the orchestra. The soloists are sized properly, and they sound natural. (A)

874 Mussorgsky, M., and Maurice Ravel: *Pictures at an Exhibition*; Scriabin, Alexander: *Poem of Ecstacy*, Chicago Symphony Orchestra, Adolph Herseth, trumpet: Chandos CHAN 8849. A very clear recording with a subtle but realistic treble-to-bass balance. The sound is very dynamic when called for with a very good sound stage and substantial depth. The hall envelopment is just what is required here. There is nice bass reproduction on the Scriabin piece. Another Chandos triumph. (A+)

875 Mussorgsky, M. and M. Ravel: *Pictures at an Exhibition*; *Night on Bare Mountain*; Rimsky-Korsakov, Nikolai: *Russian Easter Festival Overture*, Orchestre Symphonique de Montréal: London 417 299-2. Overall, this effort displays very good depth, clarity, and impact. The ensemble balance is quite good. The dynamics do not quite equal 874 or 876. (A)

876 Mussorgsky, M., and M. Ravel: *Pictures at an Exhibition*, Cleveland Orchestra: Telarc 80042. Although clear and often dynamic, this recording suffers from a somewhat diffuse sound stage and a bass drum that is a tad too boomy, yet not all that deep (an early Telarc trademark that seems to have been modified). Ironically, on smaller and less bass-potent systems the bass-drum anomaly may be an advantage. It sounded fine on mine. (B+)

877 Mussorgsky, M., and M. Ravel: *Pictures at an Exhibition*; *Night on Bald Mountain*; *Introduction to Khovanshchina*, Atlanta Symphony Orchestra: Telarc 80296. This demonstration-grade disc tops the earlier Telarc *Pictures* (see 876), which was made in 1979. The impact here is second to none, even surpassing the London and Chandos versions, although this newer Telarc release may still have too much bass-drum explosiveness for some tastes (it is considerably deeper sounding on this version than on the earlier one, however). The clarity is exceptional, given the forces massed. (A+)

878 *Negro Spirituals*; Barbara Hendricks, soprano; Dmitri Alexeev, piano: EMI 7 47026 2. This recording has a somewhat distant but still realistic sound stage. The clarity is quite good, however; the piano is sized well, and the performers are realistically positioned in relation to one another. (A)

879 Nell, Bob: *Why I Like Coffie* (with Kelly Roberty, Brad Edwards,

Jack Walrath, and Ray Anderson): New World 80419-2. There is very good piano tonality and focus on this jazz release with the rest of the ensemble smoothly integrated. Unfortunately, the single-player drum set is just too wide, marring what would otherwise be a truly outstanding recording. (B+)

880 Nelson, Steve: *Communications* (his quartet, with Mulgrew Miller, Ray Drummond, and Tony Reedus): Criss Cross Jazz 1034. A good, somewhat distant ensemble balance is apparent here with proper positioning of the individual players. Nice clarity too. The vibes (Nelson's instrument) sound a bit too close in comparison to the rest of the players, but it can be assumed he would be placed in front. (B+)

881 Nelson, S.: *Full Nelson* (with Kirk Lightsey and Ray Drummond): Sunnyside SSC 1044D. Smooth, steady, and clean, with well-positioned and well-proportioned instruments. I felt that this one was pretty much the same in technical quality as the above disc, even though the recording company is different. (B+)

882 *New Mexico Brass Quintet* (playing short works by Beveridge, Cheetham, Leudeke, Händel, Arban, and Morton): Crystal CD 560. This effort has a distant rear-of-hall perspective that does not detract from the clarity and depth of the performance. Overall, there is wonderful detail from the instruments. (A)

883 New York City Gay Men's Chorus: *Love Lives On*: Virgin Records 2-91647. Unstressed and clean, with an excellent sound stage and fine choral blend. The overall sound field is quite realistic and well imaged, including the accompanying piano, and the soloists are well positioned and properly sized.

Some 20 Hz (a rough guess) bass rumble fills the background, unfortunately, mandating a subwoofer shutdown. This effect was not apparent on my smaller system with its equalization set for a 40 Hz high-pass cut off point. (Qualified A)

884 New York Composer's Orchestra: *First Program in Standard Time*: New World 80418-2. Experimental jazz (kind of) like this is not going to be to everyone's taste, but the recording is quite clean and dynamic. The overall sound is quite clear and defined, and the sound stage is well done. The piano (always hard to integrate into a group ensemble) is properly sized and is not diffuse or phasey. (B+)

885 New York Trumpet Ensemble: *Trumpets in Stride*: Summit DCD 113. I found that this release had very clean and detailed instrumental sound on the solo parts with just a bit of sound-stage constriction in the ensemble as a whole. This kind of spread may be preferred by some intensity-stereo technique enthusiasts. (B+)

886 *New York Voices* (with Peter Eldridge, Kim Nazarian, Sara Krieger, Darmon Meader, Caprice Fox, and others): GRP GRD-9589. Punchy, wide band in frequency response, and quite articulate. There is a very good up-front sound field on this disc with the singers well integrated into the instrumental ensemble. The drums, unfortunately, are spread out all over the place. It would have been a beaut without that defect. (B+)

887 Nielsen, Carl: *The Four String Quartets*, The Kontra Quartet: BIS CD 503/504. Good clarity and spaciousness here with just a touch of string harshness that can be tamed by cutting the treble a bit. Oddly enough, such minor string harshness can often be turned to advantage with the use of a surround "ambience" synthesizer such as those produced by Lexicon and Yamaha. The ambience tends to mellow things out and put some distance between the performers and the listener. What remains is the enhanced detail that close microphone use delivers. (A)

888 Nielsen, C.: *Saul and David*, Danish National Radio Symphony Orchestra and Choir (with Aage Haugland, Peter Lindroos, Tina Kiberg, and others): Chandos CHAN 8911/12. This release displays magnificent depth and spread with outstanding detail and transparency combined with the kind of hall envelopment that is mandatory for a sense of realism. The imaging is first rate in every way, with the singers well positioned and sized properly in relation to the orchestra. This is a benchmark for other opera recordings to aim for in engineering excellence. (A+)

889 Nielsen, C.: *Symphony Number 1*; *Symphony Number 2*, Royal Scottish Orchestra: Chandos CHAN 8880. Good imaging and clarity, although the overall sound field is quite close up and a bit bright. The result is pure pleasure for some listeners and sonic overkill for others. I have no hard and fast explanation why this Chandos effort was not quite as technically pleasing to me as most of their other material, although it may be the music itself. (A)

890 Nielsen, C.: *Symphony Number 2*; *Symphony Number 3*, San Francisco Symphony Orchestra: London 430 280-2. This is close-up sound with great detail. It includes lots of dynamic impact with a good sound stage. However, the recording is just a tad bright in sections. The solo vocalists have a small part in the *Number 3*, and their positioning within the ensemble is quite good. This is a small thing, but it will matter to some listeners. (A)

891 Nielsen, C.: *Symphony Number 3*; *Symphony Number 5*, San Francisco Symphony Orchestra: London 421 524-2. Pretty much the same as the *Number 2* and *Number 3* (890). The overall sound is just a touch dry. Some people like the effect, and it works better with some sound systems (usually when they are located in rather large listening rooms) than others. As I have noted previously, surround enhancement usually does wonders with fairly dry recordings. (A)

892 Nietzsche, Friedrich: *Piano Music*, John Bell Young, piano: Newport NPD 85513. The piano music of who? I cut my philosophical teeth on Nietzsche in college (graduating to Aristotle, Spinoza, and Hegel later on) and had no idea that the man who was an early admirer of Wagner (changing his mind drastically as he grew to understand Wagner's worldview) wrote music of his own. The recording has good balance with a middistance (small-hall) listening perspective. The overall ambience is quite nice. (A)

893 Niewood, Gerry: *Share My Dream* (with Joe Beck, Jay Leonhart, Michael Camilo, Dave Weckl, Wayne Pedziwiatr, and Jim Saporito): Digital Music Products CD-450. I felt that this jazz recording was very distinct, detailed, and smooth with an excellent left-to-right sound-stage spread, a fine ensemble depth, and well-focused imaging as well as an equally fine solo saxophone sound. The piano is just a bit phasey. (A)

894 *Night Moods* (short pieces by Chopin, Fauré, Debussy, Granados, Liszt, and Griffes), Carol Rosenberger, piano: Delos D/CD 3030. This one has good piano focus and a good hall-instrument balance. Overall, there is nice clarity, presence and tonality. (A+)

895 Nirvana: *Nevermind*: Geffen DGCD 24425. This is a good example of proper rock recording techniques. The respectable vocal clarity is a high point here and is unusual in music of this kind. The sound stage is artificial, of course, but that is almost certainly what the engineers wanted. (B+)

896 Not Drowning, Waving: *Claim*: Reprise 26181-2. This is remarkably clear and dynamic soft rock with very deep bass at times. The vocals are very well done and lack the usual made-for-cheap-stereo buzziness. (A)

897 *Nova Cantica* (Latin Songs of the High Middle Ages), Schola Cantorum Basiliensis: Deutsche Harmonia Mundi 77196-2-RC. This is close up clean sound that has a fine concert-hall ambience, made more impressive when run through even a midlevel-quality surround processor and some ambience speakers. Unfortunately, traffic noise in the background will be made even more intrusive by that processor. This is an ADD recording, which once again proves that microphones and their proper placement in a good hall determine sound quality as much as (and probably more than) the type of recorder employed. This is at least true with works of this kind that are not critical in bandwidth and absolute recording-speed stability. (Qualified A+)

898 *O Tuneful Voice* (songs and duets from late eighteenth-century London); Emma Kirkby, soprano; Rufus Müller, tenor: Hyperion CDA 66497. This release displays good clarity and detail with a somewhat distant sound stage that was made even more realistic by the careful application of surround processing. While typical works of this kind do not always benefit by such treatment, this one does because of the way the hall ambience was handled by the engineer. (A)

899 *Oboe Concertos* (short works by C. P. E. Bach, Lebrun, and Mozart), The English Concert, Paul Goodwin, oboe: Archiv 431 821-2. There is an excellent sound stage, palpable ambience, and realistic clarity on this period-instrument disc. The placement of the solo oboe in the ensemble is right on the money. (A+)

900 *Old Friends* (featuring André Previn, Mundell Lowe, and Ray Brown): Telarc 83309. This release shows the results tastefully using multimicrophone techniques to record a small jazz combo. The presentation displays excellent clarity and a good sound stage, although the guitar seems a bit vague and diffuse at times. (A)

901 *The Old Hall Manuscript* (compiled c. 1410–1415), The Hilliard Ensemble: EMI 54111-2. As with many other current EMI releases, this one is very clean and clear with the vocals blended into the impressive cathedral ambience quite well. The perspective is midhall with no exaggerated left-right spread. (A+)

902 *On the Banks of the Helicon* (early music of Scotland), The Baltimore Consort: Dorian DOR 90139. Clean, transparent, and close up with maybe just a touch of diffuseness in the central instrumental image. However, the vocal soloist is tightly and properly focused at dead center and is very well recorded. The overall effect of this recording makes it quite an attention-getter. (A)

903 *On the Idle Hill of Summer* (songs by Vaughan Williams, Butterworth, Quilter, and Peel); Thomas Allen, baritone; Geoffrey Parsons, piano: Virgin Classics 91105-2. This disc delivers a front-row listening perspective, the singer and piano accurately placed in a real-world hall setting. Clear and spacious overall. (A)

904 *Opera Baroque* (highlights of operas by Monteverdi, Cesti, Cavalli, Blow, Purcell, Händel, Charpentier, Lully, and Rameau), performed independently by the Choeur et Orchestre les Arts Florissants, The London Baroque, The Deller Choir, The King's Musik, Ensemble 415, Chiara Banchini and Philharmonia Baroque Orchestra: Harmonia Mundi France 290605.07. Recorded between 1978 and 1991, this three-disc release (especially the later material) is very realistic, full, and wonderful to listen to. The imaging is uniformly excellent, and the vocalists are very well recorded and properly positioned. The sense of hall space is just right for most of the material. A class-act batch of recordings. (B to A+)

905 Orff, Carl: *Carmina Burana*, Atlanta Symphony Orchestra and Chorus: Telarc 80056. Recorded in 1980, this is another demo-grade Telarc disc of that era. It still sounds big, robust, and spacious with a nice hall ambience. The clarity is OK, considering the size of the forces involved. The solo parts are very well handled and properly sized in relation to the ensemble. (A)

906 *Organ Encores* (short works by J. S Bach, Händel, Purcell, Haydn, Schumann, Liszt, and others), Jean Guillou, organ: Dorian DOR 90112. Stunning in clarity, depth, and impact. The small background rumble from the hall (maybe a heater, air conditioner, or the organ's air pump) shows off the wide bandwidth of this recording, but the noise may be distracting to listeners with really bass-potent playback systems. (Qualified A+)

907 *Organ Works*, (a recital of works by J. S. Bach, Messiaen, Dupré, Widor, and Franck), Michael Murray, organ: Telarc 80097. This somewhat distant-sounding recording is blessed with plenty of depth and church ambience combined with alternating powerful and subtle deep bass that sometimes gets down to below 22 Hz. The Bach pieces notwithstanding, the organ used here is not your typical highly detailed and often lightweight baroque item. To get the most impact from this disc, it may be necessary to advance your amplifier gain a bit above normal. (A+)

908 *Organo Deco* (sophisticated American organ music c. 1915–1950, including material by Sowerby, Simonds, Bennett, James, Bingham, and Crandell), David Britton, organ: Delos DE 3111. Big, reverberant, dynamic, and real-organ sounding. The sound stage is wide, and the overall sound field is three-dimensional. There is some deep bass at times, needless to say. (A+)

909 *Original Arias for Soprano, Trumpet and Organ* (short works by Stachowizc, Melani, Scarlatti, Purcell, and Aldrovandini); Marie-Noëlle de Callataÿ, soprano; Alain Roelant, trumpet; Jan van Landeghem, organ: Pavane ADW 7223. Spacious, reverberant, distant, and given those characteristics, surprisingly clean. There is a very open hall sound that benefits the trumpet and organ more than the singer. This disc is a strong candidate for surround enhancement via some kind of extraction processor with a center speaker and some form of center-channel steering. (A)

910 *Orquesta Nova* (featuring music by Piazzolla, Franzetti, D'Rivera, Diamond, and others): Chesky JD-54. Chesky calls this "new vision" music and considers it more pop than classical. Maybe, but the sound is world class, no matter what kind of music it is. Depth, detail, and clarity abound in ways that few discs in any category can match. This is demo material. (A+)

911 Osbourne, Ozzy: *No More Tears*: Epic ZK 46795. Heavy-metal rock, mastered about as good as it gets by engineer Bob Ludwig. The sound is very dynamic and wide ranged in frequency response, with decent clarity, especially considering the monumental electronic processing. The vocals are just a tad oversized, but what can you expect from a blowout as big as this one? (B+)

912 Oslin, K. T.: *80's Ladies*: RCA 5924-2-R. There is a bit too much synthetic reverb in this C&W recording, but it is still decently clear and not given to excessive electrical manipulation. The voice parts are OK, but there is just a touch of pop-music vocal nasality to the sound. (B)

913 Oslin, K. T.: *Love in a Small Town*: RCA 2365-2-R. Definitely better than 912 in vocal smoothness, ensemble uniformity, fine detail, and soundstage accuracy. The effort also displays plenty of dynamic impact and drive. (B+)

914 Oslin, K. T.: *This Woman*: RCA 8369-2. Perhaps the best-engineered disc I have heard by the exceptional Ms. Oslin, maybe even a bit better than 913. There is excellent vocal clarity on this release combined with the kind of snap and dynamics that makes good C&W worth listening to. (B+)

915 *Out of the Blue(s): The Session* (with Joe Locke, Jack Wilkins, Michael Formanek, Ed Schuller, Ronnie Burrage, and George Schuller); GM 2035CD. First, let me say that this two-disc set came in a new kind of low-profile box that defied getting the discs out without almost damaging the things. The two center spindles were friction affairs that refused to loosen their respective grips. If you obtain this set, be prepared to purchase a new double box or two single-disc boxes to contain the recordings. I talked to the people at GM on the phone, and they said they were going to do something about the problem, so maybe things will be OK by the time you buy a copy. With that bit of carping out of the way, I can state that the recordings are quite good: punchy, clean, and smooth with a fine sound stage and excellent depth. A bit of bass thump (microphone feed-through, I am sure) is audible at times. The overall sound seems a bit distant, yet you can still occasionally hear one or more of the players humming along with the instrumentation. (B+)

916 Ozone, Makoto: *Starlight* (with Fujimaru Yashino, Akira Okazawa, Kohki Itoh, and others): JVC JD-3323. Punchy, smooth, and vibrant with a wide-band frequency range. There is nice imaging overall, including the drums, although the piano, excellent tonality notwithstanding, seems a bit oversized. This is Japanese pop-music audio engineering at its best. (A)

917 Palestrina, Giovanni: *Masses*, The Tallis Scholars: Gimell GIM 008. Made from a 1983 analog master tape, this recording has a clean, spacious, and somewhat distant sound that is certainly up to date. The hall ambience is particularly good. (A)

918 Palestrina, G.: *Masses*, The Tallis Scholars: Gimmell GIM 008. Similar to GIM-003 (see 917) but recorded digitally. Pretty much the same results as the above recording, which shows that microphone type and use are more important than the kind of tape recorder. There is a wonderfully spacious sound here with fine detail and clarity. The depth of the sound stage is notable. (A)

919 Palestrina, G.: *Masses*, The Tallis Scholars: Gimell GIM 020. Gimell scored big on the third try (listen to 917 and 918 to hear the first two good but not spectacular attempts), and the reason is that they moved to a different location. This result is very clear, spacious, and realistic. The close-up sound stage lends immediacy and detail to the recording. Imaging in particular is notable. These three releases are clear evidence of what a good recording environment can accomplish when all else is equal. (A+)

920 Palestrina, G.: *Missa Aeterna Christi Munera*; *Motets*, Westminster Cathedral Choir: Hyperion CDA 66490. This recording is clear and transparent with a wonderful sense of hall ambience and easily perceived depth. The sound stage has a somewhat distant perspective bit that fits right in with this music. (A+)

921 Palestrina, G.: *Missa Viri Galilaei*, La Chapelle Royale and Ensemble Organum: Harmonia Mundi France HMC 901388. This recording exhibits very realistic cathedral reverberation along with wonderful clarity, depth, and transparency. The overall sound is a bit distant. The recording responds quite well to even rudimentary surround processing. (A+)

922 Papa Doo Run Run: *California Project*: Telarc 70501. This Beach Boys sound-alike group comes across with tremendous impact and dynamic range as well as clarity. There is clearly lots of rock processing involved and maybe a bit too much thump to the bass for some tastes (more than any authentic Beach Boys album ever had), but the electrical manipulations are expertly done. The sound stage is not particularly realistic, but who cares? Compare to the Beach Boys *Surfin' USA* album (see 112). (A+)

923 Parry, Hubert: *Complete Symphonies*, London Philharmonic Orchestra: Chandos CHAN 9120-22. These six pieces (five symphonies and *Symphonic Variations*) were recorded by two engineers on four dates, but at least the recording locale was the same in every case. The sound is smooth, clean, and maybe too bright at times. The ambience is definitely large hall, and the sound-stage depth is fine, as is the left-right spread. (A)

924 Pärt, Arvo: *Cello Concerto*; *Symphonies Number 1, 2, and 3*, Bamberg Symphony Orchestra: BIS CD 434. Modern composer Pärt's music may not be for everyone, but this recording's sound is clean, three-dimensional, and close to first class. (A)

925 Patitucci, John: *On the Corner* (with Chick Corea, Al Foster, Dave Weckl, Alex Acuña, and others): GRP GRD-9583. Open, reverberant, often punchy and articulate jazz with the somewhat phasey and synthesized sound-stage idiosyncrasies exhibited by a number of other GRP releases. This is really not as bad as it seems since the effect can be subjectively pleasing when experienced on even fairly good systems in typical home listening rooms. (B+)

926 Pavone, Mario: *Toulon Days* (with Thomas Chapin, Joshua Redman, Marty Ehrlich, Steve Davis, Hotep Galeta, and Steve Johns): New World 80420-2. I felt that this release had a good jazz-style sound stage with fine clarity and depth. The bass line on this recording is delightfully punchy (and deep) at times and sneaks up on you. Even a smaller stereo system can come to life with this disc. (A)

927 Perle, George, Nicholas Thorne, and David Del Tredici: *Piano Works*, Michael Boriskin, piano: New World NW 380-2. A remarkably clean small-room sound stage presents itself in this recording of some very good modern piano pieces. Overall, this is a very realistic piece of engineering with few negative artifacts. (A)

928 Peterson, Oscar: *Last Call at the Blue Note* (his trio, with Herb Ellis, Ray Brown, and Bobby Durham): Telarc 83314. Clean clear jazz with a good sense of the nightclub's acoustics. The piano is a bit large and diffuse in relation to the other two players. Someone is humming along with the piano, probably Peterson. As I have noted before, the piano is a difficult instrument to record, and there are philosophical differences between engineers about how to handle this instrument. (A)

929 Peterson, O.: *Live at the Blue Note* (his trio, with Herb Ellis, Ray Brown, and Bobby Durham): Telarc 83304. This is another fine location recording with great clarity and realistic perspective. The sound is similar to that of 928. (A)

930 Peterson, O.: *Saturday Night at the Blue Note* (his trio, with Herb Ellis, Ray Brown, and Bobby Durham): Telarc 83306. Same comments as for 928 and 929. (A)

931 Peterson, Ralph: *Triangular* (his trio, with Geri Allen, Essiet Okon Essiet, and Phil Bowler): Blue Note CDP 7 92750-2. There is nice imaging on this jazz release with the drums and piano under reasonable technical control. There is also good ambience and acceptable stage width with a fair perceived depth to the sound field. (B)

932 Philip the Chancellor: *Songs*, Sequentia: Deutsche Harmonia Mundi 77035-2-RC. Very clear, clean, and spacious with a nice sense of hall space. This is another ADD disc from this company that highlights the importance of microphone placement and microphone quality as well as the configuration of the recording environment. "High-tech digital" is important, but the other hardware and its proper use is more important. (A)

933 Phillips, Flip: *A Real Swinger* (with Howard Alden, Wayne Wright, Dick Hyman, Jack Lesberg, and Charles Miles): Concord Jazz CCD-4358. Clean and blended with a good sound stage, well-sized drums, and a piano that is positioned properly and not bloated. The featured instrument here is the saxophone, and it sounds more than just OK. (B+)

934 *The Pilgrimage to Santiago* (A musical journey along the medieval pilgrim road to the Shrine of St. James at Santiago de Compostela), the New London Consort: L'Oiseau-Lyre 433 148-2. This one is clear, smooth, and detailed with good hall ambience and depth. Perhaps the primary highlight here is the very good vocal articulation. (A)

935 Pink Floyd: *Dark Side of the Moon*: Mobile Fidelity UDCD 517. This is another expensive "gold" reissue made from tapes recorded around 1973. There are lots of interesting sound effects on this rock recording with heavy processing of what musical material there is. In spite of its age, this one is quite detailed with an impressive but often distant sound stage. Turn the gain up a bit higher than normal to let this disc do its stuff. There is some deep bass for such an old recording. (B)

936 Pink Floyd: *Delicate Sound of Thunder*: Columbia C2K 44484. This is quite good for a live concert recording with an excellent sound stage and plenty of punch. The recorded reverberation is effective, making the disc even better with a bit L-R surround processing (Dolby, Hafler-type). The vocals are just a tad thick due to that same heavy reverb and manipulation. There is good bass on some tracks. Any listener will discover lots of "experimental-sounding" enhancement work and phase manipulations that some will love and others will hate. (B+)

937 Pink Floyd: *The Final Cut*: Columbia CK 38243. Well-handled vocals are the strong point here. The articulation is good and not so heavily processed as to be buzzy or nasal. The instrumental parts are wildly manipulated and total unreal sounding, however, even by rock-concert standards. There are some fairly good dynamics and some interesting sound effects. (B)

938 Piston, Walter: *Symphony Number 2*; *Symphony Number 6*; *Sinfonietta*, Seattle Symphony Orchestra (the two symphonies), New York Chamber Symphony (*Sinfonietta*): Delos DE 3074. The sound here is rich, full, reverberant, and real (the symphonies). The notable sound-stage depth and wide stage spread are highlights in this recording, but the dynamics are also imposing, and the frequency bandwidth is impressively broad. The *Sinfonietta*, although done at a different time and place and smaller in scale, is equally splendid. (A+)

939 Pizzarelli, John, and Bucky Pizzarelli: *Live from Studio "A" in New York City* (with Johnny Frigo): Chesky JD-1. Chesky's opening blast and the jazz release established this company's reputation among audio buffs practically overnight. This disc is very clear and clean with excellent dynamics. The good sound-stage spread is obvious, but the overall sound is slightly marred by low-level hall rumble, a flaw also found in many subsequent Chesky releases. This is no problem for most listeners (it was not audible with my smaller system with its low-bass equalizer turned off) unless their systems have potent subwoofers (which my big system certainly does). Certain surround-sound devices may also aggravate the effect. (Qualified A)

940 Pizzarelli, J.: *My Blue Heaven* (with Milt Hinton, Connie Kay, Dave McKenna, Bucky Pizzarelli, and Clark Terry): Chesky JD-38. Very clean and detailed. There is a realistic close up sound here but with some hall or studio background rumble apparent. As noted previously, Chesky very much needs to invest in a decent subwoofer for their monitoring facility. (Qualified A+)

941 *Plainchant from Prague*, Schola Hungarica: Hungaroton HCD 31085. There is notable depth and spaciousness here combined with realistic clarity and detail. After listening to a lot of music from this label. I conclude that they rank right up there with the best of the audiophile outfits. They may not always produce A+ recordings, but every one I have auditioned rates at least an A. If this is the result of the downfall of Marxism in Eastern Europe, then more than an economic renaissance is in store for that area. (A)

942 Plaxico, Lonnie: *Iridescence* (with Greg Osby, Lance Bryant, David Jones, and others): Muse MCD 5427. This is a very punchy and reverberant jazz recording with a bit more bass thump than a few would like. However, that bass is also fairly deep at times, which at least makes the recording viable on a system with good deep-range response. The bass-to-upper-range balance was actually better on my smaller system than on my larger one. The remaining instruments are well recorded (especially the sax), and the imaging and spread are fairly good. (B+)

943 *Plays of St. Nicholas*, Schola Hungarica: Hungaroton HCD 12887/88. This is a marvelously smooth, clear, reverberant, and real-sounding recording of medieval music. There is a notably fine hall ambience (as usual for this label and this ensemble) made even more impressive when run through a surround-sound processor of decent quality. (A+)

944 Popper, David: *Romantic Cello Favorites*; Janos Starker, cello; Shigeo Neriki, piano: Delos DE 3065. This production is wonderfully transparent, close up, and smooth with a fine small-hall ambience. The cello is well focused and vivid, and the piano is back just far enough to add support without overwhelming the main instrument. The small-hall ambience fits the music quite well. There is a near subsonic, low-frequency rumble that must be a large air-conditioner or heater blower. (Qualified A+)

945 Porter, Cole: *Anything Goes*, London Symphony Orchestra and the Ambrosian Singers (with Kim Criswell, Chris Groenendaal, Frederica von Stade, and others): EMI CDC 7 49848-2. There is good orchestral smoothness on this one with a good integration between the chorus, soloists, and instrumentalists. The solo vocal positioning is also quite good, and the clarity of the singers is fine. (B+)

946 Porter, C.: *Anything Goes*, Lincoln Center Theater (with Patti Lupone, Howard McGillin, Kathleen Mahoney-Bennett, and others): RCA 7769-2-RC. This release displays good stage imaging with an accommodating blend between the instrumentalists and the singers. The soloists are decently sized and clearly recorded. I thought the instrumental textures were just a bit thin and lacking in body. (B+)

947 Porter, C.: *Night and Day*; Thomas Hampson, baritone; London Symphony Orchestra; Ambrosian Chorus: EMI CDC 7 54203-2. I felt that this release had a good orchestral-vocal-choral balance as well as good solo-vocal clarity. It also displayed a realistic stage perspective with good blending between the singer and the orchestral ensemble. Good front-to-back depth. (A)

948 Porter, C.: *Nymph Errant* (with the Stephen Hill Singers, along with Kay Ballard, Fiona Fullerton, Maureen McGovern, Alexis Smith, and others): EMI CDC 7 54079-2. A good sound system will reveal the decent clarity and detail on this live recording. However, the big attraction of this disc is the hall ambience and stage depth, which are almost surround-sound like, even with only two front stereo speakers. Otherwise, the listening perspective is mid-distance, and the vocalists are properly sized in comparison with the live-performance-imaged orchestral players.

Sometimes you can hear the performers walking about the stage, and when there are a lot of them, there is a subtle and deep background rumble. I suppose this is to be expected in a recording of a live performance. (B+)

949 Porter, C.: *Overtures and Ballet Music*, The London Sinfonietta: EMI CDC 7 54300-2. This effort features an orchestra that is widely spread across the stage and well defined but with a somewhat flat depth perspective. The hall ambience is pretty well dealt with, however. (B+)

950 Porter, C.: *Porter on My Mind* (the classic songs of Cole Porter); Francis Thorne, piano and vocals; Jack Six, bass: CRI CD 585. Very smooth, clean, and detailed vocals, the piano and bass very well integrated into the mix. There is a good studio-club ambience with a nice intimate sound and well-focused, nonphasey piano. (A)

951 Poulenc, Francis: *Chamber Music*, with Pascal Ragé, Patrick Gallois, Maurice Bougue, and others: London 421 581-2. This is a nice small-ensemble sound. The piano is well sized and well located, and the hall ambience enhances the direct sound from the ensemble. It is a bit distant with the listening position just to the rear of midhall. (A)

952 Poulenc, F.: *Mass in G Major*; *Motets for Christmas and Lent*; *Four Short Prayers of St. Francis*; Robert Shaw Festival Singers; Donna Carter, soprano: Telarc 80236. An all-choral work, this recording is smooth, spacious, and very transparent with marvelous inner detail. The hall reverberation is quite strong (the recording was made in a church in France), and its influence will be liked by some listeners more than others. The direct sound field comes across as a bit diffuse, but that is no problem with works of this kind. The soloist blends perfectly with the rest of the ensemble. (A)

953 Powell, Mel: *Duplicates*; *Setting*; *Modules*, Los Angeles Philharmonic New Music Group: Harmonia Mundi France HMU 907096. Done at four time periods at two halls, the three contemporary "classical" works presented here all sound spacious and real with fine clarity. Two are double-piano pieces, so the wide-sounding piano image is intentional. (A)

954 Praetorius, Michael: *Christmas Music*; The Choir of Westminster Cathedral; The Parley of Instruments: Hyperion CDA 66200. There is a detailed and realistic orchestral sound stage on this original-instruments recording that also exhibits precisely captured hall ambience. (A+)

955 Praetorius, M.: *Dances from Terpsichore*, New London Consort: L'Oiseau-Lyre 414 633-2. This release is detailed, smooth, and quite realistic, with exemplary depth and ambience. There is very good individual-instrument imaging, an important recording attribute for music of this kind. (A+)

956 *Presenting Jian Wang* (short works by Chopin, Barber, and Schumann); Jian Wang, cello; Carol Rosenberger, piano: Delos DE 3097. This effort is smooth, rich, and transparent with a nice intimate small-room feel that is marred only by the somewhat diffuse piano. The cello sounds tight and focused, however. (A)

957 Previte, Bobby: *Claude's Late Morning* (with Wayne Horvitz, Ray Anderson, Bill Frisell, Josh Dubin, and others): Gramavision R2-79448. This jazz performance is more distant than *Empty Suits* (see 958) and a bit less dynamic and full. Some parts are quite lucid, however, and when the band settles down, the depth and ambience is decent. (B)

958 Previte, B.: *Empty Suits* (with Robin Eubanks, Steve Gaboury, Jerome Harris, and Alan Jaffee): Gramavision R2-79447. Dynamic, punchy, and forward with good clean bass and reasonably good clarity at times. The electronic rock-style, "pre-distorted" guitars used on some tracks tend to muddy things up and make this album more like rock and roll than jazz. The vocals are sized well and decently positioned, but their textures are a bit buzzy. A flawed but still pretty good technical piece. (B+)

959 Prince and the New Power Generation: *Diamonds and Pearls*: Warner 25379-2. This release is an acoustic deluge of pop-music sound with great impact and pretty good clarity, considering the monumental processing used. There is some deep bass at times. (B)

960 *The Princely Trumpet* (short works by Händel, Telemann, and others), Franz-Liszt-Kammerorchester, Edward Tarr, trumpet: Christophorus CD 74559. The somewhat distant listening position does not hurt with a recording of this kind, and the sound stage, clarity, and perspective are all fine. The trumpet positioning sounds real, and the solo sound is well integrated into the orchestra. (A)

961 Prokofiev, Sergei: *Alexander Nevsky*; *Scythian Suite*, Scottish National Orchestra and Chorus, Linda Finnie, mezzo-soprano: Chandos CHAN 8584. This one is forward, clean, bright, and front-row perfect. There is a technically sublime blending between the orchestra and chorus here, and the tremendous dynamic contrasts are expertly recorded. The solo vocalist is perfectly handled by the engineers. (A+)

962 Prokofiev, S.: *Alexander Nevsky*; *Lieutenant Kijé Suite*, Choeur et Orchestre Symphonique de Montréal, Jard van Nes, mezzo-soprano: London 430 506-2. Here we have a very well engineered sound stage with fine clarity and depth—and good integration between the choir and orchestra. The solo vocalist is perfectly integrated into the overall effort. The verdict is a toss-up between this one and 961. (A+)

963 Prokofiev, S.: *Peter and the Wolf*; Tchaikovsky, Peter: *Nutcracker Suite*, Boston Pops: Philips 412556-2. Clean and smooth with a definite close up sound stage. There is just a bit of background rumble here that will be evident only when played back on more potent woofer systems. Note that most of the Boston Pops material in this book is listed under that orchestra's name. (Qualified A)

964 Prokofiev, S.: *Piano Concertos Number 1, 4, and 5*, Royal Concertgebouw Orchestra, Boris Berman, piano: Chandos CHAN 8791. On this recording, a good solid middistance listening perspective highlights a finely focused piano image. The solo instrument is properly flanked by a tastefully spread orchestral sound stage. The clarity and depth are both quite good, and a realistic sense of hall space rounds out the program. (A)

965 Prokofiev, S.: *Romeo and Juliet* (complete ballet), Kirov Orchestra: Philips 432 166-2. A smooth, rich, balanced orchestral sound is a highlight here, with good detail to boot. The sound stage seems just a mite flat at times, but the overall job is a match for, and in many ways superior to, many of Philips's other symphonic efforts. (A)

966 Prokofiev, S.: *Romeo and Juliet* (excerpts from suites 1 and 2), Cleveland Orchestra: Telarc 80089. Overall, this one has a nice sound stage and depth, although the perspective seems a bit distant. There is good clarity in spite of the perceived distance. (A)

967 Prokofiev, S.: *Romeo and Juliet Suites 1 and 2*; *Pushkin Waltz Number 2*, Seattle Symphony Orchestra: Delos D/CD 3050. The presentation here is a broad sound stage with the violins on both left and right, as with most other Seattle Symphony recordings by Delos. This results in a pleasing blend either when heard on a sound system or enjoyed in a concert hall. Very clean sound. (A+)

968 Prokofiev, S.: *Symphony Number 1*; *Symphony Number 5*, Philharmonia Orchestra: Collins Classics 10642. A bit distant in imaging but exceptionally clean with outstanding depth and hall-sound realism. We have here a near toss-up between this one and the London effort (see 969), although if pressed, I would probably opt for the Collins disc. (A+)

969 Prokofiev, S.: *Symphony Number 1*; *Symphony Number 5*, Orchestre Symphonique de Montréal: London 421 813-2. Spacious, reverberant, full of depth, and clean. This is an outstanding example of good symphonic recording techniques. There is just a hint of hall rumble in the background that would trouble only a pair of speakers having very deep bass capabilities. (Qualified A+)

970 Prokofiev, S.: *Symphony Number 5*, Leningrad Philharmonic Orchestra: Chandos CHAN 8576. As with nearly all Chandos recordings, this one is smooth, dynamic, and clean (with a subtle and deep bass drum that is quite impressive on larger sound systems). Plenty of sound-stage breadth, depth, and overall realism. (A+)

971 Prokofiev, S.: *Symphonies* (a four-disc compilation, with *Symphonies number 1* through *7* complete, including both the 1930 and revised 1947 versions of number 4), Royal Scottish National Orchestra: Chandos CHAN 8931-34. All but number 6 were recorded at the same locale, and all were recorded in 1984-85. The sound is smooth, clean, and dynamic and slightly less forward sounding than assorted other (and especially the more recent) SNO releases. The strings throughout are marvelous, and the depth of the sound stage and the combined orchestral clarity are fine. All these recordings are roughly equal in quality. (A)

972 Prokofiev, S.: *War and Peace*, Orchestre National de France, Choeurs de Radio France (with G. Vichnievskaïa, N. Gedda, and others), Erato ECD 75480. This monumental piece (a four-disc set) is nice and smooth overall with a good sense of hall space and depth. The soloists are well positioned and properly sized in relation to the instrumentalists. Not quite state of the art but not chopped liver either. (A)

973 Puccini, Giacomo: *La Bohème*, Chorus and Orchestra of the Accademia Nazionale di Santa Cecilia (with Angelina Réaux, Barbara Daniels, Jerry Hadley, Thomas Hampson, James Busterud, Paul Plishka, and others): DGG 423 601-2. Live recordings of opera like this one often sound better than studio jobs because the staging requirements preclude excess microphone manipulation and overengineering. This disc sports a fine sound stage with realistic orchestral-vocal balance. Good clarity. (A)

974 Puccini, G.: *Songs*; Placido Domingo, tenor; Julias Rudel, piano and organ: Columbia MK 44981. This effort has a fairly good placement of Domingo and the piano support, with a front-row listening perspective that has a well-focused vocal image but a slightly diffuse piano. The organ is also diffuse, but the effect fits in with that kind of instrument. The overall tonal quality is good, Domingo's voice treated quite well by the technicians. (A)

975 Puccini, G.: *Tosca*, National Philharmonic Orchestra, Welsh National Opera Chorus (with Kiri Te Kanawa, Leo Nucci, Giacomo Aragall, and others): London 414 597-2. This recording has a somewhat distant orchestral sound that blends very well with the chorus and soloists. There is a fine stage spread with a realistic positioning of each singer. (A)

976 Puente, Tito: *Salsa Meets Jazz* (with Phil Woods and other players): Concord Picante CCD-4354. This release shows a reasonably good sound stage and imaging with a typical lack of stage depth to the obviously multimiked ensemble. The clarity is good, however, and the synthesized reverb is not all that objectionable. Overall, I feel the sound lacks the kind of percussive slam a recording of this kind of music should have. (B)

977 Pullen, Don: *New Beginnings* (with Gary Peacock and Tony Williams): Blue Note CDP 91785-2. Good depth on this jazz release with good imaging (especially the piano) and a drumset that is well focused and not swollen. The bass sounds like a real instrument with substantial output down low. The sound stage seems a bit skewed to the right. (B+)

978 Purcell, Henry: *Chamber Music*, The London Baroque: Harmonia Mundi France HMC 901327. An excellent sound stage and clarity highlight a recording that is almost certainly being done with period instruments (no mention of instrumentation in the accompanying text). (A)

979 Purcell, H.: *The Fairy Queen*, Les Arts Florissants: Harmonia Mundi France 901308/09. The small hall rumble in the background does not detract appreciably from the clarity, detail, and realistic sound stage of this recording. However, given the control the engineers should have had (after all, this is not medieval music, and it is not necessary to record it in a noisy cathedral to achieve the required effect), it is surprising that the noise was allowed to intrude on the recording. Bass-shy monitor speakers were obviously used during the mixing process. In any case, an excellent orchestral-vocal balance is achieved, and the sound has a good blend and is quite smooth. The somewhat distant sound-stage perspective is not detrimental to the effect, and this may be responsible for the lack of original-instrument clinicality to the sound. (Qualified A)

980 Purcell, H.: *Odes*, The English Concert and Choir: Archiv 427 663-2. Another clear and detailed authentic-instrument piece from Archiv. The vocal-orchestral blend is near perfect with a close-up detail that is revealing and realistic. The original-instrument sound is very well rendered with none of the usual brittleness. (A+)

981 Purcell, H.: *Songs*, Drew Minter,

Quatre Grands Concertos (982) [136]

countertenor: Harmonia Mundi France 907035. This disc has notably fine vocal clarity and detail with good positioning of the soloist in relation to the small supporting ensemble. The close up small-hall listening perspective adds to the effect. (A+)

982 *Quatre Grands Concertos pour Trompette* (short works by Désenclos, Jolivet, Chaynes, and Tomasi), Orchestre du Théâtre National de L'Opéra de Paris, Eric Aubier, trumpet: Cybella CY 824. A clear, dynamic recording with a broad sound stage. The trumpet is smooth in texture but just a tad diffuse in central focus. (A)

983 *Quel Lascivissimo Cornetto* (virtuoso solo music for cornetto), Tragicomedia, Bruce Dickey, cornetto: Accent 91730. This release is smooth and clear with good imaging. A nice hall feel rounds out the effect. (A)

984 R.E.M.: *Out of Time*: Warner 26496-2. This release features good vocal clarity combined with a typically wide but flat-sounding (multimicrophone-produced) rock-and-roll sound stage. Everything is electric, but the effect is not all that bad. (B)

985 Rachmaninov, Sergei: *Isle of the Dead*; *Symphonic Dances*, Concertgebouw Orchestra: London 410 124-2. Recorded in 1983, this pressing is dynamic, clear, and large scale. The sound just rolls over you. The overall impact of here is very impressive. It is hard to fault the engineering on this job, which shows that the London recording technique is fully at home in a really fine hall and has been so for a number of years. Unfortunately, there is just a touch of background-noise rumble, probably an air-conditioner or heater fan. Background-sound artifacts like this often sneak through the control-room checkout because many recording companies do not employ studio monitors of high enough quality, particularly for deep bass reproduction. Also, such noises may not be noticed in a large concert hall because of the psychological masking effects of the size of the place, but they will be apparent in a living room that would ordinarily not have such large-room background sounds. Finally, even if the noise is noticed during the final tape mixing operation, costs may dictate that the session cannot be economically repeated. (Qualified A+)

986 Rachmaninov, S.: *Piano Concerto Number 1*; *Piano Concerto Number 2*, London Symphony Orchestra, John Ogdon, piano: Collins Classics 10882. This release is quite transparent, spacious, and detailed with very good placement of the piano in relation to the orchestra. A good midhall listening perspective results in a realistic sound stage; the spread and depth are just right. (A+)

987 Rachmaninov, S.: *Piano Concerto Number 2*; *Piano Concerto Number 3*, Philharmonia Orchestra, Yefim Bronfman, piano: Sony SK 47183. I found this one notably smooth and transparent with a good orchestra sound stage and plenty of dynamic impact. The piano is clear and detailed but a bit too close up; somewhat large and diffuse in relation to the better-proportioned orchestral ensemble. (A)

988 Rachmaninov, S.: *Piano Concerto Number 2*; *Piano Concerto Number 3*, Pittsburgh Symphony Orchestra, Horacio Gutiérrez, piano: Telarc 80259. There is an excellent blending of the solo piano on this release integrated into a wide, clean, dynamic orchestral sound stage. (A+)

989 Rachmaninov, S.: *Piano Sonata*

Number 2; *Preludes* (op. 23 and 32); *Etudes-Tableaux* (and other, shorter works), John Browning, piano: Delos D/CD 3044. Full, rich, and detailed. The sound is middistance in perspective and located in a modest-sized hall with good you-are-there ambience and clarity. The piano is mercifully unbloated sounding and has a coherent focus. I found that some home-brewed surround processing added just enough synthesized ambience to complete the illusion, although simple stereo playback is more than good enough. (A+)

990 Rachmaninov, S.: *Symphony Number 1*, Concertgebouw Orchestra: London 411 657-2. This release displays great dynamics and wide-band response with magnificent depth, clarity, and impact. The London team is at its best with music of this kind. One of the better releases by this company, and it was done in 1982. (A+)

991 Rachmaninov, S.: *Symphony Number 2*, Scottish National Orchestra: Chandos CHAN 8423. Roughly equal to the earlier of the two Telarc versions (995) in sound quality but recorded about 5 years prior to it, in 1980. The same general comments about that Telarc release apply here, but with the subjective stage width on this one a little bit narrower. The bass-drum effects are in a class with the older Telarc also. As the Chandos-SNO team gained more experience (and almost certainly gained access to better equipment), their recordings got even better. (A)

992 Rachmaninov, S.: *Symphony Number 2*, Philharmonia Orchestra: Chandos CHAN 8520. Clean, clear, dynamic, and nearly first rate. This 1986 attempt is slightly better than the 1980 Chandos release (see 991) and a bit superior to the roughly contemporaneous first Telarc version (see 995). The dynamics are no better than the earlier release by Chandos, but the overall sound has a bit more depth and clarity. The improvements are still not enough to rate a score above those releases. (A)

993 Rachmaninov, S.: *Symphony Number 2* (and shorter works), Oregon Symphony Orchestra: Delos D/CD 3071. This effort has plenty of dynamic range and nice clarity. It seems just a tad dry for a work of this magnitude, but the bass (and the bass drum) does outclass that of the Telarc version (see 995) and runs off and leaves the Nimbus attempt (see 994). The dryness responded very well to surround processing via my big Yamaha DSP unit. (A)

994 Rachmaninov, S.: *Symphony Number 2*, BBC Welsh Symphony Orchestra: Nimbus NI 5322. Ambisonic processing gives this large-scale work a more distant listening perspective than the other recordings of this symphony reviewed here, and some listeners may not like the effect (some will love it, please note). The result is transparent and clean with nice depth. The bass drum seems a bit anemic for a work of this scale. This is another example of apparent bass bandwidth limitations of the Calrec Soundfield microphone when the unit is used in a non-complementary hall. The strong point of this recording is its fine imaging and realistic hall ambience. (B+)

995 Rachmaninov, S.: *Symphony Number 2*, Royal Philharmonic Orchestra: Telarc 80113. This effort has a very wide and spacious sound stage with great clarity, although the dynamics seem a trifle slack for a piece of this type and the bass (particularly the bass drum) seems thin for a Telarc pressing. This may be more the fault of

the recording environment than of the engineering staff. (A)

996 Rachmaninov, S.: *Symphony Number 2*, Baltimore Symphony Orchestra: Telarc 80312. There are some tremendous dynamic contrasts on this disc, with excellent clarity and great depth. At first, one wonders why Telarc decided to do this one again — until the superiority of this version over 995 is heard. The big bass drum (almost too big) is obviously there to make up for the occasionally thin sounding one in the earlier recording and maybe to show up the one in the above Delos disc (see 993). This is my first choice for this work for engineering quality. (A+)

997 Rachmaninov, S.: *Symphony Number 3*; *Symphonic Dances*, Philadelphia Orchestra: London 433 181-2. This recording is very clean and clear with plenty of dynamic impact. It may be a touch clearer and certainly has less hall noise than 985 (which duplicates the *Symphonic Dances* only), but with a tad less punch than that disc. Still, the overall sense of space, sound-stage exactness, and realism on this effort is a bit better. (A+)

998 Rachmaninov, S.: *Variations on a Theme of Chopin*; *Variations on a Theme of Corelli*, Earl Wild, piano: Chesky CD-58. The piano on this recording has a broad left-to-right sound, giving the effect of sitting very close to the instrument in a small hall. In some cases, this may come across as an in-your-listening-room effect that may appeal to some people more than others. I found that extraction-type surround enhancement helps to keep the piano where it belongs: in the hall. (A)

999 Rachmaninov, S.: *Vespers*, Robert Shaw Festival Singers, Karl Dent, tenor: Telarc 80172. There is no orchestra in this one, so it is a fine example of choral-only material with an excellent ensemble blend and a proper spatial relationship between the tenor soloist and the rest of the choir. There is fine clarity here with a wonderful church ambience. This disc got a Grammy for engineering, and it deserved it. (A+)

1000 Raitt, Bonnie: *Luck of the Draw*: Capitol C2-96111. This little gem is punchy and clean with better than average vocal clarity and sound-stage realism. The recording also has better than average bass extension for a C&W job. The vocals are more distant sounding than typical of this genera, and they blend with the orchestra better. They just seem more realistic and less amplified and artificial. The final touch is the good stereo spread and instrumental imaging, including (thankfully) the drums. (A)

1001 Rameau, Jean Philippe: *Les Boréades*; *Dardanus* (suites), Orchestra of the Eighteenth Century: Philips 420 240-2. This clear and detailed original-instrument recording highlights the talents of this fine baroque composer. Very good hall ambience and depth round out the effect. (A+)

1002 Rameau, J. P.: *Les Indes Galantes*, Orchestre de la Chapelle Royale: Harmonia Mundi France HMA 1901130. This is a good solid job with a spacious stage spread to the ensemble plus good clarity from the all-important original instruments. (A)

1003 Rameau, J. P.: *Pièces de Clavecin*, Christophe Rousset, harpsichord: L'Oiseau-Lyre 425 886-2. This transcription is close up and powerful (for harpsichord at least) with wonderful detail and clarity. The articulation is very smooth and undistorted. Unlike the recording below, a bit of home-based surround enhancement makes the ambience come across even better. This one puts you in a good front-row concert-hall seat. (A+)

1004 Rameau, J. P.: *Pièces de Clavecin*; *Suite in A*, Albert Fuller, harpsichord: Reference Recordings RR-27CD. This effort features up-close and realistic sound with state-of-the-art definition. The hall ambience on this disc is remarkable, and some may wish carefully to add home-based surround enhancement to achieve an almost eerie realism. Other listeners may feel that it is best to turn off any surround enhancements they might ordinarily use and just let the instrument occupy their listening room in a completely unforced manner. The small background hiss is unobtrusive. (A+)

1005 Rameau, J. P.: *Pièces de Clavecin en Concerts*, Trio Sonnerie: Virgin Classics 7 90749-2. This recording presents very clear sound from the period instruments. With some selections the sound stage seems shifted slightly more to the right than typical, probably a performance rather than a recording artifact. (A)

1006 Rameau, J. P.: *Les Surprises de L'Amour*, Musiciens du Louvre: Erato/Musifrance 245004-2. Here we have marvelously clear and detailed sound with good hall ambience and depth. The occasional hall rumble may be traffic noise well outside the building. Turning off your surround-enhancement processor will eliminate some of the negative aspects of the noise. Unfortunately, I found that doing so also detracted from the feeling of hall ambience and depth. From the instrumental sound quality, this appears to be a period-instrument recording, although the insert says nothing about it. (Qualified A+)

1007 Rankin, Kenny: *Because of You*: Chesky JD-63. Technically, this is one of the best vocal recordings available—of any kind. Very clean with the soloist and instrumental support very well sized and positioned. (A+)

1008 Ravel, Maurice: *Bolero*; *Rapsodie Espagnole*; *La Valse*, Orchestre Symphonique de Montréal: London 410 010-2. Nice and clean in the London Records-Montréal Symphony tradition. Also in that same tradition, just a bit lacking in depth at times, with some of the highlighted instruments just too close up. I must admit that I do not like this kind of manipulation with classical music, but some people (and certainly some engineers) love it. (A)

1009 Ravel, M.: *Daphnis et Chloé* (complete), Choeur et Orchestre Symphonique de Montréal: London 400 055-2. Although recorded in 1980, this all-digital recording still has decent clarity with a nice sense of hall space. The sound stage is adequately wide and has OK depth. (A)

1010 Ravel, M.: *Daphnis et Chloé* (complete); Diamond, David: *Elegy in Memory of Maurice Ravel*, Seattle Symphony Orchestra and Chorale: Delos DE 3110. This little jewel has a remarkable dynamic range (note the near silence of the quiet parts) plus an excellent sound stage and clarity—better in fact than the above London effort. The usual Delos blended sound stage highlights the performance. (A+)

1011 Ravel, M.: *Ma Mère l'Oye* (complete); *Valses Nobles et Sentimentales* (and other shorter works), Orchestre Symphonique de Montréal:

Ravel (1012) [140]

London 410 254-2. Nice and clean with a somewhat distant perspective. The recording has a good sound stage, although the depth seems a bit shallow. The nice unforced violin sound is welcome. (A)

1012 Ravel, M., and Francis Poulenc: *Melodies* (assorted short pieces); Jean-François Gardeil, baritone; Billy Eidi, piano: Adda 581210. This one is notable for the outstanding piano-vocal integration into a small-hall environment. The articulation is excellent, and the piano is properly sized and not the least diffuse, bloated, or fuzzy. (A+)

1013 Ravel, M.: *Piano Concerto in G Major*; *Piano Concerto for Left Hand*, Orchestre Symphonique de Montréal: Decca/London 410 230-2. Done in 1983, this disc still has up-to-date sound with good clarity, detail, and dynamic contrast. The piano is well sized in relation to the orchestra and well positioned. (A)

1014 Ravel, M.: *Piano Music, Volume 1*: Louis Lortie, piano: Chandos CHAN 8620. The piano in this release is realistically placed on the stage and has good tonality. The sound is somewhat distant, but there is a good sense of space with a good hall feel and satisfactory envelopment. (A)

1015 Ravel, M.: *Piano Music, Volume 2*: Louis Lortie, piano: Chandos 8647. The sound here is similar to that of 1014. (A)

1016 Ravel, M.: *Piano Works*, Minoru Nojima, piano: Reference Recordings RR-35CD. I thought this one had a very realistic you-are-there perspective with a very clear piano sound and a nice ambient feel. The sense of involvement is only slightly marred by a hint of background hiss and some hall rumble. (Qualified A+)

1017 Ravel, M.: *Rapsodie Espagnole*; *Ma Mère l'Oye*; *Valses Nobles et Sentimentales*; *La Valse*, Cleveland Orchestra: London 430 413-2. Clear, dynamic, and impressive. The sound stage is wonderful with realistic depth and hall envelopment. This splendid effect, combined with the impressive Telarc-like bass drum, makes one wonder if the real secret of the early Telarc recordings was the Masonic Auditorium where that company recorded material by this orchestra. (A+)

1018 Ravel, M.: *Shéhérazade*; *Ma Mère l'Oye*; *La Valse* (and other shorter works), City of Birmingham Symphony Orchestra, Maria Ewing, soprano: EMI 7 54204-2. This recording is very dynamic and smooth (especially the short *Fanfare*) with great depth and a wide bandwidth. The result is completely unlike some of the anemic EMI recordings of the past. The solo vocalist is perfectly positioned, and the sound stage is nothing but realistic. (A+)

1019 Ravel, M.: *Trio Pour Piano, Violon et Violoncelle*; Saint-Saëns, Camille: *Trio Number 1 in F Major*; Martin, Frank: *Trio Pour Piano, Violon et Violoncelle*, Guarneri Trio: Ottavo OTR C28922. These three works are given a good middistance listening perspective with fine clarity and detail. The strings have less bite than some closer-sounding recordings of this kind, but the effect simulates a real-world hall quite well. In spite of the subjective distance, the piano seems a bit diffuse. (A)

1020 Reid, Mike: *Turning for Home*: Columbia CK 46141. This release features clean and clear sound with better than average vocal realism for a C&W disc. The sound stage, although electrically contrived, works well here. (B+)

1021 *Renaissance Madrigals* (Madrigals and Canzonets from the Italian Renaissance and Baroque), Quink Vocal Quintet: Telarc 80209. Smooth and spacious with good vocal articulation. The blend between the singers and their environment results in a close up sound stage that although not as clinical sounding as some other recordings of this type, complements this particular music very well. (A+)

1022 *Renaissance Music from the Courts of Mantua and Ferrara* (assorted players performing works by Cara, Tromboncino, Spinacino, Romano, and others): Chandos CHAN 8333. This recording of obscure works has a nice concert-hall depth and a good sound stage with the vocals well blended into the instrumental ensemble. (A)

1023 Respighi, Ottorino: *Ancient Airs and Dances*; *Trittico Botticelliano*, Lausanne Chamber Orchestra: Telarc 80309. Very clean and spacious with just a hint of string harshness at times. The latter effect is rare in a Telarc recording and may be more a result of hall effects than technical limitations. In short, that may be how the material sounds live. (A)

1024 Respighi, O.: *Church Windows*; *Poema Autunnale*, Pacific Symphony Orchestra, Ruggiero Ricci, violin: Reference Recordings RR-15CD. Smooth, clear, and vibrant with good sound-stage width and realistic depth. The violin is sized correctly and is placed where it should be. (A+)

1025 Respighi, O.: *Pines of Rome*; *Roman Festivals*; *Fountains of Rome*, Philharmonia Orchestra: Chandos CHAN 8989. Spacious, reverberant, and crystal clear with a very good sound stage and good depth. The organ is absolutely spectacular at intervals. This recording will be a good test for your woofer systems, not to mention your tweeters and midranges. (A+)

1026 Respighi, O.: *Pines of Rome*; *Roman Festivals*; *Fountains of Rome*, Orchestre Symphonique de Montréal: London 410 145-2. This effort is very clear with a good sound stage and good hall acoustics. There is a very powerful low-range organ pedal (down into the middle 20s) in the *Pines* on track 4 that can thoroughly shake up bass-reflex woofers and selectively remove pictures from your listening-room walls. This recording is easily the equal of 1025. (A+)

1027 Respighi, O.: *Pines of Romes*; *The Birds*; *Fountains of Rome*, Atlanta Symphony Orchestra: Telarc 80085. Smooth and spacious in the Telarc tradition with a good sense of space around the orchestra, a characteristic of spaced-omni-microphone use that bothers some people and enthralls others. There is great imaging across the sound stage in any case, no doubt due to the careful use of a center-fill microphone. This disc does not quite have the deep bass punch of 1025 and 1026 (on the *Pines*), but it is still impressive overall. Any of these three discs should satisfy a sound nut. (A)

1028 Reubke, Julius: *Sonata for Organ*; *Sonata for Piano*, Jean Guillou, organ and piano: Dorian DOR 90106. There is remarkably clear, spacious, and reverberant sound on the organ piece and plenty of deep bass. The piano work is equally good, the instrument very well sized and positioned where it should be. The hall reverberation is perfect for the effect required. (A+)

1029 Rich, Buddy: *Live on King Street, San Francisco* (with Steve Marcus, Mark Pinto, Bob Bowlby, Mike Davis, and many others): Cafe CD 2-732. This disc was produced by the Mobile Fidelity Sound Labs team and rates a lengthier than usual review because it was promoted as a state-of-the-art sound item. Indeed, after reading the insert that came with this two-disc set, I was ready to be pinned to the wall by the recorded pyrotechnics. The listed equipment and the description of its use will give the casual reader the impression that a landmark recording was made. Unfortunately, the sound is no better than many other run-of-the-mill jazz-recording efforts. Exotic gear notwithstanding, this is still a live production (complete with audience noises) that employs an abundance of microphones to deliver a typical pan-potted one-dimensional sound stage. A surround "SQ" enhancement technique was also employed during the final mix, but the result has little bearing on how the recording interacts with a typical home playback system or even a fairly exotic one. The recording is decently clean and detailed with good instrumental tonality, but the sound stage, SQ or not, lacks depth and ambience. The drums (certainly key instruments here and the main purchasing incentive for those who buy this recording) are distant, somewhat homogenized, and lack the live-music impact one expects, but they are at least not stretched across the stage. Overall, the sound is just a bit constricted and anemic. Interestingly, running the program through a surround processor did open things up considerably, but the ratings in this book are based upon performance in a standard good-quality two-channel stereo system. (B)

1030 Rimsky-Korsakov, Nikolai: *Capriccio Espagnol*; Debussy, Claude: *Iberia*, Dallas Symphony Orchestra: Telarc 80055. This early Telarc disc is spacious and full, and slightly more diffuse than it should be. This shows that the spaced three-mike array may have more problems in some halls than others because not every recording engineered by Jack Renner has this characteristic. The overall clarity is good, and the dynamic contrasts show why this company was (and still is) an audiophile favorite. (A)

1031 Rimsky-Korsakov, N.: *The Golden Cockerel*, Choir and Orchestra of the Bolshoi: MCA AED-10391. Here we have a fairly good example of proper orchestra-chorus-soloist-hall blending. This is a live recording, so audience sounds occasionally intrude. The overall effect is smooth, clear, and detailed. (A)

1032 Rimsky-Korsakov, N.: *Scheherazade*; *Capriccio Espagnol*, Orchestre Symphonique de Montréal: London 410 253-2. This effort is slightly more dynamic and clear than the Telarc recording of the same material (see 1033). The sound stage is a bit more realistic. Unlike some of the other London-Montréal releases, the string sound seems reasonably mellow and smooth. (A)

1033 Rimsky-Korsakov, N.: *Scheherazade*; *Capriccio Espagnol*, London Symphony Orchestra: Telarc 80208. This one is clean and clear with a spacious sound stage and wonderful hall ambience. The overall sound is forward and very sharply etched at times, and possibly a bit too bright for some tastes. I felt that the trombone sections were quite realistic. (A)

1034 Rimsky-Korsakov, N.: *Scheherazade*; Glazunov, Alexander: *Stenka Razin,* The Scottish National Orchestra. Chandos CHAN 8479. This release has an expansive sound stage and astonishing depth. The listening perspective is close up but there is ample hall reverb to add bloom to the sound and the overall result is clean, smooth and dynamic. Another Chandos engineering triumph. (A+)

1035 Rivera, Paquito de: *Havana Cafe* (with Fareed Haque, Ed Cherry, Danilo Perez, David Finck, Jorge Rossy, and Sammy Figueroa): Chesky JD-60. Punchy and articulate Cuban-style jazz with excellent percussive detail. The clarinet and saxophone are very realistically recorded and ear-catching. The piano sound is equally good. (A+)

1036 Rivera, P. de: *Tico! Tico!* (with Fareed Hague, Ed Cherry, Danilo Perez, and David Finck): Chesky JD-34. In a class with *Havana Cafe* (see 1035). The clarinet sound is exemplary, and the instrumental support blends it all into a marvelously real sound stage. (A+)

1037 Rivers, Mavis: *It's a Good Day* (with Matt Catingub, Howard Alden, Alan Broadbent, Bob Magnusson, and Kevin Winard): Delos D/CD 4002. Subjectively, this jazz-vocal recording displays very clear vocals marred only by being positioned a bit too far forward of the orchestra. The lack of any substantial hall ambience might also be considered a minus. Still, the disc has marvelous inner detail, and the ambience and envelopment can be added by the intelligent use of surround-sound enhancement. (B)

1038 *Robert Noehren Premiers the New D.F. Pilzecker Organ at the Church of St. Jude* (playing short works by Widor, Brahms, J. S. Bach, Alain, Hindemith, Karg-Elert, and Messiaen): Delos D/CD 3045. This release is very reverberant and large scale with wonderful clarity, brilliance, and smoothness. The minuscule hall noise is a plus in this case (organ wind noise, I am sure) and highlights the overall realism. With surround enhancement, the illusion was quite effective. (A+)

1039 Roberts, Marcus: *Along with Three Giants*: Novus 3109-2-N. This jazz piano-solo recording was done at three locations, but there is good instrumental tonality and clarity throughout. The instrument sounds a bit oversized for its position in the ambient space of the assorted halls, but it is not phasey or diffuse in an objectionable manner. (B+)

1040 Roberts, M.: *As Serenity Approaches* (with Todd Williams, Scotty Barnhart, Ellis Marsalis, Wynton Marsalis, Ronald Westray, and Nicholas Payton): Novus 63130-2. Done at two locations, the piano solo sections are close up, well formed, and vibrant. However, at times the instrument seems a bit diffuse and unfocused. The duets between Roberts and the assorted guest players are better imaged. The piano duet with Marsalis is a joy to listen to. (B+ to A, depending on the track)

1041 Rockwell, Bob: *The Bob Rockwell Trio* (with Rufus Reid and Victor Lewis): SteepleChase SCCD 31242. This release is technically very precise, clear, and smooth with good depth and ambience. This is a much better than average jazz-trio sound. (A)

1042 Rodgers, Richard: *Five Selections from Victory at Sea* (plus assorted shorter works by other composers), Cincinnati Pops: Telarc 80175. Spacious in the usual Telarc manner, the sound typically clean but somewhat thinner (or less bloated and diffuse, depending on your feeling about Telarc recordings in general) than some other releases by this outfit. (A)

1043 Rodgers, R. and O. Hammerstein: *The King and I*, Hollywood Bowl Orchestra (with Julie Andrews, Ben Kingsley, and many others): Philips 438 007-2. Smooth and intelligible with decent depth and a workable sound-stage placement of the particulars, in spite of the obvious multimicrophone technique. At times the solo vocalists are a bit closer to us than they should be, but they are cleanly recorded, and the improved articulation will be appreciated by some. The overall sound is a bit dry (although with plenty of energy), and the reverb is obviously synthesized. (B)

1044 Rodgers, R., and O. Hammerstein: *Songbook for Orchestra* (orchestral suites), Cincinnati Pops: Telarc 80278. This is the usual spacious, somewhat diffuse Telarc sound with the good clarity we have come to expect from this recording company. If you like what Telarc has been doing lately, you will like the sound of this disc. (A)

1045 Rodney, Red: *Then and Now* (with Chris Potter, Garry Dial, Jay Anderson, and Jimmy Madison): Chesky JD-79. This jazz recording displays excellent transparency, instrumental imaging, and detail with hall acoustics that are a bit on the dry side. This characteristic will appeal to some listeners more than others because the ensemble still seems somewhat distant. Usually, the opposite is the case: when the recorded acoustics are somewhat lacking in reverberation, the sound is quite intimate, and the subjective listening perspective is fairly close. Surround enhancement with either of my processors added depth to the dry ambient effect and made the sound quite impressive. Indeed, it almost seems as if this release were designed to be run through a Yamaha or Lexicon unit. (A)

1046 Rodrigo, Joaquin: *Concierto de Aranjuez*; *Fantasía para un Gentlehombre*; Falla, Manuel de: *El Sombrero de Tres Picos — Tres Danzas*, Orchestre Symphonique de Montréal, Carlos Bonell, guitar: London 417 748-2. Recorded in 1980 and 1981, the only real defect on this disc is the overhighlighting of the guitar in relation to the orchestra. This helps clarity but cuts into the sound-stage realism of the recording. If you want to hear the guitar well, there is no denying the need for such enhancements, however. The violins have the close-microphone brightness that some people love and others detest. The dynamics are marvelous. Make no mistake, this is a recording worth hearing. (A)

1047 *Roland Auzet: Percussion Solo et Ensemble Instrumental* (assorted modern classical works by Xenakis, Taïra, and Roque-Alsina): Globo Records 140. These are very dynamic percussion pieces with great impact, clarity, and depth. This is remarkable stuff, given that this release was not touted as some kind of "audiophile, demonstration-grade recording." (A+)

1048 Rollins, Sonny: *Fallin' in Love with Jazz* (with Clifton Anderson, Jerome Harris, Mark Soskin, Bob Cranshaw, and Jack DeJohnette): Milestone MCD 9179-2. The best Rollins disc I have heard and the only one of this group good enough to make this list. This is too bad because the music is really top drawer. This one was at least clear and well focused. The drums are typically oversized. (B)

1049 *Romantic Brass Music of France and Spain* (short classical works by Albéniz, Debussy, Falla, Rodrigo, Turina, Ravel, and Granados), Empire Brass: Telarc 80301. As is typical with recordings by this company, this one is smooth and clean with a nice hall feel. I felt that the imaging was a bit diffuse, a normal characteristic of the spaced-array microphone technique usually favored by Telarc. (A)

1050 *The Romantic Trombone* (short classical pieces by Ropartz, Saint-Saëns, Jongen, Weber, and others); Christian Lindberg, trombone; Roland Pöntinen, piano: BIS CD-298. This recording has a good trombone sound that blends well with the piano and fits the small hall. There is nice on-stage focus with no perceived phasey quality to the two instruments. (A)

1051 Ronstadt, Linda: *Mas Canciones*: Elektra 61239-2. This sleeper has excellent vocal clarity and detail with good balance between the vocalist and the instrumental ensemble. (A)

1052 Rorem, Ned: *Organ Music* (including *A Quaker Reader* and *Views from the Oldest House*), Catharine Crozier, organ: Delos DE 3076. Modern organ renditions are definitely something you must get used to if you have cut your teeth on Bach and Mendelssohn. Nevertheless, technically this disc has a fine spacious sound with a realistic hall-organ mix. There is good deep bass at times, tight and well controlled with remarkable detail. The hall where this organ is located is obviously very engineer-friendly, although there is some low-level background shuddering at times, almost certainly an artifact of the organ itself. Some organ enthusiasts feel this adds to the overall realism; other listeners might consider it simply annoying. The rumble should be inaudible on smaller less bass-potent systems. (Qualified A+)

1053 Rorem, N.: *Winter Pages*; *Bright Music*, Bridgehampton Chamber Music Festival: New World 80416-2. Very clear and detailed with a nice small-hall ambience and a close up perspective. The score speaks for this review. (A+)

1054 Rosenmüller, Johann: *Sonata de Camera and Sinfonie* (1654–1682), Hespèrion XX: Astrée E 8709. These are original instruments that definitely sound like what they are. The overall sound is clear, spacious, and detailed with good depth and imaging. Some listeners may not fully appreciate the lightweight and somewhat thin sound of period instruments, but there is no denying that they come closer to the original sound than modern ones. (A)

1055 Rosenthal, Ted: *New Tunes, New Traditions* (his trio, with Billy Higgins, Ron Carter, and Tom Harrell): Ken Music 003. I felt that this jazz release was good and clean, with the piano and the rest of the combo well positioned and somewhat more distant than usual. There is a notable lack of fake sound-stage manipulation. (B+)

1056 Ross, Diana: *The Force Behind the Power*: Motown 37463-6316-2. The bass on this pop recording is a tad heavy at times, but it's still not really overbearing (nor unfortunately particularly deep) and should balance well with the rest of the sound, especially when heard on smaller systems. There is plenty of good vocal clarity and

Rossini (1057)

sound-stage balance, and that offsets the low-range excess to a large extent. This one was obviously designed to sound good on cheaper systems and car installations, and I feel that Ross deserves better. Still, not a complete loss, especially if the bass control on your preamp is backed off just a bit. (B)

1057 Rossini, Gioacchino: *Arias*; Cecilia Bartoli, mezzo-soprano; Arnold-Schönberg-Chor; Konzertvereingung Wiener Volksopernorchester: London 425 430-2. I thought this release had nice vocal positioning and sizing in relation to the orchestra and choir. It also displayed good clarity and smoothness with a better than average string sound for London. (A)

1058 Rossini, G.: *Nineteen Songs* (including the cantata *Giovanna d'Arco*); Cecilia Bartoli, mezzo-soprano; Charles Spencer, piano: London 430 518-2. This release has a good small-hall mid-distance listening perspective, with the vocal-piano blend very well done. Overall, there is a fine you-are-there feel. (A+)

1059 Rossini, G.: *William Tell* (complete), National Philharmonic Orchestra, Ambrosian Opera Chorus (with Sherrill Milnes, Luciano Pavarotti, Mirella Freni, Nicolai Ghiaurov, and others): London 417 154-2. Recorded in 1979, these discs still display sound to match all but a few current titles. There is a realistic and welcome spatial relationship between chorus and orchestra as well as proper positioning of the soloists within the sound stage. (A)

1060 Roth, David Lee: *A Little Ain't Enough*: Warner 26477-2. As one might expect, there is lots of dynamic punch on this release, which will certainly appeal to fans of Mr. Roth. The vocals are typically rock-recording buzzy, but not as bad as most. The effect is clearly intentional and will please more than a few listeners. A saving grace here is the deeper than typical bass, especially for heavy-metal rock, which normally substitutes "boominess" for depth. (B)

1061 Roth, D. L.: *Skyscraper*: Warner 25671-2. Good rock dynamics with decent deep bass. The subjective depth is fairly good (surprise!), although the sound stage is still obviously electrically synthesized and inconsistent in imaging and placement. Well, it *does* sound like a rock concert. (B)

1062 Rowles, Jimmy, and Stacy Rowles: *Looking Back* (with Eric von Essen and Donald Bailey): Delos DE 4009. A remarkably smooth, transparent, and three-dimensional jazz recording. The focus of all the instruments is good, and the drums are where they should be and are sized like real drums. This one came close to a top score. (A)

1063 Rubaja, Bernardo, and Cesar Hernandez: *High Plateaux*: Windham Hill WD-1064. This one has the WH trademark sound for sure, including plenty of console-generated electrical embellishments. Electronic manipulations notwithstanding, the transcription was still notably clear and transparent with impressive dynamic contrasts, a good left-right sound stage, and plenty of subjective envelopment. WH has turned out some technically decent material, and this is a good example. (A)

1064 Ruiz, Hilton: *A Moment's Notice* (with George Coleman, Kenny Garrett, Dave Valentin, Andy Gonzales, and others): Novus 3123-2-N. A feature on this jazz release is the widespread sound stage along with good imaging and a well-sized set of drums. The direct sound is clear but also a bit dry and analytic, certainly a candidate for some surround-style manipulations. (B)

1065 Rush: *Presto*: Atlantic 82040-2. Needless to say, this one has good impact and a room-filling sound stage. I thought the vocals were well handled for a rock recording. (B)

1066 Rush: *Roll the Bones*: Atlantic 82293-2. This is technically very well balanced rock with clear vocals and a good synthesized sound stage. The result is much less muddy than is typical of material of this kind and cleaner than *Presto* (see 1065). (B+)

1067 *The Russian Flute* (short pieces by Prokofiev, Denisov, Taktakishvili, and Amirov); Manuela Wiesler, flute; Roland Pöntinen, piano: BIS CD-419. The recording displays a good flute-piano balance with good hall envelopment that really does enhance this kind of small-scale music. There is a definite you-are-there sound, as opposed to the they-are-here effect that some engineers might strive for. (A)

1068 *Russian Piano Music* (short pieces by Tchaikovsky, Lyadov, Rachmaninov, Scriabin, and Medtner): Dmitry Paperno, piano: Cedille Records CDR 90000 01. There is a palpable and very realistic you-are-there feel to this recording, due mainly to the sound of the hall itself. There is also a decently tight, well-controlled central image with few of the usual piano phase problems. (A)

1069 *Russian Songs* (short vocal pieces by Mussorgsky, Tchaikovsky, and Rachmaninov), Sergei Baikov, bass: MCA Classics AED-10320. This disc has nice vocal clarity, tonality, and detail. The voice is just a tad too far forward to mimic faithfully what would be heard from a good seat at a live concert. (A)

1070 *The Russian Viola* (works by Rubinstein, Glinka, Glazunov, Stravinsky, and Shostakovich); Nobuko Imai, viola; Roland Pöntinen, piano: BIS CD-358. A dynamic, clear recording with a fine balance between the viola and piano. The small-hall ambience and close-up sound fit well into a typical home listening room, especially if surround-sound processing is carefully applied by the listener. (A)

1071 *Sacred and Secular Music from Six Centuries*, The Hilliard Ensemble: Hyperion CDA 66370. Wonderful depth, clarity, and ambience highlight this disc. The only flaw is the usual traffic-noise rumble evident on most of the tracks. The recording was made at two locations, and the material recorded at St. John-at-Hackney has a quieter background than the tracks cut at St. Jude's-on-the-Hill. This is interesting since another work in our listing, assorted works by John Ireland, on the Chandos label (see 598), was also done at Jude's, and it has no background noise that I could hear. The Hyperion engineers should have made the whole recording at the first location or contacted the Chandos people to discover their secret. At least the ambience and fidelity of the sound were equally good at both locations. (Qualified A+)

1072 St. Saëns, Camille: *Symphony Number 3*; Widor, Charles Marie: *Symphony Number 6* (Allegro movement only), San Francisco Symphony Orchestra, Gean Guillou, organ: Philips 412 619-2. The most notable feature of the hard-to-record first work is the very deep and clear bass pedal notes (to below 18 Hz) about 9 minutes into the *poco-adagio*. Note that they are quite subdued and require careful listening. Overall, the recording is well done with fine detail and great dynamic range. At one time, a very good subwoofer company included a sample of this disc as a free demo item with the purchase of its products. (A+)

1073 St. Saëns, C.: *Symphony Number 3*; *Phaéton*, Royal Philharmonic Orchestra, Michael Murray, organ: Telarc 80274. Nice and clean with good hall depth and spaciousness. The organ parts are fairly good and a bit better than on an earlier Telarc effort with the Philadelphia Orchestra, not in this listing. However, the organ, which was recorded separately from the orchestra (and monitored on obviously deficient Madrigal Audio Labs Proceed PDP-II D/A speakers), cannot approach the depth, power, and realism of the device reproduced on 1072. The organ on the earlier (not listed) Telarc work was also recorded separately from the orchestra. (A)

1074 Sanborn, David: *Upfront* (with Marcus Miller, Steve Jordan, Ricky Peterson, Don Alias, John Purcell, and others): Elektra 61272-2. There is lots of synthesized and electronic backup in this essentially saxophone jazz album, but the sound is crisp and detailed with plenty of live-music punch. The sound stage is broad and imaging is quite good, although the depth seems a bit two-dimensional. The saxophone is the main feature of an album like this, and its tonality and focus were excellent. (B+)

1075 Santana: *Spirits Dancing in the Flesh*: Columbia CK 46065. Clean vocals with a good sound stage. This is heavily processed rock and roll, but the result is still less fuzzy in vocal quality (and even the instrumentation) than most other albums of this weight. There was a pretty good bass line on some tracks. (B)

1076 *Sarum Chant: Missa in Gallicantu and Four Hymns*, The Tallis Scholars: Gimell CDGIM 017. Reverberant, graceful, articulate, and real sounding, this release has the kind of church ambience demanded by music of this kind. Very good depth is evident as well, imparting an almost surround-sound effect. (A+)

1077 *Saxophone Concerti* (short works by Larsson, Glazunov, and Panula), New Stockholm Chamber Orchestra: BIS CD-218. This one is clean and spacious with fine stage depth. The solo sax sounds good and is well focused. This little jewel is a fairly early full-digital item recorded in 1982. (A)

1078 Scarlatti, Domenico: *Eighteen Sonatas*, Elaine Thorburgh, harpsichord: Koch 3-7014-2. This recording displays a close up, detailed, realistic in-your-listening-room presentation. There is no phasey or diffuse quality to mar the effect either. Outstanding microphone work is clearly evident in reproducing this difficult-to-record instrument. (A+)

1079 Scarlatti, D.: *The Virtuoso Scarlatti* (fifteen sonatas for harpsichord), Igor Kipnis, harpsichord: Chesky CD-75. This is almost a demo disc since five instruments were used and the listener can note the subtle differences if his or her system is able. There are a wonderful ambience and sense of hall space around each of the instruments that highlights the detail and transparency of this recording. A note on the disc insert warns that the harpsichord is a subtle instrument and

1080 *Scherzi Musicali* (short works by Schmelzer, Biber, and Walther), Musica Antiqua Köln: Archiv 429 230-2. Here we have a brilliant and forward sound that characterizes typical original-instrument performances and recordings. The result is transparent, clean, and very detailed. The most impressive bit of recorded acoustics on this disc is the sound of the "walk-on" by the orchestra at the beginning. (A)

1081 Schiff, David: *Music of David Schiff* (including *Scenes from Adolescence*), Chamber Music Northwest: Delos DE 3058. Although done at three locations, this series is uniformly clean and detailed with exemplary imaging from the assorted players of the Chamber Music ensemble. All three locales delivered fine hall acoustics and ambience. (As noted previously, some of the DE-prefix Delos recordings were previously released with a D/CD prefix.) (A+)

1082 Schmelzer, Johann: *Balletti und Sonaten am Wiener Kaiserhof*, Clemencic Consort: Preiser 93389. This disc displayed good spread and depth with fine imaging and clarity. The baroque original instruments are presented in a fairly close up perspective. (A)

1083 Schmelzer, J., and Georg Muffat: *Sonatas*, London Baroque: Harmonia Mundi France 901220. Close up, razor sharp, and full. The image is somewhat diffuse, but the sound stage has a good spread, and the clarity is exemplary in this original-instrument recording. The hall ambience is palpable and benefits from home-based surround enhancement. There is a small background hiss that may be the result of analog recording techniques. (Qualified A)

1084 Schneiderman, Rob: *Smooth Sailing* (with Rufus Reid and Billy Higgins): Reservoir CD-114. This jazz album is detailed, quite clean, and very close up. The closeness results in a sound stage that seems a bit contrived and in your face, but the effect is OK if the playback gain is backed off just a tad. I got much better results with some surround-sound enhancement. (B)

1085 Schnittke, Alfred: *Concerto Grosso Number 3*; *Sonata for Violin and Chamber Orchestra*; *Trio Sonata*, Stockholm Chamber Orchestra: BIS CD-537. This effort is very clear and detailed with a very good handling of the soloists. The violins and the piano are notably well focused. The sound is quite dynamic at times. (A+)

1086 Schnittke, A.: *Faust Cantata*; *Passacaglia for Large Orchestra* (and shorter works), Malmö Symphony Orchestra and Chorus (with Inger Blom, Mikael Bellina, Louis Devos, and Ulrick Cold): BIS CD-437. There is a wonderful clarity and depth here with a marvelous sound stage. Fine imaging and dynamics top off the program. (A)

1087 Schnittke, A.: *Concerto Grosso Number 4*; *Symphony Number 5*, Gothenburg Symphony Orchestra: BIS CD-427. Clean and detailed with plenty of dynamic range. Good imaging is quite apparent up front, but the overall sound still has a palpable and quite realistic hall ambience and bloom. Having a good frontal image and a good sense of recorded space is not always easy to achieve. (A+)

1088 Schnittke, A.: *Symphony Number 3*, Stockholm Philharmonic

Schoenberg (1089)

Orchestra: BIS CD-477. The sound field has nice depth and clarity with a spacious and realistic hall ambience. Fine dynamics and some impressive deep bass also highlight this recording. (A+)

1089 Schoenberg, Arnold: *Intégrale de l'Oeuvre Pour Piano*, Claude Helffer, piano: Harmonia Mundi France HMA 190752. The close up piano-in-your-room sound is clear and dynamic. The accompanying booklet is vague about when this recording was made (four dates are indicated, but two of them may refer to the date the enclosed essay was written and the copyright date of the score), but it may have been as early as 1976. The total lack of obnoxious hiss and the fine sound makes me believe that it was recorded at the latest date listed, 1992. (A)

1090 Schoenberg, A.: *Pelleas und Melisande*; Webern, Anton: *Passacaglia for Orchestra*, Scottish National Orchestra: Chandos CHAN 8619. This release has very good depth and detail with a bit less of that bright, brittle, somewhat forward sound typical on some recordings made by the SNO in Henry Wood Hall. (A+)

1091 Schönberg, Claude-Michel; Alain Boublil, and Herbert Kretzmer: *Les Miserables* (original London cast recording, with Colm Wilkinson, Roger Allam, Patti LuPone, Zoe Hart, and others): Relativity Records CD 8140. Is this pop Broadway-musical sound or opera? Who cares? It's great music. Overall, this release has a wonderful sound stage with a fine balance between orchestra, chorus, and soloists. The clarity is quite good. (B+)

1092 Schönberg, C.; A. Boublil, and H. Kretzmer: *Les Miserables* (original Broadway cast recording, with Colm Wilkinson, Terrence Mann, Randy Graff, Judy Kuhn, and others): Geffen 24151-2. This recording is as well done as 1091, with just a tad more punch and just a tad less sound-stage realism and envelopment. The soloists are closer and clearer but less realistic in placements within the ensemble. (B+)

1093 Schönberg, C.; A. Boublil, and H. Kretzmer: *Les Miserables*, the Philharmonia Orchestra (worldwide performance, with Gary Morris, Philip Quast, Debbie Byrne, Tracy Shayne, and others): Relativity/First Night 88561-1027-2. This is an astonishingly successful amalgam of performers recording their respective parts at different times and locales around the world. The orchestral-choral balance is near perfect, the clarity excellent, and the breadth of the sound superior to the two versions listed previously. This disc shows what talented engineers can accomplish. It also employs an organ for some parts, and that instrument's sound is quite impressive at times. This is the complete score, by the way, on three discs instead of the two apiece the others employ. (A)

1094 Schönberg, C.; A. Boublil, and H. Kretzmer: *Les Miserables*, Philharmonia Orchestra: Relativity/First Night 88561-1099-2. A single-disc batch of excerpts from the masterpiece performance above. (A)

1095 Schönherz, Richard, and Peter Scott: *One Night in Vienna* (with Paul McCandless, Brian MacLeod, Kenneth Nash, Kurt Wortman, and Rich Girard): Windham Hill WD-1060. Transparent, sparkling, and punchy (especially the 35 Hz bass drum) with a synthesized sound stage that is pleasant to listen to even if the result comes across as almost surrealistic. (B+)

1096 Schubert, Franz: *Complete Works for Violin and Piano*; Jaime Laredo, violin; Stephanie Brown, piano: Dorian DOR 90137. This release is smooth, transparent, and blessed with excellent hall ambience. The violin images very well, and the piano blends into the background in a properly sized and properly positioned manner. (A+)

1097 Schubert, F.: *Death and the Maiden*; Beethoven, Ludwig: *String Quartet Op. 135*, Hagen Quartet: Deutsche Grammophon 431 814-2. This release has wonderful hall realism and depth with an excellent sound stage and good detail. There are no audible faults that I could hear. The recording is a strong candidate for surround enhancement. Doing so can put you right there in the hall with the Hagen players. (A+)

1098 Schubert, F.: *The Last Quartets*, Melos Quartet: Harmonia Mundi France 901408/09. This is a nice and smooth effort, with good depth and a realistic sound-stage image. (A)

1099 Schubert, F.: *Mass Number 2*; *Mass Number 6*, Atlanta Symphony Orchestra and Chorus: Telarc 80212. Very smooth and spacious. Telarc handles large-scale material like this with near-complete expertise. The disc has fine clarity, good detail, and substantial hall envelopment. The soloists are very well sized and well positioned. The recording also works well with surround decoding or enhancement. Unfortunately, the minor hall rumble in the background is also enhanced by such manipulations. (Qualified A+)

1100 Schubert, F.: *Piano Quintet in A Major, "Trout,"* and *Quartet Number 13 in A Minor*, Cleveland Quartet: Telarc 80225. Here we have a very clean and well-imaged string sound with the typically difficult-to-record piano somewhat too reverberant and bloated by comparison. Consequently, the *Quartet* is the better-sounding piece. (A+ for the latter; A for the *Quintet*)

1101 Schubert, F.: *Sonata in B-flat Major*; *Four Impromptus*, Carol Rosenberger, piano: Delos D/CD 3018. Smooth and clear with a nice small-hall ambience. The perceived sound is quite close up, with the piano clearly not positioned on a stage a long distance away from the listener and thereby subjectively small in size. While Delos has produced piano recordings in the past with a solo-instrument image a bit too fuzzy, oversized, and diffuse for my taste (especially with concertos), this one is not bad, although it still may bother some tight-image fanatics. (A)

1102 Schubert, F.: *Songs* (Hyperion Schubert Edition, Volume 7); Elly Ameling, soprano; Graham Johnson, piano: Hyperion CDJ 33007. Overall, this effort exhibits a very realistic vocal-piano integration. This is backed up by a medium-size hall ambience neatly combined with a fairly close-up subjective listening distance. (A)

1103 Schubert, F.: *String Quartet in D Minor*; *String Quartet in A Minor*, Melos Quartet: Novalis 150 058-2. Overall, this one is well sized, smooth, and transparent with a nice balance between the ensemble and the recording environment. (A)

1104 Schubert, F.: *String Quintet in C Major*, Emerson String Quartet, with Mstislav Rostropovich, cello: Deutsche Grammophon D125035. Clean, smooth, and detailed and clearly not in the negative DGG tradition of old. I was impressed by the very good sound stage and depth. (A)

Schubert (1105)

1105 Schubert, F.: *Symphony Number 1*; *Symphony Number 4*, Hanover Band: Nimbus NI 5198. This recording has a clean period-instrument tonality with a good sound stage and realistic depth. There is a realistic and enveloping hall ambience here, and the subjective listening distance is midhall rather than close up. This tends to reduce the stridency that sometimes is exhibited by this kind of instrumentation. (A)

1106 Schubert, F.: *Symphony Number 3*, *Symphony Number 5*, Hanover Band: Nimbus NI 5172. The comments for 1105 apply here. (A)

1107 Schubert, F.: *Symphony Number 5*; *Rosamunde* (excerpts), Kölner-Rundfunk-Sinfonie-Orchester: EMI CDC 7 47877-2. Nice and detailed with good smoothness and a nice sense of stage depth and small-hall ambience. The violins seem just a tad brittle to my ears. (A)

1108 Schubert, F.: *Symphony Number 5*; *Symphony Number 8* (the "Unfinished"); *German Dances*, New York Chamber Symphony of the 92nd Street Y: Delos DE 3067. Smooth and clean in the Delos tradition, with good depth and spaciousness. There is a nice sense of hall space as well. (A)

1109 Schubert, F.: *Symphony Number 5*; *Symphony Number 8*, Staatskapelle Berlin: Denon 81757 71562. The image here is focused and clean with a realistic sound stage and the kind of string-tone smoothness that works of this type demand. (A)

1110 Schubert, F.: *Symphony Number 8*; Beethoven, L.: *Symphony Number 8*, Cleveland Orchestra: Telarc 80091. This version has a somewhat distant sound stage, a novelty for Telarc. The sound is still clear, detailed, and spacious with a fine realistic texture that coincident-microphone enthusiasts would say is a bit diffuse. (A)

1111 Schubert, F.: *Symphony Number 9*, Berlin Radio Symphony Orchestra: Denon 38C37-7035. There is good clarity and detail here with a realistic if somewhat distant sound stage. Notable dynamic range. All the box-insert program notes on my copy of this disc were in Japanese. (A)

1112 Schubert, F.: *Symphony Number 9*, Chicago Symphony Orchestra: Deutsche Grammophon 413 437-2. Clean, close up, and detailed with little negative multimiking artifacts. The violin sound is quite smooth, indicating the intelligent use of accent microphones. Overall, the recording is a bit on the dry side in ambience, a characteristic of a number of other DGG discs. However, this may suit some tastes. Surround enhancement, judiciously applied, can partially compensate for the dryness. (A)

1113 Schuller, George: *Lookin' up from Down Below* (with Joe Lovano, Tiger Okoshi, Gary Valente, and Ed Schuller): GM 3013CD. Remarkably clean, smooth, transparent jazz with mostly decent imaging. The latter is unfortunately marred by the positioning of the drums (Schuller's instrument, oddly enough), which tend to wander across the stage. This would be OK if two guys were playing, but that is not the case. (B+)

1114 Schuller, Gunther: *Jumpin's in the Future* (with assorted additional jazz works by Charlie Parker, George Gershwin, and others, all arranged by Schuller): GM 3010GM. This release displays a nice spacious sound that is intimate as well. The ambience is what is required here, and there is good depth and clarity. (B+)

1115 Schuman, William: *Symphony Number 7*; Balada, Leonardo: *Steel Symphony*, Pittsburgh Symphony Orchestra: New World NW 348-2. One interesting aspect of this disc is that it was engineered and produced by the Telarc team of Renner and Woods. It has the typical Telarc spacious and reverberant sound with fine clarity. Indeed it seems to be a better recording than a number of Telarc releases. (A+)

1116 Schumann, Robert: *Lieder*; Thomas Hampson, baritone; Geoffrey Parsons, piano: Teldec 44935-2. A good realistic stage image is apparent in this release, as is the expertly recorded hall ambience. Both the piano and the vocalist sound like they are in a real concert hall and not in a contrived studio situation. The listening position is up close in the best seats in the house. (A+)

1117 Schumann, R.: *Symphony Number 1*; *Symphony Number 4*, The Authentic Orchestra: Collins Classics 50022. This period-instrument product sounds more modern than others of its type—smooth, clean, with a notable lack of high-frequency brittleness and stridency. A small-scale sound is not evident, and the sound stage is well laid out. Overall, the effect is just a bit subdued in level and a touch too distant. Advancing the gain of your amplifier will compensate to some extent. (A)

1118 Schumann, R.: *Symphony Number 1*; *Symphony Number 4*, Baltimore Symphony Orchestra: Telarc 80230. This jewel is smooth, clean, and spacious with a very "modern" orchestral sound. The sound-stage depth is typically Telarc—produced by a somewhat phasey-sounding (to some at least) spaced array but subjectively pleasing when experienced in most home listening rooms. The effect of this technique, whether with two microphones or three (or more), is highly variable and depends upon the quality of the mikes, their placement, the level adjustments of the center microphone, the hall environment, and the intelligent use of any accent units. (A)

1119 Schumann, R.: *Symphony Number 1*; *Overture, Scherzo and Finale*; *Konzertstrück for Four Horns and Orchestra*, Seattle Symphony Orchestra (with Robert Bonnevie, Mark Robbins, David Knapp, and Scott Wilson, horns): Delos DE 3084. There is exemplary clarity here with realistic depth and transparency, a typical expert engineering job by John Eargle. The horn piece is a must listening experience for students of the instrument. (A+)

1120 Schumann, R.: *Symphony Number 2*; *Symphony Number 3*, Baltimore Symphony Orchestra: Telarc 80182. Overall, maybe just a little bit better than 1118, even though this one was recorded earlier. The same orchestra and hall were involved, but there was a slightly different microphone combination, a different engineer and different monitor speakers. Every little thing adds up. (A+)

1121 Schumann, R.: *Symphony Number 2*; *Symphony Number 3*, London Symphony Orchestra: Teldec 46446-2. This one is smooth and clean but with a somewhat distant listening perspective that will appeal to some listeners more than others. The imaging is still quite good in spite of the subjective distancing, as is the sound-stage depth and hall reverb. (A)

1122 Schütz, Heinrich: *Christmas and Easter Historias*; Kammerchor Stuttgart; Musica Flata Köln; Barokorchester Stuttgart: Sony SK 45943. This effort has a very good sound stage with the vocal and choral blend just about right. The clarity is quite good. The listening position is about midway back. (A)

1123 Schuur, Diane: *Deedles* (with Dave Grusin, Stan Getz, Don Grusin, and others): GRP-D-9510. Clean, spacious, and well defined, with fine jazz-vocal tonality and a good orchestral blend. Unfortunately, the vocal and orchestral qualities appear to exist in separate worlds. The vocals are characteristically positioned: too far out in front of the orchestra, no doubt to highlight their quality, with the usual loss of sound-stage realism. (B+)

1124 Schuur, D.: *In Tribute* (with a small army of backup instrumentalists): GRP GRD-2006. Smooth and clear (including the vocals) but with the balance between the many instruments and Ms. Schuur such that she is just too far in front. This certainly highlights her fine voice, but it detracts from the live music effect—unless you consider a live performance as one that has the vocals amplified by a big nightclub sound system. (B+)

1125 Schuur, D.: *Pure Schuur* (with David Benoit, Neil Stubenhaus, Carlos Vegas, and others): GRP GRD-9628. This effort is smooth and transparent with a good synthesized blend of instruments. The vocals are a bit close in relation to the backup (although not so much as in a typical GRP-Schuur release), and the sound stage is built up electrically, but the mix is professionally done and easy to listen to. (A)

1126 Schuur, D.: *Schuur Thing* (with Dave Grusin, Stan Getz, Lee Ritenour, and others): GRP-D-9531. In the GRP-Schuur tradition, with plenty of articulation and smoothness. Those qualities are as usual combined with a too-far-forward vocal track that results in sound that is pretty good when played on smaller systems (particularly automotive ones) but not as fine as it should be on better ones. This is especially the case when finicky audio enthusiasts like me are doing the listening. (B+)

1127 Schuur, D.: *Talkin' 'Bout You* (with Dave Grusin, Tom Scott, Steve Gadd, and others): GRP GRD-9567. This release is well balanced and clean, the vocals well integrated into the obviously (and expertly) pan-potted final mix. The vocal placement seems better than average for a GRP release. (A)

1128 Schuur, D.: *Timeless* (with Gerry Vinci, Stan Getz, and many others): GRP-D-9540. This release is smoother, better balanced, and more realistic than usual with a good vocal-instrumental blend and a good sound stage. Pan-potted sound-stage manipulations can work well, and this effort is superior to most, including most other GRP releases. (A)

1129 Schuur, D.: *Diane Schuur and the Count Basie Orchestra* (with Frank Foster, Freddie Green, Sonny Cohn, Dennis Mackrel, and others): GRP GRD-9550. This is a live performance that is punchy, clean, and reverberant with a bass line that is very deep and maybe a tad too strong at times, but impressive nonetheless. On less than bass-potent hi-fi systems the mix comes across as quite balanced, but really big ones may vibrate the walls a bit too much. The requirements of the live performance seems to have put some constraints on the engineers, and Ms. Schuur's voice is well blended and properly positioned in relation to the rest of the ensemble. Overall (the heavy bass notwithstanding), the disc has impressive sound, and this is possibly the best-engineered GRP-Schuur effort. (A)

1130 Schwarz, Harvie: *In a Different Light* (with Mike Stern, John Scofield, Leni Stern, Gene Bertoncini, Winard Harper, and Leon Parker): Blue Moon R2-79153. The tracks on this jazz release were done at two locations but have pretty much the same acoustic signature. I thought the clarity and detail were OK with a middistance sense of perspective and a somewhat bland texture. The drum set is properly sized and well positioned. (B)

1131 Scofield, John: *Electric Outlet* (with Steve Jordan, David Sanborn, Ray Anderson, and Peter Levin): Gramavision R2 79404. This jazz release has a better sound stage than 1132 with a tighter, better-focused guitar sound as well as equal clarity and dynamic contrast. (B+)

1132 Scofield, J.: *Meant to Be* (his quartet, with Joe Lovano, Marc Johnson, and Bill Stewart), Blue Note CDP 7 95479 2. This one has a wide close up sound stage with a somewhat diffuse instrumental spread (particularly the guitar, which comes close to undermining the effectiveness of the whole recording) but also with decent clarity and impact. (B)

1133 Scott, Tom: *Desire* (with Vance Colaiuta, Neil Stubenhaus, Buzzy Feiten, and others): Elektra Musician 60162-2. Nicely balanced jazz with fine articulation, a smooth sound field, plenty of tastefully handled synthesized spaciousness, and good percussion impact. The vocals are well imaged and clearly recorded. Not bad for a 1982 recording. (B+)

1134 Scott, T.: *Streamlines* (with Neil Stubenhaus, Richard Tee, Eric Gale, and others): GRP GRD-9555. This recording is spacious and reverberant with a wide, well-defined (but to me, obviously synthesized) sound stage. Needless to say, the dynamics are impressive, and the presentation is dominated by a bright percussive sound. The subjective impression contrasts sharply with *Desire*, above, and *Target*, below—but this disc, although newer, is not overwhelmingly better than either of them, just different. (B+)

1135 Scott, T.: *Target* (with Harvey Mason, Neil Stubenhaus, Carlos Rios, Paul Jackson, Ernie Watts, Maria Muldaur, and quite a few others): Atlantic 80106-2. This is a very transparent direct-to-two-track (nonpanpotted) jazz recording with fine detail and good soundstaging. What we have here is tight, well-controlled sound that may be a bit too dry for some but comes across just right on my bigger system. Surround processing really opened things up, and I heartily recommend such manipulations with discs of this kind. (B+)

1136 Scott, T.: *Them Changes* (with Barnaby Finch, Eric Gale, Pat Kelley, and others): GRP GRD-9613. This release is bright, brassy, clean, and punchy with plenty of detail and a forward, up-front, well-focused saxophone image sitting in the midst of the supporting ensemble. In a nutshell, it is pretty much like *Streamlines* (see 1134). These four roughly equal but distinct-sounding discs by Tom Scott are a good example of how different engineers can manipulate the sound of the same performer. (B+)

1137 Scriabin, Alexander: *Piano Concerto in F-Sharp Minor; Symphony*

Seal (1138)

Number 3, Stockholm Philharmonic Orchestra, Roland Pöntinen, piano: BIS CD-475. The sound is distant but clear, the well-placed and finely imaged piano sound integrated into a realistic sound stage. (A)

1138 *Seal*: Sire/Warner 26627-2. There is good clarity here, especially the vocals, with a good sound stage and sometimes impressive (for a rock album) deep bass. (B+)

1139 Serrie, John: *And the Stars Go with You*: Miramar MPCD-2001. This is ethereal New Age synthesized music that has striking depth and spaciousness. Some really deep bass is apparent at times. Serrie did his own engineering on this disc, and although a bit phasey at times, those effects are probably deliberate. The material responded well to surround enhancement. (B+)

1140 *The Service of Venus and Mars* (music for the Knights of the Garter, 1340–1440), The Gothic Voices: Hyperion CDA 66238. Smooth, clean, and detailed with plenty of hall ambience and depth. As usual, this kind of recording is made even better if the listener has a surround-sound processor available to enhance things. Unfortunately, the usual church-cathedral background noise (this is another work recorded at St. Jude's) is also enhanced by such manipulations. (Qualified A+)

1141 Severinsen, Carl "Doc": *Facets* (with Ernie Watts, Lee Ritenour, Peter Erskine, Steve Kujala, Alan Pasqua, Leon Gaer, Paulinho Da Costa, and many others): Amherst 93319. This is certainly the best Severinsen album I have heard, with superior perspective, sound staging, and detail. (A+)

1142 Severinsen, Doc: *The Tonight Show Band* (with Gil Falco, Bruce Paulson, Erine Tack, Ross Tompkins, and several others): Amherst 93311. This disc has a distant perspective that eventually comes across as quite realistic and unforced, particularly if given home-based surround-processor treatment. Even a Dolby processor (a basic model or a Pro Logic unit with the center steering shut off) opens things up. The disc also responded well to enhancement by a Carver "sonic hologram" processor. (A)

1143 Severinsen, D.: *The Tonight Show Band, Volume II* (with the same crew as volume 1): Amherst 93312. This version is every bit as good as the first Tonight Show album. (A)

1144 Severinsen, D.: *The Tonight Show Band, Once More . . . with Feeling* (with Tony Bennett, Wynton Marsalis, Tommy Newsom, John Bambridge, Pete Christlieb, Snooky Young, and a slew of other first-rate performers): Amherst 94405. The lettering on the disc is AAD. If this is the case, it is proof positive that the most important thing in doing a recording, once the analog or digital tape recorder meets minimum standards, is the studio environment, microphone quality, microphone placement, and mixing. This may be the cleanest, best-recorded pop AAD disc I have ever heard, with the possible exception of *Däfos* (see 322). The sound stage in particular is very good. I do not know why the engineers chose to use an analog recorder for this job, but it did not hurt things one bit. Nearly equal to the *Facets* album (see 1141). (A)

1145 Severinsen, D.: *Unforgettably Doc*, with the Cincinnati Pops: Telarc 80304. This release has the marvelous trumpet sound we would expect from a Telarc recording of Severinsen. The orchestral accompaniment is clear, detailed, and spacious. The orchestral sound is a bit more substantial than what is usually heard on a recording by this guy. (A+)

1146 Shadowfax: *The Odd Get Even*: Private Music 2065-2-P. This rock album is clean and decently clear with a good fabricated sound stage and potent dynamics. (B+)

1147 Shankar, Ravi: *The Incredible Ravi Shankar*, playing Raga Charukauns: Chhanda Dhara SNCD 2286. The sound stage on this release appears to be positioned some distance from the listening location, but the result is still quite clean. The solo instrument is well centered and neatly focused with no spaced-array microphone phasiness. (A)

1148 Shankar, R., and Philip Glass: *Passages* (assorted musicians performing): Private Music 2074-2-P. This collaborative effort by these two modern composers (one eastern and one western) is clearly recorded with a broad sound stage. To my ears, the perceived depth is just a bit shallow. (A)

1149 Shaw, Woody: *Imagination* (with Kirk Lightsey, Steve Turre, Ray Drummond, and Carl Allen): Muse MCD 5338. Decently good and clean jazz, although the trumpet sounds overprocessed and appears to be in a larger room than the rest of the instruments. So much for the direct-to-two-track note in the insert. The piano is well focused but also sounds somewhat boxy and constricted. The drums sound clean. Barely makes the list. (B)

1150 Shearing, George: *Breakin' Out* (his trio, with Ray Brown and Marvin Smith): Concord Jazz CCD-4335. This one is forward, clear, and crisp with a good feeling of small-club ambience. The drums are well focused, but the piano seems just a touch diffuse—not a good thing considering that it is the featured item. There is good tonality to the instrument, however. (B)

1151 Shearing, G.: *Grand Piano*: Concord Jazz CCD-4281. Unlike the previous release (1150), this piano-solo disc features a well-focused piano sound, cleanly recorded and combined with an equally good nightclub small-room ambience. (B+)

1152 Shearing, G., and Ernestine Anderson: *A Perfect Match* (with Neil Swainson and Jeff Hamilton): Concord Jazz CCD-4357. There is a very good size volume-level balance between all members of this small ensemble. Even the drums are not overly spread out. Nice clarity and detail. (B+)

1153 Shew, Bobby, and Chuck Findley: *Trumpets No End* (with Art Resnick, John Patitucci, and Sherman Ferguson): Delos DE 4003. This jewel is bright, brassy (what else?), and smooth with a good jazz sound-stage focus and a proper nightclub sense of space. (A)

1154 Short, Bobby: *Late Night at the Cafe Carlyle* (with Beverly Peer and Robert Scott): Telarc 83311. This jazz release is articulate and unadulterated, particularly Short's voice, with a good instrumental-vocal balance. (A)

1155 Shorter, Wayne: *Joy Rider* (with Terri Carrington, Nathan East, and Patrice Rushen): Columbia CK 44110. Punchy, clean, and quite good in instrumental textures and blending. The highlights on this jazz release are a decent sound stage and occasionally good bass. Reverberation is heavily applied, and the synthesized effect is not objectionable. The result is anything but live-stage real, however. (B)

1156 Shostakovich, Dmitri: *Concerto Number 1, for Piano, Trumpet and Strings*, I Musici de Montréal: Chandos CHAN 8357. This release has the usual middistance to close-up listening perspective preferred by Chandos, with fine, realistic clarity and balance. The piano is well positioned in relation to the orchestra, and the trumpet is thankfully made a part of the ensemble and not pulled way out in front by an accent microphone to enhance its clarity and presence. (A)

1157 Shostakovich, D.: *Symphony Number 1*; *Symphony Number 6*, Royal Philharmonic Orchestra: London 425 609-2. Smooth and transparent with the usual large-scale London sound and an almost three-dimensional sound stage (not always a London strong point). A great dynamic range is a salient feature here. Thankfully, the violins are less cutting than typical for London, a welcome change. Ashkenazy directs this one, and it's his kind of music. (A+)

1158 Shostakovich, D.: *Symphony Number 1*; *Symphony Number 9*, London Philharmonic Orchestra: London 414 677-2. Good clarity, depth, and sound stage. The violins are, as in the recording above, smoother and less strident than typical for a London recording job. The dynamics are also quite good. I thought the previous disc had a slight edge in overall realism. (A)

1159 Shostakovich, D.: *Symphony Number 5*; *Ballet Suite Number 5 from the Bolt*, Scottish National Orchestra: Chandos CHAN 8650. This one is smooth, deep, powerful, and vibrant. It has better sound-stage depth than the Telarc release (see 1162) but is no better than that disc in clarity and tonality. This effort is more distant than that work also. The distance works well, however, and I consider this recording of the fifth one of the best. (A+)

1160 Shostakovich, D.: *Symphony Number 5*; *Festive Overture*, London Symphony Orchestra: Collins Classics 11082. Distant to the extent that higher than normal playback volume is mandatory. The result is very clear once the gain is advanced, especially the basses and cellos, with fine hall ambience and depth. The distant sound notwithstanding, I imagine that this disc will be a bit bright for some people's tastes. (A)

1161 Shostakovich, D.: *Symphony Number 5*, Concertgebouw Orchestra: London 410 017-2. This one is smooth and clean with good dynamics and a nice sense of hall space. The left-right spread is impressive. The sound is quite similar to the earlier Telarc version (see 1162). (A)

1162 Shostakovich, D.: *Symphony Number 5*, Cleveland Orchestra: Telarc 80067. A very realistic and detailed piece of work. In the best Telarc tradition, this 1981 recording has very transparent sound with great impact. The imaging is also quite good for a spaced-array microphone job, and the central focus is exemplary. (A)

1163 Shostakovich, D.: *Symphony Number 5*; *Symphony Number 9*, Atlanta Symphony Orchestra: Telarc 80215. Close up, dynamic and vibrant with even more impact than the earlier effort reviewed above. The disc delivers a good sound-stage spread and notable depth (in the Telarc tradition, of course), with marvelous clarity. The ambient background is marred by a subtle and continuous hall rumble (sounds like the air-conditioning unit) that is going to be a problem only if you have a subwoofer with significant output below 30 Hz. My smaller and larger systems would not reproduce this sound when their low-bass equalizers were set at their "bypass" modes, cutting the bass at 12 dB per octave below 45 and 35 Hz, respectively and considerably more steeply than that below 20 Hz. (Qualified A+)

1164 Shostakovich, D.: *Symphony Number 7*, Scottish National Orchestra: Chandos CHAN 8623. Recorded in a different hall than this orchestra's recording of the *Symphony 5* (see 1159), the result is still vibrant and dynamic and maybe even richer sounding. There is depth aplenty combined with a sound stage that lacks for nothing. (A+)

1165 Shostakovich, D.: *Symphony Number 7*, Dallas Symphony Orchestra: Dorian DOR 90161. This one is a bit distant but blessed with fine detail nonetheless. The sound stage is deep, and the hall ambience is near perfect. The string section is realistically "unstrident," a characteristic of nearly every Dorian symphonic recording. A lot of engineers shy away from accurately recording the violins, mainly because many listeners have never heard the things live and consider anything but a bright sound as inaccurate. (A+)

1166 Shostakovich, D.: *Symphony Number 8*, London Symphony Orchestra: Collins 12712. The low record-playback level of this disc, especially in comparison to London version (see 1167), may fool you. Turn up the gain and hear the impact. Powerful and dynamic with good clarity and depth. The bass range is especially impressive during the bass drum "whacks," and the violin smoothness is notably better than on the London disc. (A+)

1167 Shostakovich, D.: *Symphony Number 8*, Concertgebouw Orchestra: London 411 616-2. Clean, clear, and forward with a wide but somewhat flat-appearing sound stage. The violins are a bit edgy, in the London tradition. Nevertheless, one has to be impressed with the dynamic range and the left-right spread, especially considering that it was a 1983 digital effort. The overall sound is what would be heard from the front of the hall, which may account for the violin sound. (A)

1168 Shostakovich, D.: *Symphony Number 8*, National Symphony Orchestra: Teldec 74719-2. Dynamic, big, and powerful with good clarity and detail. Not as forward as the London version (see 1167), which may appeal to some listeners. Overall, however, this 1992 recording is no better than that earlier one, and I would still judge it a bit inferior to the Collins version (see 1166). (A)

1169 Shostakovich, D.: *Symphony Number 9*; *Festive Overture*; *Suite from Katerina Ismailova*, Scottish National Orchestra: Chandos CHAN 8587. In spite of being recorded in a different hall, this work is a near sonic clone of the same orchestra's recording of the *Symphony 7* (see 1164). (A+)

1170 Shostakovich, D.: *Symphony Number 10*; *Ballet Suite Number 4*, Scottish National Orchestra: Chandos CHAN 8630. In the SNO-Chandos tradition, with the usual superlatives quite appropriate. Stunningly well done with remarkable depth, detail, and dynamics. The sound stage is a bit closer than 1171's. The second movement is something I would choose to show off my stereo. I believe this is state-of-the-art sound. (A+)

1171 Shostakovich, D.: *Symphony Number 10*; *Festive Overture*, Helsinki Philharmonic Orchestra: Delos DE 3089. A somewhat distant sound stage can often work well, and that is the case here. The overall effect is just a tad dry and indicates a small hall, but the sound is also clear and balanced with excellent instrumental imaging. The somewhat withdrawn orchestral balance is probably more the result of hall acoustics than anything else. Some parts of this disc come across better than others, and I found that both of my surround processors enhanced the playback quality of this recording considerably. (A)

1172 Shostakovich, D.: *Symphony Number 10*; *Chamber Symphony*, Royal Philharmonic Orchestra: London 433 028-2. Dynamic, clean, and reverberant. This effort has a very good string tone and good depth. It is rare for a London recording to top one by Delos, but I believe this effort is a slightly superior one (see 1171). Compared to the Chandos effort (see 1170), we'll make it a toss-up. (A+)

1173 Shostakovich, D.: *Symphony Number 11*, Helsinki Philharmonic: Delos D/CD 3080. Smooth, clean, and detailed with a good sound-stage spread and good depth. The small-hall ambience of this recording highlights the nature of this work quite well. Similar in character to 1171. (A)

1174 Shostakovich, D.: *Symphony Number 11*, Gothenburg Symphony Orchestra: Deutsche Grammophon 429 405-2. Forward, detailed, and cleanly recorded with plenty of dynamic impact to contrast with the delicately handled quieter sections. There is good depth and spread too with an exciting front-row sound. This is quite an accomplishment for the usually not so impressive DGG label. (A+)

1175 Shostakovich, D.: *Symphony Number 13 (Babi Yar)*, Concertgebouw Orchestra, Choir of the Concertgebouw Orchestra: London 417 261-2. This release is smooth, full, rich, and first class with marvelous depth and clarity. I felt there was very good placement and sizing of the solo vocalists. This one is certainly an indication of what the current London engineers are capable of. (A+)

1176 Shostakovich, D.: *24 Preludes & Fugues, Op. 87*, Keith Jarrett, piano: ECM 1469/70. A very nice close up sound with a tight, nonphasey image. The ambience is perfect: small-hall and intimate. (A+)

1177 Sibelius, Jean: *Symphony Number 1*; *Karela Suite*; *Finlandia*, Oslo Philharmonic: EMI 7 54273-2. This effort displays a good sound stage spread with equally good imaging. The overall depth is about average for a good classical recording, and the clarity is fine. It is certainly better than average for an EMI/Angel release, another indication that the company is finally ready for the digital age. (A)

1178 Sibelius, J.: *Symphony Number 1*; *Symphony Number 5*, Atlanta Symphony Orchestra: Telarc 80246. Here we have a typical broad and somewhat diffuse Telarc sound stage with good depth and clarity—and realistic dynamics. The occasional intrusion of some low-level hall rumble dictates turning your subwoofer off. I have noticed this characteristic on a number of otherwise good Telarc-Atlanta discs, indicating that they would do well to employ more bass-potent monitor speakers. (Qualified A)

1179 Sibelius, J.: *Symphony Number 2*, Cleveland Orchestra: Telarc 80095. This recording has the usual

Telarc open and spacious sound with fine clarity. The effect is just a tad more diffuse and lacking in precise imaging than it should be. (A)

1180 Sibelius, J.: *Symphony Number 2*; *Finlandia*, New York Philharmonic Orchestra: Teldec 46317-2. This recording has less left-to-right spread than 1179 but with a bit more front-to-back depth and an excellent stage image (giving the impression of a coincident-array microphone job). The result is smooth, full, and rich with a fine combination of realistic orchestral detail and hall ambience. (A+)

1181 Sibelius, J.: *Symphony Number 3*; *Belshazzar's Feast Suite*; *King Christian II Suite*, Finnish Radio Symphony Orchestra: RCA 60434-2. Smoothly defined, transparent, and brilliant with a well-laid-out sound stage and good depth. The overall listening perspective is close up and front row. (A+)

1182 Sibelius, J.: *Symphony Number 4*; *Canzonetta*; *The Oceanides*, Gothenburg Symphony Orchestra: BIS CD-263 (also available from the Musical Heritage Society as 512873A). This outstanding disc is smooth, spacious, and full of depth and dynamic contrasts. The hall image is enveloping and realistic. Overall, quite clean and revealing of abundant detail. (A+)

1183 Sibelius, J.: *Symphony Number 5*, Philharmonic Orchestra: London 410 016-2. This release has great depth and clarity with just a bit of sub–25 Hz hall rumble intruding from the background that will make you want to switch off your subwoofer. Doing so should not affect the instrumental sound. (Qualified A)

1184 Sibelius, J.: *Symphony Number 7*; *Kuolema*; *Night Ride and Sunrise*, Gothenburg Symphony Orchestra: BIS CD-311. Although the microphone arrangement for this disc differs somewhat from that of 1182 (fewer elements appear to have been used), the overall result is quite similar. As in that disc, the sound is smooth, spacious, deep, and dynamic with good clarity. (A+)

1185 Simon, Carly: *Coming Around Again*: Arista ARCD 8443. Nice and smooth pop sound with plenty of synthesized reverb and an enveloping sound stage. There is some nice and fairly deep bass at times. The all-important vocals are pretty smooth with some midrange emphasis. (B+)

1186 Simon, C.: *Spoiled Girl*: Epic EK 39970. This one is reverberant, punchy, and fairly smooth. There is just a bit of buzziness and sibilance in the voice, but the central image is OK, and the sound stage is broad and enveloping. A recording like this does well when played back on a typical automotive system. (B)

1187 Simon, Paul: *Graceland*: Warner 25447-2. Punchy, reverberant, and somewhat more distant on some tracks than others. The effect is similar to having a more distant seat at an electrified concert. The tracks that are more forward are not necessarily better, just different. Overall, the sound stage is obviously synthesized but still well defined. The vocals are quite well recorded. (B+)

1188 Simon, P.: *Hearts and Bones*: Warner 23942-2. This release is fairly clear and clean with good percussive dynamics. The sound stage is wildly synthesized but the vocals are well imaged and reasonably free from microphone and mixer artifacts. (B)

1189 Simon, P.: *The Rhythm of the Saints*: Warner 26098-2. This one has a highly synthesized and spacious sound stage with lots of percussion coming from all over. There is fair detail and transparency with decent vocal focus and clarity. It's not a great recording job, but it's not chopped liver either. (B)

1190 Skynyrd, Lynyrd: *1991*: Atlantic 82258-2. There is good impact on this one combined with plenty of solid rock-style bass. The latter has the kind of large-room reverb that imparts a live-concert feel to a presentation of this type. I also thought the clarity was better than average for a rock effort, and there was good left-to-right spread. A recording like this reacts positively to surround enhancement. (B+)

1191 Slaughter: *Stick It Live*: Chrysalis F2 21816. There is plenty of satisfying rock-and-roll dynamics on this one and decent depth too. The vocals are typically lost in the reverb but still come across with the kind of impact aficionados cherish. (B)

1192 Smetana, Bedrich: *The Complete Czech Dances*: Antonin Kubalek, piano: Dorian DOR 90122. This effort exhibits very clean sound with a fine blend of solo piano and hall ambience. The recording has a definite you-are-there (in a small hall) sound-stage perspective. (A+)

1193 Smetana, B.: *Má Vlast*, Milwaukee Symphony Orchestra: Telarc 80265. Spacious to the point of being a tad diffuse in central imaging but with great depth and clarity. Some buffs will love the direct-sound phasey quality, and others will be somewhat put off by it. In some listening rooms the effect can be quite pleasing. (A)

1194 Smith, Hale: *Innerflexions*; Silver, Sheila: *Sonata for Cello and Piano*; Hoffman, Joel: *Duo for Viola and Piano*: CRI CD 590. There is fine clarity and depth on this recording of works by these contemporary composers. The sound stage is quite good with excellent imaging from most of the instruments, although the piano seems just a tad diffuse on the *Sonata*. (A)

1195 Smith, Marvin: *Keeper of the Drums* (with Steve Coleman, Robin Eubanks, Mulgrew Miller, Ralph Moore, Lonnie Plaxico, and Wallace Roney): Concord Jazz CCD-4325. This jazz disc is smooth, clean and a bit distant, but not enough to ruin the effect. The good overall hall ambience makes the distance seem plausible, and the left-to-right imaging is quite good with the exception of the drums, which are just too wide across the stage to mimic realism. The drums do have more punch than in 1196. This is interesting because I believe the one reviewed here is the older of the two. (B+)

1196 Smith, Marvin: *The Road Less Traveled* (with James Williams, Robert Hurst, Wallace Roney, Steve Coleman, Ralph Moore, Robin Eubanks, and Kenyatte Abdur-Rahman): Concord Jazz CCD-4397. A nice sound stage, but the subjective effect is a bit distant. The overall sound is good and clean, but the drums are less dynamic than they should be in a performance of this kind. They sound electrically compressed. What's more, they appear to be physically too wide compared to the size of the rest of the combo and definitely too broad of beam in light of their lack of dynamic impact. A drum set should not stretch clear across the sound stage in a recording with this kind of left-to-right ensemble spread. (B)

1197 Snidero, Jim: *Storm Rising*

(with Mulgrew Miller, Peter Washington, and Jeff Hirshfield): Ken Music 006. This release is clean, vibrant, and close up in perspective with fine imaging and a good bass line. (B+)

1198 *Solo Cantatas* (short works by Monteverdi, Vivaldi, Haydn, and Rossini); Teresa Berganza, mezzo-soprano; English Chamber Orchestra: Claves CD 50-9016. The excellent sound stage and depth of this release enhances the easily discernible sense of instrumental realism. The overall blend is smooth, clear, and balanced. As with most fine recordings, this one has a good midhall listening perspective. (A+)

1199 *Sonate Concertate in Stil Moderno* (virtuoso instrumental music by Castello and Scarani), Concerto Palatino: Accent 9058-D. This presentation displays wonderful depth, a realistic sound-stage spread, and a real-hall sense of envelopment. The notable instrumental clarity of this recording is just what is needed for music of this kind. (A+)

1200 Sondheim, Stephen: *Into the Woods*, original London-cast recording (with Julia McKenzie, Imelda Staunton, Patsy Rolands, and Clive Carter): RCA 60752-2-RC. A feature here is the wide sound stage and the very close up perspective. This recording presents a front-row seat for sure. The Dolby surround encoding (another feature) works very well, although standard stereo playback also worked in an exemplary manner. More recordings are appearing with this technique, and I feel this is a very good thing. This is eminently clear and detailed sound combined with an impressive dynamic range. (A)

1201 *A Song for Francesca: Music in Italy, 1330–1430*, The Gothic Voices: Hyperion CDA 66286. Smooth, clean, and just a bit more forward than ideal — also than what is usually found on other discs produced by Hyperion. The vocals are just a touch edgy at times, although this characteristic may actually aid in articulation when the disc is played on speaker systems having a slightly muted treble (very common). The usual low-level hall-sound "grunge" (or traffic noise) fills out the background, which should be no problem if the playback speakers have less than room-shaking deep bass capabilities. (Qualified A)

1202 *The Sound of Cellos* (the Yale Cellos play favorites by Pachelbel, Vivaldi, Albinoni, Rachmaninoff, Händel, Joplin, Popper, and Veracini): Delos D/CD 3042. This performance displays a solid full sound with plenty of detail and bite. The recording is very smooth overall with a nice hall ambience that comes across even better with home-playback surround enhancement. (A)

1203 Sowerby, Leo: *Organ Music* (including *Fantasy for Flute Stops, Requiescat in Pace, Symphony in G Major*), Catherine Crozier, organ: Delos D/CD 3075. This jewel sounds open and reverberant with a realistic placement of the organ in the hall. The depth is notable, as is the subtle deep bass. If you have a surround-sound device, using it makes this marvelous disc sound even better. (A+)

1204 Spies: *By Way of the World* (with Paul Freeman, Richard Hahn, David Witham, Jon Crosse, Jay Anderson, and numerous guest players): Telarc 83305. Another un-Telarc-like multimicrophone jazz-pop disc that employs the same Dolby-compatible Shure "HTS Stereosurround" process that ProArte uses on some of its recordings. The result is superclear with great impact and detail and an interesting although not particularly realistic hall ambience. More recordings using this process will certainly be made in the future, and it should also work well for minimalist-microphone-recorded classical material. (A+)

1205 Spies: *Music of Espionage* (with Steve Schaeffer, Mike Hamilton, Abraham Laboriel, Alan Deremo, and quite a few others): Telarc 85503. This is the earlier of the two Spies albums listed here, and it still has all the impact of and clarity of the second one. There was no surround encoding on this first attempt, but running the results through a decoder at your end will open things up even more. There is lots of percussive force and even though the overall effect is multimicrophone synthesized, the disc is hi-fi demo in quality and a lot of fun. (A+)

1206 Spinal Tap: *Break Like the Wind*: MCAD 10514. Send-up-album or not (love the title), this group has given us a recording with impressive impact, good clarity, and a decent sound-stage spread. We need more rock and roll like this. (B+)

1207 Starer, Robert: *Concerto for Cello and Orchestra*; Wernick, Richard: *Viola Concerto*; Wilson, Thomas: *Concerto for Piano and Orchestra*, ProArte Chamber Orchestra of Boston: CRI CD 618. This one has a fairly realistic sound stage with good detail and a proper small-hall ambience. The instruments used in the three solo parts all image well and are suitably placed in relation to the ensemble, although the piano is a bit more diffuse than it should be. (A)

1208 *Stars and Stripes: Marches, Fanfares and Wind Band Spectacular*, Cleveland Symphonic Winds: Telarc 80099. This early Telarc digital effort is very realistic, clear, and vibrant with the usual spaced-array sense of hall envelopment. A remarkable achievement, and it was recorded in 1978–79! This disc is a good example of why Telarc has become such a dominant force in the recording world. Whatever one thinks of the three-spaced-microphone technique, this recording has a lot to offer. (A)

1209 *Steelheart*: MCAD-6368. There is lots of impact on this rock release with good deep bass at times. The stage impression is broad and spacious. (B+)

1210 Steely Dan: *Gaucho*: Mobile Fidelity UDCD 545. Another "gold" reissue that is much better than this company's release of the earlier Steely Dan album *Aja*. Good clarity, sound-stage spread, and dynamics. Gold's nice, but they could have done as good a job more cheaply if they had stuck with aluminum. I know the purer metal lasts longer, but is this disc really time-capsule material? (B+)

1211 Steps Ahead: *NYC* (with Mike Mainieri, Steve Kahn, Tony Levin, Steve Smith, and others): Capitol/Intuition CDP 7 91354 2. There is nice percussive detail and impact on this one. The sound stage is typically contrived, but it does have a decent lateral spread, and the reverb is not overdone. It is certainly better than average for a Capitol recording. (B)

1212 Stern, Mike: *Jigsaw* (with Bob Berg, Michael Brecker, Jim Beard, Jeff Andrews, Peter Erskine, Dennis Chambers, and Manolo Badrena): Atlantic 82027-2. Punchy, clean, well-blended jazz with good synthesized depth and decent imaging except for Stern's guitar, which often seems to be coming from the whole area between the speakers and seems phasey to boot. Pretty good otherwise. (B+)

1213 Stern, M.: *Odd or Even* (with Lincoln Goines, Bob Berg, Dennis Chambers, Ben Perowsky, and Don Alias): Atlantic 82297-2. Dynamic, smooth, and well done. The electric guitar is big and robust and dominates the sound field, but the other instruments are distinct and clean and well laid out. The synthesized sound stage works with music of this kind. (A)

1214 Stern, M.: *Time in Place* (with Bob Berg, Michael Brecker, Jim Beard, Jeff Andrews, Peter Erskine, Don Alias, and Don Grolnick): Atlantic 81840-2. Much less stage spread than 1213 with a much more distant listening perspective. The record is clean and clear nonetheless, but is generally more subdued and less technically interesting. (B)

1215 Still, William Grant: *Selected Works*, Videmus: New World Records 80399-2. This is an excellent example of works by modern black composer William Grant Still, showing off the sound of a solo piano, violin, and baritone voice. This disc has good clarity, the vocals and instruments well placed. The blending of these is also very well handled. I felt that the nice hall feel was made even better with a bit of surround enhancement. It is often true that smaller ensembles are better helped by such manipulations than larger ones. (A)

1216 Sting: *The Soul Cages*: A&M 7502-16405-2. This release is very well balanced, clear, and dynamic for a rock disc. It has a wide-range response with a very wide stage spread, almost as if the master tape had been run through a Carver, Lexicon, or Sound Concepts cross-talk-canceling device before being transferred to disc. Both the Q-Sound and Roland RSS encoding processes can achieve this kind of effect, and they may have been used to produce this disc. Surround enhancement, via a processor attached to your home system, is almost a must to get the full impact of this recording since the additional enhancement really fills out the sound field to the rear. (A)

1217 Stradella, Alessandro: *San Giovanni Battista*, Les Musiciens du Louvre: Erato 45739-2. There is good vocal imaging and clarity here with a close-to-listener sound stage that works well with this kind of music. The instrumental parts are positioned well and exhibit equally fine detail. (A+)

1218 Strata Institute: *Cipher Syntax* (with Steve Coleman, Greg Osby, Dave Gilmore, and others): JMT 834 425-2. Punchy, detailed, often cutting, and quite variable from track to track. Some pieces are tightly focused, and others are more diffuse and phasey. Clearly an experiment in modern jazz that often sounds quite impressive—and from an analog master, yet. (B+)

1219 Strauss, Johann: *Die Fledermaus*, Vienna Philharmonic Orchestra and Choir (with Wolfgang Brendel, Kiri Te Kanawa, Tom Krause, and others): Philips 432 157-2. This release has nice orchestral textures, a decent stage spread, and a fine instrumental balance. The solo vocals are well positioned and properly sized most of the time. However, they occasionally seem to swell to hall-filling dimensions in direct proportion to their need to sound louder. The engineers are offering more assistance here than they should. Nevertheless, the clarity of the work is notable, and the overall quality of the recording makes for a fulfilling experience. (A)

1220 Strauss, J.: *The Virtuoso Johann Strauss* (paraphrases and arrangements of assorted Strauss melodies by Rosenthal, Tausig, Godowsky, and Schultz-Evler), Thomas Labé, piano: Dorian DIS-80102. This disc exhibits an excellent piano tonality with a very good you-are-there sound stage combined with realistic hall ambience. There is just a bit of stage-induced microphone feedback at times. As in most cases, this should not unsettle a typical sound system, one that lacks a big subwoofer. (Qualified A)

1221 Strauss, Richard: *Also Sprach Zarathustra*; *Dance of the Seven Veils*; *Four Symphonic Interludes from Intermezzo* (the title on the box cover is *Thus Spake Zarathustra*), Seattle Symphony Orchestra: Delos D/CD 3052. Here we have an excellent blend of instruments with outstanding depth, clarity and perspective. Needless to say, there is very impressive deep bass on the first piece. This is an exceptionally well-done recording. (A+)

1222 Strauss, R.: *Also Sprach Zarathustra Tod und Verklärung*, Vienna Philharmonic Orchestra: Telarc 80167. This one is well recorded, clean, and dynamic, with a realistic sound stage. On a work of this scale, the intelligent use of the three-omni array can produce impressive results. The deep bass, although impressive, does not quite match that of 1221. (A)

1223 Strauss, R.: *Concerto for Oboe and Small Orchestra*; *Le Bourgeois Gentilhomme*, Stockholm Sinfonietta: BIS CD-470. Each of these pieces was recorded at different times and places with somewhat different recording techniques. In the BIS tradition, both are spacious and somewhat diffuse, a characteristic that can be complementary to the music in a small listening room but a bit overblown in a larger one. The clarity and dynamics are quite good. (A)

1224 Strauss, R.: *Don Juan*; *Don Quixote*, Chicago Symphony Orchestra: Erato 45625-2. This recording displays a very good delineation of assorted individual instruments working within the orchestra. The hall ambience is good, and the sound-stage spread is OK. Both pieces give the listener a midhall seat. (B+)

1225 Strauss, R.: *Don Juan*; *Don Quixote*, Vienna Philharmonic Orchestra: Telarc 80262. This effort is superior to most of the competition (and a number of other Telarc recordings) in clarity, depth, and breadth of sound stage and string realism. It is definitely better than 1224. (A+)

1226 Strauss, R.: *Don Juan*; *Till Eulenspiegel*; *Tod und Verklärung*, Detroit Symphony Orchestra: London 400 085-2. This disc, recorded in the early 1980s, has the expensive large-hall sound that London is noted for and these pieces require. The presentation is clear and dynamic, although the stage depth could be a tad better and the treble may sound a bit brittle on some sound systems. (A)

1227 Strauss, R.: *Don Quixote*; *Till Eulenspiegel*, Symphonieorchester des Bayerischen Rundfunks: RCA 60561-2. The overall sound here is smooth, clear, and a bit distant with good depth and spread. The *Eulenspiegel* is not quite in a class with the above version on the much older London release (see 1226). (B+)

1228 Strauss, R.: *Ein Heldenleben*;

Macbeth, Seattle Symphony Orchestra: Delos DE 3094. A wide, deep, and transparent overall sound are evident on both pieces. Two engineers shared this two-work recording job, and each of them did OK. The result is just a bit lacking in hall reverberation for such large-scale hall-filling works. I just did not think the recording was quite in a class with some of the really notable Delos efforts. Surround processing of almost any kind helps works like these that lack an expansive reverb. (A)

1229 Strauss, R.: *Ein Heldenleben*; *Four Last Songs*; Vienna Philharmonic Orchestra, Arleen Augér, soprano: Telarc 80180. A marvelous-sounding large-scale recording with a detailed yet spacious sound stage. The solo violin and the solo vocal are realistically blended and fit into the orchestral sound stage the way they should. This recording shows what Telarc can produce when the chips are down. (A+)

1230 Strauss, R.: *Der Rosenkavalier*, Staatsopernchor and Staatskapelle Dresden (with Kiri Te Kanawa, Kurt Rydl, Anne Sofie von Otter, Franz Grundheber, Barbara Hendricks, and others): EMI 7 54259-2. Brilliant, brassy, and vibrant. The large-scale sound is reverberant and suits this kind of music, and the soloists are extremely well handled and relate to the sound stage as they should. I found that surround enhancement, via either of my home-system processors, made the excellent overall sound even more alive. Another sign of the recording practices of the "new" EMI. (A+)

1231 Stravinsky, Igor: *Apollo* (1947 version); *Concerto in D for String Orchestra* (1946 version); *Cantata*, London Sinfonietta and Chorus, with Yvonne Kenny, soprano; and John Aler, tenor (on the *Cantata* only): Sony SK 46667. This release is very clean, close up, and three-dimensional with palpable hall depth. In the choral pieces, the blend between the orchestra, choir, and soloists is near perfect. This fine effort shows what Sony can produce when they concentrate on microphone techniques and do not let the supposed advantages of "20-bit processing" lull them into not thinking about the proper way to stage a recording. (A)

1232 Stravinsky, I.: *Dances Concertates*; *Suite de Pulcinella*, The Avanti Orchestra: BIS CD-292. This is a good example of a "purist" two-microphone recording technique. Done right, with recordings that do not demand really tight central images, it is obvious that the simple spaced array can deliver the goods. This disc displays fine depth and clarity with only a hint of central-image phasiness. (A)

1233 Stravinsky, I.: *Firebird Suite*; Borodin, Alexander: *Music From Prince Igor*, Atlanta Symphony Orchestra: Telarc 80039. An early (1978) digital release, this recording is still notable for clarity and depth. The sound field displays particularly good bass reproduction, somewhat better than the London complete *Firebird* (see 1237) and only a bit inferior to the later Telarc release (see 1234). (A)

1234 Stravinsky, I.: *Firebird Suite*; *Pétrouchka*, Baltimore Symphony Orchestra: Telarc 80270. This new Telarc *Firebird* shows how much things have progressed since the still very good "early digital" Telarc (see 1233). This effort is demo-grade stuff with great impact and clarity and an absolutely realistic sound stage. The low bass on the opening of the *Bird* is only the beginning of a disc that defines the current state of the art. The *Pétrouchka* is equally remarkable in sound quality. This release just gives more bang for the buck than the earlier one. It is obvious that the Baltimore Symphony and Telarc are in for a remarkable period of creativity. (A+)

1235 Stravinsky, I.: *Firebird* (complete ballet); *Le Chant du Rossignol*, Danish National Radio Symphony Orchestra: Chandos CHAN 8967. This effort displays a smooth, clean, reverberant, powerful sound with good depth. Nevertheless, Chandos has delivered better results on a number of other recordings, and given this company's track record, I attribute the lack of a top score to the acoustics of this particular hall. (A)

1236 Stravinsky, I.: *Firebird* (complete ballet); *Song of the Nightengale*, Seattle Symphony Orchestra: Delos D/CD 3051. There is great detail and impact on this disc along with a broad sound stage, spacious ambience, and notable clarity. Nevertheless, the recording quality is not quite up to that of the later Telarc version of the *Suite* (see 1234) but certainly equal to the earlier one. (A)

1237 Stravinsky, I.: *Firebird* (complete ballet), Orchestre Symphonique de Montréal: London 414 409-2. This version is clear and brilliant with great depth and a decent stage perspective. The brilliance is not overbearing, however and comes across quite nicely on my larger system and seems only slightly too bright on my smaller one. Just a very small background noise intrudes occasionally. It sounds suspiciously like automobile traffic. (Qualified A)

1238 Stravinsky, I.: *Firebird* (complete ballet), Philharmonia Orchestra: Teldec 44932-2. Excellent depth, clarity, and hall perspective are hallmarks of this recording. The sound is a bit subdued in the high frequencies when compared to the London version (see 1237), but on the whole I would still judge it to be more or less equal to that release. It is just different from perfection in the opposite direction. (A)

1239 Stravinsky, I.: *Pétrouchka* (1911 version); *Symphony in Three Movements*, London Symphony Orchestra: Nimbus NI 5088. This is another Ambisonic recording that has a distant near-the-back-of-hall perspective. The presentation is distinctly lightweight and lacks the big-orchestra punch that some listeners will feel is required, at least with *Pétrouchka*. It is important to remember, however, that the 1911 version of this work was a bit of a lightweight anyway and was not the same as what resulted from the 1947 rewrite. The latter is far more commonly heard these days, and the sound here may not be to everyone's taste, particularly to those enamored of spaced-array microphone techniques and heavy-duty impact. In any case, the clarity of the instrumentation and the sound-stage imaging mimic a real-world hall very well. The subjective depth of this presentation is notable, the front of the orchestra clearly sounding closer than the rear sections. In relation to the other versions available, I found that this recording came across better on my smaller system than on my larger one. It also responded well to Yamaha-processor surround enhancement. (B+)

1240 Stravinsky, I.: *Pétrouchka* (1947 version); *Divertimento* (1949 revision), Orchestre de Paris: Philips 432 145-2. This rendition is smooth, clean, and close up with good dynamics and a good hall feel. Notwithstanding the shortness of this review compared to 1239, I feel that this is a better-engineered recording of *Pétrouchka* than that one, even allowing for the revision differences. (A+)

1241 Stravinsky, I.: *Pétrouchka* (1947 version); *Divertimento from the Fairy's Kiss*, Dallas Symphony Orchestra: ProArte CDS 596. This recording makes use of Shure's "Stereo-Surround" recording-encoding process, which is a Dolby-compatible surround enhancement system. While this effort sounds very good when played on a standard stereo, it is actually designed to be at its best when played back through a Dolby-type decoder with at least four (and preferably five) speakers. There is a broad, deep, and realistic hall sound when played on any decent system, and the overall result is very clear and clean with impressive dynamics and a wide-band frequency response. (A+)

1242 Stravinsky, I.: *Pulcinella*; *Octet*; *Renard the Fox*, London Sinfonietta; Sony Sk 45965. Although made at two studio locations, all three pieces display a beautiful and accurate sound stage with excellent clarity and depth. There is a notably accurate placement of the vocal and instrumental soloists combined with the kind of small-hall ambience that works of this kind demand. (A)

1243 Stravinsky, I.: *The Rake's Progress*, London Sinfonietta and Chorus, plus assorted soloists: Decca/London 411 644-2. Here we have a close up sound that is clear and smooth. The soloists are well placed, and the sound stage is wide and has more depth than what would ordinarily be expected from what looks like a multimicrophone job in the accompanying photo. (A)

1244 Stravinsky, I.: *Le Sacre du Printemps* (standard English translation: *The Rite of Spring*); Prokofiev, Sergei: *Scythian Suite*, Dallas Symphony Orchestra: Dorian DOR 90156. The balance of bass-to-mid-to-treble is very unlike what is common in other versions and is quite lifelike. This is an exceptionally dynamic and realistic disc, having none of the prominent and often strident high frequencies found on many other classical recordings. It's nice to not hear the violin sound shoved into your face. The overall impression is clean and transparent with good depth and spread and tremendous impact when the music requires. The only weakness some sound enthusiasts might notice is a slight lack of hall reverb—easily excusable if one is happy to have a recording that mimics the sound of a smaller hall and easily correctable if one has a good surround processor. Mine turned this excellent disc into a sonic masterpiece. (A+)

1245 Stravinsky, I.: *Le Sacre du Printemps*, Detroit Symphony Orchestra: London 400 084-2. This is a good recording when one considers its decade-old sound, with high-impact dynamics and clarity. Overall, I felt that it was just a tad two-dimensional. Superior conducting by Antal Dorati probably has a lot to do with the perceived engineering excellence. (A)

1246 Stravinsky, I.: *Le Sacre du Printemps*; *Firebird Suite*, London Symphony Orchestra: Nimbus NI 5087. The low overall playback level of this disc requires a higher than usual setting of the playback volume control. However, the sound is clear, brilliant, and transparent and displays a realistic hall bloom and ambience. The overall listening perspective is somewhat distant, although the strings to the left seem somewhat closer to the listener than they should be (an artifact of this kind should not happen with the Calrec Soundfield microphone used for a Nimbus Ambisonic recording). As with many Nimbus discs, this recording has a rather lightweight chamber-orchestra sound that will appeal to some listeners more than others. As with any recording with this type of sound, surround enhancement can work wonders. (A)

1247 Stravinsky, I.: *Le Sacre du Printemps*, Cleveland Orchestra: Telarc 80054. This is a good early Telarc recording, particularly in dynamic range. The sound stage is broad and diffuse in the company tradition, but that kind of image is not out of place here. The clarity is good in spite of the slight lack of central focus. (A)

1248 Stravinsky, I.: *Le Sacre du Printemps*; *Pulcinella Suite*, Atlanta Symphony Orchestra: Telarc 80266. This later Telarc release again shows the advances in the recording art that have occurred since the earlier Telarc work (1247). This version has great impact combined with a fine sense of hall space, detail, and depth, although still not quite up to the standard set by 1244. In the new Telarc tradition for sure. (A+)

1249 Stravinsky, I.: *Le Sacre du Printemps* (version for two pianos); *Concerto For Two Pianos*, Vladimir Ashkenazy and Andrei Gavrilov, pianos: London 433 829-2. Here we have a close up but you-are-there sound with fine detail and dynamics. There is good piano tonality, and the use of two of the instruments allows for a broad sound stage that some engineers apparently try to achieve with only one piano. Each of these instruments is well focused and imaged properly. (A)

1250 Stravinsky, I.: *The Soldier's Tale*, Scottish Chamber Orchestra: Nimbus NI 5063. This effort has excellent depth and an enveloping hall feel due to the Ambisonic recording process. The "direct" signal here is quite detailed and well imaged and contrasts markedly with the more diffuse sound stage of 1251. The up-front realism is apparent on even a two-channel system. There is nice real-world clarity here, especially in the spoken parts. (A+)

1251 Stravinsky, I.: *The Soldier's Tale* (excerpts); Prokofiev, Sergei: *Classical Symphony*; Shostakovich, Dmitri: *Piano Concerto Number 1*, Los Angeles Chamber Orchestra: Delos D/CD 3021. Digitally recorded in 1980 (and engineered by Marc Aubort), this effort displays fine ensemble tonality combined with a sense of stage envelopment. The spaced-array technique's supposedly phasey-sounding qualities are not subjectively a problem for the most part, and the sound stage is wide, deep, and realistic. However the solo piano is a bit diffuse, highlighting an obvious weakness in what may be a simple two-microphone technique. Even a three-spaced-microphone technique can have problems with piano concertos. (A+ for the Stravinsky and Prokofiev; A for the Shostakovich)

1252 Streisand, Barbra: *The Broadway Album*: Columbia CK 40092. Smooth and clean with a good, broad (but not like Broadway) synthesized sound stage. The vocals are obviously what count here, and Ms. Streisand's voice is nice and clear and far enough forward to set her off from the large supporting ensemble but not so up front to be too unrealistic. The microphone chosen to record her was a fairly good one; it has little unwanted sibilance or midrange emphasis. (B+)

1253 Sullivan, Maxine: *Swingin' Sweet* (with the Scott Hamilton Quintet, including John Bunch, Chris Flory, Phil Flanigan, and Chuck Riggs): Concord Jazz CCD-4351. A live performance like this one typically has a distant sound quality when recorded, but decent hall ambience is an often positive consequence. On this release there is notable clarity and realistic sound-stage depth on the instrumentals. The vocals are well located in relation to the quintet, but the microphone used for them is a bit "tizzy." This recording is kinder to Sullivan than the Mobile Fidelity reissue of one of her earlier releases. I found that surround processing had a very positive effect. (B)

1254 *Sumer Is Icumen In* (Chants Médiévaux Anglais), The Hilliard Ensemble: Harmonia Mundi France 901154. This disc displays a fine sound-stage spread and depth with a wonderful hall ambience. The clarity is exemplary, and the tonality is realistic. A very small ambient noise intrudes at times, but its texture is of "hall space" and actually enhances the realistic effect in this case. (A+)

1255 Swanson, Ric, and Urban Surrender: *Windsock* (with Larry Coryell and Richie Cole): American Gramophone AGCD-687. This bit of New-Age material was smooth and reverberant with a nice sense of synthesized space. (B)

1256 Talking Heads: *Speaking in Tongues*: Sire 9 23883-2. This is an example of the kind of clarity (combined with impact) a good rock album should exhibit and is not bad for a 1983 recording. This is also an example proving that at least some engineers knew what they were doing so many years ago. Overall, there is a rather distant sound on this disc, with fine synthesized depth. Turn up your amplifier gain to bring the performance into your listening room. The recording responded very positively to surround enhancement. (A)

1257 Tallis, Thomas: *Complete English Anthems*, The Tallis Scholars: Gimell CDGM-007. This gem is smooth, detailed, and blessed with realistic ambience and depth. A benchmark recording for the sound of a small choral group in a moderately sized church. (A+)

1258 Tallis, T.: *The Lamentations of Jeremiah*, The Hilliard Ensemble: ECM 1341-833 308-2. This is a very clean and close-up choral work. The recording has a wonderful sense of hall ambience and space as well as excellent front-to-back depth, particularly with surround enhancement. At times, low-frequency background artifacts subtly intrude (almost sounds like traffic noise). This would be an enhancement of realism if one wanted to feel he or she was in the hall during rush hour. (Qualified A+)

1259 Tallis, T.: *The Lamentations of Jeremiah*, The Tallis Scholars: Gimell GIM 025. Overall, this disc displays a nice sense of hall space and proper ensemble positioning combined with good clarity. Very good imaging between the speakers. (A)

1260 Tana, Akira, and Rufus Reid: *Yours and Mine* (with Rob Schneiderman, Jesse Davis, and Ralph Moore): Concord Jazz CCD-4440. There is a nice sound-stage presence and clarity on this release with good blending between the players. The listening perspective is just a bit distant with some instruments (the sax, for instance) and a bit close up with others (the piano).

The drums are often too widely spread out, given the left-right image of the rest of the ensemble. Too bad, since that is Tana's instrument. (B+)

1261 Tavener, John: *The Protecting Veil*; Britten, Benjamin: *Third Suite for Cello, op. 87*, London Symphony Orchestra, Steven Isserlis, cello: Virgin Classics 7 91474-2. This is a very spacious and clean recording with an exceptional reproduction of the cello. Tavener, a contemporary composer, is not the same person as the Renaissance composer John Taverner listed below. (A+)

1262 Taverner, John: *Missa Gloria Tibia Trinitas*, The Tallis Scholars: Gimell CDGM-004. Remarkable clarity, smoothness, depth, and ambience are multiple highlights here—the latter so well done that the result has a surround-sound effect, even with only two front stereo speakers. Note that the first track of this disc (totaling 15 seconds and entitled "ambience") contains nothing but silence. (A+)

1263 Taverner, J.: *Western Wynde Mass*; *Te Deum* (and other short works), The Sixteen: Hyperion CDA 66507. This disc is somewhat distant but still clear, smooth, and detailed. Overall, it has a nice hall ambience and very good depth. (A)

1264 Taylor, Deems: *Through the Looking Glass*; Griffes, Charles: *Poem for Flute and Orchestra* (and other, smaller works on this album, the cover title of which is *The Musical Fantasies of Charles Griffes and Deems Taylor*): Seattle Symphony Orchestra (with Bernard Shapiro, oboe; Scott Goff, flute; and Victoria Bogdashevskaya, piano): Delos DE 3099. This release is smooth, open, and clean with the usual Seattle-Delos sound stage: wide, blended, and with plenty of depth and ambience. The recent Seattle-Delos recordings have all been excellent. (A+)

1265 Tchaikovsky, Peter: *1812 Overture*; *The Tempest*; *Hamlet*, Oregon Symphony Orchestra: Delos D/CD 3081. This recording is extremely articulate and detailed with wonderful depth and stage spread—and first-rate imaging, perhaps just a bit better than the famous old Telarc version (see 1266). The artillery shots of the *1812*, while impressive in their own way and more than good enough for an artistic expression of high quality, are no match for the older Telarc effort. (A+)

1266 Tchaikovsky, P.: *1812 Overture*; *Capriccio Italien*, Cincinnati Symphony Orchestra: Telarc 80041. This selection was digitally recorded in 1978 and was first released as an LP. It was considered for years a state-of-the-art test for phono cartridges. While the *1812* is the most famous item on this hi-fi show favorite, the *Capriccio* is artistically better and equal as a "test" item for anything but your woofers. Needless to say, this effort displays the typically good Telarc-style spaciousness and depth. The cannon shots are fun but really tell you little about anything but the peak-power capabilities of your system, although this disc cannot help but earn its high score because of them. The shots vary in level considerably and should come from several points on the sound stage. It is important to remember that the playback level of this disc is set purposely low to accommodate the loud peak-level cacophony of cannon blasts that come near the end. If you set the gain for an initial loud playback, you could damage your woofers during the finale. Watch it! (A+)

1267 Tchaikovsky, P.: *The Nut-*

cracker (complete), London Symphony Orchestra: Telarc 2CD-CD-80137. This compact disc is clean, smooth, and dynamic—and considerably better than the videotape version, which also had a grainy picture. (A)

1268 Tchaikovsky, P.: *The Nutcracker* (complete), Orchestra of the Royal Opera House: Conifer ROH 304/5. This effort is clear and detailed with a midhall listening perspective. I felt that it lacked the necessary forceful front-row impact, which will suit some listeners and alienate a few others. (A)

1269 Tchaikovsky, P.: *The Nutcracker Suite*; *Romeo and Juliet*, Cleveland Orchestra: Telarc 80068. Over a decade old, this recording still captivates with its clarity and spacious envelopment. The sound stage is broad, and the spaced-microphone recording arrangement does a fine job of synthesizing ambience in a home listening environment. (A)

1270 Tchaikovsky, P.: *Piano Concerto Number One*; Prokofiev, Sergei: *Piano Concerto Number Three*, Jon Kumura Parker, piano; Royal Philharmonic Orchestra: Telarc 80124. There is a nice balance here between the orchestra and soloist, with just a hint of midstage piano fuzziness. The orchestral sound has the usual Telarc breadth, depth, and spaciousness combined with a close up feel. I thought that the other Telarc effort (1271) was superior, however. (A)

1271 Tchaikovsky, P.: *Piano Concerto Number One*; Rachmaninoff, Sergei: *Rhapsody on a Theme of Paganini*, Baltimore Symphony Orchestra, Horacio Gutiérrez, piano: Telarc 80193. A bit more distant than the Teldec job (see 1272) and certainly more so than the other Telarc recording (see 1270). The piano is better focused than in either of the other recordings, a critical factor for me. The orchestra has all the clarity, detail, and spaciousness you could ask for. Another Baltimore-Telarc triumph. (A+)

1272 Tchaikovsky, P.: *Piano Concerto Number One*; Rachmaninoff, S.: *Piano Concerto Number Two*, London Symphony Orchestra, Alexei Sultanov, piano: Teldec 46281-2. A fine hall sense of ambience, substantial orchestral depth, and accurate sound staging highlight this recording. There is a good midhall listening perspective, with the piano clear and well focused. However, its extreme clarity in relation to the somewhat more withdrawn orchestral sound gives the impression that the instrument is just a bit farther in front than it should be. This positioning was obviously the result of careful consideration by the engineer. Similarly, my judgement of its positioning was made after careful consideration. By itself, the orchestral sound is very dynamic and realistic, and not giving this recording an A+ involved some rather extended listening. (A)

1273 Tchaikovsky, P.: *Pique Dame* (The Queen of Spades), Boston Symphony Orchestra (with Vladimir Atlantov, Mirella Freni, Sergei Leiferkus, Maureen Forrester, and others): RCA 60992-2. This sound on this release is clearly etched and detailed, yet with a somewhat withdrawn orchestral image. The vocals are excellent, however, and are properly sized and well placed. The ambience around the voices is quite realistic. (A)

1274 Tchaikovsky, P.: *Romeo and Juliet; Francesca da Rimini*, Gewandhausorchester Leipzig. Teldec 76456-2. The sound here is close up, detailed, dynamic, and fairly good in terms of stage depth and left-right imaging. Nice string tone. Extraction-type surround enhancements can make the illusion of being there even better, although a good synthesizing processor, which will increase the ambience of what is already on the disc, can have an even greater impact on the sound. (A)

1275 Tchaikovsky, P.: *The Seasons*, Antonin Kubalek, piano: Dorian DOR 90102. This is a marvelous piano recording with the you-are-there impression just about perfect. There is fine hall ambience and equally good clarity, the piano properly located and sized for a midhall listening position. (A+)

1276 Tchaikovsky, P.: *Serenade in C for Strings*; Pachelbel, Johann: *Kanon*; Borodin, Alexander: *Nocturne for String Orchestra*; Vaughan Williams, Ralph: *Fantasia on Greensleeves*, Saint Louis Symphony Orchestra: Telarc 80080. This disc exhibits a very fine string tone, which is obviously important in a recording of this kind. Overall, it is clean and smooth and is certainly in the Telarc tradition. Not bad for a recording made in the early 1980s. (A)

1277 Tchaikovsky, P.: *Symphony Number 4*; *Romeo and Juliet Fantasy Overture*, USSR Ministry of Culture Symphony Orchestra: Erato 45620-2. Close up, bright, and very clean with great dynamic range. The sound stage exhibits excellent imaging and depth, and the sense of hall space is enveloping. This one has less bass impact than the Telarc effort below (see 1278), but it is still first class. Not every recording needs lots of bass punch to be a winner in the realistic-sound sweepstakes. (A)

1278 Tchaikovsky, P.: *Symphony Number 4*; *Romeo and Juliet Fantasy Overture*, Baltimore Symphony Orchestra: Telarc 80228. This latest Telarc Tchaikovsky *Fourth* has tremendous impact, power, depth, detail, and hall ambience—all wrapped up in one neat package. Bass nuts will say that it clearly outclasses all the efforts by the competition, particularly in percussive dynamics. However, it is also by a small margin probably the best in everything else technical that matters. The front-row perspective heightens the effect. (A+)

1279 Tchaikovsky, P.: *Symphony Number 5*, Orchestre Symphonique de Montréal: London 425 503-2. This is a smooth, clean, and transparent recording with just a touch of the violin harshness that continues to plague many of the classical CDs produced by otherwise competent engineers. On some systems such an effect may be offset by mellow-sounding speakers. However, some near-field monitors may tend to sound glassy at times. (A)

1280 Tchaikovsky, P.: *Symphony Number 5*, Royal Philharmonic Orchestra: Telarc 80107. Similar in positive respects to 1279 but with the string harshness tamed. Indeed, the string tones on both sides of the orchestra are very well handled. Overall, this recording is smooth and detailed with plenty of hall ambience and depth. (A+)

1281 Tchaikovsky, P.: *Symphony Number 6*; Scriabin, Alexander: *Poèm de L'Extase*, Philadelphia Orchestra: EMI CDC 7 54061-2. This one is quite smooth and transparent with very good sound-stage depth and imaging. The result is not quite as dynamic and rich as 1282, but this version has just a little bit better instrumental delineation. The recording is a cut above 1283, especially in depth and smoothness. (A+)

1282 Tchaikovsky, P.: *Symphony Number 6*; *Romeo and Juliet*, Orchestre Symphonique de Montréal: London 430 507-2. This London-Montréal release is smooth, clean, and dynamic. It is not so dry as 1283 and has more impact. It also has a fine sound stage and good depth combined with balanced and realistic clarity. (A+)

1283 Tchaikovsky, P.: *Symphony Number 6*, Philharmonia Orchestra: London 411 615-2. Not bad for an early (1981) London digital job. The somewhat flat-appearing sound stage is salvaged by good detail and good dynamic impact. Overall, the recording is a bit dry, the strings just a tad brittle. As in quite a few other cases, I found that both of these characteristics can be partially corrected with a bit of listener-applied surround enhancement. The quality of the fix will depend on the kind of equipment one has, but with dry recordings the most effective procedure is to *add* synthetic reverberation rather than try to *extract* ambience from the recording itself. How much of an audible problem the slightly brittle violin sound can be will be determined by the quality of the playback speakers and how they are placed. (A)

1284 Tchaikovsky, P.: *Swan Lake* (complete), London Symphony Orchestra: Sony S2K 46592. This release is clear and transparent with good dynamics, an excellent sound stage, and good instrumental balances. A note on the CD box states that this recording uses "20-bit technology." As I have pointed out before (189, 1231), this has little audible effect when compared to a properly operating 16-bit system. A well-tuned 16-bit digital recorder can do a subjectively "perfect" job of capturing what any orchestra can produce. Good microphone types and placement as well as intelligent mixing techniques are responsible for this disc's quality. (A+)

1285 Tchaikovsky, P.: *Swan Lake*; *Sleeping Beauty* (suites), Royal Philharmonic Orchestra: Telarc 80151. This release exhibits the typical Telarc broad and spacious sound stage with good depth and clarity. The bass drum is just a tad boomy (another occasional Telarc trademark), which may work to good effect on smaller sound systems that are a bit bass shy or "overdamped" in the bass. (A)

1286 Tchaikovsky, P.: *Trio in A Minor, op. 50*; Alyabiev, Alexander: *Trio in A Minor*, The Borodin Trio: Chandos CHAN 8975. (This is the second time the Borodin Trio has done the Tchaikovsky work for Chandos, the other being CHAN 8348, which I have not heard.) This newer version has outstanding sound-stage depth combined with fine clarity. The instrumental images are exceptional, and the ensemble is surrounded by a palpably real hall ambience. (A+)

1287 Tchaikovsky, P.: *Trio in A Minor*; Arensky, Anton: *Trio in D Minor*; Andres Cardenes, viola; Jeffrey Solow, cello; and Mona Golabek, piano: Delos DE 3056. This performance is wide staged (actually, subjectively a bit too wide for the perceived listening distance) with good string clarity and a very good piano focus. (A)

1288 Tchaikovsky, P.: *Violin Concerto in D*; Sibelius, Jean: *Violin Concerto in D Minor*, Boston Symphony Orchestra, Viktoria Mullova, violin: Philips 416 821-2. This effort displays good orchestral depth, transparency, and spread, the violin very clear and articulate but also a bit closer to the listener in relation to the rest of the ensemble than it should be. Even the orchestra presents a definite front-row perspective, which means that the violin is subjectively close indeed. A continuous rumbling noise permeates the background (sounds like traffic). It's getting harder to find a quiet concert hall all the time. (Qualified A)

1289 Tcherepnin, Alexander: *Symphony Number 4*; *Suite for Orchestra*; *Romantic Overture*, Czecho-Slovak State Philharmonic Orchestra: Marco Polo 8.223380. This release is close up and clean with good imaging, a nice spread, and a pleasant hall-orchestral balance. (A)

1290 Telemann, Georg Philipp: *Bläserkonzerte* (concertos for woodwind instruments), Camerata Köln: Deutsche Harmonia Mundi 77201-2-RC. This original-instruments recording is clean and clear with marvelous instrumental delineation. The hall ambience is just what is required for this kind of music. The recording is certainly up to the usual standards for this label. (A+)

1291 Telemann, G. P.: *Chamber Music*, Chandos Baroque Players: Hyperion CDA 66195. Virtuoso playing and very clear sound make this period-instruments disc a real pleasure to listen to. The sound stage, no doubt due to the coincident-source microphonc tcchnique, seems just a bit narrow and constricted, but the hall ambience is excellent. (A)

1292 Telemann, G. P., and George Frideric Händel: *Concertos for Recorder, Baroque Bassoon and Strings*, Drottingholm Baroque Ensemble: BIS CD-271. This one is a bit big, rich, and spacious for a baroque recording, but some listeners will feel that the reverberation works well here, particularly if some L-R surround enhancement (Dolby or even a Hafler "ambience extraction" device, for instance) is used during playback. This moves some of the reverb out and around the listener and makes it more workable. The sound stage is quite good with excellent ensemble clarity. (A)

1293 Telemann, G. P.: *Domestic Music* (volume 3 of a series), Collegium Musicum 90: Chandos CHAN 0525. This is a smooth, detailed, close up, clean rendition by a fine original-instrument ensemble. There is some low-level background noise that sounds like traffic outside the concert hall. As usual, turning off your subwoofer or surround processing gear will eliminate most of the rumble. I think we can assume that the two earlier volumes of this series approach this one in sound quality. (Qualified A+)

1294 Telemann, G. P.: *Ino*; Händel, G. F.: *Apollo e Dafne*, Concentus Musicus Wien, with Roberta Alexander and Thomas Hampson, vocalists: Teldec 44633-2. The strong point here is the wonderful vocal realism, topped off with a fine orchestral blend in the background. The result is clean, clear, and vibrant. The instruments are original types, of course. (A+)

1295 Telemann, G. P.: *The Paris Quartets*, American Baroque: Amon-Ra CDSAR-39. (Also on Musical Heritage Society 512698K.) The period instruments sound clean and detailed, and the recording is endowed with a rather close up perspective and small-hall acoustics. (A)

1296 Telemann, G. P., and G. F. Händel: *Trio Sonatas*, Hans Maria Kneihs, recorder (with Daniel Spector, Angelika Klinger, Mark Peters, and

Wolfgang Zerer): Camerata 32CM-133. The Telemann piece was recorded in 1981 and sounds every bit as good as the Händel, which was recorded in 1990. Both were also recorded in different halls. The result shows good balance, ambience, and depth with a clear and transparent sound. (A)

1297 Telemann, G. P.: *Trumpet Concertos*, English String Orchestra, John Wallace, trumpet: Nimbus NI 5189. This is a fine example of Ambisonic surround recording using a Calrec coincident-source microphone array (note that you will need an Ambisonic decoder in your system to get the full effect, but stereo-only playback is still magnificent). The result is very clean and realistic with the kind of ambience and sound stage that good engineers strive for. The trumpet is where it is supposed to be and is the right size for the dimensions of the orchestra. The stereo sound can be made even more realistic with "standard" surround decoding (even Dolby or a Hafler hookup) or with Lexicon or Yamaha-style ambience synthesis. (A+)

1298 Terry, Clark: *Having Fun* (with Red Holloway, Major Holly, John Campbell, and Lewis Nash): Delos DE 4021. This release is marvelously clear and detailed with excellent imaging. The tonality here is beautiful, and the piano and drums are perfectly sized. The studio ambience is expertly handled, and the trumpet sounds real. Front-rank jazz sound. (A+)

1299 Terry, C.: *Live at the Village Gate* (with Jimmy Heath, Paquito D'Rivera, Don Friedman, Marcus McLauren, and Kenny Washington): Chesky JD-49. Maybe a bit cleaner than the earlier JD-2 (see 1300), even though this release is not a controlled studio-recording situation. The overall sound is very dynamic and realistic. Live recordings like this one often respond very well to surround-sound enhancement, although processing with center-channel steering may not always work to best effect (the whole sound stage sometimes collapses into the center channel). (A+)

1300 Terry, C.: *Portraits* (with Don Friedman, Victor Gaskin, and Lewis Nash): Chesky JD-2. This is an early Chesky release that is clean and articulate (especially the trumpet) but with a somewhat subdued, distant sound. Even so, the stage effect is almost three-dimensional. (A)

1301 Tesla: *Five Man Acoustical Jam*: Geffen 9 24311-2. This one is pretty clean for a live recording, especially for rock. There is a pretty good sound stage and decent instrumental delineation. (B)

1302 Tesla: *The Great Radio Controversy*: Geffen 9 24224-2. Similar to the above release but with somewhat greater dynamics, good spacious effects, and an adequate frequency-response bandwidth. The modest improvements are not enough to bump up the score from that one. (B)

1303 Tesla: *Mechanical Resonance*: Geffen 9 24120-2. Like the other recordings above, this one has a wide, resonant sound stage. The presentation has good impact with vocal clarity also good for such a reverberant sound field. (B)

1304 Thomson, Virgil: *Symphony on a Hymn Tune*; *Symphony Number 2*; *Five Tenor Solos From the Opera Lord Byron*, Monadnock Festival Orchestra (symphonies only), Budapest Symphony Orchestra, Martyn Hill, tenor (orchestral-vocal material):

Albany TROY 017-2. The orchestral textures of this recording are bright, clear, detailed, and impressive with an outstanding instrumental focus and a fine hall ambience. There is also a deep, wide, realistic sound stage, which at times almost seems like surround sound. For hi-fi showpiece buffs, there are some tremendous dynamic contrasts in the Monadnock Festival sections. As a final treat, there is first-rate near-perfect engineering of the tenor vocals in combination with their clean and realistic blending into the instrumental textures of the Budapest group. This is a front-rank recording. (A+)

1305 *Three-Way Mirror* (with Airto Moreira, Flora Purim, Joe Farrell, and others): Reference Recordings RR-24CD. The players on this disc include many of the group that produced the *Däfos* recording (see 322). This one was also engineered by Keith Johnson. The sound is transparent, clean, and well balanced, but without the often room-shaking impact of the earlier disc. (A+)

1306 The Timeless All-Stars: *Essence* (with Bobby Hutcherson, Harold Land, Curtis Fuller, Cedar Walton, Buster Williams, and Billy Higgins): Delos D/CD 4006. There is an excellent sound stage on this release with a very realistic you-are-there perspective. This is notably transparent sound with the kind of detail that highlights the performance of a good playback system. Other recording companies should spend time studying Delos recording techniques. (A+)

1307 Tippett, Michael: *The Blue Guitar*; Britten, Benjamin: *Nocturnal*; Schafer, R. Murray: *Le Cri de Merlin*, Norbert Kraft, guitar: Chandos CHAN 8784. The instrument on this release is subjectively a bit far from the listener rather than given the more close up presentation favored by some engineers. This sense of space, combined with the right amount of hall ambience, adds a fair degree of realism to solo-instrument recordings of this kind. To top things off, the clarity is fine with a good sharp focus. (A)

1308 *To Catch a Christmas Star* (assorted choral songs of Christmas), Roger Wagner Chorale; University Handbell Choir of California State University, Long Beach (with William Beck, organ; and David Christensen, carillon): Delos D/CD 3072. There is an overall wonderful choral-instrumental blend here (even with the carillon recorded separately from the other material and mixed in later) with fine ensemble imaging, excellent clarity, and a good sense of hall space. (A+)

1309 Tormé, Mel: *Mel Tormé, Rob McConnell and the Boss Brass* (with Moe Koffman, Dave Woods, Jerry Roth, Eugene Amaro, Ron Hughes, and others): Concord Jazz CCD-4306. Punchy, dynamic, and clean with a good sound-stage image. The vocals are usually well positioned and cleanly recorded, but occasionally Tormé seems a bit closer to the listener than the positioning of his supporting ensemble would dictate. (B+)

1310 Tormé, M., and George Shearing: *An Elegant Evening*: Concord Jazz CCD-4294. Lucid, clean, and unstressed with the piano and vocals well imaged and sized well in relation to each other. The voice, however, has an "amplified" texture to it that is not as good as it would be live and unelectrified. However, it probably is like what one would hear at a typical live stage show where amplifiers, microphones, loudspeaker systems, and engineers often conspire to color the sound. (B+)

1311 Tormé, M. and G. Shearing: *A Vintage Year* (with John Leitham and Donny Osborne): Concord Jazz CCD-4341. Open, smooth, and clear, this program, apparently recorded outdoors, seems to have a certain synthesized indoor ambience added that fills out the effect nicely. The drums and piano are well focused, and the vocals, although a bit close, are equally tight. An odd background rumble-thumping effect is highlighted by any surround processing you may be adding yourself, and it is a good idea to deenergize any subwoofer you may be using or at least back off on your bass control a bit. Most systems should not have a problem with the noise. (Qualified B+)

1312 Toto: *The Seventh One*: Columbia CK 40873. This pop release is nice and punchy with excellent instrumental articulation and a good solid bass line that substitutes generous depth for midbass boom. The synthesized sound field is tight and well controlled, and the vocals are very well handled. This is a fine example of the way rock can be recorded. (A)

1313 *A Touch of Class: Popular Classics Transcribed for Guitar* (works by J. S. Bach, Respighi, Mozart, Cutting, Albinoni, Vivaldi, Debussy, Satie, Yacoh, and Meyers), Angel Romero, guitar, with Lito Romero on some tracks: Telarc 80134. As expected, this recording has very clear sound with the solo image well centered and decently focused. The latter is something Telarc occasionally has trouble with when handling solo-instrument work. A good sense of hall envelopment tops things off. (A)

1314 *Toy Matinee*: Reprise 26235-2. The vocals and instrumentation are quite clear on this one with good, decently deep bass for a rock album. There is no reason for not putting deep bass on a wide-band medium like the CD, even when the music is rock and roll. Some rock lovers do have speaker systems with deep-bass potential. (B+)

1315 The Tragically Hip: *Road Apples*: MCAD 10173. I thought this rock release had good vocal clarity and impact, and the stage spread is also good. The bass is solid but not as deep as it could be. (B)

1316 Travis, Randy: *No Holdin' Back*: Warner Bros. 25988-2. Travis's voice is clear enough here to offset some of the typically reverberant synthesized country-sound processing that can be a real annoyance when listened to on a good playback system. The disc barely makes the grade here, but it is somewhat better than most other albums by him I have put through their paces. (B)

1317 Travis, R.: *Old 8 x 10*: Warner 25738-2. This one is pretty much the same as 1316, but with a bit less nasality to the vocals. It more easily made the list than the other effort but was not enough better to rate a higher score. The sound of the instrumental backup was not too bad on either album. (B)

1318 *Trompete und Orgel* (short works by Mancini, J. S. Bach, Telemann, Werner, and others); Joachim Pliquett, trumpet; Arvid Gast, organ: Christophorus CD 74574. This release is clean and brilliant with a nice sense of space and depth. The trumpet-organ balance is excellent, which shows great restraint by the engineer. I thought this release slightly outpointed 1319. (A+)

1319 *Trompet et Orgue* (short works

The Trumpet in Baroque (1320) [180]

by Purcell, Händel, Telemann, and others); Bernard Soustrot, trumpet; François-Henri Houbart, organ: Pierre Verany 789103. Overall, this recording has a nice clean sound with a somewhat distant listening perspective. The trumpet is well positioned in relation to the much larger-sounding organ. (A)

1320 *The Trumpet in Baroque Chamber Settings* (short works by Albinoni, Scarlatti, Corelli, Hertel, Finger, and Corbett), Anthony Plog, trumpet: Centaur CRC 2068. This recording has the clean, transparent, and close-up sound that is to be expected of an assortment of baroque restored instruments playing a variety of baroque pieces. A nice hall ambience fills out the sound field. (A)

1321 *Trumpet Collection* (assorted short period pieces on original instruments), The Clarion Ensemble: Amon Ra CD-SAR 30. Overall, this one is very clear with excellent imaging and depth. Note that the original trumpets employed here have a unique sound and are quite unlike modern instruments. The effect will not be to everyone's taste, even trumpet freaks. (A)

1322 *Trumpet Spectacular* (short works by Rossini, Clarke, J. S. Bach, Rimsky-Korsakov, Puccini, and others), Cincinnati Pops Orchestra, Doc Severinsen, trumpet: Telarc 80223. This marvelous disc presents a wide-range, wide-stage rendition of a number of popular classics by a well-known performer. The trumpet playing is clear and well focused and blends in with the orchestra perfectly. The hall envelopment is quite good. (A+)

1323 Tucker, Tanya: *What I Do I Do with Me*: Capitol. CDP 7 95562-2. The somewhat cryptic title cannot detract from the decent engineering quality of this disc and the down-to-earth vocals of Tucker. The sound is spread out well and fairly clear, although it does suffer from a touch of the immoderate reverberation and overdriven vocal projection typical of C&W albums. I believe it sounded a bit more at home on my smaller system than on my bigger one. (B)

1324 *Twentieth Century Works for Unaccompanied Violoncello*, Ivan Monighetti, cello: Chant du Monde LDC 278 1059. This is a very clean cello sound, with the instrument placed in a well-defined you-are-there environment. While this is a single-instrument transcription with good in-hall ambience built into the sound field, the need for an even better sense of space is important enough to make surround enhancement something to consider. The recording works well in stereo, but I found that adding some surround processing moved the instrument into a more three-dimensional setting. (A)

1325 Tye, Christopher: *Cathedral Music*, Winchester Cathedral Choir: Hyperion CDA 66424. There is fine detail and striking transparency on this recording of the works of sixteenth-century composer Christopher Tye. Those qualities are combined with excellent hall ambience and a realistic sense of sound-stage depth. The vocals are notably lacking in recorded sound manipulation. (A)

1326 Tyner, McCoy, Avery Sharpe, and Louis Hayes: *Bon Voyage*: Timeless SJP-260. This fine jazz release was unstressed and clean with a well-focused stage image and a good left-right spread. (B+)

1327 Tyner, M.: *44th Street Suite* (with David Murray, Arthur Blythe,

Ron Carter, and Aaron Scott): Red Baron AK 48630. I felt that this one was good, clean, and sonically penetrating with decent imaging and a manageable jazz sound stage. The piano is typically diffuse and a bit bloated, but the drum set is at least under spatial control; it stays the proper size in relation to the rest of the combo. (B+)

1328 Tyner, M.: *New York Reunion* (his quartet, with Joe Henderson, Ron Carter, and Al Foster): Chesky JD-51. There is an ultralucid, realistic, and close-up sense of space in this recording, but there is also a substantial amount of low-frequency room rumble that will be clearly audible when the disc is played back on systems having flat bass response to below 25 Hz. The effect will not be apparent with smaller speakers, fortunately, although some bass-reflex models might tend to produce a bit of below-woofer-resonance distortion. Chesky should stop spending so much time and money on refining their 128-times oversampling recorders and other goodies and invest in a good subwoofer for their monitoring work. Turn down or shut your subwoofer off for this one. (Qualified A+)

1329 Vaché, Warren, and Beaux-Arts String Quartet: *Warm Evenings* (with Jack Gale, Ben Aronov, Lincoln Milliman, and Giampaolo Giagi): Concord Jazz CCD-4392. This fine example of the recording art is smooth and clean with imaging that is quite good. There is notable depth to the sound stage. (A)

1330 Vai, Steve: *Passion and Warfare*: Relativity CRT-1037. There is plenty of punch and reverberation on this rock album. It gets on the list mainly because of its remarkable synthetic sound-stage manipulation. It also has fairly deep bass at times. (B)

1331 Valentin, Dave: *Mind Time* (with Early Klugh, Lincoln Goines, Robbie Gonzalez, Bill O'Connell, Ted Lo, Richard Martinez, Robbie Ameen, and Giovanni Hildalgo): GRP GRD 9554. This is a very well done studio job with fine synthesized ambience as well as excellent detail and clarity. On the whole, GRP does a better job with jazz and pop than most other labels. (A)

1332 Vangelis: *Chariots of Fire* (orchestral suite): Polydor 800 020-2. Mostly synthesizer music performed by the composer (apparently analog mastered in 1981). Incidentally, Vangelis is his first name; his last name is Papathanassiou. The overall sound is smooth and dynamic with some potent (and sometimes fairly deep if you listen closely) bass. The sound stage is of course totally contrived, but it is certainly what the composer intended. (B+)

1333 Van Halen: *OU812*: Warner W2 25732. This recording starts out sounding distant and a bit thin, then gets better. The overall sound character changes radically as the performance moves from song to song, and the later tracks have good depth and impact with potent deep bass. I felt that even though things improve along the way, the overall sense of ensemble positioning remains a bit distant, even at high volume levels. There is some very heavy phase and amplifier distortion tricks on some tracks that many rock buffs seem to like. (B to B+)

1334 Van Zant, Johnny: *Brickyard Road*: Atlantic 82110-2. Some tracks on this rock-and-roll release are a tad rough sounding, and yet others have fine vocal/instrumental clarity and blending. This is probably the result of heavy after-session manipulation by maybe more than one person. (B)

1335 The Vaughan Brothers: *Family Style*: Epic ZK 46225. This rock disc was recorded at several locations by several engineers but was mastered by Bob Ludwig. His expertise probably saved things. Some tracks come across as a bit thin, but others are well balanced, and the vocals throughout the disc are quite clear. (B)

1336 Vaughan, Stevie Ray: *The Sky Crying*: Epic 47390. This pop-rock album displays clean vocals (except, for some bizarre reason, the first track) and good instrumental delineation. (B)

1337 Vaughan Williams, Ralph: *Fantasia on a Theme by Thomas Tallis* (plus other short works by Satie, Barber, Fauré, and Grainger), Saint Louis Symphony Orchestra: Telarc 80059. Produced in 1981, this disc still exhibits a wonderful smoothness combined with fine depth, ambience, and detail. It contains the Barber *Adagio*, which is as finely done here as it was eight years later when recorded by the same orchestra on the EMI label (85). (A)

1338 Vaughan Williams, R.: *Overture: The Wasps*; *The Lark Ascending*; Delius, Frederick: *Florida Suite*, English String Orchestra: Nimbus NI 5208. Good and clear with a somewhat distant sound (in the Nimbus tradition). The hall ambience on this disc is enveloping and realistic (also in the Nimbus tradition). The Ambisonic recording technique works well in this case and sounds fine even when played back on a conventional stereo system. (A)

1339 Vaughan Williams, R.: *Songs* (plus additional short material by Butterworth, Howells, and Hely-Hutchinson); Shura Gehrman, bass; Adrian Farmer, piano: Nimbus NI 5033. This is an excellent example of what Ambisonic processing, via the Calrec microphone (even with a 1980–81 master tape) can do with small-scale material. The result is smooth and transparent with the voice and piano very realistically positioned in a real-world small hall. Ambisonic decoding is not required to obtain magnificent results from this recording. There is some surprisingly dynamic sound at times. (A)

1340 Vaughan Williams, R.: *Symphony Number 1 (A Sea Symphony)*, The Philharmonia Orchestra, London Symphony Chorus (Margaret Marshall, soprano; Stephen Robert, baritone): Virgin Classics VC 7 90843-2. As required with material of this kind, this recording delivers great impact combined with fine depth and clarity. The solo vocalist parts are important features of this work, and they are recorded as they should be with excellent positioning and a realistic size relationship to the instrumental ensemble. (A+)

1341 Vaughan Williams, R.: *Symphony Number 1*, London Symphony Orchestra and Chorus: Chandos CHAN 8764. This release is dynamic, clear, spacious, and impressive. The hall acoustics are realistically handled, and the solo vocals are magnificently recorded and properly blended into the ensemble. (A+)

1342 Vaughan Williams, R.: *Symphony Number 2*; *The Lark Ascending*, Royal Philharmonic Orchestra: Telarc 80138. In this example of high-quality sound we have some beautifully clean, low-level detailed sections that lead into equally transparent and three-dimensional areas of great dynamism. Recordings with this kind of soft-to-loud range are one reason the compact disc displaced the LP as the preferred playback medium. The hall acoustics are beautifully rendered as well. Telarc is known for its ability to reproduce very smooth string tones, and these are particularly well done. (A+)

1343 Vaughan Williams, R.: *Symphony Number 3*; *Oboe Concerto*, London Symphony Orchestra (Yvonne Kenny, soprano; David Theodore, oboe): Chandos CHAN 8594. Smooth, clean, and vibrant with a good soundstage spread and good depth. The vocalist is very well sized and correctly positioned for a wonderful dramatic effect. In addition, the oboe is well handled and sounds detailed and clear. The Chandos engineers have traditionally been good at striking a proper balance between large ensemble and featured soloists. (A)

1344 Vaughan Williams, R.: *Symphony Number 3*; *Symphony Number 4*; *Fantasia on Greensleeves*, Philharmonia Orchestra, with Linda Hohenfeld, soprano: RCA 09026-61194-2. This release is full, rich, and close up with a wide bandwidth and great dynamic range. The sound stage seems a bit flat. The soprano soloist was recorded at a different time and place from the rest of the ensemble, but the blend is quite good. (A)

1345 Vaughan Williams, R.: *Symphony Number 5*; *Fantasia on a Theme of Thomas Tallis*, Royal Philharmonic Orchestra: Telarc 80158. The usual Telarc sound: smooth, clean, and transparent with a good sense of hall space. The hall ambience here may be more related to the effects of the spaced-microphone array on the direct signal than the recorded sound of the environment, but the subjective result is good nonetheless. Music like this requires a clean string sound, and this disc delivers. (A+)

1346 Vaughan Williams, R.: *Sinfonia Antarctica (Symphony Number 7)*; *Toward an Unknown Region*, London Symphony Orchestra and Chorus: Chandos CHAN 8796. As usual with material from this label, this effort has a very fine orchestral spread and detail combined with a proper sense of hall space. There is a subtle deep bass from the organ, at times (into the low 20s I would imagine). I felt the sound was just a bit more refined than on the Chandos-LSO recording on the *Symphony Number 3* (see 1343). (A+)

1347 Vaughan Williams, R.: *Symphony Number 9*; *Piano Concerto in C Major*, London Symphony Orchestra, Howard Shelley, piano: Chandos CHAN 8941. Like 1346, this one is spacious, clean, and transparent. As expected from a Chandos recording of a concerto, the solo piano is well integrated into the orchestral sound. (A+)

1348 Vaughan Williams, R.: *The Wasps* (overture); *Serenade to Music* (orchestral version); Delius, Frederick: *Assorted short works*, London Philharmonic Orchestra: Chandos CHAN 8330. This one has a nice sound stage with a good midhall listening perspective and a nice sense of envelopment. The stage depth is also notable as is the subtle, often deep bass. The violins sound quite smooth. (A)

1349 *Venetian Music at the Habsburg Court in the 17th Century* (short works by Neri, Buonamente, Valentini, Bertali, and Priuli), Musica Fiata: Deutsche Harmonia Mundi 77086-2-RC. This effort has nice original-instrument clarity with a good combination of stage spread, imaging, and depth. (A)

1350 Verdi, Giuseppe: *Falstaff*,

Symphonieorchester des Bayerischen Rundfunks (with Rolando Panerai, Marilyn Horne, Sharon Sweet, Alan Titus, Frank Lopardo, and others): RCA 60705-2. In this release we have a properly sized sound stage with the assembled singers at a nice midhall listening distance. There is good overall clarity, and the hall acoustics envelop the presentation quite nicely. This recording presents a fairly realistic positioning of the entire ensemble with no in-your-face soloists. Engineers often strive for the opposite effect because it usually has an edge in vocal articulation. (A)

1351 Verdi, G.: *La Forza del Destino*, Philharmonia Orchestra, Ambrosian Opera Chorus (with Rosalind Plowright, Agnes Baltsa, José Carreras, Renato Bruson, Juan Pons, Paata Burchuladze, and others): Deutsche Grammophon 419 203-2. A number of DGG opera recordings in the past (as well as many of their straight orchestral works) were overengineered with each and every instrumental group given its own microphone and recording track. The result was often hyperdetailed clarity but no sense of space or depth. That is not the case here. There is a very realistic orchestral-vocal balance in this release that still preserves clarity, and all of it blended into an excellent sound stage with a fine sense of envelopment. (A)

1352 Verdi, G.: *Luisa Miller*, Metropolitan Opera Orchestra and Chorus (with Aprile Millo, Placido Domingo, Vladimir Cherna, Florence Quivar, and others): Sony Classical S2K 48073. While this release is exceptionally clean and transparent and has a good soundstage spread (important characteristics for any opera recording), there appeared to be a notable lack of hall reverberation and envelopment. I also felt that the soloists were a bit more in front of the orchestral-choral support than some listeners might like. It should be noted that this kind of dry and forward characteristic is considered by some engineers a good thing since it tends to enhance vocal clarity and make the work more enjoyable in a home listening situation. These views are seconded by a number of knowledgeable listeners, including many of those who often struggle to hear the soloists at live performances. Thus, the recording favors articulation over an absolute sense of you-are-there hall realism. For those who wish a little more reverb, I found that the recording benefited greatly when manipulated by my larger Yamaha DSP unit. (B+)

1353 Verdi, G.: *Requiem*, Atlanta Symphony Orchestra and Chorus (with Susan Dunn, Diane Curry, Jerry Hadley, and Paul Plishka): Telarc 80152. As one would expect from a Telarc recording of this work, this effort has tremendous impact with a near-perfect balance among soloists, choir, and orchestra. The sound stage is free of any subjective phasey quality, probably because of the overall scale of the work. A skillful use of accent microphones combined with a separate spaced array for the chorus allows the engineer to avoid the kind of central-image artifacts that might plague a straight three-omni technique. (A+)

1354 Verdi, G.: *Rigoletto*, Orchestra e Coro del Teatro Comunale di Bologna (with June Anderson, Luciano Pavarotti, Leo Nucci, Nicolai Ghiaurov, and others): London 425 864-2. This presentation is clean and clear, but with an often much too front-row-center listening perspective for the vocal soloists in relation to the more distant-sounding orchestra. Although this recording is a good one to evaluate the up-close human voice, it is not one I would choose to demonstrate a realistic operatic sound stage. During some of the passages, the orchestra is acoustically "moved to the rear" (obviously by means of mixer adjustments) to preserve vocal clarity. The strong point of this recording is the fine vocal articulation. (B+)

1355 Verdi, G.: *La Traviata*, Philharmonia Orchestra and Ambrosian Opera Chorus (with Renata Scotto, Sarah Walker, Cynthia Buchan, Alfredo Kraus, Renato Bruson, and others): EMI CDS 7 47538 8. The somewhat distant sound-stage perspective in this 1982 DDD recording does not reduce its realistic impact. However, it is realism as heard from the back rows of the hall. Most opera, live or recorded, sounds better with the singers *and* the orchestra listened to fairly close up since the soloists can be understood (and in a live performance seen) better. There is a good orchestral-vocal blend here. (A)

1356 Victoria, Tomás: *O Magnum Mysterium*; *Ascendens Christus in Altam*, Westminster Cathedral Choir: Hyperion CDA 66190. These are remarkably clear and realistic recordings of works by Renaissance composer Tomás Luis de Victoria. The hall envelopment is excellent, the sound stage is focused well, and there is very good choral blending. (A+)

1357 Victoria, T.: *Requiem*, The Tallis Scholars: Gimell GIM-012. This effort is nice and clean with a good sense of hall space. I felt the stage image was somewhat distant. This effect will be appreciated by many listeners. (A)

1358 Vierne, Louis: *Symphony Number 6*; Reger, Max: *Second Sonata in D Minor*, David Craighead, organ: Delos DE 3096. This is an absolutely stunning state-of-the-art engineering job. The sound is smooth, transparent, reverberant in just the right way, and blessed with optimum ambience. Outstanding church acoustics and impressive bass are clearly evident. (A+)

1359 Villa-Lobos, Heitor: *Music For Flute*, William Bennett and Friends: Hyperion CDA 66295. This effort displays a wide, spacious sound stage with fine depth and clarity. The flute is well positioned in relation to the grouping. (A)

1360 Villa-Lobos, H.: *Quatuors a Cordes, Numbers 4, 5, and 6*, Bessler-Reis Quartet: Le Chant du Monde LDC 278 901. This recording is very clean and clear with a close up, front-row listening perspective. Good depth and imaging. (A)

1361 Villa-Lobos, H.: *Valsa Da Dor*; *Bachiana Brasileira Number Four*; *Ciclo Brasileiro*, Alma Petchersky, piano: Academy Sound and Vision CDDCA-607. This disc displays a clean you-are-there sound with good small-hall ambience and the piano well located in relation to the listener. (A)

1362 Viola Works: *Paul Cortese, Viola*, with Jon Klibonoff, piano (assorted short pieces by Carter, Bergsma, Hovhaness, Rochberg, and Persichetti): Crystal CD 636. This effort has a realistic and small sound stage combined with good instrumental imaging and a well-integrated hall ambience. The clarity is top grade. (A+)

1363 *The Virtuoso Trumpet* (short works by Arban, Françaix, Tisné, Honegger, Maxwell-Davies, Rabe, and Hartmann); Håkan Hardenberger, trumpet; Roland Pöntinen, piano: BIS

Virtuoso Trumpet (1364) [186]

CD-287. This is a supremely accurate reproduction of the sound of two difficult-to-record instruments. The imaging is precise, and the music is presented on a you-are-there sound stage with just the right hall envelopment. (A+)

1364 *Virtuoso Trumpet* (short works by Neruda, Endler, Molter, and Telemann), German Bach Soloists, Wolfgang Basch, trumpet: ProArte CDG 3299. I felt that this recording displayed an excellent sound stage with superior placement of the solo trumpet in relation to the rest of the ensemble. Clean, clear, just right. When given some decent surround-sound enhancement, the whole recording becomes even more three-dimensional. (A+)

1365 *Virtuoso Trumpet Concertos* (short works by Biber, Molter, Fasch, M. Haydn, W. A. Mozart, and L. Mozart), Philharmonia Orchestra, John Wallace, trumpet: Nimbus NI 5121. This is a brilliant, realistic, clear example of baroque and early classical music. Excellent depth and ambience combined with fine dynamic contrasts highlight this paradigm of Ambisonic reproduction, even when played through only two front speakers. The Calrec microphone is at its best with music of this kind. (A+)

1366 Vitry, Philippe de: *Motets and Chansons*, Sequentia: Deutsche Harmonia Mundi 77095-2-RC. This release displays excellent vocal clarity and spaciousness combined with a nice sense of stage depth. All of this fine quality is coming from an ADD recording and proves the importance of good microphones, their proper use, and the quality of the hall or studio in obtaining good sound. High-tech digital is great, but the other hardware is often underrated, at least for music of this kind, which often lacks extreme dynamic range and a wide-frequency bandwidth. (A)

1367 Vivaldi, Antonio: *Cello Concertos, Volume 1* (including *Concerto For Cello in D Minor* and *Concerto For Cello in C Minor*), Toronto Chamber Orchestra, Ofra Harnoy, cello: RCA 7774-2-RC. This release is very smooth, transparent, and revealing with a good sense of hall space and depth. The cello is extremely well focused and sized perfectly in relation to the supporting players. (A+)

1368 Vivaldi, A.: *Choral Works*, Budapest Madrigal Choir, Liszt Ferenc Chamber Orchestra: Hungaroton HCD 11695-2. This ADD production again proves that it is engineering expertise, microphone quality, microphone placement, and hall acoustics that determine the merit of a recording. There is a wonderful enveloping ambience here with vocal clarity and sound-stage depth aplenty. (A+)

1369 Vivaldi, A.: *Il Cimento dell' Armonia e dell'Inventione* (14 concertos, including *The Four Seasons*), Raglan Baroque Players: Virgin Classics 7 90803-2. This set of period-instrument instrumental works is detailed, clean, and robust. The hall ambience is complementary to the presentation. (A)

1370 Vivaldi, A.: *Concerti a Due (Six Concertos)* with assorted featured players), Wiener Akademie: Novalis 150 074-2. This state-of-the-art authentic-instruments recording is demo grade all the way. None of that "tinny" sound here. The sound-stage spread, clarity, hall envelopment, and depth are all front rank. I felt that the effect of realism was made even more impressive with a bit of surround enhancement, but the overall ambience and depth is such that the recording almost seems surround-sound with just two stereo speakers. (A+)

1371 Vivaldi, A.: *Concertos*, London Chamber Orchestra: Virgin Classics 7 91167-2. This effort displays a typically bright and clear baroque sound. The instrumental textures are very detailed with good imaging, a nice sense of hall space, and excellent stage depth. There are a number of other fine instruments in this ensemble, but if you want to hear two Stradivarius violins in action, this is your record of choice. (A+)

1372 Vivaldi, A.: *Flute Concertos*, I Solisti Veneti, Jean-Pierre Rampal, flute: Columbia MK 39062. Recorded by Erato, this disc has a nice sound stage, good ensemble depth, and fine solo-instrument imaging—possibly somewhat better than on the release by Harmonia Mundi (see 1374) but not enough to give it a better score. The latter has a somewhat better sound-stage spread and sense of hall space. (A)

1373 Vivaldi, A.: *Flute Concertos*; Camerata Köln; Karl Kaiser, flute; Michael Schneider, recorder: Deutsche Harmonia Mundi 77156-2-RC. This is an exceptionally clean and three-dimensional original-instruments recording. There is a remarkably good sound-stage presentation combined with the kind of hall envelopment that makes music like this work. The instrumental focus is adequately tight, given the perceived listening distance. In terms of that music of this kind requires, this disc surpassed both 1372 and 1374 and holds its own with 1370. (A+)

1374 Vivaldi, A.: *Flute Concertos*, Philharmonia Baroque Orchestra, Janet See, flute: Harmonia Mundi USA HMC 905193. This series of flute works is very clean and transparent with a broad stage spread and a nice sense of space. The clearly recorded baroque flute is up front in perspective but is just a tad diffuse. To get an idea of a slightly more realistic sense of recorded hall space with at least some of these works, compare this disc to *Concerti a Due* (see 1370). (A)

1375 Vivaldi, A.: *Four Seasons*; *Flute Concerto in D*; *Harpsichord Concerto in A Major*, The Connecticut Early Music Festival Ensemble (Jörg-Michael Schwarz, violin; Igor Kipnis, harpsichord): Chesky CD-78. Here we have an extremely articulate and transparent original-instrument sound with the kind of front-row sound stage that live-music patrons pay extra money for. Note the highly defined, very revealing, almost etched-in-space violin. Fine depth and ambience highlight the panorama, and the harpsichord sounds real. What else can I say? Go buy this disc. (A+)

1376 Vivaldi, A.: *Four Seasons*, Boston Symphony Orchestra: Telarc 80070. Another early Telarc digital recording (1981) that still possesses formidable clarity, detail, and a blended and spacious hall ambience. The listening perspective is somewhat distant, and the string sound is unforced and rendered in the modern manner, very much in contrast to 1375. The performance is marvelous, the orchestral sizing somewhat large (rather than original-instrument small), and the sound is close to state of the art. (A)

1377 Vivaldi, A.: *Gloria, RV 588*; *Gloria, RV 589*, The Hanover Band and Christ Church Cathedral Choir: Nimbus NI 5278. This recording is smooth and distant with the usual original-instrument and (to some) slightly

Vivaldi (1378)

thinned-out sound. This is *not* a recording deficiency but a characteristic of the hall acoustics and ensemble itself. The clarity is notable, and hall ambience is quite good. (A)

1378 Vivaldi, A.: *Motets*, Mária Zádori, soprano (with support from a period-instrument ensemble): Quintana 903063. There are very fine instrumental textures here, the soloist a bit close up but very clearly recorded as a consequence. The hall ambience is good. (A)

1379 Vivaldi, A.: *Six Concertos*, I Musici de Montreal: Chandos CHAN 8651. This release is very clean with excellent stage depth and a fine sense of hall space. There is just a hint of background noise on the first track, probably an artifact of the small organ that is a part of the ensemble. (A+)

1380 *Vladimir Horowitz: The Last Recording* (playing works by Haydn, Chopin, Liszt, and Wagner): Sony Classical SK 45818. This effort is close up and detailed with fine piano tonality. However, the instrument sounds too close at times since its mechanical noise is often audible. Piano recordings may or may not be helped by surround enhancement. One that is as closely recorded as this probably comes across better with your system's surround-sound processing turned off. (A)

1381 Vollenweider, Andreas: *Book of Roses*: Columbia CK 48601. There is remarkable clarity and a wide-band frequency-response range on this highly processed, clearly electrically manipulated New Age disc. Lots of sound effects round things out. If one accepts it for what it is (not live-sounding music), it comes across as a nice piece of technical work. (A)

1382 Wagner, Richard: *Music of Wagner* (orchestral selections), Minnesota Orchestra: Telarc 80083. This is a typical "middle period" (1983) Telarc recording with a spacious, reverberant, and somewhat diffuse sound field. The perceived sound-stage depth is good. (B+)

1383 Wagner, R.: *Parsifal*, Berlin Philharmonic, Choir of the German State Opera (with José van Dam, John Tomlinson, Matthias Hölle, Sigfried Jerusalem, and others): Teldec 74448-2. This effort displays very accurate orchestral sound with good depth and a very good left-right spread. There is also a good sense of orchestral-choral blending. The vocal solo clarity is good, as is the left-right positioning of the performers on the stage, although they are sometimes placed a bit closer to the listener than the distance to the orchestra and the choir would dictate (at a live opera performance, all of the singers will usually be a bit farther from the audience than the orchestra, which will be in a pit area in front of the stage). The engineering trade-off is as usual: vocal clarity over stage realism. (A)

1384 Wagner, R.: *The Ring Without Words* (orchestral highlights from the Ring Cycle), Berlin Philharmonic Orchestra: Telarc 80154. Like the earlier Telarc recording above, this one is for Wagner nuts who cannot understand German or those fluent in the language who would care less about the words. This disc has marvelous clarity combined with often tremendous dynamic range. It is also quite clearly recorded with a good subjective sound stage. The Telarc recording philosophy was made for music like this, and the company's current recording policies expertly implement that view. This is a significant improvement over the earlier Telarc release (see 1382). (A+)

1385 Waller, Fats: *Dick Hyman Plays Fats Waller*: Reference Recordings RR-33CD. This is one of the better jazz-piano recordings. Crystalline, clean, and totally lacking the phasey, diffuse quality that mars so many other solo-piano recordings. (A+)

1386 Walton, Cedar: *Cedar Walton Plays*, (with Ron Carter and Billy Higgins): Delos D/CD 4008. This is a praiseworthy example of the way small-combo jazz should be recorded. Clean and transparent with realistic depth, enveloping stage spread, and excellent dynamics. The bass line is marvelous, and the piano treatment is unusual, near perfect. The drums sound like real drums. (A+)

1387 Walton, William: *Façade 1 & 2*, The City of London Sinfonia: Chandos CHAN 8869. Clean, clear, and close up, the speaking parts perhaps subjectively a bit too close to the listener in relation to the instruments. There is a good sense of hall space, however, and good imaging. (A)

1388 Walton, W.: *Henry V*, Orchestra and Chorus of the Academy of St. Martin in the Fields: Chandos CHAN 8892. The up-close sound on this release is clear, bright, and dynamic. Narrator Christopher Plummer's voice is well positioned, and the hall ambience adds to the effect of his actually speaking in a large-space environment. (A)

1389 Walton, W.: *In Honour of the City of London* (and other shorter works), The Bach Choir, Philharmonia Orchestra: Chandos CHAN 8998. This recording is vibrant, spacious, somewhat distant, yet quite real sounding if one favors a near-back-of-the-hall location. There is also a fine blend between the chorus and orchestra. (A)

1390 Walton, W.: *Orchestral Works* (including *Portsmouth Point Overture, Capriccio Burlesco*, and *Music For Children*), London Symphony Orchestra: Chandos CHAN 8968. Clean, dynamic, smooth, and vibrant. The accurate orchestral reproduction is combined with a very realistic hall envelopment and depth. The disc has the palpable ambience we have come to expect from the latest material from Chandos. (A+)

1391 Walton, W.: *Symphony Number 1*, Royal Philharmonic Orchestra: Telarc 80125. Big and spacious, clear and detailed. The sense of hall space is particularly notable. Telarc's occasional central-image diffuseness seems to be missing here, probably because of the nature of the music and maybe the hall acoustics — but also possibly because of refinements in the company's recording technique. (A+)

1392 Ward, Robert: *Symphony Number 6*; *Appalachian Ditties and Dances*; *Lamentation*; *Dialogues*, Saint Stephen's Chamber Orchestra (with Stephen Shipps, Eric Larson, and the Amadeus Trio): Bay Cities BCD-1015. The recording is detailed and smooth with excellent ensemble focus and a realistic hall ambience on both the larger- and smaller-scaled works. There is good overall piano and string imaging with the ensemble placed in a small-hall setting. (A)

1393 Warlock, Peter: *Songs*; Benjamin Luxon, baritone; David Willison, piano: Chandos CHAN 8643. This one is close up and detailed with a good blend between the soloist and the piano. The singer and his accompaniment are properly placed and correctly sized. A good sense of hall ambience rounds out the effect. (A+)

1394 Warnes, Jennifer: *Famous Blue*

Raincoat, Songs of Leonard Cohen: RCA/Cypress PD90048. This fine effort displays stunningly smooth, realistic pop-music sound. The vocals have a remarkable clarity, and the sound stage blends well with them. This disc has some surprisingly strong and deep bass at times. The recording has been popular with audio buffs for some time, and for good reason. (A+)

1395 Warnes, J.: *The Hunter*: Private Music 82089-2. This is an absolutely superior-quality pop album with clear vocals, wide-band sound, and a good sound stage. One of the technically best pop recording jobs of its kind. (A+)

1396 Washington, Grover Jr.: *Then and Now* (with Marvin Smith, Ron Carter, Herbie Hancock, and others): Columbia CK 44256. This jazz release is smooth and articulate with good depth and detail. Unfortunately, both the piano and the drums are a bit too spread out in relation to the rest of the ensemble, although the width of the latter is not too much of a problem. A spread-out piano bothers me, though. There is some powerful bass at times. (B+)

1397 *Water Music of the Impressionists*, (short piano pieces by Ravel, Liszt, Debussy, and Griffes) Carol Rosenberger, piano: Delos CD-3006. This recording has a very realistic and reverberant stage perspective, the piano sounding fairly close (it also may sound a bit diffuse on some systems). If your hi-fi can generate the required high levels, the piano sounds as if the instrument were in your listening room. If you have a system with a good subwoofer, you may find that just a bit of hall rumble will be audible on this 1979 recording. (Qualified A)

1398 *Watkins Ale: Music of the English Renaissance*, The Baltimore Consort: Dorian DOR 90142. The instruments used here are modern copies of period types. The result displays excellent close up clarity, depth, and realistic sound stage. At times, the ensemble imaging seems just a tad diffuse in the center. The vocals themselves are superbly rendered with a final central focus. Just a hint of stage-induced "thumping" occasionally intrudes. To a great extent, this is due to the superior clarity of this disc. Even its flaws are realistic. (Qualified A+)

1399 Weill, Kurt: *Street Scene*, Scottish Opera Orchestra and Chorus: London 433 371-2. This is a "new technology" London effort with good orchestral clarity, realistic depth, and a broad sound-stage spread. The vocals are well positioned and properly sized in relation to the instrumentalists and have good clarity. The synergism is quite good, a cut above what is found in many earlier London classical recordings. (A+)

1400 Weiss, Michael: *Presenting Michael Weiss* (his quintet, with Tom Kirkpatrick, Ralph Lalama, Ray Drummond, and Kenny Washington): Criss Cross Jazz 1022. This release displays very clear and close-up instrumental delineation at the expense of some stage depth and accurate ensemble imaging. This is an example of the good and the bad aspects of the multimicrophone recording technique. (B)

1401 Wess, Frank, and Harry Edison: *Dear Mr. Basie* (their orchestra, with Joe Newman, Al Aarons, Snooky Young, Ray Brown, and many others): Concord Jazz CCD-4420. The sound here is attention-getting: punchy, clean, bright, and brassy. There is a very good sound stage in this live recording with better depth than typical for a jazz release. (A)

1402 Weston, Randy: *Portraits of Duke Ellington* (with Jamil Nasser, Idris Muhammad, and Eric Asante): Verve 841 312-2. There are some tremendous dynamic contrasts on this jazz recording, with surprisingly deep bass from the drums. I also thought the work had a nice piano sound with good overall clarity. Unfortunately, there is some low-frequency stage noise, probably microphone feed-through from a stand. (Better studio speaker monitors, more of a rarity than one might think, would have pinpointed the problem for the engineers.) This recording was made at the same as 1403 and 1404. (Qualified B+)

1403 Weston, R.: *Portraits of Thelonious Monk* (with Jamil Nasser, Idris Muhammad, and Eric Asante): Verve 841 313-2. There is good real-world nightclub ambience here plus good clarity. Overall, the sound is similar to the recording reviewed in 1402. Track 2 has a particularly noticeable bit of stage-induced low-bass vibration that mars the performance. (Qualified B+)

1404 Weston, R.: *Self Portraits* (with Jamil Nasser, Idris Muhammad and Eric Asante): Verve 841 314-2. Like 1402 and 1403, this release has a decent sound stage with the instruments well located between the speakers. The perspective is a bit distant, giving the effect of listening from the back of the studio (or jazz club). Also like the other two, there is just a bit of stage rumble that in this case seems to be triggered by the activity of the bongo player. (Qualified B+)

1405 *What Sweeter Music: Carols for the Year Round* (short works by Smedley, Abell, Stamm, Ayer, Sowerby, Vaughan Williams, Rutter, Britten, and others), Memphis Boychoir, Memphis Chamber Choir: Pro Organo CD 7031. The result here is very smooth but somewhat distant with good hall ambience, depth, and clarity. The organ accompaniment is well done, blending in with the rest of the ensemble the way it should. (A)

1406 *Where Silence Reigns* (short works by Bauer, Babbitt, and Geller), Griffin Music Ensemble: GM 2032CD. This recording is very detailed and clear with an outstanding sound stage on the first two works. These pieces were recorded at three times at two halls, but all three are fine examples of modern recording technology capturing the nuances of modern serious music. (A+ for Bauer and Babbitt; A for the Geller material)

1407 Whigham, Jiggs: *The Jiggs Up* (with Bud Shank, John Clayton, George Cables, and Jeff Hamilton): Capri 74024-2. This release has a close up and very smooth and mellow piano sound that is, as usual for jazz recordings of this kind, somewhat oversized in relation to the rest of the ensemble. At least it is not phasey. The drums are, thankfully, well focused. (B+)

1408 *White Man Sleeps* (short works by Volans, Ives, Hassell, Lee, Johnston, Coleman, and Bartók), Kronos Quartet: Elektra-Nonesuch 9 79163-2. This disc sounds smooth and blended with good depth and with a close-up somewhat dry feel that is satisfactorily intimate. This is a characteristic that complements music of this kind. Note that this "classical" material is quite modern (a bit advanced for traditional tastes, I would imagine), and although the Kronos Quartet name headlines the album, none of the music was written by the group members. (A)

1409 *White Trash*: Elektra 61053-2. There are good dynamic contrasts and plenty of stage spread on this one, the vocals typically overmodulated and strongly projected. The instrumental delineation is better than average for a rock album. (B)

1410 Williams, Hank Jr.: *Maverick*: Curb/Capricorn 26806-2. This is very well done C&W with fine vocal and instrumental delineation and smoothness. (B+)

1411 Williams, James: *Magical Trio 1* (with Ray Brown and Art Blakey): Emarcy 832 859-2. I felt this release displayed a very good piano tone, although the instrument is just too widely spread out. The drums are excellently recorded, however, as is the bass. The tonal blend of this jazz disc is its strong point, and it would have scored much higher if it were not for the piano bloating. The effect is lessened on smaller stereo systems. (B)

1412 Williams, Joe: *I Just Want to Sing* (with Thad Jones, Eddie Davis, Benny Golson, John Collins, Jerry Peters, Norman Simmons, John Heard, and Gerryck King): Delos D/CD 4004. There are some very clean vocals here combined with an excellent sound stage, marvelous depth, and a wide-frequency bandwidth. This recording is quite realistic sounding, another example of the Delos recording team's abilities when dealing with jazz material. I believe that this is one of the best-sounding jazz discs available, the one that I use when I am looking for a reference to evaluate other recordings of this kind. (A+)

1413 Williams, J.: *In Good Company* (with Marlena Shaw, Shirly Horn, and many others): Verve 837 932-2. This release is clean, distinct and yet somewhat distant. It has a very smooth sound field that delivers a good jazz nightclub feel. It lacks the presence, openness, and depth of 1412 and 1414, however. (B+)

1414 Williams, J.: *Nothin' But the Blues* (with Red Holloway, Eddie Vinson, Jack McDuff, Phil Upchurch, Ray Brown, and Gerryck King): Delos CD 4001. Done in 1983, most of the comments attached to 1412 apply here. Overall, this disc has great depth, spread, and clarity. I felt that it was just a bit rougher sounding than the later release. (A)

1415 Williams, Tony: *Angel Street* (with Wallace Roney, Billy Pierce, Mulgrew Miller, and Charnett Moffett): Blue Note CDP 7 48494-2. This is possibly the best of the Tony Williams jazz albums reviewed here, with good clarity and a well-focused sound stage. The drums and piano are both treated well. Recordings with this kind of tight imaging tend to respond well to manipulations by your home surround processor. (B+)

1416 Williams, T.: *Civilization* (with Wallace Roney, Billy Pierce, Mulgrew Miller, and Charnett Moffett): Blue Note CDP 7 46757-2. Nice and clean with a better sound stage than the recording discussed below. Under normal conditions, I would say there is too much drum spread, but the liner notes indicate that a drum machine was used in addition to regular drums, so the spread may actually mimic what one would hear at an electrified performance. (B+)

1417 Williams, T.: *Foreign Intrigue* (with Wallace Roney, Donald Harrison, Mulgrew Miller, and Ron Carter): Blue Note CDP 7 46289-2. This release seems a bit rougher and more congested at times than the above works by Williams (mixing problems, mainly), but the overall sound is blended well, and the bass line sneaks through with some fairly deep notes when required. I found that running the program through my more elaborate surround processor in either of its "jazz" modes opened up the program considerably. Often, lesser-quality discs respond well to such manipulations. If you have a number of marginal recordings, seriously consider upgrading your system with some kind of surround-enhancement device and additional speakers. (B)

1418 Willson, Meredith: *Music Man*, Cincinnati Pops, Indiana University Singers: Telarc 80276. This wonderful recording is clean, clear, dynamic, and spacious but with the solo vocals occasionally a bit too close. There are some good sound effects. (A)

1419 Wilson, Nancy: *Forbidden Lover* (with Carl Anderson assisting on some vocals): Columbia CK 40787. This is a very effective studio-sound multimicrophone job. There is a punchy and startlingly realistic bass line at times, which should still come across well without the need of a big subwoofer. Overall, Wilson's excellent voice is well treated by the engineers. This is a better recording job than her *Keep You Satisfied* album, which did not make the list. (B+)

1420 Wilson, N.: *Godsend*: Denon 7188. This pop release is clean and quite smooth with an electrically synthesized reverb that will be loved by some and hated by others. I felt that it had better bass balance than *I'll Be A Song* (see 1421), with some impressive depth on occasion. (B+)

1421 Wilson, N.: *I'll Be a Song*: Denon 7061. This one is smooth and very clean with maybe too much thump to the kick bass. However, on a smaller, less bass-potent stereo, the latter may be a plus factor. That was the case when the work was played on my smaller system, when the electronic equalizer subwoofer was set to its "filter-only" mode and the bass below 40 Hz attenuated. The sound stage is quite good, although the vocals are typically a bit too far forward in relation to the supporting ensemble. (B+)

1422 Wilson, Thomas: *Piano Concerto; Introit (Towards the Light)*, Scottish National Orchestra, David Wilde, piano: Chandos CHAN 8626. This is a well-sized and balanced piano-concerto album with good orchestral clarity and depth. The Chandos engineers continue to do a fine job of putting a solo instrument into an orchestral setting. (A)

1423 *Wind Quintets by Barber, Saeverud, Jolivet and Hindemith*, Bergen Wind Quintet: BIS CD-291. Smooth and clear with a fine if somewhat distant sound stage and good stage depth. Some BIS recordings seem to have the phasey and diffuse-sounding central image that characterizes a spaced-array microphone pickup, but this one is reasonably tight and well focused. (A)

1424 Winter, Paul: *Earthbeat* (with the Paul Winter Consort and Dmitri Pokrovsky Singers): Living Music LD-0015. There is remarkable clarity in this mixture of Russian folk and American jazz. There is also a good sound-stage spread, although the imaging is somewhat diffuse. Some parts were recorded in Moscow, and the American material was apparently overlaid at a studio in New York. It is certainly an interesting piece of work. (B+)

1425 Wonder, Stevie: *Innervisions*: Mobile Fidelity UDCD 554. This is another remastered and expensive "gold" disc. Produced when the master tapes were nearly two decades old, this reissue still has plenty of impact, good vocal clarity, and an enveloping sound stage. There is also some impressive bass at times. I think it is great that a recording like this was reissued, but the gold substrata makes it cost too much. The gold has no effect on the sound. (B+)

1426 Woods, Phil: *Evolution* (his Little Big Band, with Tom Harrel, Nick Brignola, Nelson Hill, Hal Crook, Hal Galper, Steve Gilmore, and Bill Goodwin): Concord CCD-4361. Nothing of microphone harshness or serious distortion intrudes on this clear and realistic-sounding jazz sound stage. The studio sound is somewhat dry, but as I have noted a number of times before, it can really come to life when even rudimentary surround processing is applied, be it a cross-feed-cancellation circuit such as the Carver hologram or the Polk SDA feature, or via more elaborate "synthesizing" processors such as those produced by Lexicon, Onkyo, and Yamaha. (A)

1427 Woods, P.: *Here's to My Lady* (his Little Big Band, with Tommy Flanagan, George Mraz, and Kenny Washington): Chesky JD-3. This is jazz saxophone realism that must be heard to be believed. There is great clarity and detail here with a realistic (read deep and spacious) sound stage. A well-defined piano image tops off the effort. (A+)

1428 Woods, P.: *Flash* (his Quintet + One, with Tom Harrell, Hal Galper, Steve Gilmore, Bill Goodwin, and Hal Crook): Concord Jazz CCD-4408. This release is good and clean with plenty of bite. The overall blend is a bit thin and distant, a defect that is correctible with the bass control of your pre-amp or receiver. (B)

1429 Woods, P.: *Real Life* (his Little Big Band, with Steve Gilmore, Bill Goodwin, Jim McNeely, Tom Harrell, Hal Crook, and Nick Brignola): Chesky JD-47. Another Chesky winner with a remarkably three-dimensional sound stage. The ensemble sounds very unclouded and clean with fine dynamics. As might be expected, the imaging is notably good, and the sax sound is on the nose. This jazz effort is right up there with JD-3 (see 1427). (A+)

1430 Xenakis, Iannis: *Kraanerg*, Alpha Centauri Ensemble: Etcetera KTC 1075. While this very modern "serious" music is not for everyone, some parts of it are revealing of playback-system anomalies, and the recording itself is quite good overall. The technical standouts here are the remarkable sound stage and exacting instrumental textures. (A)

1431 Yellow Jackets: *Four Corners* (with Russell Ferrante, Jimmy Haslip, Marc Russo, and William Kennedy, with several guests assisting): MCA 5994. There is some clear and punchy sound on this pop-jazz disc. The recording displays a very satisfactory and wide dynamic range that comes across as more than simply rock-and-roll-type punch. This is sharply etched sound that shows the MCA engineers wanted a performance that sounded good on better-grade home audio systems as well as car stereos. (A)

1432 Yellow Jackets: *Greenhouse* (with Russell Ferrante, Jimmy Haslip, William Kennedy, and such guest musicians as Bob Mintzer, Vince Mendoza, Alex Acuña, and a few others): GRP

GRD 9630. There is a good sound stage and depth here, and the clarity is quite good. This album is more modern-sounding jazz than the material on the other YJ discs reviewed here. (A)

1433 Yellow Jackets: *Politics* (with Russell Ferrante, Jimmy Haslip, Marc Russo, and William Kennedy): MCA 6236. Most Yellow Jackets discs are DDD, but this ADD effort holds its own with the others. It seems a bit less punchy than 1431 (but still plenty potent) and actually seems to have a somewhat better sound stage. (B+)

1434 Yellow Jackets: *Shades* (with Russell Ferrante, Jimmy Haslip, Ricky Lawson, Marc Russo, and several guest players): MCA 5752. This one is clear, dynamic, and vibrant with typical YJ attention to sound quality. (B+)

1435 Yellow Jackets: *The Spin* (with Marc Russo, Jimmy Haslip, Russell Ferrante, and William Kennedy): MCA 6304. Ditto to 1434. (B+)

1436 Yes: *Big Generator*: ATCO 90522-2. This rock album is spacious with good dynamic contrasts as well as decent bass at times. The vocals are a bit distant and overly reverberant. (B)

1437 Yes: *Union*: Artista ARCD-8643. The vocals here are a tad rough, but the detail is still clear and articulate (probably intentional to enhance automotive or small home-system listening). The overall ensemble has a good sound stage and plenty of rock punch. In addition, the left-mid-right imaging is surprisingly well done. The recording also responds well to surround enhancement. (B)

1438 *Your Friendly, Neighborhood Big Band* (with Matt Catingub, Mavis Rivers, and many others): Reference Recordings RR-14CD. The sound here is distant to the extent that you *must* crank up the volume well above normal for the full impact of this disc to come across. And come across it does. The result is a phenomenally realistic and dynamic jazz-band sound stage with great depth, envelopment, and imaging. The orchestral balance and impact of this disc parallel what you would hear from a good seat at a live concert. One of the best. Remember to hang on. (A+)

1439 ZZ Top: *Recycler*: Warner 26265-2. This impressive effort displays fine clarity combined with a really good rock-concert sound stage. This is modern rock sound at its best. Excellent rock-grade (often deep) bass. (B+)

1440 ZZ Top: *The Six Pack*: Warner 25661-2. While the dynamics, upper-range smoothness, and wide-band response of the early 1970s recordings on disc number one of this remastered three-disc reissue are a bit limited by up-to-date standards, it is educational to chart the improvements in the above qualities in the later recordings. Most important for a rock album, however, is the impressive sound stage and imaging found on all of the recordings here, a tribute to the recording engineers and mastering expert Bob Ludwig, who also worked on *Recycler* (see 1439). (B for disc 1; B+ for discs 2 and 3)

1441 Zappa, Frank: *The Best Band You Never Heard in Your Life*: Barking Pumpkin Records D2 74233. This release exhibits a good sound stage, decent clarity, and typical Zappa dynamics. The vocals are unrealistically forward sounding, unfortunately, but probably enhance the effect Zappa was after. Remember, rock music is not necessarily supposed to sound like an exact replica of what would be heard at a live acoustic-instrument concert. (B+)

1442 Zappa, F.: *Boulez Conducts Zappa* (*The Perfect Stranger* and other works), Ensemble Intercontemporain and the Barking Pumpkin Digital Gratification Consort: Barking Pumpkin D2-74242. (Previously released in 1984 as EMI 47125-2.) Zappa classical? You bet and fairly well recorded too. The sound of this recording is close up, detailed, and dynamic — and conducted by Pierre Boulez, yet. Note that this is not music for everyone, even Zappa pop-music lovers. The sound stage seems to lack some depth, although the left-right spread is wide and the imaging precise. (A)

1443 Zappa, F.: *Them or Us*: Ryko RCD 40027. What we have here is certainly one of the better-recorded avant-garde pop discs. This is very detailed sound reproduction with substantial impact — but also heavily processed and not really "real" sounding. (B+)

1444 Zappa, F.: *We're Only in It for the Money/Lumpy Gravy*: Ryko RCD 40024. Like the above disc, which was DDD, this Ryko AAD reissue is quite clear but heavily manipulated at the mixing box. Both of these Zappa discs often have rather unusual musical content. Not for children — or some adults, either. (B+)

1445 Zeitlin, Denny: *In the Moment* (with David Friesen, Peter Donald, and Joel DiBartolo): Windham Hill WD-0121. This one is close up, detailed, and smooth. The one glaring fault that keeps this AAD jazz recording from scoring higher is the somewhat oversized and phasey-sounding quality of the featured instrument on this disc, the piano. (B)

1446 Zemlinsky, Alexander von: *Symphony in B-Flat Major*, Slovak Philharmonic Orchestra: Marco Polo 8.220391. Overall, this recording has a marvelous degree of stage depth and spread with excellent clarity and detail. Just a bit of brittleness in the violin sound is the only salient defect. The hall acoustics are a bit dry, but some listeners like the effect, and I found that this actually worked to the recording's favor when I applied surround processing via my Yamaha DSP unit. (A)

1447 *Zigeunerlieder* (songs by Brahms, Spohr, Stolz, Tchaikovsky, Liszt, Schumann, and Dvořák); Kristin Thiesen, soprano; Audun Kayser, piano: Thorofon CTH 2096. This recording displays good vocal focus and imaging with an equally good sense of hall space and depth. The piano and vocal sounds dovetail properly. (A)

Appendix A: Test and Sampler Recordings

Needless to say, the recordings below will have some very compelling sounds. A few are strictly "test" discs; the rest are "samplers" designed to attract listeners to more complete works by the companies that produce them. A few are combinations of both. All come with inserts containing information about the techniques used to make the recordings, and some of those are miniature tutorials on recording and sound-system theory.

All the discs to follow contain material that will fully exercise even the most potent stereo systems. The test segments on some are often fun to work with and are both educational and important in determining if a system is operating up to snuff. I believe that any serious sound enthusiast should own at least a couple of test discs to use as measurement tools and reference standards for good recorded sound.

A lot of samplers and digital-test discs are available these days, and more are appearing all the time. This is a cross section of the better ones, those I had on hand or had access to at the university library where I work. I am aware that a number of good ones have been left out.

Bravura (includes pieces by Respighi, Strauss, and Lutoslawski, played by several different orchestras): Delos DE 3070. This is a showpiece, demo-type album with great impact, impressive dynamics, and a wide-band frequency range. The enclosed flyer has important data on how each of the segments was produced. While not a "test disc" in the strict sense, this production is a fine educational tool for those interested in learning about why certain microphone and hall configurations interact as they do. It should also entice you into buying the complete versions of the assorted samples. (A+)

Chesky Jazz Sampler, Volume 1: Chesky JD-37. A must for buffs who want to evaluate imaging and want good examples of advanced recording techniques. The vertical imaging demonstration is entertaining and will reveal weaknesses in speaker sound-staging capabilities and placement asymmetries. (Listen to this test section on several different systems to get an idea of what it should sound like.) The functional but also notorious "Bonger" test should be used only to evaluate the low-level artifacts of your CD player since the initial part of the test signal made on the custom processor was overdriven and distorted during the recording process. The absolute-phase comparison is irrelevant if your system has low asymmetric (even-order) harmonic distortion and you listen well into

Appendix A

the *reverberant* field, although it may be meaningful if you listen with headphones or occupy the *direct* listening field of speakers designed for that kind of use. Absolute phase is important mainly to paranoid audiophiles who want to "hear" things. Chesky's use of 128-times oversampling is also pretty much audibly inconsequential (although I am certain that its effects are measurable). Their hyping of the technique is just that — hype. Their good sound comes mainly from the proper use of good microphones, adhering to "minimalist" microphone techniques, and careful attention to mixing. (A+)

Chesky Jazz Sampler, Volume 2: Chesky JD68. More remarkable tests and excerpts from Chesky. The imaging and sound-stage tests are revealing. The tests on D-A converters and digital cables meant nothing to me, but maybe your system can resolve such nuances, although it pays to keep a cool head as you try to spot such things. As usual, the musical selections are first class. (A+)

Demonstration of Stereo Microphone Techniques: Performance Recordings PR-6-CD. If you want to hear what a number of microphone types and placement techniques sound like, this 19-minute disc is the recording for you. This is one of the most educational "test" tools available and a must for any audio buff who wants to learn more about the sound of "purist" recordings. The main goal of the producers was to demonstrate the stereo imaging produced by a variety of recording methods. A secondary goal was to demonstrate the kind of tonal quality available from several microphone types. The first goal was magnificently achieved, the second less so.

A weak point in the production is the lack of any data on how microphones in halls behave in properly handling ambience, especially that reflected from the sides and rear. However, dealing with reflected ambience, given the small scale of the sound stage and the tools used, was obviously not a goal of the producers. I felt that one glaring deficiency was the lack of any example of the "Decca Tree" recording technique, which places the center microphone of a three-capsule array considerably in front of the flanking mikes. There was an example of a standard three-omni-in-a-row configuration, similar to what is used by Telarc, although the spacing between the capsules was much smaller. Still, this disc is worth every penny of its almost dollar-per-minute cost. (A+)

Denon Digital Audio Check CD: Denon 33C39-7441. This is a fine combination sampler-test disc that contains twelve tracks of excerpts from the Denon catalog plus a series of test sequences on fourteen additional tracks that will be helpful in setting up a basic stereo system (speaker phase, balance, centering). Perhaps the most helpful item is the low-level test sequence, which will help the system owner to evaluate the D-A converter in his or her CD player. (A)

The Digital Domain: A Demonstration: Elektra 9 60303-2. This is a good selection of electronic music and test sequences by the Stanford University Center for Computer Research in Music and Acoustics. The opening jet-plane sequence should be run at low volume at first to give the operator an idea of the sound levels involved and prevent speaker damage. For sound-effects nuts, this piece alone will be worth the price of the disc. Test tones are also available (sine waves, pink noise, etc.), which can help you calculate volume control–power output settings if you have power meters on your amplifier or receiver. They can also assist you in adjusting an equalizer if

Appendix A

you have an RTA. (A real-time analyzer presents a continual readout of the signal amplitude in evenly divided spectral bands.)

An important warning should be made here about the square-wave test on track 19. This should *not* be played through speakers at all since even a small advancement of the volume control could fry some speaker drivers. An announcement on track 18 warns about possible speaker damage on the next track, but it is still possible to punch a programming-sequence button by mistake and immediately land your speakers in a lot of trouble. The test tone should have been on the same band as the announcement—directly following it—making any kind of accidental sonic disaster more difficult. (A+)

Engineer's Choice (a sampler featuring twenty-two excerpts of material recorded by engineer John Eargle): Delos DE 3506. It's hard to beat this one. These are masterful examples of what Eargle is capable of. The insert that comes with the disc gives interesting information on the microphone techniques used as well as the recording environments encountered. (A+)

Gems of Jazz (a sampler featuring Joe Williams, Cedar Walton, Red Holloway, Bunky Green, and others): Delos DE 3507. This disc features wonderful sound throughout and is an example of what recording engineer work is all about. This is not just a sampler to take with you to evaluate systems at your local dealer. It is also a sampler to listen to and enjoy over and over. If owning this disc does not make you want to collect the complete recordings highlighted here, you are just not into good jazz and good sound. (A+)

Hi-Fi News and Record Review Test Disc II: HFN 015. This is an excellent series of tests and musical passages engineered by Tony Faulkner. However, two warnings are in order. First, some very clean test tones (running from 2 Hz to 20 KHz) are recorded at maximum level (0 dB), which requires keeping the volume fairly low during playback unless you want to blow a speaker driver. Levels this high may also overload certain signal processors, especially equalizers, installed in an external processor or tape loop. Second, the central image in the early spoken "walk-around" test sections (both stereo and Ambisonics) are slightly skewed to the left side, an odd error that is not the fault of your system. Further into the test sequence, an excellent central-image test copied from an earlier Denon test disc will validate the problem with the first series and accurately evaluate central imaging balance. (Qualified A+)

In Sync: ProJazz Sampler 2 (selections by the Tokyo Union Big Band, The Michel Camilo Trio, Ronnie Cuber, Ronnie Foster, and quite a few others): ProJazz CDJ 599. This release has plenty of punch when needed with fine clarity, good depth, and well-etched detail. These selections are taken from the ProJazz catalog. The sound quality is variable. (B+ to A)

King of Instruments (a listener's guide to the art and sciences of recording the organ, with short excerpts from J. S. Bach, Buxtehude, Sowerby, Rorem, and others along with written descriptions by John Eargle of the recording techniques employed): Delos DE 3503. This is a remarkable series of excerpt recordings taken from the Delos catalog. A variety of microphone techniques were used to make this disc, and these are clearly described in the accompanying insert. Needless to say, this is an outstanding educational guide to the art and science of recording organs and an equally outstanding example of state-of-the-art recorded sound. (A+)

Appendix A

An Organ Blaster Sampler (excerpts from J. S. Bach, Jongen, Widor, Soler, Franck, and others), Michael Murray, playing several organs: Telarc 80277. There is variable quality on this sampler disc, ranging from good to great. Some of the stuff here has a tremendous impact and will highlight the potential of any world-class sound system. (B+ to A+, depending on the piece and the organ)

Soul of the Machine (The Windham Hill Sampler of New Electronic Music): Windham Hill WD-1700. This is a good cross section of this company's material with an assortment that is indicative of what WH can turn out when it wants to. Every one of the selections has fine tonality, a good left-right sound-stage spread, and exemplary detail and transparency. Most are not realistic in the live-music sense, of course, but they are certainly impressive as works in themselves. (A)

Stereophile Test CD: STPH 002-2 (available from the magazine). This item was produced by the staff of *Stereophile* magazine and contains interesting and educational excerpts from recordings made over the years by Gordon Holt, John Atkinson, Robert Harley, Peter Mitchell, and Brad Meyer. The statement on subjective testing by Gordon Holt at the beginning of the disc is far more cerebral than any of the more extreme "subjectivist" essays that have appeared in the magazine during the last few years.

Some of the recorded selections are very fine indeed, and the descriptions are worthwhile. The disc also has some *very* interesting comparisons of eighteen commonly used microphones (done during the Holt reading of his stand on subjective testing), although it is too bad that only one B&K and no highly regarded Schoeps units or the Calrec Soundfield model were included. In addition, the warble-tone test section is not much help since the device used to produce it was out of whack during its production (there has been a lot written in some of the other hobby journals about this goofup). Both correlated and "uncorrelated" pink-noise tones are also available, the latter helpful in setting up certain kinds of L-R surround processors and doing stereo sound-field measurements with an RTA. Some of the comments about critical A-B testing in the accompanying booklet are misleading, unfortunately. While I am the last person to feel at home complimenting the doings of most of the staff of *Stereophile*, I must admit that for the most part this is a very helpful disc. (A+)

Stereophile Test CD2: STPH 004-2 (available from the magazine). This is technically and philosophically similar to the first *Stereophile* disc, although the content is somewhat different. New music example tracks are included, and the disc includes one of the best recordings of acoustic guitar I have ever heard. The overall playback level seems excessively low (probably a wasted attempt by the producers to eliminate any chance of digital overload), but the chance of hearing any noise from your amp or digital artifacts from your CD player (as the gain of the former is turned up to compensate) is eliminated by the mostly hissy-sounding AAD or ADD source material. While these are quite good in terms of perspective, depth, clarity, and ambience, they all lose a lot because of that hiss. (Background noise of this kind seems to be a "badge of honor" for a few current tweak-oriented CD producers who are obsessed with analog recording gear and tube electronics.) According to the insert that comes with the disc, the producers are quite aware of the noise and state that most of it is the result of the tube microphones. The highly touted "EAR" microphones used in some of the recordings also seem, at least to my ears, a bit harsh at times, although in the first *Stereophile* disc I thought they sounded a bit muffled.

The pink-noise sections are useful (particularly the stereo, uncorrelated sequence) especially if one has a microphone-fed RTA to help in placing and equalizing speakers. This section can also be useful in double-checking surround-speaker levels, although an RTA is still needed for proper tweaking. The harmonic-distortion, test-tone comparisons are interesting, but their impact is limited since similar tests done with musical material would be far less conclusive, due to masking effects. It is interesting how subjectivist "tweak" audio buffs are interested in using test tones when they support their views and oblivious to them when they do not. Steady-state "pure" tones are academically interesting, but they are poor tools for evaluating the subjective effects of distortion on complex musical signals. These guys should know better. The tests dealing with digital "jitter" are nonsense. They also blew a chance to evaluate some important microphones that were left off the first disc. (A)

The Symphonic Sound Stage: A Listener's Guide to the Art and Science of Recording the Orchestra (eleven excerpts from symphonic performances, all engineered by John Eargle or Marc Aubort): Delos D/CD 3502. These short passages can help a knowledgeable listener quickly evaluate important aspects of audio-system performance, particularly (of course) the speakers and their placement. These are very realistic examples of the state of the recording art accompanied by worthwhile descriptions of the techniques used. Full-length versions of some of these pieces are listed in the main review list. (A+)

A Video Standard (A twelve-inch laser-video disc designed to "Optimize Your Audio/Video System") Reference Recordings LD-101. Although this is not a "compact" disc, it is included here for its audio as well as video abilities. This disc is equal to thousands of dollars of test hardware (assuming you have a "combi" player) and combined with its encyclopedic instruction manual, is a veritable tutorial in video and audio. The color and resolution charts will help you to align a TV monitor expertly, and the audio sections are nearly as helpful. (Note, however, that because there is no pause or warning prior to their appearance during the moving program, the video stills will automatically flash past rapidly during normal play. To lock into them, you must quickly hit the "still" button on your player and then move back and forth through the sequence of tests as required by means of the player's frame-advance feature.) The audio tests are workable, but some of them move along rapidly and require engaging the "loop-through" feature of your player to keep repeating them. Be prepared to read the manual carefully. (A+)

Appendix B: Record-Review and Equipment Journals

Most *music-oriented* magazines (either music journals that contain a few record reviews or record-review journals that specialize in them) are wonderful if one desires information on the world of music in general or wishes to know about the artistic aspects of a recorded performance. However, in many cases the reviews printed by these publications give you only a brief sketch of sound quality, either because the reviewer is uninterested in engineering or because he or she has a sound system that is incapable of resolving the detail necessary to tell a poor recording from a good one or a good one from a great one. In some cases, the reviewers attend live concerts regularly and consider the sound of any recording substandard.

The *audio-oriented* magazines currently available usually do a better job of analyzing the "sound" of the discs they review than the music-oriented journals. Indeed, a substantial number of music lovers would say that they put too much stress on engineering idiosyncrasies and not enough on the aesthetic qualities of the performance. However, while audio-oriented journals as a whole cater to equipment junkies more than music lovers, the reviews that the best ones contain are often incisive and accurate when it comes to electrical *and* artistic merits.

Ironically, quite a few of the equipment-oriented publications are inadequate in evaluating the hardware needed to build a fine system, especially loudspeakers. Many of them are written for and edited by individuals who are in possession of many half-truths about audio.

Here is a summary of some journals I am familiar with that were in print when this book was being written.

The Absolute Sound (irregular). The audio bible for the equipment extremist and die-hard subjectivist buffs, this journal usually has pretty good record reviews that stress artistic qualities as well as sound. Unfortunately, the editorial position for some has been that LP (grooved vinyl) recordings are more "true" to accurate sound than CDs. Fortunately (and mysteriously), this has not negatively affected the quality of their CD reviews, and when they say a recording sounds good, it usually does. However, that same editorial position *has* affected their opinions about audio hardware, and much of the stuff they print on the subject is silly. All kinds of music are reviewed.

American Record Guide (bimonthly). A record-collector's journal, the *ARG* has reviews that are usually impeccable in artistic expertise. However, the comments about sound quality are variable, depending on which of the many reviewers that work for the magazine is doing the review. Even when sound is mentioned, it is usually only as part of a brief statement at the end of the review that terminates with something like "up-to-date sound" or "more than adequate recorded sound." When *High Fidelity* magazine folded a few years back, the companion journal, *Musical America*, was nearly lost. It has now merged with the *ARG*, and the combination has become a must for serious record collectors and serious lovers of classical music. I have written a number of essays on the technical aspects of audio for this magazine.

Andrew Marshall's Audio Ideas Guide (quarterly). This Canadian-based journal is mainly equipment oriented, but a few record reviews are usually included in each issue. The magazine is strongly oriented toward audio quality, and the discussions of sound recordings are usually fine. Unfortunately, the information on hardware for home playback is often meaningful only to those whose ideas about audio are fantasy oriented. There is lots of pseudo-science in the equipment commentaries, particularly those dealing with CD players and amplifiers. The speaker-system reviews cater to the "direct-sound" crowd rather than individuals who listen to more distantly placed speakers in typical living rooms. All kinds of music are reviewed.

Audio (monthly). This magazine is an audio-enthusiast journal, and the reviews always include comments on sound quality—and those comments are usually quite accurate. The artistic evaluations are variable, however. The equipment coverage is variable also, with some of the test reports and technical essays in the world-class category and some of it subjective fantasy (the "oracle" column, usually, for example). The speaker tests cater to the "direct-field" crowd. All kinds of music are reviewed.

The Audio Critic (irregular). Mainly hardware oriented, the magazine is an often continuous polemic against the lunatic fringe in audio. As such, it is a valuable antidote for people who are easily influenced by propaganda and might be potential big-spending victims of the subjectivist "tweak" magazines. Some of the technical essays are very accurate and informative. The record reviews are sound oriented and are informative and accurate. The disc reviews stress classical with some pop and jazz thrown in.

CD Review (monthly). Once called *Digital Audio*. For a few months in the early 1990s, this magazine deleted the dual-category (performance-sound) record-review procedure that it had been using for a number of years. In 1993, it reinstated the dual-category system (but with two five-point rather than two ten-point scales) probably due to reader pressure. During the single-scale "middle" period, it was difficult for anyone to know if a recording were well engineered or not. Indeed, some releases gained a top score (five out of a possible five stars) without having particularly good sound. The current policy returns to the more sensible procedure, and the reviews are often quite informative in reporting what a recording sounds like. At one time, the equipment reviews by the likes of Ken Pohlmann (on digital gear) and Dave Moran (on speakers) were very helpful, but the data on hardware printed in the magazine now is nearly useless. The journal's physical layout is often very difficult to wade through. All kinds of music are reviewed.

Classic CD (monthly). Each issue of this journal comes with a "sampler"

Appendix B [204]

CD that contains a dozen or so excerpts from the most significant recordings reviewed in that issue. In addition, many other discs are reviewed, the total usually topping two hundred. As with most such journals, the comments on sound quality must be searched for as the review is read. If the sampler-disc feature continues, this would certainly have to be considered a good magazine for sound buffs. It also contains many outstanding essays on the musical scene as well as interviews with notables in the industry. The layout is sometimes a bit confusing, with "glitz" taking precedence over readability. Classical music is stressed.

Consumer's Research Magazine (monthly). While this is a general consumer-product-oriented publication, each issue usually has a short section of record reviews. They are typically incisive and accurate and always rate the performance and sound quality. Classical music is stressed.

Downbeat (monthly). The stress here is on the live-music jazz scene, and the magazine contains many excellent interviews and essays. The record reviews are incisive but usually lack much information on the quality of the engineering.

Fanfare (bimonthly). Similar in format and style to the *American Record Guide*, this journal specializes in material for record collectors. Typical reviews have comments about recorded sound on a par with what is found in that journal. Typically, *Fanfare* will have hundreds of reviews per issue, and a single copy may have over three hundred pages. At one time the equipment commentators were lunatic fringe in the extreme (except in my case; I once wrote a regular "audio-dementia-antidote" column for the magazine), but equipment is stressed very little now, and the guy who does write about it seems levelheaded. Classical music is stressed, but some jazz, film music, and video material are also reviewed.

Gramophone (monthly). This British journal caters to record collectors, is available in the United States by subscription, and is full of reviews that are excellent in performance aesthetics. The sound-quality comments must be hunted for, but they are usually quite cogent and meaningful. The sections on audio hardware are limited and mainly of use to British buffs. Classical music is stressed.

Hi-Fi News and Record Review (monthly). Another British journal, this one is more equipment oriented than *Gramophone* and has record reviews that are along the lines of what is found in the American journals *Audio* and *Stereo Review*. The magazine has even produced an interesting test disc (see Appendix A). While the equipment evaluation reports done in the magazine are often positively silly, it is a fairly good buy for buffs seeking data on recorded sound quality and specific reviews. All kinds of music are reviewed.

High Performance Review (quarterly). A combination of excellent record reviews by musically knowledgeable critics (usually over one hundred per issue) combined with equipment reviews of limited value. This is particularly true concerning amplifiers and CD players. These are usually high-end units, and the testers do electrical measurements that show nearly all of them to be close to identical—and then do subjective listening tests that supposedly "reveal" often less than subtle differences in the sound. One interesting thing about this procedure is that the listening tests are usually done with recordings that are discussed in detail, and the equipment reviewers often indicate that a certain player or amplifier will reveal nuances in a performance that were missed by other hardware. This is simply nonsense since most amplifiers (at least if they are designed properly and working within their power limitations) and CD players are functionally identical. The speaker tests done by the magazine cater to the "direct-field" school. Surprisingly, the "regular" record reviews in the magazine seldom discuss sound quality in detail. Nevertheless, they are certainly helpful, and their quantity alone makes the magazine worth subscribing to. However, remember to take the equipment comments with a full grain of salt. All kinds of music are reviewed.

Jazz Times (monthly). This journal surveys the worlds of current live-music jazz. Excellent essays and personal interviews are common. The recorded-music review section is not particularly large, but the writings are to the point and expertly handled. Needless to say, little is mentioned about sound quality. Jazz is stressed in the reviews.

Musician (monthly). This publication contains information about the current pop and jazz scene with fine essays, interviews, and announcements. The record reviews, although musically comprehensive, typically stress the artistic over the technical. The recordings reviewed are pop and jazz.

Notes: The Quarterly Journal of the Music Library Association (bimonthly). This academically oriented journal is usually found in music libraries and will often have a section containing brief summaries of reviews by many of the other magazines listed here. It serves mainly as an excellent reference guide to those reviews, but sound quality is sometimes noted in the short summaries. The magazine also contains many fine reviews of books on music. Classical music is stressed.

Opera (monthly). This fine British journal deals mainly with information about the world of live opera. However, it does contain a few record reviews, and those are done by individuals with outstanding credentials for evaluating the artistic merits of a recording. Unfortunately for sound buffs, the stress is rarely (if ever) on the technical aspects. If a recording sounds "OK," that is good enough. The recordings reviewed are mainly opera.

Opera News (monthly or biweekly, depending on the time of year). This is another opera-specialty journal that usually has only a couple of pages of lengthy reviews in each issue. The few that are done are written by experts on opera who ordinarily have only a passing interest in the sound quality of what they review, provided it meets rather minimal standards. Sound, when mentioned, usually gets only a brief "fine sound" comment or something similar. While the stress here is mostly on opera, there are also frequent reviews of material by the likes of Gershwin, Porter, and so on.

Opera Quarterly. A fine music journal containing basic and detailed information about the world of live opera in addition to reviews of performances, interviews with opera personalities, historical discographies, and a few in-depth scholarly reviews of opera recordings. Like the other opera journals above, the stress is on performance and not on sound quality.

Request (monthly). A pop-music magazine (stressing rock and country) that deals mostly with the current live-music scene via interviews and essays. The record reviews are strictly pop oriented, and although they cover the music's artistic merits (or lack of) quite well, they deal very little with sound quality. Music videos are also reviewed. The occasional essays on equipment are shopping oriented.

The Speaker: The Magazine of the Boston Audio Society (irregular). Mostly concerned with information on the audio scene and the industry itself, this fine little magazine often has important data on current events and audio equipment. When record reviews appear, they usually stress engineering analyses over aesthetic qualities, and the findings are precise and informative. You get the magazine when you join the BAS, and members are all over the country. All kinds of music are reviewed.

Stereo Review (monthly). Like *Audio*, this is primarily an upscale enthusiasts' magazine, and sound quality is always at least mentioned in the record reviews. Unfortunately, the info is often hard to locate in the sometimes lengthy writeups, and the comments are sometimes at odds with what I have found. The review and essay sections on audio hardware are usually quite good, although somewhat limited in the depth of analysis at times. The regular editorial comments by equipment tester Julian Hirsch should be required reading by all audio enthusiasts. All kinds of music are reviewed.

Stereophile (monthly). This is *the* major "audio subjectivist" magazine. The record reviews are quite good and stress sound quality. However, the technical material usually leaves much to be desired since the stress is on subjective evaluations as opposed to the more clinical, instrumental, "objective-measurement-oriented" tests I prefer. The magazine often has lengthy and absolutely pointless essays on the philosophical virtues of subjective testing. I must admit, though, that the industry information features and newsletter material are a must for audio buffs wanting to keep us with the latest gossip, and the "letters" section is usually more entertaining than most TV comedy shows — and of course the information on record sound quality will not mislead. All kinds of music are reviewed.

Stevenson Classical Compact Disc Guide (quarterly). This is a large compendium of excerpted reviews from a number of other journals listing both summarized performance and sound-quality information. In addition, short original reviews by the magazine's staff are included, as are listings of discs that received outstanding ratings. This journal is a must for individuals looking for an index to longer reviews as well as a quick reference guide for shopping. The stress is on classical, with some music videos also summarized.

The Strad (monthly). Another fine British magazine that stresses the world of classical-music stringed instruments. It contains scholarly essays on the subject plus discographies, interviews, and a smattering of lengthy and well-written record reviews. Like most music-oriented journals, the emphasis is on performance and not on engineering. The reviews deal mainly with recordings that feature the sound of stringed instruments.

Tempo (quarterly). Still another fine British music magazine that contains serious essays and interviews dealing with contemporary music theory. The record reviews are limited, but they are artistically revealing. Unfortunately, little is said about sound quality in those reviews.

Appendix C: A Short List of Outstanding Discs

To satisfy audio types who are in a hurry, I have put together this listing of "supersound" discs that includes many (but not all) of the highly rated discs in the main listings. Not included here are test and sampler recordings, since they are assumed to be pretty super to begin with and readers can turn to Appendix A for the necessary information. The listings here are purposely sketchy to save space and therefore lack detailed information. For that data, use the review numbers to find the complete information in the main section.

Abercrombie, John: *Current Events*: ECM 1311 **(1)**.
American Tribute: Summit DCD 127 **(12)**.
Azahara: Flamenco Guitar Recital: Nimbus NI-5116 **(30)**.
Bach, Johann Christian: *Three Quartets*; *Sextet*: Archiv 423 385-2 **(34)**.
Bach, Johann Sebastian: *Brandenburgische Konzerte*: Archiv 423 116-2 **(42)**.
Bach, Johann Sebastian: *Cantata BWV 63*; *Cantata BWV 65*: Dorian DOR 90113 **(43)**.
Barber, Billy: *Lighthouse*: Digital Music Products CD-455 **(81)**.
Bartók, Bela: *Concerto for Orchestra*: Delos DE-3095 **(91)**.
Bartók, Bela: *Music for Strings, Percussion and Celesta*; *Divertimento*; *The Miraculous Mandarin*: London 430 352-2 **(98)**.
Basie, Count (his orchestra, led by Frank Foster): *Live at El Morocco*: Telarc 83312 **(105)**.
Berlioz, Hector: *Symphonie Fantastique*: Telarc CD-80271 **(156)**.

Bernstein, Leonard: *Arias and Barcarolles*; Gershwin, George: *An American In Paris*; Barber, Samuel: *Overture to "The School for Scandal:"* Delos DE-3078 **(160)**.
Bernstein, Leonard: *Chichester Psalms*; Barber, Samuel: *Agnus Dei*; Copland, Aaron: *In the Beginning*; *Three Motets*: Hyperion CDA 66219 **(163)**.
Billings, William: *Anthems and Fuging Tunes*: Harmonia Mundi France 907048 **(169)**.
Boston Pops: *By Request*: Philips 420 178-2 **(182)**.
Britten, Benjamin: *Song Cycles*: Chandos CHAN 8514 **(209)**.
Britten, Benjamin: *War Requiem*; *Sinfonia da Requiem*; *Ballad of Heroes*: Chandos CHAN 8983/4 **(210)**.
Brock, Jim: *Tropic Affair*: Reference Recordings RR-31CD **(212)**.
Caram, Ana: *The Other Side of Jobim*: Chesky JD-73 **(235)**.
Carmina Burana: The Great Mystery of the Passion: Harmonia Mundi France 901323/24 **(240)**.

Appendix C

Cephas, Johns, and Phil Wiggins: *Bluesmen*: Chesky JD-89 **(249)**.
Chopin, Frédéric: *The Four Scherzi and Other Works*: Dorian DOR 90140 **(267)**.
Copland, Aaron: *Fanfare for the Common Man*; *Rodeo*; *Appalachian Spring*: Telarc CD-80078 **(294)**.
Corelli, Archangelo: *Concerti Grossi Numbers 1-6*: Harmonia Mundi France HMU 907014 **(299)**.
Corigliano, John: *Symphony Number 1*: Erato 45601-2 **(307)**.
Daniels, Eddie, and Gary Burton: *Benny Rides Again*: GRP GRD-9665 **(324)**.
Debussy, Claude: *La Mer*; Roussel, Albert: *Symphony Number 4*; *Sinfonietta*; Milhaud, Darius: *Suite Provençal*: Chandos CHAN 9072 **(334)**.
Dire Straits: *Brothers in Arms*: Warner Bros. 25264-2 **(348)**.
Elgar, Edward: *Symphony Number 1*; *Pomp and Circumstances Marches Numbers One and Two*: Telarc CD-80310 **(373)**.
Enya: *Watermark*: Geffen 9 24233-2 **(384)**.
The Essence: Digital Music Products CD-480 **(386)**.
Fagen, Donald: *The Nightfly*: Warner 23696-2 **(389)**.
Flim and the BB's: *Big Notes*: Digital Music Products CD-454 **(414)**.
Flim and the BB's: *The Further Adventures of Flim and the BB's*: Digital Music Products CD-462 **(415)**.
Gabriel, Peter: *Security*: Geffen 2011-2 **(434)**.
Gershwin, George: *Marni Nixon Sings Gershwin*: Reference Recordings RR-19CD **(450)**.
Gershwin, George: *Piano Improvisations*: Special Music SCD 6039 **(452)**.
Gillespie, Dizzy: *To Diz With Love*: Telarc 83307 **(464)**.
Green, Bunky: *Healing the Pain*: Delos DE 4020 **(476)**.
Grusin, Dave: *The Gershwin Connection*: GRP GRD-2005 **(485)**.
Grusin, Dave and Don: *Sticks and Stones*: GRP GRD-9562 **(488)**.
Händel, George Frideric: *Giulio Cesare* (Julius Caesar): Harmonia Mundi France 901385/87 **(507)**.
Hanson, Howard: *Symphony Number 5*; *Symphony Number 7*; *Mosaics*; *Piano Concerto in G Major*: Delos DE 3130 **(527)**.
Harrell, Tom: *Passages*: Chesky JD-64 **(532)**.
Hersch, Fred: *Forward Motion*: Chesky JD-55 **(564)**.
Hindemith, Paul: *Organ Works*; Distler, Hugo: *Spielstücke*; Kropfreiter, A.F.: *Toccata Francese*: Argo 417 159-2 **(573)**.
Hohner, Robert (his Percussion Ensemble): *Different Strokes*: Digital Music Products CD-485 **(576)**.
Holst, Gustav: *Suite Number 1 in E-Flat*; *Suite Number 2 in F*; *A Moorside Suite*; *Hammersmith*: Reference Recordings RR-39CD **(586)**.
Ireland, John: *A London Overture*; *These Things Shall Be*: Chandos CHAN 8879 **(598)**.
Jarvis, John: *Something Constructive*: MCAD-5963 **(617)**.
Liszt, Franz: *Christus*: Hungaroton 12831-33-2 **(670)**.
Liszt, Franz: *Sonata in B Minor* (and other, shorter pieces): Etcetera KTC 2010 **(680)**.
Mahler, Gustav: *Symphony Number 5*: Teldec 46152-2 **(720)**.
Mays, Bill, and Ray Drummond: *One to One 2*: Digital Music Products CD-482 **(751)**.
Mendelssohn, Felix: *Organ Works*: Argo 414 420-2 **(768)**.
Mintzer, Bob: *Art of the Big Band*: Digital Music Products CD-479 **(795)**.
Mozart, Wolfgang Amadeus: *Die Zauberflöte*: Telarc 80302 **(864)**.

Appendix C

Mussorgsky, Modest, and Maurice Ravel: *Pictures at an Exhibition*; Scriabin, Alexander: *Poem of Ecstacy*: Chandos CHAN 8849 **(874)**.
Nielsen, Carl: *Saul & David*: Chandos CHAN 8911/12 **(888)**.
Opera Baroque: Harmonia Mundi France 290605.07 **(904)**.
Orquesta Nova: Chesky JD-54 **(910)**.
Papa Doo Run Run: *California Project*: Telarc 70501 **(922)**.
Piston, Walter: *Symphony Number 2*; *Symphony Number 6*; *Sinfonietta*: Delos DE-3074 **(938)**.
Prokofiev, Sergei: *Alexander Nevsky*; *Scythian Suite*: Chandos CHAN 8584 **(961)**.
Rachmaninov, Sergei: *Symphony Number 2*: Telarc 80312 **(996)**.
Rachmaninov, Sergei: *Vespers*: Telarc CD-80172 **(999)**.
Rankin, Kenny: *Because of You*: Chesky JD-63 **(1007)**.
Ravel, Maurice: *Daphnis et Chloé* (complete); Diamond, David: *Elegy In Memory of Maurice Ravel*: Delos DE 3110 **(1010)**.
Respighi, O.: *Pines of Rome*; *Roman Festivals*; *Fountains of Rome*: Chandos CHAN 8989 **(1025)**.
Rivera, Paquito de: *Havana Cafe*: Chesky JD-60 **(1035)**.
Scarlatti, Domenico: *Eighteen Sonatas*: Koch 3-7014-2 **(1078)**.
Schonberg, Claude-Michel: *Les Miserables*: Relativity/First Night 88561-1027-2 **(1093)**.
Schumann, Robert: *Symphony Number 1*; *Overture, Scherzo and Finale*; *Konzertstrück for Four Horns and Orchestra*: Delos DE-3084 **(1119)**.
Severinsen, Doc: *Facets*: Amherst 93319 **(1141)**.
Severinsen, Doc: *The Tonight Show Band, Once More ... with Feeling*: Amherst 94405 **(1144)**.
Short, Bobby: *Late Night at the Cafe Carlyle*: Telarc 83311 **(1154)**.
Shostakovich, Dmitri: *Symphony Number 5*; *Ballet Suite Number 5 from The Bolt*: Chandos CHAN 8650 **(1159)**.
Shostakovich, Dmitri: *Symphony Number 10*; *Ballet Suite Number 4*: Chandos CHAN 8630 **(1170)**.
Spies: *By Way of the World*: Telarc 83305 **(1204)**.
Spies: *Music of Espionage*: Telarc 85503 **(1205)**.
Strauss, Richard: *De Rosenkavalier*: EMI 7 54259-2 **(1230)**.
Stravinsky, Igor: *Firebird Suite*; *Pétrouchka*: Telarc 80270 **(1234)**.
Stravinsky, Igor: *Le Sacre du Printemps*; Prokofiev, Sergei: *Scythian Suite*: Dorian DOR 90156 **(1244)**.
Tallis, Thomas: *Complete English Anthems*: Gimell CDGM-007 **(1257)**.
Taverner, John: *Missa Gloria Tibi Trinitas*: Gimell CDGM-004 **(1262)**.
Tchaikovsky, Peter: *Symphony Number 4*; *Romeo and Juliet Fantasy Overture*: Telarc 80228 **(1278)**.
Terry, Clark: *Having Fun*: Delos De 4021 **(1298)**.
Thomson, Virgil: *Symphony on a Hymn Tune*; *Symphony Number 2*; *Five Tenor Solos From the Opera Lord Byron*: Albany TROY 017-2 **(1304)**.
The Timeless All-Stars: *Essence*: Delos D/CD 4006 **(1306)**.
Vierne, Louis: *Symphony Number 6*; Reger, Max: *Second Sonata in D Minor*: Delos DE 3096 **(1358)**.
Virtuoso Trumpet Concertos: Nimbus NI 5121 **(1365)**.
Vivaldi, Antonio: *Concerti a Due (Six Concertos)*: Novalis 150 074-2 **(1370)**.
Vivaldi, Antonio: *Four Seasons*; *Flute Concerto in D*; *Harpsichord Concerto in A Major*: Chesky CD-78 **(1375)**.
Waller, Fats: *Dick Hyman Plays Fats Waller*: Reference Recordings RR-33CD **(1385)**.
Walton, Cedar: *Cedar Walton Plays*: Delos D/CD 4008 **(1386)**.

Appendix C

Warnes, Jennifer: *Famous Blue Raincoat, Songs of Leonard Cohen*: RCA/Cypress PD90048 **(1394)**.

Warnes, Jennifer: *The Hunter*: Private Music 82089-2 **(1395)**.

Williams, Joe: *I Just Want to Sing*: Delos D/CD 4004 **(1412)**.

Woods, Phil (his Little Big Band): *Here's To My Lady*: Chesky JD-3 **(1427)**.

Woods, Phil (his Little Big Band): *Real Life*: Chesky JD-47 **(1429)**.

Your Friendly, Neighborhood Big Band: Reference Recordings RR-14CD **(1438)**.

Appendix D: Evaluation Hardware Used

Since this book is about recorded sound quality, some data on the test gear used is required. Obviously, a wide-bandwidth, high-definition system is needed to evaluate a recording. However, a smaller, less capable (but still good) system is important if one wishes to determine how recordings will sound on more typical home systems. To do this book, systems of both kinds were employed.

The author's *small* system sits in a 1,900-cubic-feet room and consists of a combination of Carver, Yamaha, and AudioSource electronics, RDL satellite speakers (four AV-1 minispeakers, stacked two to a side as short line sources) and Allison subwoofers. The latter consists of two Allison Model 1/3, 10-inch woofers in custom cabinets equalized by an Allison ESW (Electronic Subwoofer) for flat response to 40 Hz in the filter-only mode and to 20 Hz in the equalized mode. The main-sub combination is tied together with an Allison MS-205 crossover network. Four small Radio Shack speakers handle the surround "effects." They are located near the ceiling, up and down the side walls. The inputs to this system consist of a cheap CD player and a good VHS Hi-Fi VCR. The hookup also includes a good but cheap 27-inch TV monitor and laservideo player. The total amplified audio power available is about 260 watts, with 200 of that available for the main speakers.

Except for the adjustable subwoofer bass potential, this system exemplifies what can be accomplished by any budget-oriented audio enthusiast for a reasonable sum—say, $1,500 ("retail") for good midlevel audio equipment. Another $1,500 ("retail") would obtain the video gear. It was effective in determining if any artifacts detected with the large system would be audible with typical smaller ones.

The *large* system sits in a 3,400-cubic-feet room and consists of a combination of Carver, Yamaha, and dbx electronics and critically sited Allison "main" speaker systems (top-of-the-line IC-20s) equalized by an Allison ESW for flat response down to 18 Hz. The system also has another pair of Allison speakers (three-way AL-125s) bracketing a 45-inch Mitsubishi TV monitor. These handle the center channel material when the program (usually video, but also Dolby-encoded audio) calls for it. The four "effects" speakers are also Allison models (LC-120s), and they are located down the length of the side walls, fairly high up. The total amplified audio power available is about 850 watts, with 100 watts to each of the two center-channel speakers and 250 to each main speaker. The inputs to this conglomeration consists of Technics and Sony CD players, a Pioneer LaserVideo (Combi) player, and a fine Panasonic Hi-Fi VCR.

As capable as these two systems are, it is important to remember that all the

Appendix D [212]

preliminary listening evaluations were done with the large system *operating in the basic stereo mode with no surround processing applied*. The small-system backup checks were also done in the stereo mode. Assorted surround enhancements were usually tried with whatever system was involved *after* each recording was rated to ascertain its ability to be surround manipulated. However, the surround evaluations had no influence on the final scores.

To see that everything in both systems was operating properly, a significant number of recordings were also auditioned by me on a good friend's large "audiophile" system that was even more impressive "on paper" (at least to high-end buffs) than my main system. This assembly consisted of a pair of KEF 107 speakers (with the K-UBE equalizer), two Adcom "monoblock" amplifiers, and a top-of-the-line Sony compact disc player driving the amps directly through its variable output (no preamp). All of this gear was expertly positioned in a 3,500-cubic-feet room intelligently treated with Sonex sound-absorbing material.

Outstanding as this system is (and taking into consideration the different radiation patterns of its speakers), I still consider it roughly equal to the stereo-only part of my larger one, and listening to numerous high-quality recordings on it confirmed my views of the over 3,000 potentially excellent titles that were auditioned for this book and the over 1,400 that were accepted.

Appendix E: Microphone Pickup Patterns

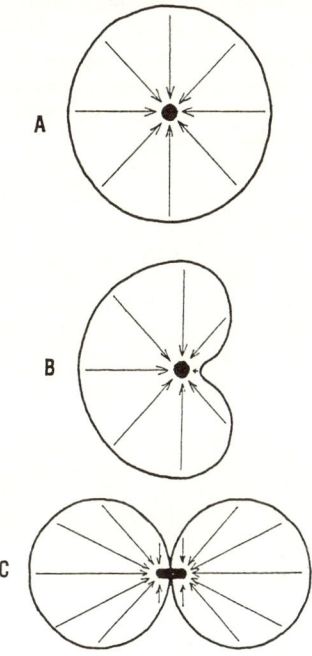

A number of microphone pickup patterns are discussed in the reviews. While there are a huge number of good microphones available for serious recording, the most common will have patterns similar to those sketched here and discussed below, or a subtle variant. Recording engineers may use as few as two or more than a dozen microphones to record a work.

The pickup pattern in diagram A is that of an *omnidirectional* microphone. By recording wide-bandwidth signals equally from all directions, it can have an impressively flat frequency response until the highest frequencies are encountered. This design lends itself to spaced-array configurations that require both time and intensity clues (see Appendix F). Omni microphones are usually used for recording classical music rather than pop.

Appendix E

The microphone in diagram B exhibits a *cardioid* (heart-shaped) pickup pattern. By detecting more sound from the front (and to an extent the sides) than from the rear, it allows the recording engineer to control intensity levels better and reduce interference from adjacent sources. A design like this lends itself well to multiple-microphone work (nearly universal with pop music), individual-instrument recording, and "accent" use in classical recording. The directionality of the design may not be absolutely consistent at all frequencies, and this usually results in an overall frequency response that is inferior to good omnidirectional microphones. However, for many kinds of work, such deficiencies may not be important. Cardioid microphones are also good for certain kinds of spaced-array work (see Appendix F).

The microphone in diagram C is a *figure-8* or bidirectional type. By picking up information from the front and rear, but not the sides, it allows the engineer to record small-area frontal sounds as well as hall ambience simultaneously coming from the rear while ignoring additional information arriving from other areas (see Appendix F). However, it is important to note that the sounds from the rear are recorded 180 degrees out of phase with those from the front. Properly used in a two-capsule configuration, this microphone can impart a great deal of spacious ambience to the sound of a recording while maintaining well-focused imaging. Because of their "side-null" design, good bidirectional microphones may have a very uniform frequency response right into the top octaves. This design is popular with a number of "purist-technique" classical-music recording engineers.

Three other types not pictured here are the *subcardioid*, which combines features of the omni and the cardioid and has a pattern that looks like an off-center omni, the *supercardioid*, and the *hypercardioid*. The latter two combine characteristics of the cardioid and the figure-8, with the front lobe larger than the rear. The latter two also have reduced side sensitivity compared to the cardioid but have more than the figure-8. All three of these types may be used when rear- and/or side-information levels provided by the omni, cardioid, or figure-8 types are not quite right for a situation.

It is important to remember that these sketches illustrate microphone behavior *in only one dimension*. To the real world, they operate in a three-dimensional manner. The cardioid, for example, has a pattern that is shaped somewhat like a tomato, the figure-8's sensitivity range resembles a dumbbell, and the omni's pattern resembles a tennis ball.

There are high-quality versions of each of six types discussed above, and a number of models available to the engineer have adjustability features that make them adaptable to a variety of recording situations.

Appendix F: Microphone Placement

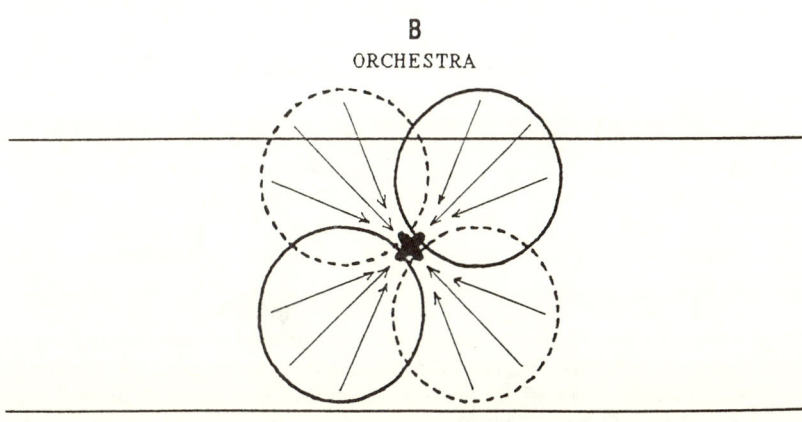

Appendix F [216]

While engineers who record most pop, jazz, and C&W music use multiple-microphone techniques to capture the sound of every performer, most classical (and some jazz) recording engineers prefer the "minimalist" or "purist" technique, which is said to capture more accurately the depth and ambience of the recording space as well as the precise location of the instruments. The sketches on page 215 explain two popular purist techniques.

Diagram A shows the relative location of the microphones used in a spaced three-module, "omnidirectional" array. Each used in this arrangement is equally sensitive in all directions. The dotted lines give you an idea of their respective pickup patterns. Typically, the left- and right-side microphones may be 5 to 12 feet apart, but some outfits space them as much as 18 feet from each other. Spaced microphones, as can be seen in this sketch, are sensitive to both intensity and time-of-arrival differences. Normally, the latter are of paramount importance unless the spacing is quite wide.

One problem with a spaced configuration is that sounds reaching the left microphone from the right side will be recorded mostly out of phase from the signals reaching the right microphone from the right side and vice versa. The relative levels of the more distant out-of-phase signals should be lower than the main signals, but they may still impart a diffuse or "phasey" quality to the central-area image. In such an arrangement, a center microphone (as pictured here) is sometimes employed to help "tighten" those diffuse midpoint images, particularly soloists. With some large-group recordings, the single center mike may be replaced by two more spaced units. Central-image problems like this are inherent in the spaced-array technique. In any case, a big advantage of spaced "omni" microphones is the warm, subjectively spacious, wide-range, undistorted sound they can produce.

Diagram B shows one type of "coincident" crossed figure-8 (X-Y or Blumlein) microphone array. The dotted-line circle shows the pickup pattern for the left channel, and the solid-line circle shows the pattern for the right channel. In a configuration like this, front-back-sensitive directional microphones are placed *very* close together (usually located one right above the other) to reduce left-right time-of-arrival differences to zero. Figure-8 microphones set up in this way receive sounds from the front (orchestra) as well as from the back (hall or audience) area where they are also aimed. The individual capsules do not pick up a lot of sound from the sides and pretty much ignore sound from the part of the orchestra or hall where they are not aimed. As can be seen in this sketch, coincident microphones will be sensitive mostly to intensity differences, which is why recordings made with them are called "intensity stereo." It is important to remember that the figure 8s shown here are "dipoles." The typically more distant hall-reflected rear signals are recorded out of phase from those of the front, imparting a spacious quality when compared to the more focused front signals. One big advantage of this configuration is the strong, stable phantom-center image that will be formed with two-speaker stereo playback.

Another coincident-source technique, the "M-S" (Mid/Side or Mono/Stereo), commonly has a cardioid (see Appendix E) microphone aimed forward and a figure-8 module oriented left-right. The forward-aimed module picks up the central image and the left-right-aimed one produces a different signal that is "matrixed" into the whole. (A variant uses a figure-8, supercardioid, or hypercardioid module for the central area coverage. The rear-aimed lobe then picks up additional hall ambience, and the overall effect is similar to what is achieved with the figure-8 setup.) Properly handled, the M-S technique has the advantage of easily controlling the central image strength and stereo spread, important when recording soloists. The engineer can make changes after the recording session to highlight the central image or increase the spread. Such flexibility cannot be achieved with crossed figure-8s or outward-angled cardioids and is possible only with spaced microphones if a central module is employed. The big disadvantage of the M-S technique, at least if a cardioid is used for the central image, is that the polar-pattern-related frequency-response differences between the two types of microphones will result in overall frequency-response anomalies that are greater than the sum of the parts. The M-S system is popular in Europe.

The ORTF microphone placement system (developed some years back by the Office de Radiodiffusion-Télévision Française) uses directional, mostly front-sensitive (cardioid, super- or hypercardioid) microphones spaced a bit more than 6½ inches apart and angled toward the sides at about 110 degrees from each other. These cover a pattern similar to the stage-aimed part of the figure-8 configuration shown in diagram B, with a little more sensitivity to sounds from the sides but little response to hall ambience from the audience area. The slight spacing imparts some of the pleasant high-frequency phasiness of the spaced array to the recording while achieving some of the sharp imaging qualities of the coincident array. Lower frequencies, because of the wave lengths involved, behave mostly as if recorded by a coincident array. The ORTF system can work well when recording small ensembles in smaller halls, as can the similar NOS (Nederlandsche Omroep Stichting) system from the Netherlands, which places the microphones about a foot apart. When these kind of techniques are employed for larger works, some engineers will position additional main-channel microphones off to the sides of the central pair. During the final mix, carefully blending the output of the flanking microphones with the primary signals will add width or spaciousness to the ensemble.

No matter what kind of main array is used, many classical-music recording engineers will place an extra microphone or two out in the audience area to pick up all the reflections that add ambience to the recording. Because those signals will be on different tape tracks from the front microphone information, they can be added to the end result as required during the final mix (with the proper delay time, reverberation, and levels, of course).

When soloists are involved in a large-scale recording, many engineers also locate additional (usually cardioid-type) microphones close to one or more of them to ensure that their sound will not be too submerged in the overall blend. Again, those accent microphones will be on separate tape tracks and will have their signals properly combined during the final mix. "Properly combining" is a key phrase here. If the instruments being picked up by the accent microphones are toward the rear of the orchestra, the careful engineer will delay their signals electrically to synchronize their arrival times with those being received by the main array some distance away. If this is not done, the result will be reduced clarity and a flattened stage image.

Bibliography

Not every item listed here deals specifically with recorded sound, recording practices, or microphone technology, but each essay and significant parts of each book will be helpful to those who want information on recording speaker-room-listener interactions, why recordings sound like they do, and how to make the recordings you play on your system sound better.

Books

Ballou, Glen, editor: *Handbook for Sound Engineers*, Sams, 1987.
Bartlett, Bruce: *Introduction to Professional Recording Techniques*, Sams, 1987.
Benson, K. Blair, editor: *Audio Engineering Handbook*, McGraw-Hill, 1988.
Beranek, Leo L.: *Music, Acoustics and Architecture*, Wiley, 1962.
Berg, Richard E.: *The Physics of Sound*, Prentice-Hall, 1982.
Blauert, Jens: *Spatial Hearing: The Psychoacoustics of Human Sound Localization*, MIT Press, 1983.
Borwick, John: *Microphones: Technology and Techniques*, Focal Press, 1990.
Camras, Marvin: *Magnetic Recording Handbook*, Van Nostrand Reinhold, 1988.
Clifford, Martin: *Microphones*, 3rd edition, Tab Books, 1986.
Davis, Don: *Sound System Engineering*, 2nd edition, Sams, 1987.
Davis, Gary, and Ralph Jones: *The Sound Reinforcement Handbook*, published for Yamaha by Hal Leonard Publishing Corporation, 1987.
Dickreiter, Michael: *Tonmeister Technology*, Temmer Enterprises, 1989.
Eargle, John: *Handbook of Recording Engineering*, Van Nostrand Reinhold, 1986.
Eargle, John: *Handbook of Sound System Design*, ELAR, 1989.
Eargle, John: *The Microphone Handbook*, ELAR, 1981.
Eargle, John: *Music, Sound and Technology*, Van Nostrand Reinhold, 1990.
Everest, F. Alton: *The New Stereo Soundbook*, Tab Books, 1992.
Ferstler, Howard W.: *High Fidelity Audio-Video Systems: A Critical Guide for Owners*, McFarland, 1991.
Huber, David: *Microphone Manual: Design and Application*, Sams, 1988.
Huber, David, and Robert Runstein: *Modern Recording Techniques*, 3rd edition, Sams, 1989.
Jones, Steve: *Rock Formation: Music, Technology and Mass Communication*, Sage, 1992.
Jorgensen, Finn: *The Complete Handbook of Magnetic Recorders*, 3rd edition, Tab Books, 1988.
Miller, Allen Wayne: "Choral Recordings as History" (a study of the recording techniques of five choral ensembles), Ph.D diss., Florida State University, 1992.

Nisbett, Alec: *The Use of Microphones*, 3rd edition, Focal Press, 1989.
Olson, Harry F.: *Music, Physics and Engineering*, Dover, 1967.
Rumsey, Francis and Tim McCormick: *Sound and Recording: An Introduction*, Focal Press, 1992.
Runstein, Robert: *Modern Recording Techniques*, Sams, 1986.
White, Glenn: *The Audio Dictionary*, 2nd edition, University of Washington Press, 1991.
Woram, John M.: *Sound Recording Handbook*, Sams, 1989.
Zaza, Antony: *Mechanics of Sound Recording*, Prentice-Hall, 1991.

Magazine Articles

Aczel, Peter: "Seminar 1989" (a two-part series of roundtable interviews with audio experts Bob Carver, Dave Clark, John Eargle, Stanley Lipshitz, and Peter McGrath), two 1989 issues of *The Audio Critic*. Write the publisher: P.O. Box 978, Quakertown, PA 18951.
Allison, Roy: "Loudspeakers and Real Rooms" (an analysis of room/loudspeaker interactions), *Hi-Fi News and Record Review* (British), December 1989.
Allison, Roy: "Marking the Boundaries" (concludes the series on room-speaker interactions, *Hi-Fi News and Record Review* (British), April 1990.
Allison, Roy: "Room For Improvement" (a continuation of "Loudspeakers" on room-speaker interactions), *Hi-Fi News and Record Review* (British), February, 1990.
Bartlett, Bruce: "Good Sound: What Is It?" *High Performance Review*, Spring 1987.
Bartlett, Bruce, and Michael Billingsley: "An Improved Microphone Array Using Boundary Technology: Theoretical Aspects," *Journal of the Audio Engineering Society*, volume 38, numbers 7-8, July-August 1990.
Bartlett, Bruce: "Stereo Imaging," *High Performance Review*, Winter 1992-93.
Berlant, Bert: "Loudspeaker Directionality and the Perception of Reality," *Journal of the Audio Engineering Society*, volume 33, number 5, May 1985.
Canby, Edward Tatnall: "Looking for Mr. Good Mike" (microphones and their use in live performances), *Audio*, December 1991.
Davis, Don: "The LEDE Concept" (an analysis of the live-end-dead-end listening-room-treatment procedure and theory), *Audio*, August 1987.
Davis, Mark: "Audio Specifications and Human Hearing," *Stereo Review*, May 1982.
Eargle, John: "The First Step to Great Sound" (a top recording engineer discusses his techniques), *Stereo Review*, December 1993.
Eargle, John: "Stereo Microphone Techniques," *db*, June, 1981.
Eargle, John: "Testing, 1, 2, Testing" (a discussion of recording techniques plus a review of two test discs), *Audio*, February 1991.
Everest, F. Alton: "Coloration of Room Sound by Reflections," *Audio*, March 1993.
Everest, F. Alton: "The Uneasy Truce Between Music and the Room," *Audio*, February 1993.
Feldman, Leonard, and John Sunier: "Surround Sound Without the Pictures" (an analysis and review of a number of audio-only Dolby recordings), *Audio*, December 1991.
Ferstler, Howard W.: "The Compact Disc," *American Record Guide*, May-June 1988.

Bibliography

Ferstler, Howard W.: "Sound Dispersion" (a discussion of speaker performance in real-world rooms), *Stereo Review*, October 1990.

Ferstler, Howard W.: "Subwoofers," *American Record Guide*, Fall 1987.

Fielder, Louis, and Eric Benjamin: "Subwoofer Performance for Accurate Reproduction of Music," *Journal of Audio Engineering Society*, volume 36, number 6, June 1988.

Gillen, Marilyn: "Ludwig Cleans Up with Gateway" (a look at Bob Ludwig's recording and mixing studio), *Billboard*, volume 105, number 16, April 17, 1993.

Gillen, Marilyn: "Remix & Match: Dave Way Forges New Paths in R & B" (a study of the remixing techniques of engineer Dave Way), *Billboard*, volume 105, number 26, June 26, 1993.

Greisinger, David: "Theory and Design of a Digital Audio Signal Processor for Home Use" (a useful analysis of surround sound), *Journal of the Audio Engineering Society*, volume 37, number 1/2, January–February 1989.

Herrold, Robert: "Microphones: Start with the Basics," *Audio*, April 1985.

Hibbing, Manfred: "XY and MS Microphone Techniques in Comparison," *Journal of the Audio Engineering Society*, volume 37, number 10, October 1989.

Howland, Rick: "Mechanics Hall, Meetinghouse for Music" (a discussion of concert-hall acoustics, with one hall used as a paradigm), *Audio*, January 1993.

Julstrom, Stephen: "An Intuitive View of Coincident Stereo Microphones," *Journal of the Audio Engineering Society*, volume 39, number 9, September 1991.

Kumin, Daniel: "Stop! You're Surrounded," *CD Review*, July 1993.

Lander, David: "Tom Jung: The Digital Music Man" (an interview with DMP's top recording engineer), *Audio*, August 1988.

Lipshitz, Stanley: "Stereo Microphone Techniques ... Are the Purists Wrong?" (a seminal analysis of coincident and spaced-array techniques), *Journal of the Audio Engineering Society*, volume 34, number 9, September 1986.

Masters, Ian: "The Basics: Magnetics and Music—How the Sound Gets from There to Here," *Stereo Review*, December 1989.

Meyer, E. Brad: "The Amp/Speaker Interface," *Stereo Review*, June 1991.

Meyer, Jürgen: "The Sound of the Orchestra," *Journal of the Audio Engineering Society*, volume 41, number 4, April 1993.

Mitchell, Peter: "All About Subwoofers, Part 1," *Stereo Review*, June 1992.

Mitchell, Peter: "All About Subwoofers, Part 2," *Stereo Review*, July 1992.

Mitchell, Peter: "Digital Sound: Myth and Reality," *Opus*, October 1985.

Mitchell, Peter: "The Ground Floor" (a discussion of subwoofers and deep bass), *Stereophile*, March 1993.

Mitchell, Peter: "A Sensible Guide to Upgrading: From Two-Speaker Stereo to a Surround-Sound Home Theater," *Stereo Review*, February 1993.

Nash, Michael: "Grateful Tapers: An Informal History of Recording the Dead" (a history and analysis of the techniques used to record the rock group Grateful Dead), *Audio*, January 1988.

Pisha, B.V., and Charles Bilello: "Designing a Home Listening Room," *Audio*, September 1987.

Ranada, David: "Interviewing the Best Interviewees in Audio, Part 1" (conversations with audio experts John Eargle, Roy Allison, Kevin Voecks, and Floyd Toole, dealing with sound recording and related subjects), *The Audio Critic*, Spring 1993.

Rananda, David: "Interviewing the Best Inverviewees in Audio, Part 2" (conversations with audio experts Mark Davis and Robert Carver, dealing with sound recording and related subjects), *The Audio Critic,* Spring, 1993.

Ranada, David: "Sounding Off" (a talk with recording engineer John Eargle), *High Fidelity*, September 1988.

Swedien, Bruce, "Grammy Recording Forum: Modern Engineering Production Techniques (excerpts from the third annual forum, New York City, October 5, 1991), reprinted in *NARAS Journal*, Spring 1992.

Theile, Günther: "On the Naturalness of Two-Channel Stereo Sound," *Journal of the Audio Engineering Society*, volume 38, number 10, October 1991.

Toole, Floyd: "Caged Sound" (an analysis of the relation between listeners, speakers, and the listening room), *High Fidelity*, March 1988.

Toole, Floyd: "Good Sound: How to Evaluate Speaker Performance," *Stereo Review*, September, 1992.

Toole, Floyd: "Listening Tests — Turning Opinion into Fact" (a study of the subjective performance of loudspeakers and how we hear them), *Journal of the Audio Engineering Society*, volume 30, number 6, June 1982.

Toole, Floyd: "Loudspeakers and Rooms for Stereophonic Sound Reproduction" (a paper delivered at the eighth AES international conference, May 1990), available from the society.

Toole, Floyd, and Sean Olive: "The Detection of Reflections in Typical Rooms," *Journal of the Audio Engineering Society*, volume 37, numbers 7–8, July–August 1989.

Voelker, Ernst-Joachim: "Control Rooms for Music Monitoring," *Journal of the Audio Engineering Society*, volume 33, number 6, June 1985.

Whyte, Bert: "Halls for All" (concert-hall acoustics), *Audio*, July 1993.

Woszczyk, Wieslaw: "Microphone Arrays Optimized for Music Recording," *Journal of the Audio Engineering Society*, volume 40, number 11, November 1992.

Index

Numbers refer to entry numbers not page numbers.

A&M Recordings 175, 388, 473, 1216
ASV Recordings 648
ATCO Recordings 1436
Aarons, Al 1401
Abdur-Rahman, Kenyatte 1196
Abe, Keiko 666
Abell, Jack 1405
Abercrombie, John 1, 2, 470, 533, 695, 755
About Home 356
Academy of Ancient Music 501, 508, 557, 827, 828, 849
Academy of St. Martin in the Fields 135, 262, 365, 773, 798, 1388
Academy Sound and Vision Recordings 1362
Accademia Claudio Monteverdi 804
Accent Recordings 983, 1199
Aci, Galatea e Polifemo 497
Acuña, Alejandro (Alex) 287, 752, 925, 1432
Adagio 85, 1337
Adda Recordings 1012
Adler, Bruce 446
Adrenalize 340
African Exchange Student 441
After Hours 230
Agnus Dei 163
Aguilera de Heredia, Sebastían 748
Ah Via Musicom 623
Ainsley, John 474, 592
Aja 1210
Akiyoshi, Toshiko 4
Alain, Jehan 1038
Albany Recordings 1304
Albéniz, Isaac 5, 1049
Albert, Stephen 6
Albinoni, Tomaso 250, 1202, 1313, 1320
Albrici, Vincenzo 602
Alden, Howard 7, 933, 1037
Aldrovandini, Giusseppe Antonio 909

Aldwell, Edward 73
Aler, John 150, 1231
Alexander, Jason 449
Alexander, Roberta 1294
Alexander Nevsky 961, 962
Alexander's Feast 503
Alexeev, Dmitir 878
Alias, Don 375, 1074, 1213, 1214
Allam, Roger 1091
Allen, Carl 1149
Allen, Geri 8, 9, 931
Allen, Thomas 357, 903
Allman Brothers Band 10
Along with Three Giants 1039
Alpha Centauri Ensemble 1430
Also Sprach Zarathustra 1221, 1222
Alternative Express 22
Always in My Heart 655
Alyabiev, Alexander 1286
Amadeus Trio 1392
Amaro, Eugene 1309
Amazonia 234
Ambisonic Recording System 30, 94, 95, 123, 124, 233, 265, 295, 553, 555, 596, 603, 798, 994, 1239, 1246, 1250, 1297, 1338, 1339, 1365; *see also* pages 9, 199
Ambrosian Opera Chorus 1059, 1351, 1355
Ambrosian Singers 945, 947
Ameen, Robbie 1331
Ameling, Elly 28, 1102
American Baroque 1295
American Composers Orchestra 177
American Creed 290
American Gramophone Recordings 1255
American in Paris 160, 454, 455
American Theater Orchestra 490
Amherst Recordings 1141-1144
Amirov, Fikret 1067

Index

Amon Ra Recordings 471, 847, 1295, 1321
Amor Brujo 391
Amores 628
Amsterdam Baroque Orchstra 848
Ancient Airs and Dances 1023
And the Stars Go With You 1139
Anderson, Carl 1419
Anderson, Clifton 1048
Anderson, Elizabeth 76
Anderson, Ernestine 13, 1152
Anderson, Jay 1045, 1204
Anderson, June 162, 864, 865, 1354
Anderson, Ray 879, 957, 1131
Anderson, Wessell 739
Andress, Tuck 14, 15, 16
Andrews, Jeff 145, 146, 1212, 1214
Andrews, Julie 1043
Angel Recordings *see* EMI/Angel
Angel Street 1415
"Anima" Moscow Chamber Choir 789
Années de Pèlerinage Duexième Année-Italie 669
Anonymous 4 380
Anthems and Fuging Tunes 169
Antilles Recordings 354, 625, 812, 814
Anything Goes 945, 946
Apollo 1231
Apollo e Dafne 1294
Appalachian Ditties and Dances 1392
Appalachian Spring 288, 289, 292, 294
Arabesque Recordings 769
Aragall, Giacomo 975
Araiza, Francisco 135, 543
Araro, Eugene 756
Arban, Jean-Baptiste 241, 882, 1363
Archiv Recordings 34, 42, 118, 301, 501, 503, 514, 518, 521, 548, 551, 552, 834, 840, 842, 845, 846, 899, 980, 1080
Are You Experienced? 654
Arensky, Anton 1287
Argenta, Nancy 54
Argo Recordings 177, 281, 291, 573, 768
Arias for Montagnana 498
Arista Recordings 433, 658, 1185, 1437
Arlen, Harold 180, 183
Armstrong, James 576
Armstrong, Nancy 836
Arnold-Schönberg-Choir 53, 1057
Aronov, Ben 1329
Art Ensemble of Chicago 21, 22, 23
Art of Fugue 36
Art of the Big Band 795
Arts Florissants 260, 457, 699, 904, 979
As Serenity Approaches 1040
Asante, Eric 1402-1404
Ascendens Christus in Altam 1356

Ashkenazy, Vladimir 1249
Ashmore, Lawrence 409
Astley, Rick 26
Astoria: Portrait of the Artist 142
Astrée Recordings 1054
Asylum Recordings 668
Atlanta Boy Choir 211
Atlanta Symphony Orchestra 52, 57, 84, 117, 150, 192, 211, 294, 296, 397, 544, 575, 723, 777, 877, 905, 1027, 1099, 1163, 1178, 1234, 1248, 1353
Atlantic Recordings 314, 382, 441, 445, 470, 597, 606, 644, 729, 799, 1065, 1066, 1135, 1190, 1212-1214, 1334
Atlantov, Vladimir 1273
Atkins, Chet 258
Atys 699
Aubade Héoïque 652
Auber, Daniel-François-Esprit 186
Aubier, Eric 982
Aubort, Marc 129, 524, 1251
Auger, Arleen 696, 1229
Aurora 29
Austin, Ivy 449
Austro-Hungarian Haydn Orchestra 555
Authentic-Instrument Recording *see* Original-Instrument Recording
Authentic Orchestra 1117
Auzet, Roland 1047
Avanti Orchestra 1232
Ayer, John 1405

BBC Philharmonic Orchestra 467
BBC Welsh Symphony Orchestra 993
B-52's 31
BIS Recordings 48, 229, 318, 351, 541, 615, 628, 746, 747, 783, 887, 924, 1050, 1067, 1070, 1077, 1085, 1087, 1088, 1137, 1182, 1184, 1223, 1232, 1292, 1363, 1423
BMG Recordings 26, 306, 589
Babbitt, Milton 1406
Baby I'm Yours 759
Bach, Carl Philipp Emanuel 32, 33, 899
Bach, Johann Christian 34
Bach, Johann Sebastian: Keyboard 45, 47-50, 73, 74, 76, 684; Orchestral/Choral Works 39, 43, 51-59; Orchestral Works 36, 41, 42, 46, 585, 1322; Organ Works 38, 40, 44, 60-67, 69, 72, 440, 906, 907, 1038; Small Ensemble Music 34, 38, 76; Solo Instrument 68, 70, 71, 75, 318, 1313, 1316; Solo Vocal 35
Bach, Wilhelm Friedemann 77

Index

Bach at Bryn Mawr 38
Bach at St. Bavo's 40
Bach Choir 1389
Bach Choir of Bethlehem 43
Bach Festival Orchestra 43
Bachiana Brasileira Number Four 1361
Back to the Beautiful 312
Badrena, Manolo 1212
Baikov, Sergei 1069
Bailey, Donald 1062
Baird, Julianne 381, 871
Bang Tango 80
Baker, Anita 78
Balada, Leonardo 1115
Baldwin, Dalton 696
Ball, Larry 606
Ballard, Kay 948
Ballet Suite Number 5 from the Bolt 1159
Balletti und Sonaten am Wiener Kaiserhof 1082
Baltimore Consort 902, 1398
Baltimore Symphony Orchestra 156, 373, 996, 1118, 1120, 1234, 1271, 1278
Baltsa, Agnes 1351
Bamberger Symphoniker 746, 747, 924
Bambridge, John 1144
Banchieri, Adriano 436
Baptist, Rick 415
Baptista, Cyro 234
Barber, Bill (senior) 416
Barber, Billy 81, 82, 414–419
Barber, Samuel 83–87, 160, 163, 524, 781, 956, 1337, 1423
Barking Pumpkin Digital Gratification Consort 1442
Barking Pumpkin Records 1441, 1442
Barnhart, Scotty 1040
Barockorchester, Stuttgart 59, 1122
Baron, Joey 429, 493, 566
Barrett, Brent 466
Barrett, William 161
Barron, Kenny 207, 806, 808
Bartók, Bela 68, 90–103, 1408
Bartoli, Cecilia 826, 1057, 1058
Barton, Steve 689, 690
Baryton Music 560
Basch, Wolfgang 250, 1364
Basie, Count 104–110, 535
Basin Street 231
Baskerville, Priscilla 330
Bass Depth Highlighted 1, 26, 61, 62, 65–67, 113, 139, 144, 182, 183, 187, 190, 192, 212, 218, 219, 248, 258, 276, 310, 315, 341, 344, 353, 354, 358, 359, 373, 378, 382, 384, 410, 414, 445, 462, 469, 473, 486–489, 540,
567, 573, 583, 586, 590, 592, 623, 630, 658, 687, 691, 693, 701, 758, 759, 768, 783, 800, 818, 874, 877, 896, 907, 908, 926, 935, 936, 942, 959, 970, 977, 993, 996, 1000, 1017, 1025–1028, 1052, 1060, 1061, 1072, 1088, 1095, 1129, 1138, 1139, 1166, 1185, 1203, 1209, 1221, 1233, 1234, 1312, 1314, 1330, 1332, 1333, 1346, 1348, 1358, 1394, 1396, 1402, 1417, 1419, 1420, 1425, 1439, 1457, 1459, 1460
Bassini, Rubins 484
Bassoon Music 593, 1292
Battle, Kathleen 35, 637, 833
Baude Cordier (14th century) 277
Bauer, Marion 1406
Bavarian Dances 371
Bavarian Radio Symphony Orchestra 709
Bax, Arnold 111, 342
Bay Cities Recordings 305, 522, 1392
Bayo, Maria 19
Beach Boys 112, 922
Beard, Jim 1212, 1214
Beatles 540
Beaux Arts String Quartet 1329
Beaux Arts Trio 395
Bebop & Beyond 113
Bebop Lives! 809
Because of You 1007
Beck, Jeff 114
Beck, Joe 893
Beck, William 1308
Becker, Carla 576
Beethoven, Ludwig van: Orchestral/Choral Works 115, 117, 118; Orchestral Works 127–136, 1110; Piano Concertos 119, 120, 130; Small Ensemble Music 116, 123–126, 194, 1097; Solo Piano 45, 121, 122, 684; Solo Vocal 28
Before We Were Born 429
Beirach, Richie 755
Belafonte, Harry 137
Belden, Bob 138
Belgrave, Marcus 9
Bella Domna 139
Bellian, Michael 1086
Bellini, Vincenzo 561
Bellstedt, Hermann 241
Belmont Chorale 491
Belshazzar's Feast Suite 1181
Bénédiction de Dieu dans la Solitude 678
Bennett, Richard Rodney 141
Bennett, Robert Russell 908

Bennett, Tony 142, 143, 1144
Bennett, William 1359
Bennett/Berlin 143
Benny Rides Again 324
Benoit, David 144, 1125
Benson, George 143
Berg, Bill 414–419
Berg, Bob 145, 146, 534, 1212–1214
Berganza, Teresa 1198
Bergen Wind Quintet 1423
Bergeron, Wayne 400
Bergsma, William 1362
Berio, Luciano 147, 148
Berlin, Irving 185
Berlin Philharmonic Orchestra 710, 719, 831, 1383, 1384
Berlin Radio Symphony Orchestra 1111
Berliner, Jay 656
Berlioz, Hector 149–157
Berman, Boris 964
Bernart de Ventadorn 158
Bernhardt, Warren 159
Bernstein, Leonard 27, 87, 160–163, 181, 184, 186
Bertali, Antonio 1349
Bertoncini, Gene 1130
Bessler-Reis Quartet 1360
Best, Martin 158
Best Band You Never Heard in Your Life 1441
Bevan, Tom 402
Beveridge, Thomas 882
Biber, Heinrich von 79, 89, 165–167, 1080, 1365
Bierach, Richard 664
Big Band 796
Big Generator 1436
Big Notes 414
Billings, William 169
Billy the Kid 288, 293
Bilson, Malcom 840, 842, 845, 846
Bingham, Seth 908
Biorhythms 469
Birds 1027
Bizet, Georges 170, 171
Black and Blue 536
Black Hawk Recordings 400
Blakey, Art 172, 1411
Blamires, David 788
Blanchard, Terance 191
Bläserkonzerte 1290
Blazer, Judy 447
Bley, Paul 173, 174
Blier, Steven 161
Blom, Inger 1086
Blow, John 904
Blue Guitar 1307

Blue Light 285
Blue Moon Recordings 113, 1129
Blue Note Recordings 9, 220, 222, 375, 483, 562, 563, 695, 731, 732, 737, 758, 931, 977, 1132, 1415–1417
Bluebell Recordings 682, 683
Blues Traveler 175
Bluesmen 249
Blumenthal, Daniel 648
Blythe, Arthur 1327
Boccherini, Luigi 176
Body and Soul 400
Bogdashevskaya, Victoria 1264
La Bohème 973
Böhn, Ole 245
Boîte à Joujoux 333, 337
Boîto, Aristo 150
Bolcom, William 177, 631
Bolero 1008
Bolling, Claude 178
Bon Voyage 1326
Bonell, Carlos 1046
Bonincini, Giovanni 602
Bonnevie, Robert 1119
Boogie Down 13
Book of Roses 1381
Les Boréades 1001
Boris Godounov 873
Boriskin, Michael 927
Borodin, Alexander 179, 1233, 1276
Borodin Trio 1286
Boss Brass 756, 1309
Boston Baroque 506, 511
Boston Early Music Festival Orchestra 836
Boston Pops 180–190, 963
Boston Symphony Orchestra 119, 131, 1273, 1288, 1376
Boublil, Alain 1091–1094
Bougue, Maurice 951
Boulez, Pierre 1442
Boulez Conducts Zappa 1442
Bourgeois Gentilhomme 1223
Bowie, Lester 21, 22
Bowlby, Bob 1029
Bowler, Phil 931
Bowman, James 474, 509
Boylan Heights 283
Bozzacco, Gino 610
Brackeen, Joanne 191
Brahms, Johannes 100, 192–204, 387, 665, 1038, 1447
Braja, Leandro 234
Brake, Brian 263
Brandenburg Concertos 41, 42
Brandenburg Consort 46
Brasileiro 779

Index

Break Like the Wind 1206
Breakin' Out 1150
Brecker, Michael 2, 205, 223, 237, 375, 483, 1212, 1214
Brecker, Randy 375, 483, 795, 798
Brendel, Alfred 681
Brendel, Wolfgang 1219
Brewer, Alfred 381
Brickyard Road 1334
Bridge 621
Bridge, Frank 342
Bridge Recordings 134, 246
Bridgehampton Chamber Music Festival 1053
Bright Music 1053
Brightman, Sarah 689, 690
Brignola, Nick 207, 1426, 1429
Brinker, Ray 401
Britten, Benjamin 208-211, 1261, 1307, 1405
Britton, David 440
Brno Philharmonic Orchestra 134
Broadbent, Alan 1037
Broadway Album 1252
Brock, Jim 212
Bronfman, Yefim 987
Brooks, Garth 213
Broom, Bobby 220, 222
Brothers in Arms 348
Brown, Baron 275, 276
Brown, Dean 275
Brown, Donald 172, 228
Brown, Garnett 535
Brown, Ray 168, 535-538, 900, 928-930, 1150, 1401, 1411, 1414
Brown, Stephanie 1096
Browning, John 85, 679, 989
Brubeck, Dave 168
Bruckner, Anton 214-216
Bruson, Renato 1351, 1355
Bryant, Lance 942
Buchan, Synthia 1355
Budapest Madrigal Choir 1368
Budapest Symphony Orchestra 103, 1304
Buens, Doug 394
Buffett, Jimmy 217
Buffett, Peter 218
Bullock, Hiram 219
Bullock, Robin 588, 726
Bunch, John 494, 1253
Bunnell, Jane 160
Buonamente, Giovanni Battista 1349
Buono, Nick 610-612
Burchuladze, Paata 831, 1351
Burgess, Sally 652, 754
Burnett, Richard 471, 847
Burrage, Ronnie 915

Burrell, Kenny 220-222
Burton, Gary 223, 327, 485, 626
Bury, Alison 303
Bush, Sam 413
Busoni, Ferruccio 224
Busterud, James 973
Bustijn, Pieter 530
Butt, John 72
Butterworth, George 595, 903, 1339
Buxtehude, Dietrich 37, 225-227
By Way of the World 1204
Byard, Jaki 421
Bylsma, Anner 32
Byrd, Donald 228
Byrne, Debbie 1093, 1094

CMP Recordings 469, 664
CPE Recordings 378
CPO Recordings 825
CRD Recordings 869
CRI Recordings 654, 950, 1194, 1207
Cabezón, Antonio de 748
Cables, George 810, 812, 814, 1407
Caccini, Guilio 871
Café 374, 375
Cafe Recordings 1029
Cage, John 229, 628
Caldera, Antonio 378
Calderazzo, Joey 732
California EAR Unit 399
California Project 922
Callata, Marie-Noëlle de 909
Calloway, Cab 168
Calm Sea and Prosperous Voyage 775
Calrec Soundfield Microphone 94, 95, 268, 371, 669, 776, 993, 1246, 1297, 1339, 1365; *see also* page 9
Cambria Recordings 698
Camerata Academica des Mozarteums Salzburg 861
Camerata Köln 1290, 1373
Camerata Recordings 1296
Camilo, Michael 893
Camouflage 797
Campbell, John 230, 459, 1298
Campion, Thomas 381
Canadian Brass 231, 232
Candid Recordings 421, 808
Candide 162
Canning, Tom 701
Cantata 1231
Canticle of Freedom 290
Cantos de España 5
Canzonetta 1182
Capitol Recordings 213, 475, 524, 623, 1000, 1211, 1323

Index

Capri Recordings 1407
Capriccio Burlesco 1390
Capriccio Espagnol 1030, 1032, 1033
Capriccio Italien 1266
Capriccio Recordings 365
Capricorn Recordings 1408
Cara, Marchetto 1022
Caram, Anna 234-236
Cardenes, Andres 1287
Carle, Frankie 188
Carley, Dale 107, 108
Carlton, Larry 237
Carlton, Todd 401
Carmen 170, 171
Carmina Burana 905
Carnival Overture 365, 367
Carr, Colin 769
Carr, Kenny 259
Carreras, José 1351
Carrington, Chris 347
Carrington, Terri 1155
Carroll, David 447
Carter, Benny 242
Carter, Clifford 370
Carter, Clive 1200
Carter, Donna 952
Carter, Elliot 243-246, 1362
Carter, Ron 274, 285, 441, 468, 562, 563, 607, 608, 702, 791, 808, 1055, 1327, 1328, 1386, 1396, 1417
Carver Electronics 705
Cash, Johnny 258
Castello, Dario 1199
Cathcart, Patti 14, 16
Catingub, Matt 1037, 1438
Cavalli, Pier Francesco 871, 904
Cedar Walton Plays 1386
Cedille Recordings 1068
Cello Music 25, 28, 32, 70, 71, 76, 116, 307, 342, 345, 360, 385, 549, 560, 635, 769, 924, 956, 1104, 1194, 1202, 1207, 1261, 1324, 1367
Centaur Recordings 363, 1320
Cephas, John 249
Cesti, Marc Antonio 904
Chabrier, Emmanuel 427
Chaffee, Gary 469
Chamber Music Northwest 202, 1081
Chamber Symphony 1172
Chambers, Dennis 145, 1212, 1213
Chambers, Joe 312
Chaminade, Cecile 420
Chandos Baroque Players 1291
Chandos Recordings 37, 54, 90, 101, 111, 199, 209, 210, 226, 333, 334, 342, 372, 405, 420, 467, 504, 587, 594, 595, 598, 599, 614, 635, 636, 641, 647, 712, 716, 802, 874, 888, 889, 923, 961, 964, 970, 971, 991, 992, 1014, 1015, 1022, 1025, 1034, 1090, 1156, 1159, 1164, 1169, 1170, 1235, 1286, 1293, 1307, 1341, 1343, 1346-1348, 1379, 1387-1390, 1393, 1422
Channel Classics Recordings 70, 116, 271, 499, 838, 839, 843, 844
Chant 665
Chant du Ménestrel 636
Chant du Rossignol 1235
Chant du Monde Recordings 1324, 1360
Chapelle Royal de Paris 767
Chapin, Harry 255-257
Chapin, Thomas 926
Chariots of Fire 1332
Charles, Ray 258, 259
Charpentier, Mark-Antoine 260, 261, 904
Chase, Stephanie 194
Chastain, Don 456
Chateauneuf, Paula 869
Chaynes, Charles 982
Cheatham, Doc 464
Cheek, John 150, 544
Cheetham, John 12, 882
Cherna, Vladimir 1352
Cherry, Ed 1045, 1036
Cherubini, Luigi 262
Chesky, David 236, 263, 264
Chesky Recordings 71, 234-236, 249, 263, 264, 266, 356, 532, 564, 634, 656, 697, 765, 910, 939, 940, 998, 1007, 1035, 1036, 1045, 1079, 1299, 1300, 1328, 1375, 1427, 1429
Chestnut Brass Company 624
Chevy Chase Elementary School Chorus 873
Chhanda Dhara Recordings 1147
Chiara Banchini 904
Chicago Fire 459
Chicago Symphony Orchestra 56, 92, 98, 647, 708, 722, 724, 874, 1112, 1224
Chichester Psalms 163
Childs, Billy 326, 476
Chilingirian Quartet 101
Choeur et Orchestre Régional de Cannes-Provence-Alpes-Côte d'Azur 308
Choeurs de Radio France 972
Choeurs et Orchestre National de Lyon 115, 396
Choir and Orchestra of the Bolshoi 1031
Choir of New College Oxford 509

Index

Choir of the German State Opera 1383
Chopin, Frédéric 45, 265–269, 684, 894, 956, 1380
Chor der Deutschen Oper Berlin 831
Choral Arts Society 873
Choral Ensemble of the Schola Cantorum Basiliensis 278
Choristers of Liverpool Cathedral 754
Choristers of St. Paul's Cathedral 210
Chorus and Orchestra of the Accademia Nazionale di Santa Cecilia 973
Chorus of Opera North 652
Christ Church Cathedral Choir 1377
Christensen, David 1308
Christie, James 836
Christlieb, Pete 730, 1144
Christmas and Easter Historias 1122
Christmas Music 190, 738, 952, 954, 1122, 1308
Christophorus Recordings 273, 379, 748, 960, 1318
Christus 670
Chrysalis Recordings 1191
Church Windows 1024
Ciclo Brasileiro 1361
Ciconia, Johannes 271
Cimento dell'Armonia e dell'Inventione 1369
Cincinnati Pops Orchestra 168, 579, 1042, 1044, 1145, 1322, 1418
Cincinnati Symphony Orchestra 171, 216, 393, 455, 706, 1266
Cipher Syntax 1218
City of Birmingham Symphony Orchestra 1018
City of London Sinfonia 420, 595, 1387
Civilization 1416
Claim 896
Clapton, Eric 272
Clarinet Music 202, 327, 409, 459, 593, 828–830, 1035, 1036
Clarion Ensemble 1321
Clark, James 134
Clarke, Herbert 241
Clarke, Jeremiah 1322
Classical Quartet 853
Classical Symphony 1251
Claude's Late Morning 957
Claves Recordings 19, 1198
Clayton, John 13, 1407
Clayton-Hamilton Jazz Orchestra 13
Clemencic Consort 1082
Cleveland Quartet 770, 852, 1100
Cleveland Symphonic Winds 585, 1218

Cleveland Symphony Orchestra 155, 224, 364, 718, 876, 966, 1017, 1110, 1162, 1179, 1247, 1269, 1274
Clift, Karen 511
Closer Than They Appear 634
Cobb, Jimmy 422, 808
Cobham, Billy 274–276
Cocina Caliente 287
Cohen, Marc 138, 816
Cohn, Sonny 106–108, 1129
Colaiuta, Vince 326, 1133
Cold, Ulrick 1086
Cole, Kevin 448
Cole, Nat King 280
Cole, Natalie 280
Cole, Richie 1255
Coleman, George 1064
Coleman, Ornett 787, 1408
Coleman, Steve 312, 577, 578, 1195, 1196, 1218
Coleridge-Taylor, Samuel 281
Coles, Johnny 809
Collegium Musicum 90 54, 1293
Collegium Vocale de Gand 767
Collegium Vocale, Gent 58
Colley, Scott 564
Collins, John 1412
Collins Classics Recordings 343, 387, 707, 713, 749, 968, 986, 1117, 1160, 1166
Colman, Denardo 787
Columbia Recordings 49, 100, 142, 143, 178, 231, 241, 258, 259, 284, 285, 286, 316, 329, 349, 451, 453, 542, 608, 621, 627, 655, 702, 734–736, 738–744, 936, 937, 974, 1020, 1075, 1155, 1252, 1312, 1372, 1381, 1396, 1419
Comin' from a Good Place 610
Coming Around Again 1185
Communications 880
Complete Czech Dances 1192
Complete English Anthems 1257
Conant, Richard 134
Concentus Musicus Wien 53, 515, 1294
Concertgebouw Orchestra 133, 147, 203, 721, 964, 985, 990, 1034, 1161, 1167, 1175
Concerti a Due 1370
Concerti a Due Cori 501
Concertino 362
Concerto da Camera in C Minor 522
Concerto for Organ, Harp and Strings 522
Concerto for Two Pianos and Orchestra 472
Concerto in F 454

Index

Concerto Köln 507
Concerto Palatino 1199
Concerto Vocale 261
Concierto de Aranjuez 1046
Concord Jazz Recordings 4, 13, 191, 312, 430, 437, 438, 492, 494, 435–438, 629, 760, 866, 933, 1150–1152, 1195, 1196, 1253, 1260, 1309–1311, 1329, 1401, 1426, 1428
Concord Picante Recordings 410, 976
Conifer Recordings 1268
Connecticut Early Music Festival Ensemble 1375
The Connells 283
Connick, Harry 284–286
Consort Musicke 803, 805
Consortium Classicum 593
Conte, Luis 287, 410, 415
Contemporary Recordings 221, 230, 459, 531, 533, 534, 619, 809, 810, 811, 813, 815
Cool 606
Coolman, Todd 230, 437, 459, 806, 807
Copeland, Keith 313, 629
Copenhagen Boys Choir 712
Copland, Aaron 163, 181, 288–297, 472, 696
Corbett, William 1320
Corea, Chick 298, 485, 925
Corella, Douglas 576
Corelli, Archangelo 299–304, 602, 1320
Corigliano, John 305–307
Cornysh, William 309
Cortese, Paul 1362
Corydon Singers 163
Coryell, Larry 1255
Cosmic Thing 31
Costello, Dario 404
Coull String Quartet 771
Countdown 791
Cowell, Henry 229
Cowell, Stanley 312, 313, 625
Craighead, David 1358
Crandell, Robert 908
Crane, Lacy 626
Cranshaw, Bob 313, 1048
Crawdaddy 329
Crawford, Michael 314–316, 689, 690
Crawford, Tim 108
Cray, Robert 317
Crazy for You 446
Crazy People Music 734
Creation 543, 544
Crescent City Christmas Card 738
Cri de Merlin 1307
Criss Cross Jazz Recordings 667, 880, 1400

Criswell, Kim 945
Crone, Tan 600
Crook, Hal 1426, 1428, 1429
Cross Currents 374
Crosse, Jon 1204
Crozier, Catherine 248, 1052, 1203
Crusaders, The 319
Crystal Recordings 882, 1362
Culture Club 320
Cunelier (14th century) 277
Cunning Little Vixen 614
Current Events 1
Curry, Diane 1353
Curveball 639
Cutting, Francis 1313
Cybella Recordings 982
Cycles 145
Czech Philharmonic Orchestra 362, 614
Czecho-Slovak State Philharmonic Orchestra 1289

DIW Recordings 21–23, 702
Da Costa, Paulinho 1141
Däfos 322, 539, 1144, 1305
Dalberto, Michel 678
Dallas Symphony Orchestra 297, 1030, 1165, 1241, 1244
Dallas Wind Symphony 586
Damn Right, I've Got the Blues 489
Dance Cubana 472
Dance of the Seven Veils 1221
Dance Panels 288
Dance Suite 92, 95, 103
Dance Variations for Two Pianos and Orchestra 472
Dances Concertantes 1232
Dances from Terpichore 955
Dances of Galánta 96, 647
Dancin' on Coals 80
Daniels, Barbara 973
Daniels, Eddie 168, 324–327, 377, 485
Danish National Radio Symphony Orchestra 712, 888, 1235
Daphnis et Chloé 1009, 1010
Dardanus 1001
Dark Side of the Moon 935
Darling Buds, The 329
d'Ascoli, Bernard 265
Davis, Andrew 25
Davis, Anthony 330
Davis, Art 476
Davis, Charlie 415, 422
Davis, Eddie 1412
Davis, Gregory 349
Davis, Jesse 1260

Index

Davis, Mike 1029
Davis, Quin 611
Davis, Sa 274–276
Davis, Stanton 23
Davis, Steve 926
Deadrock Symphony Orchestra 446
Dean, Billy 331, 332
Dean, Michael 513
Dear Mr. Basie 1401
Death and the Maiden 1097
Death and Transfiguration see *Tod und Verklärung*
Debriano, Santi 312
Debussy, Claude 187, 251, 333–339, 894, 1030, 1049, 1313, 1397
Decade of Decadence 822
Decca Recordings *see* London Recordings
Deedles 1123
Deep Breakfast 701
Def American Recordings 424
Def Leppard 340, 341
Definitive Thad Jones 659, 660
DeFranco, Buddy 459
DeGroote, Steven, 101
DeJohnette, Jack 206, 207, 374, 578, 616, 702, 787, 1048
Delage, Maurice 465
Delicate Sound of Thunder 936
Delicious Vinyl Recordings 740
Delius, Frederick 342, 343, 372, 1338, 1348
Deller Choir 904
De Los Angeles, Victoria 387, 390
Delos Recordings 6, 38, 60, 91, 92, 94, 96, 126, 129, 130, 132, 141, 143, 160, 172, 202, 225, 248, 290, 293, 344, 345, 359, 392, 440, 476, 481, 520, 523, 525–527, 549, 550, 553, 679, 696, 749, 860, 894, 908, 938, 944, 956, 967, 989, 993, 1010, 1037, 1038, 1052, 1062, 1081, 1101, 1108, 1119, 1153, 1171, 1173, 1202, 1203, 1221, 1228, 1236, 1251, 1264, 1265, 1287, 1298, 1306, 1308, 1358, 1386, 1397, 1412, 1414
Del Tredici, David 927
DeMerle, Les 611
Denham, Vince 423
Denisov, Edisson 1067
Denley, Catherine 54, 509
Denon Recordings 29, 104, 106, 145, 146, 151, 152, 157, 287, 374, 396, 468, 493, 505, 506, 678, 727, 836, 854–858, 1109, 1111, 1420, 1421
Dent, Karl 999
Departure #2 313

Deremo, Alan 1205
Désenclos, Alfred 982
Desire 1133
Detroit Symphony Orchestra 97, 334, 482, 1226, 1245
Deutsche Grammophon Recordings 35, 162, 215, 336, 338, 543, 637, 717, 778, 785, 790, 831, 1097, 1104, 1112, 1174, 1351
Deutsche Harmonia Mundi Recordings 55, 89, 165, 214, 250, 278, 321, 546, 897, 932, 1290, 1349, 1366, 1373
Deutschler, Ursula 19
Devos, Louis 1086
Dial, Garry 1045
Dialogues 1392
Diamond, David 305, 344, 345, 910, 1010
Diamonds and Pearls 959
Diaz, Bessón 436
DiBartolo, Joel 1445
DiBlasio, Denis 401, 403
Dick Hyman Plays Fats Waller 1385
Dickey, Bruce 983
Different Strokes 576
Digital Duke 377
Digital Music Products Recordings 81, 82, 159, 386, 414–416, 418, 419, 576, 750, 751, 795–797, 893
Digital Works 606
DiMeola, Al 346, 347
D'India, Sigismondo 871
Dire Straits 348
Dirty Dozen Brass Band 349
Disley, John 592
Dison, Eric 104, 108
Dispa, Michel 28
Distler, Hugo 573
Diva 658
Divertimento 1240
Divertimento from the Fairy's Kiss 1241
Dmitri Pokrovsky Singers 1424
Dr. Feelgood 823
Dodd, Tommy 610
Dolby™ Noise Reduction 792
Dolby™ Pro Logic 237, 298, 324, 431, 609, 731, 796, 1142, 1299; *see also* page 8
Dolby™ Surround Sound 3, 237, 252, 298, 431, 490, 512, 609, 782, 796, 936, 1142, 1200, 1204, 1241, 1292, 1296; *see also* page 8
Domingo, Placido 655, 974, 1352
Don Giovanni 831
Don Juan 1224–1226
Don Quixote 1224, 1225, 1227
Don Sanche 671

Index

Donald, Peter 1445
Don't Be Afraid of the Dark 317
Don't Try This at Home 205
Dorian Recordings 43, 61, 62, 198, 267, 381, 588, 726, 871, 902, 1028, 1096, 1165, 1192, 1220, 1244, 1275, 1398
Double Image 810
Double Vision 609
Douglas, Jerry 413
Dowland, John 351, 352
The Dowland Consort 351
Drake, Julius 208
Dread Zeppelin 353
Dream 14
Drew, Kenny 354
Drewes, Billy 752
Drewes, Glen 659, 660
Drive 413
Drottingholm Baroque Ensemble 1292
Drummond, Ray 386, 422, 438, 533, 534, 568, 619, 750, 751, 880, 881, 1149, 1400
Drums 628
Dubin, Josh 957
Duesing, Dale 160
Dufey, Guillaume 355
Dumas, Tony 326
Duncan, Stuart 413
Dunhill Recordings 256, 257
Dunlap, Bruce 356
Dunn, Susan 1353
Duo for Viola and Piano 1194
Duotones 433
Duparc, Henri 357
Duplicates 953
Dupré, Marcel 358, 440, 907
Durham, Bobby 928-930
Durón, Sebastián 748
Duruflé, Maurice 359, 397
Dvořák, Antonin 25, 360-367, 1447
Dvořák and Friends 361
Dylan, Bob 540

ECM Recordings 1, 2, 47, 74, 570, 574, 577, 578, 616, 1176, 1258
EMI/Angel Recordings 85, 136, 153, 254, 262, 288, 297, 350, 355, 446, 524, 618, 691, 754, 772, 835, 862, 878, 901, 945, 947-949, 1018, 1107, 1177, 1230, 1281, 1355, 1441
Eargle, John 60, 91, 129, 526, 553; *see also* pages 199, 201
Earthbeat 1424
East, Hathan 425, 1155
Eastman Philharmonia Orchestra 306
Eastmond, Barry 461

Eaton, Cleveland 107, 110
Edison, Harry 495, 496, 1401
Edwards, Brad 879
Edwards, Ross 666
Egan, Mark 370, 470
Egmond, Max van 55
Ehrlich, Marty 926
Eidi, Billy 1012
Eight Poems of Emily Dickinson 289
1812 Overture 1265, 1266
80's Ladies 912
88 Basie Street 107
Eine Kleine Nachtmusik 832
Eisenach, Johann Jakob von 282
Eldridge, Peter 886
Electric Outlet 1131
Elegant Evening 1310
Elegy in Memory of Maurice Ravel 1010
Elegy in Memory of Serge Koussevitsky 523
Elektra Recordings 78, 255, 280, 429, 779, 822-824, 1051, 1074, 1133, 1409, 1453
Elektra-Nonesuch Recordings 45, 73, 83, 328, 398, 447, 449, 456, 465, 1408
Elgar, Edward 371-373, 595
Elias, Eliane 374, 375
Elkins, Gerry 275, 276
Ellington, Edward Kennedy "Duke" 185, 189, 377, 1402
Ellington, Mercer 377
Ellington, Steve 437
Elliot, Chris 378
Ellis, Herb 535, 928-930
Elwes, John 55
Emarcy Recordings 626, 1411
Emerson String Quartet 338, 1104
Empire Brass 436, 1049
Empty Suits 958
Endler, Johann Samuel 1364
Endlessly 461
Enescu, Georges 90
Engel, Max 165
English Baroque Soloists 51, 118, 834, 840, 842, 845, 846, 859
English Chamber Orchestra 594, 691, 830, 850, 1198
English Concert 34, 301, 503, 514, 518, 521, 548, 551, 552, 899, 980
English Mass 592
English Northern Philharmonia 652
English String Orchestra 87, 371, 1297, 1338
English Symphony Orchestra 292
Enja Recordings 412
Ensemble Alcatraz 328

Index

Ensemble Aurora 870
Ensemble Clement Janequin 656
Ensemble Divitia Cologne 499
Ensemble et Orchestre de la Chapelle Royal 58, 633, 921
Ensemble InterContemporain 243, 1442
Ensemble Organum 240, 252, 253, 277, 279, 369, 620, 782, 921
Ensemble Project Ars Nova 20, 601
Ensemble Venance Fortunat 432
Ensemble 415 302, 904
Entführung aus dem Serail 833
Enya 382-384
Epic Recordings 10, 113, 320, 638, 911, 1086, 1335, 1336
Erato Recordings 243, 307, 714, 848, 873, 972, 1006, 1217, 1224, 1277, 1372
Erb, Donald 12, 385
Ericsson, Hans-Ola 783
Erskine, Peter 1, 2, 29, 114, 146, 159, 223, 324, 753, 795, 797, 1141, 1212, 1214
Eschete, Ron 536, 537
Essence 1306
Essiet, Okon Essiet 931
Estes, Gene 725
Etcetera Recordings 33, 208, 600, 680, 684, 1430
Eubanks, Kevin 667
Eubanks, Robin 577, 958, 1195, 1196
Euphonic Sounds: The Scott Joplin Album 631
Europa Recordings 804
Evans, Bill 370, 470
Evidence Recordings 568
Evolution 1426
EWI, Akai 205, 206
Ewing, Maria 336, 1018
Extreme 388
Eye of the Beholder 298

FSM Recordings 404, 428
Façade 1 & 2 1387
Facets 1141
Faddis, John 464, 535
Fagen, Donald 389
Fairy Queen 979
Faith Hope Love 644
Falco, Gil 1142, 1143
Falla, Manuel de 390-393, 465, 1046, 1049
Fallin' in Love with Jazz 1048
Falstaff 1350
Family Style 1335
Famous Blue Raincoat, Songs of Leonard Cohen 1394

Fancy Pants 108
Fanfare for the Common Man 290, 294
Fantasia in G Major 585
Fantasia on a Theme by Thomas Tallis 1337, 1345
Fantasia on Greensleeves 1276, 1344
Fantasia para un Gentilhombre 1046
Fantasie in A 630
Fantasy for Flute Stops 1203
Fantasy Variations on a Theme of Youth 525
Fantini, Girolamo 602
Farmer, Adrian 1339
Farmer, Art 619
Farrell, Eileen 394
Farrell, Joe 1305
Fasch, Johann Friedrich 1365
Faulkner, Tony 129
Fauré, Gabriel 187, 395-397, 427, 894, 1337
Faust Cantata 1086
Faust Symphony in Three Character Portrayals 672
Favre, Christian 674
Feather on the Breath of God 569
Feeling Good 172
Feinstein, Michael 398
Feiten, Buzzy 1133
Felder, Wilton 319
Feldman, Lawrence 797
Feldman, Morton 399
Felix, Delbert 735, 736
Ferguson, Maynard 400-403
Ferguson, Sherman 1153
Ferrabosco, Alfonso 381
Ferrante, Russel 1431-1435
Festive Overture 1160, 1169, 1171
Fialkowska, Janina 677
Fiddler's Child 614
Field, Gregg 110
Field, John 405-407
Field, Lucille 698
Fields, Brandon 423
Fi Fi Goes to Heaven 191
Final Cut 937
Finch, Barnaby 1136
Finck, David 234, 236, 263, 1035, 1036
Findley, Chuck 1153
Finger, Gottfried 250, 1320
Fink, Bernada 507
Finlandia 1177, 1180
Finlandia Recordings 408
Finnerty, Barry 374
Finnie, Linda 961
Finnish Radio Symphony Orchestra 408, 1181

Index

Finzi, Gerald 409, 595
Fiqueroa, Sammy 1035
Firebird 1233-1238, 1246
Firkusny, Rudolf 362
First Concerto for Flute and Percussion 628
First Program in Standard Time 884
Fischer, Brent 410
Fischer, Clare 410
Fischer-Dieskau, Dietrich 515
Fisher, Gillian 474
Fisher, Steve 401
Five Man Acoustical Jam 1301
Five Tenor Solos From the Opera Lord Byron 1304
Flanagan, Tommy 411, 412, 1427
Flanigan, Phil 494, 1253
Flash 114, 1428
Fleck, Bela 413
Die Fledermaus 1219
Flim and the BB's 414-419
Florida Suite 1338
Flory, Chris 494, 1253
Flute Music 24, 71, 178, 306, 420, 526, 628, 726, 1067, 1203, 1264, 1359, 1372-1375
Folia 443
Fonè Recordings 323
For My Broken Heart 757
Forbidden Lover 1419
Force Behind the Power 1056
Ford, Mark 423
Ford, Ricky 421, 422
Ford, Robbin 423
Foreign Intrigue 1417
Form 531
Formanek, Mike 565, 915
Forrester, Maureen 25, 1273
44th Street Suite 1327
Forward Motion 564
Forza del Destino 1351
Foster, Al 191, 228, 325, 327, 354, 411, 562, 563, 814, 815, 925, 1328
Foster, Frank 104-106, 1129
Foster, Ronnie 646
Fountain, Eli 9
Fountains of Rome 1025-1027
Four Corners 1431
Four Horseman 424
Four Last Songs 1229
Four Piano Blues 295
Four Seasons 1369, 1376, 1377
Four Short Prayers of St. Francis 952
Four Symphonic Interludes from Intermezzo 1221
Fowler, Beth 456
Fowler, Bruce 511

Fox, Caprice 886
Frager, Malcom 269
Françaix, Jean 1363
Franck, César 254, 426, 630, 907
Francs-Juges Overture 498
Franz-Liszt-Kammerorchester 273, 379
Franzetti, Carlos 910
Freddie Hubbard Quintet 468
Free 26
Freeman, Paul 1204
Freiburger Barockorchester 513
Freni, Mirella 1059, 1224
Frescobaldi, Girolamo 870
Friedlander, Erik 564
Friedman, Don 1299, 1300
Friendship 258
Friesen, David 1445
Frigo, Johnny 939
Frink, Laurie 797
Frisell, Bill 429, 752, 753, 957
Frishberg, Dave 430
From Day to Day 792
From Kirk to Nat 667
Fulbert de Chartres 432
Full Nelson 881
Fuller, Albert 1004
Fuller, Curtis 619, 1307
Fullerton, Fiona 948
Funérailles 681
Furlanetto, Ferruccio 851
The Further Adventures of Flim and the BB's 415

GM Recordings 915, 1113, 1114, 1406
GRP Recordings 144, 223, 237, 274-276, 298, 319, 324, 325, 326, 327, 370, 377, 462, 484-488, 645, 886, 925, 1123-1129, 1134, 1136, 1331, 1432
Gable, Tony 433
Gaboury, Steve 958
Gabriel, Peter 434, 435
Gabrieli, Giovanni 404, 436
Gächinger Kantorei and Bach-Kollegium, Stuttgart 39
Gadd, Steve 609, 753, 1127
Gaer, Leon 1141
Gale, Elizabeth 515
Gale, Eric 1134, 1136
Gale, Jack 1329
Gale, Warren 113
Galeta, Hotep 926
Gallois, Patrick 951
Galper, Hal 437, 438, 1426, 1428
Galway, James 306

Gardeil, Jean-François 1012
Gardner, Derrick 105
Garino, Gérard 671
Garrett, Kenny 9, 172, 441, 1064
Garrett, Margo 637
Garrison, David 447, 451
Garson, Michael 442
Gaskin, Victor 1300
Gasparo Recordings 427, 491
Gast, Arvid 1318
Gáti, Istvan 671
Gaucho 1210
Gavrilov, Andrei 1249
Gayaneh 641
Gedda, Nicolai 682, 683, 873, 972
Geffen Recordings 384, 434, 435, 685, 692, 752, 753, 786–788, 800, 895, 1092, 1301, 1302, 1303
Gehrman, Shura 1339
Geller, Timothy 1406
Geminiani, Francesco 443, 444
Generation 220
Genesis 445
George, Michael 474, 509
German Bach Soloists 1364
German Dances 1108
Gershwin, George: Orchestral Music 160, 453, 454, 455, 482, 618, 1114; Piano Music 448, 452; Stage Shows 446, 447, 449, 451, 456; Vocal 450, 637
Gershwin, Ira 446, 447, 449, 451, 456
Gershwin Connection 485
Gesualdo, Carlo 457, 458
Getting Down to Business 228
Getting There 2
Getz, Stan 1123, 1126, 1128
Gewandhausorchester Leipzig 128, 1274
Ghiaurov, Nicolai 1059, 1354
Ghirlande Profane 804
Ghirlande Sacre 804
Giagli, Giampaolo 1329
Gibbons, John 76
Gibbs, Gerry 230, 459
Gibbs, Leonard 607
Gibbs, Terry 459
Gideon, Miriam 698
Gilbert, William 460
Gilford, Jack 451
Gillespie, Dizzy 143, 242, 461–464, 807
Gilmore, Dave 1218
Gilmore, Steve 1426, 1428, 1429
Gimell Recordings 309, 458, 632, 917–919, 1076, 1257, 1259, 1262, 1357
Giovanna d'Arco 1058
Girard, Rich 1095
Girl Crazy 447

Girls Girls Girls 824
Giuffre, Jimmy 173, 174
Giulio Cesare 507
Give It What U Got 219
Gjevang, Anne 712
Glass, Alan 433
Glass, Philip 1148
Glasser, David 104
Glazounov, Alexander 27, 466, 635, 636, 1034, 1070, 1077
Glennie, Evelyn 666
Gliere, Reinhold 467
Glinka, Mikhail 186, 1070
Globo Records 1047
Godard, Benjamin 420
Godowsky, Leopold 1220
Godsend 1420
Goff, Scott 1264
Goines, Lincoln 795, 1213, 1331
Golabek, Mona 1287
Gold, Ernest 579
Gold Medal Collection 255
Goldberg Variations 47–50
Golden Cockerel 1031
Goldstein, Gil 370
Golson, Benny 463, 468, 619, 1412
Golub, David 769
Gomez, Eddie 159, 325, 374
Gondek, Juliana 513
Gonzales, Andy 1064
Gonzalez, Robbie 1331
Goodrick, Mick 469
Goodrum, Randy 487
Goodwin, Bill 725, 1426, 1428, 1429
Goodwin, Paul 512, 899
Gordon, Dexter 143
Gordon, Irving 189
Gorshin, Frank 447
Goscalch (14th century) 277
Gothenburg Symphony Orchestra 1087, 1174, 1182, 1184
Gothic Voices 247, 439, 569, 653, 704, 733, 763, 1140, 1201
Göttingen Festival 513
Gottlieb, Danny 370, 470
Gottschalk, Louis 471
Gould, Glenn 49
Gould, Morton 181, 472
Gounod, Charles 254
Graae, Jason 456
Graceland 1187
Graff, Randy 1092
Gragnani, Filippo 593
Grainger, Percy 1337
Gramavision Recordings 330, 957, 958, 1131
Granados, Enrique 387, 894, 1049

Index [236]

Grand Canyon Suite 293, 482
Grand Piano 1151
Grand Serenades, Numbers 1 and 2 593
Grant, Amy 473
Grant, Peter 656
Great Radio Controversy 1302
Great White 475
Green, Adolph 162
Green, Benny 700
Green, Bill 535
Green, Bunky 476
Green, Freddie 110, 1129
Greenhouse 1432
Greer, Lowell 194
Gregorian Chant *see* medieval chants
Grey, Al 495, 496
Grieg, Edvard 170, 481
Griffes, Charles 604, 894, 1264, 1397
Griffin Music Ensemble 1406
Grillo, Giovanni Battista 404
Groenendaal, Chris 945
Groener, Harry 446
Grofé, Ferde 293, 482
Grolnick, Don 145, 146, 483, 796, 1214
Gruberova, Edita 833
Grundheber, Franz, 1230
Grusin, Dave 484–488, 1123, 1126, 1127
Grusin, Don 485, 488, 1123
Guarneri Trio 1019
Guiding Spirit 221
Guido de Lange (14th century) 277
Guildhall String Ensemble 409
Guillou, Jean 61, 62, 906, 1028, 1072
Guitar Music 1, 2, 7, 16, 30, 220–222, 234, 235, 237, 242, 264, 272, 356, 469, 593, 608, 623, 655, 697, 786, 798, 1046, 1131, 1132, 1212–1214, 1307, 1313
Gulbenkian Orchestra 603
Gumbs, Onaje 275
Guthrie, Woodie 181
Gutiérrez, Horacio 988, 1271
Guy, Buddy 489
Guzelimian, Armen 604

Hadden, Nancy 868
Haden, Charles 8, 206, 531, 566, 787
Hadley, Jerry 162, 490, 754, 973, 1353
Hagans, Tim 732
Hagen Quartet 1097
Haggard, Merle 258
Haggett, Monica 303
Haguenauer, Jean-Louis 127
Hahn, Reynaldo 427
Hahn, Richard 1204
Hairston, Jester 491

Hakim, Omar 346, 486
Hall, Barry Lee 377
Hall, Doug 470
Hall, Jim 492, 493
Hamari, Júlia 671
Hamilton, Jeff 13, 430, 537, 580, 1152, 1407
Hamilton, Mike 1205
Hamilton, Scott 494, 866, 1253
Hamlet 1265
Hamlisch, Marvin 185, 189
Hammersmith 586
Hammerstein, Oscar 1043, 1044
Hampson, Thomas 604, 665, 947, 973, 1116, 1294
Hampton, Lionel 495, 496
Hancock, Herbie 758, 1396
Handbell Choir of California State University, Long Beach 1308
Händel, George Frideric: Choral/Instrumental 53, 497–500, 507–509, 510, 511, 513, 515–517, 904, 1294; Instrumental 89, 501–506, 512, 514, 518, 519, 520, 521, 585, 882, 960, 1202, 1292, 1296, 1319; Solo Instrument 71, 906; Solo Vocal 25, 637
Händel and Haydn Society Chorus 836
Händel and Haydn Society Players 502
Handy, Craig 138
Hanover Band 268, 558, 775, 776, 1105, 1106, 1377
Hanson, Howard 522–527
Haque, Fareed 1035, 1036
Harbison, John 83
Hardenberger, Håkan 27, 1363
Hargrove, Roy 812
Harjanne, Jouko 408
Harmonia Mundi France Recordings 44, 58, 72, 77, 115, 127, 169, 194, 240, 252, 253, 260, 261, 277, 279, 299, 300, 302, 308, 369, 380, 390, 457, 498, 507, 510, 513, 516, 517, 620, 633, 657, 699, 762, 767, 782, 904, 921, 953, 978, 989, 981, 1002, 1083, 1089, 1098, 1254
Harmonia Mundi UK Recordings 497
Harmonia Mundi USA Recordings 376, 1375
Harmonie Ensemble 361
Harnoy, Ofra 25, 1367
Harold in Italy 149
Harp Music 522, 526, 528
Harper, Heather 210
Harper, Winard 354, 1130
Harper Brothers 529
Harpsichord Music 19, 33, 47, 48, 71, 74–77, 499, 530, 871, 872, 1003, 1004, 1078, 1079, 1375

Harrell, Lynn 385
Harrell, Tom 493, 531–534, 1055, 1426, 1428, 1429
Harris, Gene 535–538
Harris, Hilda 330
Harris, Jeff 759
Harris, Jerome 958, 1048
Harris, Keven 349
Harris, Roy 290
Harrison, Donald 1417
Harrison, Lou 628
Hart, Anthony 463
Hart, Bill 438, 534
Hart, Mickey 322, 539
Hart, Zoe 1091
Hartmann, Karl Amadeus 801, 1363
Háry János Suite 647
Haslip, Jimmy 1431–1435
Hassell, Jon 1408
Haugland, Aage 888
Hauta-Aho, Teppo 408
Havana Cafe 1035
Havens, Richie 540
Having Fun 1298
Haydn, Joseph: Orchestral/Choral Works 543–545, 1198; Orchestral Works 273, 542, 548–559, 561; Small Ensemble Music 541, 546, 547, 560, 906; Solo Piano 1380
Haydn, Michael 1365
Hayes, Louis 813, 1326
Haynes, Roy 786
Haywood, Lorna 211
Headley, Erwin 869
Healing the Pain 476
Healing the Wounds 319
Heard, John 1412
Heart in Motion 473
Hearts and Bones 1188
Heartsongs 565
Heath, Jimmy 1299
Hebrides Overture 775
Heilmann, Uwe 863
Heldenleben 1228–1229
Helffer, Claude 1089
Helicon 588
Helmrich, Dennis 71
Helsinki Philharmonic Orchestra 1171, 1173
Hely-Hutchinson, Victor 1339
Henderson, Joe 228, 562, 563, 743, 791, 815, 1328
Henderson, Scott 298
Henderson, Steve 666
Hendricks, Barbara 254, 715, 864, 865, 878, 1230
Hendricks, Jon 758

Henry, Doug 394
Henry V 1388
Herbig, Gary 442
Here's To My Lady 1427
Hernandez, Cesar 1063
Hersch, Fred 327, 564–566
Herseth, Adolph 874
Hertel, Johann Wilhelm 1320
Hespèrion XX 1054
Hiawatha 281
Hicks, John 567, 568
Hicks, William 610, 612
Hiérophonie 229
Higgins, Billy 386, 809, 811, 1055, 1084, 1306, 1386
Higgins, Michael 401
Higgs, David 38
High Plateaux 1063
High Tension Wires 821
High Voltage 401, 402
Highlights from the Phantom of the Opera 689
Hildalgo, Giovanni 1331
Hildegard of Bingen 569
Hill, Martyn 210, 1304
Hill, Nelson 403, 1426
Hilliard Ensemble 355, 703, 762, 901, 1071, 1254, 1258
Hillier, Paul 570
Hindemith, Paul 571–575, 1038, 1423
Hing, Kenny 104
Hinton, Milton 421, 495, 496, 736, 940
Hirsh, Albert 305
Hirshfield, Jeff 138, 565, 1197
His Majestie's Clerkes 169
Hitzlberger, Thomas 672
Hoch, Beverly 862
Hoffman, Joel 1194
Höffner, Anton 282
Hoggard, Jay 221
Höhne, Carl 27
Hohner, Robert 576
Holberg Suite 481
Holland Dave 207, 577, 578, 629, 786
Hölle, Matthias 1383
Holloway, Red 1298, 1414, 1455
Holly, Major 1298
Hollywood Bowl Orchestra 1044
Holman, Bill 580
Holman, Peter 602
Holst, Gustav 581–586
Homilius, Gottfried August 270
Honegger, Arthur 587, 1363
Honey 806
Hong Kong Philharmonic Orchestra 466
Hooked 475
Hope 731

Index

Horigome, Yuzuko 861
Horn, Shirly 1413
Horn Music 194, 436, 648, 830, 1119
Horne, Marilyn 1350
Hornsby, Bruce 589–591
Horowitz, Vladimir 1380
Horszokowski, Mieczyslaw 45
Horvitz, Wayne 957
Houbart, François-Henri 1319
Hough, Stephen 307, 594
Hovhaness, Alan 1362
Howard, Leslie 673
Howe, Ted 212
Howell, Gwynne 56
Howells, Herbert 592, 1340
Hoyle, Ted 71
Hudson, Benjamin 776
Huelgas Ensemble 321
Hughard, Jim 430
Hughes, Luther 144, 536
Hughes, Ron 1309
Hulting, Billy 402
Hummel, Johann Nepomuk 273, 542, 561, 593, 594
Humphrey, John 544
Hungarian Radio and Television Chorus 670, 671
Hungarian State Opera Orchestra 670, 671
Hungarian State Symphony Orchestra 94, 95, 102, 103, 670
Hungarian Youth Ensemble Choir 675
Hungaroton Recordings 11, 36, 103, 140, 368, 431, 478–480, 560, 663, 670, 671, 675, 766, 941, 943, 1368
Hunt, Loraine 510, 516, 517
Hunter 1395
Hurford, Peter 573, 768
Hurst, Robert 9, 732, 734, 737, 740, 741, 743, 792, 1196
Hutcherson, Bobby 815, 1306
Hyman, Dick 933, 1385
Hymns, Carols, and Songs About Snow 15
Hymnus Paradisi 592
Hyperion Recordings 46, 139, 158, 163, 167, 200, 201, 247, 311, 357, 439, 443, 509, 528, 547, 558, 569, 592, 602, 649, 652, 653, 673, 703, 704, 733, 763, 771, 898, 920, 954, 1071, 1102, 1140, 1201, 1263, 1291, 1325, 1356, 1359
Hysteria 341

I Just Want to Sing 1412
IMP Recordings 474
I Never Went Away 141
INXS 597
IRS Recordings 17, 18, 353
Iberia 5, 1030
Ibert, Jacques 27, 420
Idenstram, Gunnar 64
Idomeneo 834
Iles, Alex 400
I'll Be a Song 1421
Images Pour Orchestre 339
Imagination 1149
Imai, Nobuko 199, 1070
Imboden, Tris 410
Immaculate Collection 705
In a Different Light 1130
In Good Company 1413
In Honor of the City of London 1389
In Process 700
In the Beginning 163
In the Moment 1445
In the Mood for Swing 242
In the Year of the Dragon 8
In Tribute 1124
Incredible Ravi Shankar 1147
Indes Galantes 1002
Indiana University Singers 1418
Innerflexions 1194
Innervisions 1425
Ino 1294
Intégrale de l'Oeuvre pour Piano 1089
Interlude 4
Intima Recordings 401, 402
Into the Woods 1200
Introduction to Khovanshchina 877
Introit 1422
Invisible Touch 445
Invitation to a Concert 437
Ireland, John 595, 598–600
Iridescence 942
Irwin, Dennis 4, 660–662, 700
Isaac, Heinrich 436
Isle of the Dead 985
Israel, Yoron 221
Isserlis, Steven 1261
Italian Cantatas 508
Itoh, Kohki 916
It's a Good Day 1037
Ives, Charles 291, 603, 604, 1408

JMT Recordings 1218
JVC Recordings 580, 916
Jackson, Anthony 346
Jackson, Dave 220, 222
Jackson, Javon 700
Jackson, Joe 605

Index

Jackson, Milt 259
Jackson, Paul 609, 646, 1135
Jackson, Randy 433
Jacobs, René 55
Jaffee, Alan 958
Jamal, Ahmad 606
James, Bob 425, 607–609
James, Harry 610–612
James, Philip 908
Janácek, Leos 362, 364, 613, 614
Janácek Opera Choir 134
Janácek Philharmonic Orchestra 363
Jansen, Rudolf 28
Jarman, Joseph 21, 22, 23
Jarre, Maurice 579
Jarrett, Keith 47, 74, 616, 1176
Jarvis, John 617
Jason, Neil 608
Jazz Forum All Stars 808
Jazz Messengers 172
Jazztet 619
Jerusalem, Sigfried 1383
Jeux 335, 337
Jiggs Up 1407
Jigsaw 1212
Jim Hall's Three 492
Jo, Sumi 863
Jobim, Antonio 236
Joel, Billy 631, 622
Johns, Steve 926
Johnson, Anthony 515, 862
Johnson, Cliff 416
Johnson, Eric 623
Johnson, Flim 414–419
Johnson, Francis 624
Johnson, Graham 1102
Johnson, J.J. 625
Johnson, Jimmy 326, 415, 417, 419
Johnson, Keith 676, 1305
Johnson, Marc 1, 2, 223, 324, 626, 695, 725, 731, 752, 753, 1132
Johnson, Robert 381
Johnston, Ben 1408
Jolivet, André 420, 627, 628, 982, 1423
Jonas, Dorothy 472
Jones, David 942
Jones, Della 392
Jones, Elvin 567, 743
Jones, George 258
Jones, Hank 386, 495, 496, 629
Jones, Harold 536
Jones, Rodney 220, 222
Jones, Thad 659, 660, 1412
Jones, Victor 461
Jones, Warren 291
Jongen, Joseph 630, 1050
Joplin, Scott 631, 1202

Jordan, Dan 403
Jordan, Steve 1074, 1131
Josquin des Prez 632, 633
Journeyman 272
Joy Rider 1155
Judas Maccabaeus 509
Juliard String Quartet 244
Jumpin's in the Future 1114
Junghänel, Konrad 165
Just Between Us 259
Just Jazz 495

K., Sara 634
Kabalevsky, Dmitri 186, 635
Kahn, Steve 1211
Kaiser, Karl 1373
Kakuk, Balázs 560
Kalinnikov, Vasily 636
Kammerchor Stuttgart 59, 1122
Kander, John 180
Kanon 1276
Kansas City Shout 109
Kaplan, Mark 769
Karela Suite 1177
Karg-Elert, Sigfrid 1038
Kashkashian, Kim 574
Kassoff, Russell 794
Kathleen Battle Sings Mozart 835
Kawamoto, Glenn 212
Kay, Connie 940
Kaye, Judy 161
Kayser, Audun 1447
Keavy, Stephen 602
Kee, Piet 37, 226
Keen, Catherine 393
Keeper of the Drums 1195
Keezer, Geoff 639, 640
Kellaway, Roger 325, 327
Kelly, Pat 1136
Ken Music Recordings 700, 1055, 1197
Kennard, Julie 592
Kennedy, William 1431–1433, 1435
Kenny G (real name Kenny Gorelick) 437
Kenny, Yvonne 136, 1231, 1343
Keri, Larry 451
Kern, Jerome 189
Kettel, Gary 666
Khachaturian, Aram 635, 641
Kiberg, Tina 888
Kiko 693
Kikoski, David 145
Kilgore, Robby 146
Kim, Earl 465
Kindertotenlieder 706
King, B.B. 237, 642, 643

Index

King, Gary 607, 608
King, Gerryck 1412, 1414
King and I 1043
King Christian II Suite 1181
King James Version 611
King's Consort 474, 509
King's Musick 904
King's Singers 350
Kings X 644
Kingsley, Ben 1043
Kipnis, Igor 1079, 1375
Kirkby, Emma 497, 508, 509, 704, 805, 827, 898
Kirkland, Kenny 206, 462, 645, 734, 735
Kirkpatrick, Tom 1400
Kirov Orchestra 965
Kiss My Axe 346
Kitagawa, Kiyoshi 529
Kite, Christopher 268, 776
Klibonoff, John 1362
Klinger, Angelika 1296
Klugh, Earl 607, 608, 646, 1331
Knapp, David 1119
Kneihs, Hans Maria 1296
Knowles, Gregory 666
Knowles, Nancy 24
Knoxville Summer of 1915 83
Koch Recordings 161, 472, 593, 1078
Kochan, Günter 251
Kocian Quartet 854, 855
Kodály, Zoltán 96, 647
Koechlin, Charles 648
Koffman, Moe 756, 1309
Kölner-Rundfunk-Sinfonie-Orchester 1107
Kolodner, Ken 588
Komen, Paul 116
Kontra Quartet 887
Konzertvereingung Wiener Staatsoperchor 515, 838
Konzertvereingung Wiener Volksopernorchester 1057
Koopman, Ton 63, 227, 303
Koor van de Nederlandse Bachvereniging 848
Korchhof, Lutz 75
Korngold, Erich Wolfgang 579, 649
Koslowsky, Johanna 500
Kraanerg 1430
Kraft, Norbert 1307
Kraus, Alfredo 1355
Kraus, Michael 863
Krause, Tom 1219
Krebs, Johann Ludwig 270
Krenek, Ernst 650
Kretzmer, Herbert 1091-1094

Krieger, Sara 886
Krommer, Franz 361
Kronos Quartet 1408
Kroon, Steve 263
Kropfreiter, Augustinus 573
Kroumata Percussion Ensemble 229, 628
Krüger, Irmtraud 748
Krystall, Marty 29
Kubalek, Antonin 198, 1192, 1275
Kuhn, Judy 1092
Kujala, Steve 1141
Kun, Hu 87
Kuolema 1184

LaBarbera, Joe 142, 143
Labé, Thomas 1220
Labelle, Dominique 836
Laboriel, Abraham 1205
Lacefield, Jim 442
Lachrimae, or Seaven Teares 351
Lack, Fredell 305
Lacy, Steve 651
Lady Be Good 449
Lady Be Good: First Recordings of the Unknown George Gershwin 448
Lai de la Fonteinne 703
Lalama, Ralph 1400
Lambert, Constant 652
Lament 811
Lament for Beowulf 526
Lamentation 1392
Lamentations of Jeremiah 1258, 1259
Lan Doky, Niels 534
Land, Harold 1306
Landmark Recordings 228, 791, 792
Landmarks 695
Landrum, Kenny 263
Lane, Jennifer 517
Lane, Piers 201
Lang, David 654
Langosch, Paul 142, 143
Langridge, Philip 210
Lanier, N 381
Laredo, Jamie 850, 1096
Largo, Pat 611
Lark Ascending 1338, 1342
Larmore, Jennifer 507
Larson, Eric 1391
Larsson, Lars-Erik 1077
Lashkary, Iraj 606
LaSpina, Steve 592, 593, 656
Last Call at the Blue Note 928
Last Protest Singer 256
Late Night at the Cafe Carlyle 1154
Laughter and Lust 605
Laurens, Guillemette 55

Index

Lausanne Chamber Orchestra 1023
Lawrence-King, Andrew 528, 869
Lawson, Rickey 1434
Lazy Afternoon 629
Leavel, Beth 446
Lebrun, Ludwig August 899
Lecuona, Ernesto 655
Ledbetter, Victor 511
Ledford, Mark 788
Lee, John 461
Lee, Peggy 656
Lee, Thomas 1408
Lee, Will 146, 375
Leeds Festival Chorus 652
Lees, Benjamin 305
Lefty's Roach Soufflé 286
Legend 599
Lehrndorfer, Franz 165
Leiferkus, Sergei 1273
Leitham, John 1311
LeJeune, Claude 657
Lembranças 410
Leningrad Philharmonic Orchestra 970
Lennox, Annie 658
Leonhart, Jay 656, 759, 866, 893
Lerios, Cory 433
Le Roux, François 336
Lesberg, Jack 933
Lester Bowie's Brass Fantasy 23
Let Them Eat Cake 451
Let's Eat Home 430
Levee Low Moan 739
Levin, Peter 1131
Levin, Robert 574
Levin, Tony 1211
Levy, Jules 241
Lewis, Mel 7, 659-662
Lewis, Roger 349
Lewis, Victor 625, 639, 1041
Lexicon 23, 53, 447, 543, 809, 887, 1045, 1216, 1297, 1427
Liberty Recordings 331, 332
Liebman, David 533, 664
Lieutenant Kijé Suite 962
Life of a Trio 173, 174
Lighthouse 81
Lightsey, Kirk 422, 667, 881, 1149
Lin, Cho-Liang 850
Lincoln, Abby 812
Lincoln Center Theater 946
Lincoln Portrait 290
Lindberg, Christian 318, 1050
Lindberg, Jakob 541
Linden, Japp te 303
Lindley, David 668
Lindroos, Peter 888
Lindsay, Arto 429

Linkola, Jukka 408
List, Eugene 455
Listen Here! 537
Liszt, Franz: Choral 675; Orchestral/Choral 670, 671; Organ 248, 674, 906; Solo Piano 127, 669, 672, 673, 676-681, 684, 894, 1380, 1397; Songs 682, 683, 1447
Liszt at the Opera 673
Liszt Ferenc Chamber Orchestra 36, 1368
Little Ain't Enough 1060
Little Big Band 1426, 1427, 1429
Little Consort 271
Little Feat 686, 687
Live at the Blue Note 929
Live at the Regal 642
Live at the 6th Tokyo Music Joy '90 23
Live at the Village Gate 1299
Live from Studio "A" in New York City 939
Live in Australia 622
Live Oak and Company 694
Live on King Street, San Francisco 1029
Liverpool Oratorio 754
Living Music Recordings 1424
Lloyd Webber, Andrew 184, 314, 689-691
Lo, Ted 234, 1331
Lock Up 692
Locke, Joe 915
Logan, Stacy 446
London Baroque Ensemble 497, 904, 978, 1083
London Chamber Orchestra 1371
London Classical Players 136, 153, 772, 861
London Overture 598
London Philharmonic Orchestra 599, 635, 764, 923, 1158, 1348
London Recordings 56, 92, 93, 97, 98, 147, 149, 196, 203, 335, 339, 364, 366, 391, 482, 572, 581, 708, 718, 721, 724, 826, 833, 863, 875, 890, 891, 951, 962, 969, 975, 985, 990, 997, 1008, 1009, 1011, 1013, 1017, 1026, 1032, 1046, 1057, 1058, 1059, 1157, 1158, 1161, 1167, 1172, 1175, 1183, 1226, 1237, 1243, 1245, 1249, 1279, 1282, 1283, 1354, 1399
London Sinfonietta 148, 245, 420, 618, 949, 1231, 1242, 1243
London Symphony Orchestra 129, 130, 162, 197, 210, 315, 316, 337, 343, 360, 392, 598, 707, 713, 837, 945, 947, 986, 1033, 1121, 1160, 1166, 1239, 1246,

Index

1261, 1267, 1272, 1284, 1341, 1343, 1346, 1347, 1390
Lookin' Up from Down Below 1113
Looking Back 1062
Lopardo, Frank 1350
Loriod, Yvonne 785
Lortie, Louis 1014, 1015
Los Angeles Chamber Orchestra 129, 520, 860, 1251
Los Angeles Philharmonic Orchestra 367, 453, 715, 953
Los Lobos 693
Lost Art 661
Lost Spindle 694
Lott, Felicity 56
Lovano, Joe 531–533, 695, 780, 1113
Love in a Small Town 913
Love Lives On 883
Lovesome Thing 812
Low, Mundell 900
Lubin, Steven 194
Luck of the Draw 1000
Ludus Danielis 323
Ludwig, Bob 31, 340, 911, 1335, 1440
Ludwig, Christa 336
Luedeke, Raymond 882
Lufkin, Daniel 402
Luft, Lorna 447
Luisa Miller 1352
Lukács, Péter 560
Luker, Rebecca 456
Lully, Jean Baptiste 699, 748, 904
Lumambo, Romero 264, 697
Lundquist, Tjörborn 229
Lupone, Patti 946, 1091
Lute Music 75, 352, 381, 541
Luxon, Benjamin 209, 211, 372, 1393
Lyadov, Anatoly 1068
Lynch, Brian 700
Lynch, Ray 701
Lyric Suite 481

MCA Recordings 80, 205, 217, 461, 617, 622, 756, 757, 805, 818, 821, 1031, 1069, 1206, 1209, 1315, 1431, 1433–1435
Ma Mère l'Oye 333, 1011, 1017, 1018
Má Vlast 1193
McBee, Cecil 191, 567
Mabern, Harold 702
Macbeth 1228
McBride, Christian 354
McCandless, Paul 1095
McCartney, Paul 754
McClure, Ron 755
McConnell, Rob 430, 756, 1309

MacDonald, Ralph 608
McDougald, Kenny 433
MacDougall, Jamie 509
MacDowell, Edward 604
McDuff, Jack 1414
McEntire, Reba 757
McFarlane, Ronn 381
McFerrin, Bobby 463, 758
McGillin, Howard 946
McGlohon, Loonis 394
McGovern, Maureen 451, 759, 948
McGuire, James 544
Machaut, Guillaume 703, 704
McJeff 755
McKenna, Dave 760, 940
McKenzie, Julia 1200
Mackrel, Dennis 107, 1129
McLauren, Marcus 1299
McLeod, Brian 1095
McLeod, John 666
McLurine, Marcus 221
McNair, Sylvia 57, 834
McNeely, Jim 771, 1429
Madison, Jimmy 1045
Madonna 705
Madrigaux à 5 Voix 457
Maffett, Jonathan 287
Maghostut, Malachi 22
Magic Trio 1 1411
Magnificat 51–53
Magnusson, Bob 1037
Mahler, Gustav: Symphonies 134, 707–724; Vocal 25, 665, 706
Mahoney-Bennett, Kathleen 946
Mai-Dun 599
Maier, Franzjosef 165
Mainieri, Mike 1211
Major Changes 813
Makowicz, Adam 725
Le Malade Imaginaire 260
Malmö Symphony Orchestra 615, 1086
Malone, Russell 285
Mancini, Francesco 1318
Mancini, Henry 727
Manhattan Blues 421
Manhattan Transfer 729, 758
Mann, Terence 1092
Mantooth, Frank 730
Marcal, Armando 788
Marco Polo Recordings 466, 1089, 1446
Marcoulescou-Stern, Yolanda 427
Marcus, Steve 1029
Margitza, Rick 731, 732
Marienthal, Eric 485
Marini, Biagio 870
Marks, Alan 295, 669
Marni Nixon Sings Gershwin 450

Index

Marquez, Sal 485
Marsalis, Branford 191, 377, 462, 486, 645, 734–736
Marsalis, Ellis 737, 742, 1040
Marsalis, Red 464
Marsalis, Wynton 241, 542, 627, 738–744, 814, 1040, 1144
Marshall, Eddie 4
Marshall, Margaret 1340
Martin, Frank 420, 1019
Martin, Mel 113
Martin Best Ensemble 233
Martinez, Richard 1331
Martinů, Bohuslav 745, 746
Mas Canciones 1051
Masakowski, Steve 731
Mascagni, Pietro 254
Mason, Harvey 425, 607, 608, 1135
Masques et Bergamasques 396
Mass in B Minor 54–57
Massenet, Jules 28
Masters of Reality 747
Mastersound Recordings 25
Mathis, Edith 543
Mathis de Maler 572
Matthäus Passion 58
Matthews, Ronnie 814
Mattila, Karita 135
Maverick 1410
Maxwell-Davies, Peter 749, 1364
Mayorga, Lincoln 450
Mays, Bill 750, 751
Mays, Lyle 752, 753, 788
Mazeppa 674
Meader, Darmon 886
Meant to Be 1132
Mechanical Resonance 1303
Medici String Quartet 123, 124
Medieval Music 3, 11, 20, 137, 140, 252, 253, 277, 368, 380, 431, 477–480, 663, 762, 763, 867, 868, 934, 941, 943, 1071, 1076, 1254
Medtner, Nilolay 764, 765, 1068
Melani, Allessandro 909
Meliora Quartet 522
Melos Quartet 1098, 1103
Memos from Paradise 325
Memphis Boychoir 1405
Memphis Chamber Choir 1405
Mendelssohn, Felix: Orchestral 772–777; Organ 248, 768; Piano 27; Small Ensemble 769–771, 778; Vocal 28, 254, 665, 767
Mendes, Sergio 779
Mendoza, Vince 780, 1432
Mennin, Peter 305
Menotti, Gian Carlo 83, 781

Mephisto Waltz 676, 677
La Mer 334, 335
Mercer, Johnny 394
Mercury Recordings 317, 340, 341, 820
Meridian Recordings 512
Meslanges 657
Messe de Notre Dame 703
Messiaen, Olivier 783–785, 907, 1038
Messiah 510, 511
Metheny, Pat 206, 786–788
Metropolitan Opera Orchestra and Chorus 1352
Meyers, Stanley 1313
Miaskovskii, Nicolai 789
Michael Crawford Performs Andrew Lloyd Webber 315
Micheljew, Alexander 360
Midsummer Night's Dream 777
Migration 486
Mikado 460
Miki, Minoru 666
Milan, Susan 420
Miles, Barny 346
Miles, Charles 933
Milestone Recordings 1048
Milhaud, Darius 334, 618, 790
Militello, Bob 580
Miller, Glenn 188
Miller, Marcus 319, 609, 1074
Miller, Mulgrew 324, 441, 468, 791, 792, 815, 880, 1195, 1197, 1415–1417
Milliman, Lincoln 1329
Millo, Aprile 1352
Milnes, Sherrill 1059
Milwakee Symphony Orchestra 1193
Mind Time 1331
Mingus, Charlie 793
Minnelli, Liza 794
Minnesota Orchestra 1382
Minter, Drew 513, 516, 517, 981
Mintz, Billy 442
Mintzer, Bob 483, 780, 795–797, 1432
Minz, Shlomo 778
Mirabai Songs 83
Miraculous Mandarin 94, 96, 97
Miramar Recordings 1139
Mironov, Jeff 759
Les Miserables 1091–1094
Missa Aeterna Christi Munera 920
Missa Choralis 675
Missa Gloria Tibi Trinitas 1262
Missa in Angustiis 545
Missa La Sol Fa Re Mi 632
Missa "L'Homme Armé" 355
Missa Pange Lingua 632
Missa Viri Galilaei 921
Mitchell, Dick 410, 580

Mitchell, Grover 110
Mitchell, Joni 800
Mitchell, Roscoe 21, 22, 23
Mobile Fidelity Recordings 112, 137, 608, 642, 793, 935, 1029, 1210, 1253, 1425
Mobley, Bill 640
Modules 953
Moeran, Ernest 802
Moffett, Charnett 441, 639, 645, 1415, 1416
Moll, Kurt 863
Molter, Johann Melchior 250, 282, 1364, 1365
Moments Like This 656
Moment's Notice 1064
Monadnock Festival Orchestra 1294
Monighetti, Ivan 1324
Monk, Thelonious 113, 651, 1403
Monte, Tony 656
Monteverdi, Claudio 803-805, 871, 904, 1198
Monteverdi Choir 51, 118, 192, 834
Mood Indigo 814
Moody, James 495, 496, 796, 797
Moore, Ralph 354, 625, 1195, 1196, 1260
Moorside Suite 586
Moranelli, Mark 808
Moravec, Ivan 267
More Monk 651
Moreira, Airto 322, 539, 731, 1305
Morgan, Ann 726
Morgan, Frank 809-815
Morgan, Lanny 580
Morgan, Rachael 600
Morgan Creek Recordings 687
Morley, Thomas 381
Morris, Gary 816-819, 1093, 1094
Morrison, Ann 449
Morrison, Richard 836
Morrison, Van 820
Morse, Steve 821
Morton, Ferdinand "Jelly-Roll" 882
Mosaics 527
Mosca, John 659, 660, 661
Moscow Radio Grand Symphony Orchestra 179
Moscow Virtuosi 801
Motets à Voix Seule et à Deux Voix 261
Motets for Christmas and Lent 952
Motian, Paul 8, 531, 532
Mötley Crüe 822-824
Motown Recordings 1056
Moulana, Sheik Chinna 872

Moye, Famoudou 22
Mozart, Leopold 825, 1365
Mozart, Wolfgang Amadeus: Orchestral/Choral Works 117, 831, 833, 834, 836, 848, 849, 862-865; Orchestral Works 542, 828, 829, 830, 832, 850, 856-861, 899, 1365; Piano Concertos 838-846; Small Ensemble Music 318, 829, 847, 852-855, 1313; Solo Vocal/Orchestral 637, 826, 827, 835, 837, 851
Mraz, George 354, 411, 412, 1427
Muffat, Georg 1083
Muhammad, Idris 1402-1404
Mukherjee, Budhaditya 596
Muldaur, Maria 1135
Müller, Rufus 898
Mulligan, Gerry 168, 866
Mullova, Viktoria 68, 1288
Murphy, Jon 544
Murray, David 1327
Murray, Michael 40, 65-67, 426, 630, 907, 1073
Muse Recordings 422, 942, 1149
Music & Arts Recordings 361
Music for Children 1390
Music for Strings, Percussion and Celesta 93, 98, 99
Music for the Royal Fireworks 585
Music for the Theater 296
Music Man 1418
Music Masters Recordings 624
Music of Espionage 1205
Music of Wagner 1382
Music West Recordings 700
Musica Alta Ripa 500
Musica Antiqua Köln 42, 1080, 1122
Musica Antique Praha 88
Musica Fiata 404, 1349
Musica Mensurata 428
Musica Viva Recordings 677
Musical Fantasies of Charles Griffes and Deems Taylor 1264
Musical Heritage Society Recordings 471, 477, 847, 1295
Musici de Montréal 504, 587, 1156, 1379
Musicians of Swann Alley 376
Musiciens du Louvre 1006
Musicmasters Recordings 242, 659, 660, 661, 662
Musikproduktion Dabringhaus und Grimm Recordings 79, 500, 650
Mussorgsky, Modest 873-877, 1069
Mustafa, Melton 105, 106
My Blue Heaven 940
My Name is Makowicz 725

Index

Myaskovsky *see* Miaskovskii
Myers, Leah Ann 134
Myslivecek, Josef 361

NYC 1211
Narada Recordings 218
Nash, Kenneth 1095
Nash, Lewis 735, 812, 1298, 1300
Nash, Ted 660, 662
Nasser, Jamil 1402-1404
National Philharmonic Orchestra 542, 975, 1059
National Symphony Orchestra 872, 1168
Nautilus Recordings 403
Nazarian, Kim 886
Negri, Joo 394
Neidlinger, Buell 29
Nell, Bob 879
Nelson, Steve 639, 640, 880, 881
Nelson, Willie 258
Nelson Mass 545
Neon 416
Neri, Massimiliano 1349
Neriki, Shigeo 944
Neruda, Johann Baptist Georg 1364
Nevermind 895
New Albion Recordings 20, 399, 601
New Beginnings 977
New Budapest String Quartet 200, 201
New Faces 462
New London Consort 166, 238, 239, 934, 955
New Stockholm Chamber Orchestra 1077, 1085
New Tunes, New Traditions 1055
New York Chamber Symphony 6, 132, 288, 344, 525, 526, 938, 1108
New York Choral Artists 361, 451
New York Chorinhos 264
New York City Gay Men's Chorus 883
New York Composer's Orchestra 884
New York Ensemble for Early Music 323
New York Philharmonic Orchestra 584, 720, 1180
New York Reunion 1329
New York Trumpet Ensemble 885
New World Records 385, 879, 884, 926, 927, 1053, 1115, 1215
Newman, Alfred 579
Newman, Anthony 69, 120
Newman, Joe 1401
Newport Recordings 69, 120, 892
Newsom, Tommy 1144
Niedermeyer, Louis 254

Nielsen, Carl 887-891
Nietzsche, Friedrich 892
Niewood, Gerry 656, 893
Night and Day 947
Night on Bare Mountain 874, 876
Night on the Town 589
Night Ride and Sunrise 1184
Night Ride Home 800
Nightfly 389
Nightlines 487
Nights at the Vanguard 411
Nights in the Gardens of Spain 392
Nimbus Recordings 30, 87, 94, 95, 123, 124, 233, 265, 268, 292, 295, 360, 371, 555, 582, 596, 603, 669, 749, 774, 776, 798, 993, 1105, 1106, 1239, 1246, 1250, 1297, 1338, 1339, 1365, 1377
1991 1190
Nirvana 895
Nixon, Marni 289
No Guru, No Method, No Teacher 820
No Holdin' Back 1316
No More Tears 911
Nobody Said It Was Easy 424
Nocturnal 1307
Nocturne for String Orchestra 1276
Noehren, Robert 60, 226, 1038
Nojima, Minoru 676, 1016
Nojima Plays Liszt 676
Nonesuch Recordings *see* Elektra-Nonesuch Recordings
Nonet for Strings 292
Norman, Chris 588, 726
Norton, Nick 282
Not Drowning, Waving 896
Notare, Karen 393
Nothin' But the Blues 1414
Nouvel Ensemble Moderne 664
Novalis Recordings 39, 63, 179, 227, 709, 1103, 1370
Novus Recordings 567, 806, 807, 1039, 1040, 1064
Nucci, Leo 975, 1354
Nuova Era Recordings 164
Nurturer 9
Nussbaum, Adam 755
Nutcracker 963, 1267-1269
Nymph Errant 946
Nymphs and Satyr Ballet Suite 522

O Magnum Mysterium 1356
ORTF Recording Technique 553 *see also* page 217
OU812 1333

Index

Oak Ridge Boys 258
Oatts, Dick 414–419, 661, 662
Oboe Music 499, 512, 526, 828, 899, 1223, 1264, 1343
Obradors, Fernando 696
Ocasio, Tito 441
Oceanides 1182
O'Connell, Bill 1331
O'Connor, Mark 413
O'Conor, John 121, 122, 406, 407, 841
Octet 1242
The Odd Get Even 1146
Odd or Even 1213
O'Dette, Paul 352
Of Thee I Sing 451
Ogdon, John 986
O'Hara, Paige 451
Ohlsson, Garrick 224
L'Oiseau-Lyre Recordings 166, 238, 239, 502, 508, 557, 827, 828, 849, 867, 868, 934, 955, 1003
Ojeda, Bob 105, 106
Okazawa, Akira 916
Okoshi, Tiger 484, 1113
Old American Songs 291, 295
Old 8 x 10 1317
Oliveira, Carlos 236
Oliveira, Elmar 524
Olympia Recordings 789
O'Mahony, Beverly 701
Omega Recordings 631
On a Different Level 207
On the Corner; 925
One by One 218
One Night in Vienna 1095
One on One 608
One to One 750, 751
Open Up: Whatcha Gonna Do for the Rest of Your Life? 349
Optimism Recordings 730
Opus 111 Recordings 176
Oratorio Society of Washington 873
Orchestra Anima Eterna 838, 839, 843, 844
Orchestra e Coro del Teatro Comunale di Bologna 1354
Orchestra of St. Lukes 35, 83, 330, 451, 519, 556, 559
Orchestra of the Age of Enlightenment 32, 41, 554
Orchestra of the Eighteenth Century 1001
Orchestra of the Royal Opera House 1268
Orchestre de Chambre Ferenc Liszt 99
Orchestre de la Bastille 785
Orchestre de la Chapelle Royale 1002
Orchestre de la Suisse Romande 714
Orchestre de Paris 1240
Orchestre du Capitole de Toulouse 790
Orchestre du Théâtre National de l'Opéra de Paris 982
Orchestre National de France 972
Orchestre Rèvolutionnaire et Romantique 192
Orchestre Symphonique de Montréal 93, 149, 335, 339, 391, 875, 962, 969, 1008, 1009, 1011, 1013, 1026, 1032, 1046, 1237, 1279, 1282
Ordóñez, Antonia 393
Oregon Symphony Orchestra 993, 1265
Orff, Carl 905
Orford String Quartet 126
Organ Music 37, 39, 40, 44, 60–69, 72, 117, 225, 226, 227, 248, 270, 358, 359, 373, 378, 426, 440, 522, 573, 592, 598, 614, 630, 674, 690, 723, 748, 754, 768, 783, 906–909, 974, 1025, 1026, 1028, 1038, 1052, 1072, 1073, 1093, 1094, 1203, 1308, 1318, 1319, 1346, 1358, 1379, 1405, 1458, 1459
Original-Instrument Recordings 32, 34, 41, 42, 46, 51, 53, 54, 70, 72, 116, 118, 119, 134, 136, 153, 165, 166, 193, 268, 301, 302, 304, 351, 443, 444, 499, 501–503, 510–512, 514, 517, 518, 521, 547, 548, 551, 552, 554, 557, 558, 560, 699, 772, 775, 776, 803, 827, 828, 834, 838, 840, 842, 847–849, 853, 859, 862, 870, 899, 954, 978–980, 1001, 1002, 1005, 1006, 1054, 1080, 1082, 1083, 1105, 1117, 1290, 1291, 1293, 1294, 1295, 1320, 1321, 1349, 1369, 1370, 1373, 1375, 1377, 1378, 1398
O'Rourke, Mígeál 405
Orozco, Raphael 5
Orpheus 674
Orquestra de Cambra Teatre Lliure 390
Ortiz, Gumbi 347
Osborne, Donny 1311
Osbourne, Ozzy 911
Osby, Greg 942, 1218
Oslin, K.T. 912–914
Oslo Philharmonic Orchestra 1177
Ostrovsky, Paul 778
O'Sullivan, Jerry 145
Othello Overture 365
Other Side of Jobim 235
Ottavo Libro de Madrigali 1638 803
Ottavo Recordings 1019
Ottone 513
Out of Time 984

Index

Out West! 293
Outdoor Overture 289
Ovalle, Jayme 696
Overture for a Masque 802
Owl Recordings 173, 174
Ozone, Makoto 626, 916

Pablo Recordings 107, 108, 109, 110
Pachelbel, Johann 187, 1202, 1276
Pacific Symphony Orchestra 289, 781, 1024
Padveen, Tom 610
Paganini, Niccolo 68, 241, 684
Paisiello, Giovanni 387
Paladihe, Émile 25
Palistrina, Giovanni 917–921
Panula, Jorma 1077
Papa Doo Run Run 922
Papathanassiou, Vangelis *see* Vangelis
Paperno, Dmitry 1068
Paris Quartets 1295
Párkáyi, Tibor 560
Parker, Charlie 1114
Parker, Jon Kimura 1270
Parker, Leon 1130
Parker, Eric 599
Parley of Instruments 167, 602, 954
Parry, Hubert 923
Parsifal 1383
Parsons, Geoffrey 387, 665, 903, 1116
Pärt, Arvo 924
Pasqua, Alan 1141
Passacaglia for Large Orchestra 1086
Passacaglia for Orchestra 1090
Passages 532, 1148
Passion and Warfare 1330
Pastorale 630
Pastorale for Oboe, Harp and Strings 526
Patitucci, John 144, 298, 327, 485, 925, 1153
Paul Cortese, Viola 1362
Paul Winter Constort 1424
Paulson, Bruce 415, 1142, 1143
Pavane Recordings 909
Pavarotti, Luciano 1059, 1354
Pavone, Mario 926
Pay, Antony 826
Payne, Joseph 44, 48
Payton, Nicholas 1040
Peacock, Gary 616, 977
Peacock Variations 647
Pedziwiatr, Wayne 893
Peel, Graham 903
Peer, Beverly 1154
Pelléas et Mélisande 336

Pelleas und Melisande 1090
Peña, Paco 30, 798
Penderecki, Krzysztof 801
Penerai, Rolando 1350
Penland, Ralph 326, 476
Peplowski, Ken 7, 629
Perahia, Murray 100
Percussion Highlighted 93, 97–100, 212, 229, 275, 276, 287, 298, 322, 344, 414–419, 482, 576, 585, 586, 610–612, 628, 666, 679, 872, 1029, 1047, 1133, 1189, 1265, 1266
Perez, Daniel 531, 532, 1035, 1036
Perfect Match 1152
Perfect Stranger 1441
Pergolesi, Giovanni 387,
Period-Instrument Recording *see* Original-Instrument Recording
Perle, George 927
Perlman, Itzhak 35
Perowsky, Ben 1213
Perry, Eugene 330
Perry, Herbert 330
Perry, Phil 731
Perry, Rich 564
Per-se-vere 730
Persichetti, Vincent 1362
Pesco, Paul 607
Petchersky, Alma 1361
Peter and the Wolf 963
Peters, Jerry 1412
Peters, Mark 1296
Peterson, Oscar 928–930
Peterson, Ralph 931
Peterson, Ricky 1074
Petite Band 55
Pétrouchka 1234, 1239–1241
Pezel, Johann Christoph 250
Phaéton 1073
Phantom of the Opera 690
Phantom Unmasked 314
Philadelphia Symphony Orchstra 997, 1281
Philharmonia Baroque Orchestra 299, 300, 498, 510, 516, 517, 904, 1374
Philharmonia Orchestra 582, 613, 627, 717, 856, 858, 968, 987, 1025, 1093, 1094, 1183, 1238, 1283, 1340, 1344, 1351, 1355, 1365, 1389
Philidor, André Danican 282
Philip the Chancellor 932
Philips Recordings 27, 28, 51, 68, 128, 133, 135, 180–183, 185, 186, 187, 188, 190, 193, 303, 395, 454, 477, 545, 681, 710, 719, 837, 859, 963, 965, 1001, 1043, 1072, 1219, 1240, 1288
Phillips, Flip 933

Index

Philomusica Antiqua 120
Piano Concerto for Left Hand 1013
Piano Concerto in A Minor 481
Piano Music Highlighted 4, 5, 8, 9, 13, 25-28, 45, 49, 50, 73, 81, 82, 86, 100, 101, 102, 116, 119-122, 127, 130, 141, 144, 159, 161, 168, 173, 174, 178, 189, 194, 195, 196, 198, 199, 201, 206, 208, 209, 212, 224, 230, 264, 265, 266-269, 284, 286, 291, 295, 305, 307, 310, 312, 313, 318, 342, 354, 362, 372, 387, 392, 395, 405-407, 427, 437, 438, 448, 450, 452-455, 468, 471, 472, 481, 485, 522, 525, 527, 531, 533, 537, 538, 550, 553, 564-566, 568, 571, 574, 594, 599, 600, 604, 640, 645, 648, 659, 660, 664, 665, 669, 672-674, 676-684, 696, 728, 737, 750-752, 755, 760, 761, 764, 765, 769, 776, 778, 780, 784, 785, 791-793, 810-815, 838-846, 866, 878, 879, 892, 894, 903, 927, 928-931, 933, 944, 950, 951, 953, 956, 964, 977, 986-989, 998, 1012, 1013-1016, 1019, 1028, 1035, 1039, 1040, 1050, 1058, 1067, 1068, 1070, 1089, 1096, 1100, 1101, 1102, 1116, 1137, 1150-1152, 1156, 1176, 1192, 1194, 1207, 1214, 1220, 1249, 1251, 1264, 1270-1272, 1275, 1287, 1310, 1311, 1340, 1347, 1361-1363, 1380, 1385, 1386, 1393, 1397, 1402, 1407, 1411, 1415, 1422, 1427, 1445
Piano Variations 295
Piazzolla, Astor 910
Picchi, Giovanni 404
Picture This 274
Pictures at an Exhibition 874-877
Pièces de Clavecin 1003-1005
Pieces of Blue and The Blues 222
Pied Piper Fantasy 306
Pierce, Billy 640, 1415, 1416
Pierce, Joshua 472
Pierre Verany Recordings 1319
Pines of Rome 1025-1027
Pink Floyd 935-937
Pinto, Mark 1029
Pique Dame 1273
Piston, Walter 472, 938
Pittsburgh Symphony Orchestra 454, 988, 1115
Pizzarelli, Bucky 939, 940
Pizzarelli, John 939, 940
Plain Brown Wrapper 817
Planet Drums 539
Planets 581-584
Plass, Joe 433

Plaxico, Lonnie 462, 942, 1195
Pliquett, Joachim 1318
Plishka, Paul 873, 973, 1353
Plog, Anthony 282, 1320
Plowright, Rosalind 1351
Plummer, Christopher 1388
Poèm de L'Extase 1281
Poem for Flute and Orchestra 1264
Poem of Ecstacy 874
Poema Autunnale 1024
Politics 1433
Polk SDA Speakers 705
Polozov, Vyacheslav 873
Polydor Recordings 689, 690, 1332
Polygram Recordings 8
Pomp and Circumstance Marches 371, 373
Pons, Juan 1351
Pöntinen, Roland 27, 318, 1050, 1067, 1070, 1137, 1363
Popkin, Ralf 513
Popper, David 944, 1202
Porcaro, Jeff 237
Porgy and Bess 482
Pornograffitti 388
Porter, Cole 188, 945-950
Porter on My Mind 950
Portrait 438
Portraits 1300
Portraits of Duke Ellington 1402
Portraits of Freedom Music of Aaron Copland and Roy Harris 290
Portraits of Thelonious Monk 1403
Portsmouth Point Overture 1390
Posnak, Paul 452
Posthorn Serenade 832
Potter, Chris 1045
Poulenard, Isabelle 55
Poulenc, Francis 951, 952, 1012
Powell, Jim 660, 661
Powell, Mel 953
Powell, Shannon 284, 286
Power Play 275
Power Trio 567
Powers, Patrick 136
Praetorius, Michael 954, 955
Prague Chamber Orchestra 832
Preiser Recordings 1082
Prélude à l'après-midi d'un faune 335, 337
Preludes for Piano 453
Preludio Recordings 674
Presenting Michael Weiss 1400
Presto 1065
Preston, Brian 522
Previn, Andre 454, 900
Previte, Bobby 957, 958

Index

Prima, Louis 188
Prince 959
Prince Igor 1233
Priuli, Giovanni 1349
Private Music Recordings 1146, 1148, 1395
Pro Arte Chamber Orchestra of Boston 1207
Pro Organo Recordings 1405
ProArte Recordings 448, 1241, 1364
Proensa 570
Prokofiev, Sergei: Orchestral 963, 964–971, 1244, 1251, 1270; Orchestral/Choral 961, 962, 972; Small Ensemble 801, 1067
Protecting Veil 1261
Puccini, Giacomo 973–975, 1322
Puente, Tito 976
Pugh, Jim 394
Pulcinella (suite and complete) 1232, 1241, 1248
Pullen, Don 977
Pulse 229
Puquet, Michel 827
Purcell, Henry 904, 906, 909, 978–981, 1319
Purcell, John 1074
Purcell Band 443
Purcell Quartet 443
Pure Schuur 1125
Purim, Flora 322, 539, 1305
Pushkin Waltz 967
Pyle, Cheryl 532

Q-Sound System 705
Quaker Reader 1052
Quality Recordings 315
Quantum Recordings 432
Quast, Philip 1093, 1094
Quatours a Cordes 1360
Queen of Spades see *Pique Dame*
Question and Answer 786
Quiet City 292
Quilter, Roger 595, 903
Quink Vocal Quintet 1021
Quintana Recordings 3, 99, 478, 1378
Quintergy 625
Quivar, Florence 1352

RCA Recordings 76, 86, 148, 214, 232, 306, 362, 409, 490, 590, 591, 666, 722, 759, 801, 806, 829, 912, 913, 914, 946, 1181, 1200, 1227, 1273, 1344, 1350, 1367, 1394

Rabe, Folke 1363
Rabello, Raphael 697
Rachmaninoff, Sergei: Choral 999; Orchestral 985, 990–997, 1202; Piano 998, 1068; Piano Concerto 986–989, 1271, 1272; Solo Vocal 637, 1069
Radio-Sinfonie-Orchester, Frankfurt 151, 152
Rāg Jhiñjoti 596
Rāg Ramkali 596
Raga Charukauns 1157
Ragé, Pascal 951
Ragin, Derek Lee 208, 499, 507
Raglan Chamber Players 1369
Raimondi, Ruggero 873
Rainey, Tom 564
Raitt, Bonnie 1000
Rake's Progress 1243
Rameau, Jean Philippe 904, 1001–1006
Ramey, Samuel 135, 291, 831
Rampal, Jean-Piérre 178, 1372
Random Abstract 735
Rankin, Kenny 1007
Raphael Ensemble 649
Rapsodie Espagnole 1008, 1017
Ravel, Maurice 333, 427, 465, 874–877, 1008–1019, 1049, 1397
Rawls, Lou 259
Rayo-X 668
Razor's Edge 577
Reach, Pierre 50
Real Life 1429
Real Swinger 933
Real Time 619
Réaux, Angelina 973
Recorder Music 1292, 1296, 1373
Recycler 1439
Red Baron Recordings 1327
Redman, Joshua 926
Reedus, Antony 441, 640, 700, 880
Reference Recordings 154, 212, 289, 322, 394, 442, 450, 586, 676, 781, 1004, 1016, 1024, 1305, 1385, 1438
Reflections 815
Reger, Max 25, 1358
Reid, Mike 1020
Reid, Rufus 625, 640, 667, 1041, 1084, 1260
Reigel, Kenneth 873
Reincken, Jan Adam 530
Reinhold, Günter 784
Relativity Records 1091, 1093, 1094, 1330
Remember When the Music 257
Remembrance 529
Remler, Emily 144

Index

Renaissance Music 350, 528, 1021, 1022, 1071, 1262, 1263, 1325, 1356, 1357, 1398
Renard the Fox 1242
Renner, Jack 519, 1030, 1115
Renzi, Mike 656, 759, 866
Representing the Mambo 686
Reprise Recordings 31, 272, 383, 688, 896, 1314
Requiescat in Pace 1203
Reservoir Recordings 207, 1084
Resnick, Art 1153
Respighi, Ottorino 1023–1027, 1313
Reubke, Julius 248, 1028
Reutter, Johann Georg von 378
Reverie 164
Rhapsody for Orchestra "Taras Bulba," 364
Rhapsody in Blue 453, 454, 455
Rhapsody on a Theme of Paganini 1271
Rheinberger, Josef 358
Rhythm of the Saints 1189
Ricci, Ruggiero 781, 1024
Riccio, Giovanni Battista 404
Rice, Tony 413
Rich, Buddy 1029
Richmond, Mike 761
Richter, Franz Xaver 378
Ries, Tim 400
Riggs, Chuck 494, 1253
Right Time 494
Rigoletto 1354
Riley, Ben 421
Riley, Herlin 285, 606, 739, 741, 742, 744
Rimsky-Korsakov, Nikolai 241, 875, 1030–1034, 1322
Ring Without Words 1384
Rio After Dark 236
Rio Grande 652
Rios, Carlos 298, 486, 1135
Rite of Spring see *Le Sacre du Printemps*
Ritenour, Lee 425, 484, 485, 1126, 1141
Ritual Observances 385
Rivera, Paquito de 236, 463, 910, 1035, 1036, 1299
Rivers, Mavis 1037, 1438
Rizner, Fred 829
Road Apples 1315
Road Less Traveled 1196
Robbin, Catherine 511
Robbins, Mark 1119
Robert, Stephen 1340
Robert Shaw Festival Singers 999
Roberts, Marcus 739, 740–742, 744, 1039, 1040
Roberty, Kelly 879

Robinson, Justin 529
Rochberg, George 1362
Rochester Chamber Orchestra 522
Rockwell, Bob 1041
Rodby, Steve 788
Rodeo 288, 293, 294
Rodgers, Richard 185, 189, 1042–1044
Roditi, Claudio 464
Rodney, Red 1045
Rodrigo, Joaquin 1046, 1049
Roelant, Alain 909
Roger Wagner Chorale 1308
Rogers, Nigel 352
Rogers, Patsy 698
Roker, Mickey 538
Roland RSS System 707
Rolfe, Anthony 211, 834
Roll the Bones 1066
Rollins, Sonny 1048
Roman Carnival Overture 156
Roman Festivals 1025, 1026
Romanian Folk Dances 95
Romano, Eustachio 1022
Romantic Cello Favorites 944
Romantic Overture 1289
Romeo and Juliet 151, 965–967, 1269, 1274, 1277, 1278, 1282
Romero, Angelo 1313
Romero, Lito 1313
Roney, Wallace 172, 354, 1195, 1196, 1415, 1417
Ronstadt, Linda 1051
Roos, Lars 682, 683
Ropartz, Guy 1050
Ropin' the Wind 213
Roque-Alsina, Carlos 1047
Rorem, Ned 1052, 1053
Rosamunde 1107
Rosauro, Ney 666
Rosenberger, Carol 130, 392, 525, 527, 550, 553, 894, 956, 1101, 1397
Der Rosenkavalier 1230
Rosenkranz-Sonaten 165
Rosenmüller, Johann 1054
Rosenthal, Moriz 1055, 1220
Ross, Diana 1056
Rossi, Luigi 871
Rossini, Gioacchino 186, 254, 318, 1057–1059, 1198, 1322
Rossy, Jorge 1035
Rostropovich, Mstislav 1104
Roth, David Lee 1060, 1061
Roth, Jerry 1309
Rothko Chapel 399
Rounder Recordings 413
Roussel, Albert 334
Rousset, Christophe 77, 1003

Index

Rowan, Peter 413
Rowlands, Patsy 1200
Rowles, Jimmy 1062
Rowles, Stacy 1062
Royal Liverpool Philharmonic Orchestra 592, 754
Royal Philharmonic Orchestra 195, 204, 314, 358, 472, 583, 655, 835, 995, 1073, 1157, 1172, 1270, 1280, 1285, 1342, 1345, 1391
Royal Philharmonic Pops Orchestra 727
Royal Scottish National Orchestra 90, 636, 716, 889, 961, 971, 991, 1034, 1090, 1159, 1164, 1169, 1170, 1422
Rozario, Patricia 713
Rozsa, Miklos 579
Rubaja, Bernardo 1063
Rubinstein, Anton 251, 1070
Rückert Lieder 706
Rudel, Julias 974
Ruiz, Hilton 728, 1064
Rush 1065, 1066
Rushen, Patrice 1155
Russian Easter Festival Overture 875
Russo, Marc 1431, 1433-1435
Rutter, John 1405
Rydl, Kurt 1230
Rykodisc Recordings 322, 539, 540, 1443, 1444
Sabre Dance 641

Sacks, Steve 234, 236
Le Sacre du Printemps 1244-1249
Saeverud, Harald 1423
Saffer, Lisa 513
Sail Away 533
Saint James Baroque Players 512
Saint Louis Symphony Orchestra 85, 86, 170, 288, 385, 524, 711, 1276, 1337
Saint Saëns, Camile 187, 360, 420, 427, 1019, 1050, 1072, 1073
Saint Stephen's Chamber Orchestra 1392
Salomaa, Petteri 136
Saloman String Quartet 547, 847
Salsa Meets Jazz 976
Saluzzi, Dino 347
Salzburger Barockensemble 79
Sameth, Hene 134
Sample, Joe 319
Sampson, David 12
San Francisco Symphony Orchestra 572, 630, 890, 891, 1072
San Giovanni Battista 1217
Sanborn, David 146, 487, 609, 1074, 1131

Sanchez, Michitos 410
Sándor, György 102
Sandström, Sven-David 628
Sant'Ambrogio, Sara 161
Santana 1075
Saporito, Jim 893
Sarabande 566
Satie, Erik 187, 1313, 1337
Saturday Night at the Blue Note 930
Saul 515
Saul & David 888
Sax, Doug 403
Saxophone Music 207, 223, 421, 422, 433, 441, 468, 476, 494, 538, 651, 664, 695, 734-736, 791, 806, 809-815, 893, 933, 942, 1035, 1084, 1087, 1134-1136, 1260, 1427-1429
Saxotic Stomp 422
Scarani, Giuseppe 1199
Scarlatti, Alessandro 387, 909, 1320
Scarlatti, Domenico 1078, 1079
Scenes from Adolescence 1081
Scenes from the Southside 590
Schaeffer, Steve 1205
Schafer, R Murray 1307
Schatz, Mark 413
Scheherazade 1032-1034
Scher, Tony 346
Schiff, David 1081
Schlick, Barbara 507
Schmelzer, Johann Heinrich 79, 166, 1080, 1082, 1083
Schmidt, Andreas 706, 862
Schneider, Michael 1373
Schneiderman, Rob 1084, 1260
Schnittke, Alfred 801, 1085-1088
Schoenberg, Arnold 649, 1089, 1090
Schola Antiqua 866, 867
Schola Cantorum Basiliensis 897
Schola Hungarica 140, 368, 431, 478-480, 663, 766, 941, 943
Schola of the Hofburgkapelle, Vienna 477
Schönberg, Claude-Michel 184, 1091-1094
Schönherz, Richard 1095
Schöpfung 543, 544
Schubert, Franz: Orchestral/Choral Works 1099; Orchestral Works 1105-1112; Small Ensemble Music 318, 1096-1098, 1100, 1103, 1104; Solo Piano 684, 1101; Solo Vocal 25, 28, 254, 1102
Schuller, Ed 915, 1113
Schuller, George 915, 1113
Schuller, Gunther 12, 1114
Schulz-Evler, Adolf 1220

Index

Schuman, William 1114
Schumann, Robert: Orchestral 1117–1121; Organ 248, 906; Piano 684; Small Ensemble 199, 251, 318, 956; Vocal 25, 665, 1116, 1447
Schunk, Gary 646
Schütz, Georg 672
Schütz, Heinrich 1122
Schütz Choir of London 136, 862
Schuur, Diane 1123–1129
Schuur Thing 1126
Schwartz, Harvie 469, 1130
Schwarz, Michael 1375
Scofield, John 223, 534, 780, 1131, 1132
Scott, Aaron 1327
Scott, Peter 1095
Scott, Robert 1154
Scott, Stephen 529
Scott, Tom 1127, 1133–1146
Scottish Chamber Orchestra 549, 550, 553, 561, 749, 774, 841, 864, 865, 1250
Scottish Opera Orchestra 1399
Scotto, Renata 1355
Scriabin, Alexander 874, 1068, 1137, 1281
Scythian Suite 961, 1244
Sea 636
Sea Symphony 1341, 1342
Seasons 1275
Seaton, Lynn 7
Seattle Symphony Orchestra 6, 91, 96, 160, 290, 293, 344, 345, 481, 523, 525–527, 938, 967, 1010, 1119, 1221, 1228, 1236, 1264
Second Rhapsody for Orchestra 453
Second Sonata in D 1358
Security 434
See, Janet 1374
Seeger, Ruth Crawford 698
Segerstam, Leif 408
Self, Jim 251
Self Portraits 1404
Selma y Salaverde, Bartolomé 869
Selon Mexico 297
Sequentia 932, 1366
Serenade for Flute, Harp and Strings 526
Serenade in C for Strings 1276
Serenade to Music 1348
Serendipity 442
Serkin, Rudolf 119
Serrie, John 1139
Setting 953
Seventh One 1312
Severinsen, Carl "Doc" 168, 1141–1145, 1322
Shades 1434
Shades of Gray 82

Shades of Rio 697
Shades of the World 10
Shadowfax 1146
Shadows 'n' Dreams 760
Shake Me Up 687
Shaking the Tree 435
Shank, Bud 1407
Shankar, Ravi 1157, 1148
Shapiro, Bernard 1264
Share My Dream 893
Sharon, Ralph 142, 143
Sharp, John 212, 307
Sharp, William 161
Sharpe, Avery 811, 1318
Shaughnessy, Ed 168
Shaw, Marlena 1413
Shaw, Rich 401
Shaw, Woody 1149
Shayne, Tracy 1093, 1094
Shearing, George 1150–1152, 1310, 1311
Shéhérazade 1018
Sheffield Labs Recordings 610–612, 725
Shelley, Howard 1347
Shelton, Lucy 6
Shepherd Moons 383
Shew, Bobby 730, 1153
Shimell, William 56, 652
Shipps, Stephen 1392
Shirley-Quirk, John 210
Shola Hungarica 3, 11, 140, 368, 431, 478–480, 663, 766, 941, 943
Short, Bobby 1154
Short Stories 146
Shorter, Wayne 758, 1155
Shostakovich, Dmitri: Orchestral 1157–1175, 1251; Piano 1176; Small Ensemble 1070, 1156
Shuffle Off to Buffalo 378
Sibelius, Jean 1177–1184, 1288
Siete Canciones Populares Españolas 390
Silver, Sheila 1194
Silvertone Recordings 489
Simmons, Norman 1412
Simon, Carly 1185, 1186
Simon, Paul 1187–1189
Simonds, Bruce 908
Simpson, Marietta 57
Sinfonia Antarctica 1346
Sinfonia Varsovia 857
Sinfonieorchester des Norddentschen Rundfunks Hamburg 214
Sinfonie-Orchester Frankfurt 157
Sinfonietta 334, 613
Sinfonye 137, 311
Sire Recordings 1256
Sisu 229

Six, Jack 950
Six Maeterlinck Songs 721
Six Pack 1440
Six Prussian Sonatas 33
Sixteen 1263
Sky Crying 1336
Skynyrd, Lynyrd 1190
Skyscraper 1061
Slatkin, Leonard 86
Slaughter 1191
Slavonic Rhapsodies 363
Sleeping Beauty 1285
Slovak Chamber Orchestra 825
Slovak Philharmonic Orchestra 1446
Smedley, Bruce 1405
Smedvig, Rolf 561
Smetana, Bedrich 1194, 1194
Smith, Alexis 948
Smith, Bob 795
Smith, Hale 1194
Smith, Hopkinson 303
Smith, Marvin 468, 577, 619, 1150, 1195, 1196, 1396
Smith, Norm 602
Smith, Philip 666
Smith, Steve 1211
Smithson String Quartet 546
Smooth Sailing 1084
Smulyan, Gary 659–661
Snidero, Jim 700, 1197
Snow, Phoebe 487
Snyder, Barry 305
So Far So Close 375
Soft Lights and Hot Music 662
Soft Lights and Sweet Music 866
Soldier's Tale 1250, 1251
Soler, Antonio 748
Solisti Italiani 505
Solisti Veneti 1372
Soloff, Lew 377
Solow, Jeffrey 1287
Solti, Georg 100
Sombrero de Tres Picos 391, 392, 1046
Something Constructive 617
Something Different This Way Comes 692
Sonare-Quartett 650
Sonata da Camera and Sinfonie 1054
Sonatas pour Flûte à Bec et Basse Continue 497
Sondheim, Stephen 184, 1200
Song X 787
Song of the Nightengale 1236
Songbook for Orchestra 1044
Songs of a Wayfarer 706
Sony Recordings 59, 75, 102, 183, 184, 189, 197, 244, 337, 444, 530, 715, 850, 851, 861, 987, 1122, 1231, 1242, 1284, 1352, 1380
Soskin, Mark 1048
Soul Cages 1216
Soul Note Recordings 651
Sound Concepts Electronics 705
Soundstream Recording System 722
Sousa, John Philip 183
Soustrot, Bernard 1319
Sowerby, Leo 440, 908, 1203, 1405
Spaulding, James 421
Speak Low 808
Speaking in Tongues 1256
Special Music Recordings 452
Spector, Daniel 1296
Speculum Musicae 246
Spence, Patricia 510, 513
Spencer, Charles 1058
Sperger, Johannes 378
Spielstücke 573
Spies 1204, 1205
Spin 1435
Spinacino, Francesco 1022
Spinal Tap 1206
Spirits Dancing in the Flesh 1075
Spirituals 491
Spohr, Ludwig 1447
Spoiled Girl 1186
Spontaneous Inventions 758
Spring 636
Staatskapelle Berlin 1109
Staatsopernchor and Staatskapelle Dresden 1230
Stachowizc, Peter Damian 909
Stamm, Ruth 796, 1405
Standard Time 740–742
Standing Room Only 490
Stardust 468
Starer, Robert 1207
Starker, János 91, 345, 549, 944
Starlight 916
Start Here 780
State of the Tenor 562, 563
Staunton, Imelda 1200
Steel Symphony 1115
Steele-Perkins, Cristan 602
Steely Dan 1210
SteepleChase Recordings 313, 755, 761, 1041
Steiner, Max 180, 579
Steinsky, Ulrike 864, 865
Stephen Hill Singers 958
Steps Ahead 1211
Stern, Mike 146, 1130, 1212–1214
Stevens, Halsey 251
Stevens, John 12
Stewart, Bill 695, 1132

Index

Stick It Live 1191
Sticks and Stones 488
Still, William Grant 1215
Still Harry After All These Years 612
Still Life (Talking) 788
Sting 1216
Stirps Jesse 432
Stockholm Philharmonic Orchestra 1088, 1137, 1223
Stoltzman, Richard 409, 829
Stolz, Robert 1447
Stone, Dave 610, 611
Stones 818
Stories 534
Storm 403
Storm Rising 1197
Stow, Bill 394
Stradella, Alessandro 602, 1217
Straight Street 702
Strata Institute 1218
Strathclyde Concerto 749
Strauss, Johann 1219, 1220
Strauss, Richard: Opera 1230; Orchestral 1221, 1222, 1224–1229; Small Ensemble 1223; Vocal 25, 28, 637, 696
Strauss, Ron 701
Stravinsky, Igor: Orchestral 83, 1232–1241, 1244–1251; Orchestral/Choral 1231; Small Ensemble 618, 801, 1070, 1242, 1243; Vocal 465
Streamlines 1134
Street Dreams 753
Street Scene 1399
Streisand, Barbra 1252
Strike Up the Band 232, 456
Stripling, Byron 106
Stubenhaus, Neil 1125, 1133–1135
Styne, Jule 184
Suite for a Large Orchestra 363
Suite for Orchestra 1289
Suite from Katerina Ismailova 1169
Suite from the Opera "Merry Mount" 526
Suite in A 1004
Suite Provençal 334
Sullivan, Arthur 460
Sullivan, Maxine 1253
Sultanov, Alexei 1272
Summers, Bob 107
Summers Last Will and Testament 652
Summit Brass 12, 571
Summit Recordings 12, 251, 282, 571, 830, 885
Sunnyside Recordings 138, 565, 566, 639, 640, 881
Supraphon Recordings 88
Surfin' USA 112, 922

Surprises de l'Amour 1006
Susanna 516
Sutherland, Peter 726
Swainson, Neil 1152
Swallow, Steve 173, 174
Swan Lake 1284, 1285
Swanson, Rick 1255
Sweelinck, Jan Pieterszoon 226, 530
Sweet, Sharon 1350
Sweet and Lovely 807
Swenson, Joseph 76
Swingin' Sweet 1253
Symphonic Dances 985, 997
Symphonic Metamorphosis 572
Symphonie Fantastique 152–156
Symphonieorchester des Bayerischen Rundfunks 545, 1227, 1350
Symphony in Three Movements 1239
Symphony on a Hymn Tune 1304
Symphony Orchestra of Russia 789
Szabo, Frank 110

TVT Recordings 283
Tack, Ernie 1141, 1142
Tactus Recordings 870
Tafelmusik 444
Tag, Christian Gotthilf 270
Taira, Yoshihisa 229, 1047
Taktakishvili, Otar 1067
Talk to Your Daughter 423
Talkin' 'Bout You 1127
Talking Heads 1256
Tallis, Thomas 1257–1259
Tallis Scholars 309, 458, 632, 917–919, 1076, 1257, 1259, 1262, 1357
Talvi, Ilkka 6
Tana, Akira 492, 806, 807, 1260
Tanaka, Toshimitsu 666
Tanglewood Festival Chorus 190
Tarack, Gerald 794
Taras Bulba 613, 614
Target 1135
Tarr, Edward 273, 379, 748, 960
Tartini, Giuseppe 561
Tasso Lamento and Trionfo 674
Tate, Buddy 495, 496
Tate, Grady 495, 496, 866
Tausig, Karl 1220
Tavener, John 1261
Taverner, John 1262, 1263
Taylor, Art 412
Taylor, Deems 1264
Tchaikovsky, Peter: Orchestral 963, 1265–1269, 1274, 1276–1285, 1288; Orchestral/Vocal 1273; Piano Solo 1068, 1275; Piano Concerto 1270–

Index

1272; Small Ensemble 1286, 1287; Vocal 1069, 1447
Tcherepnin, Alexander 1289
Tears of Joy 16
Te Kanawa, Kiri 754, 837, 975, 1219, 1230
Tee, Richard 1134
Teeter, Lara 449
Telarc Recordings 40, 52, 57, 65, 66, 67, 84, 105, 117, 119, 121, 122, 131, 150, 155, 156, 168, 170, 171, 192, 195, 204, 211, 216, 224, 269, 294, 296, 358, 367, 373, 393, 397, 406, 407, 426, 436, 455, 460, 463, 464, 495, 496, 506, 511, 519, 544, 556, 559, 561, 575, 579, 583, 585, 630, 706, 711, 723, 728, 749, 770, 777, 794, 832, 841, 852, 864, 865, 876, 877, 900, 905, 907, 922, 928–930, 952, 966, 988, 995, 996, 999, 1021, 1023, 1027, 1030, 1033, 1042, 1044, 1049, 1073, 1099, 1100, 1110, 1115, 1118, 1120, 1145, 1154, 1162, 1163, 1178, 1179, 1193, 1204, 1205, 1208, 1222, 1225, 1229, 1233, 1234, 1247, 1248, 1266, 1267, 1269, 1270, 1272, 1274, 1276, 1278, 1280, 1285, 1313, 1322, 1337, 1342, 1345, 1353, 1376, 1382, 1384, 1391, 1418
Teldec Recordings 53, 125, 515, 584, 604, 665, 720, 1116, 1121, 1168, 1180, 1238, 1272, 1274, 1294, 1383
Telemann, Georg Philipp: Orchestral 1294, 1297; Small Ensemble 89, 960, 1290–1293, 1295, 1296, 1318, 1319, 1364; Solo Instrument 71, 250
Tempest 1265
Tenebrae Responsories for Holy Saturday 458
Terfel, Bryn 598
Terry, Clark 377, 495, 496, 730, 940, 1298–1300
Tesarowicz, Romuald 873
Tesla 1301–1303
Testament of Tristan 158
Tetzlaff, Christian 613
Theodore, David 1343
These Rooms 493
Thielmans, Toots 626
Theisen, Kristin 1447
Thelonica 412
Them Changes 1136
Them or Us 1443
Then and Now 1045, 1396
Theodora 517
There Is Always One More Time 643
These Things Shall Be 598
Thick in the South 743

Third Suite for Cello 1261
This Is a Recording 417
This Is New 732
This Is Now 326
This Time the First Four Years 320
This Woman 914
Thomas, David 497, 498, 517
Thomas, Jeffrey 517, 836
Thomas, Michael Tilson 453
Thompson, Phil 394
Thomson, Virgil 27, 1304
Thorburgh, Elaine 1078
Thorne, Francis 950
Thorne, Nicholas 927
Thornton, Jon 212, 394
Thornton, Steve 327
Thorofon Recordings 784, 1447
Three-Cornered Hat see *El Sombrero de Tres Picos*
Three Transcendental Etudes 677
Through the Looking Glass 1264
Thus Spake Zarathustra see *Also Sprach Zarathustra*
Tico!! 1036
Till Eulenspiegel 1226, 1227
Tilney, Colin 871
Time In Place 1214
Timeless 1128
Timeless All Stars 1306
Timeless Recordings 1326
Times Like These 223
Tiomkin, Dmitri 180
Tippett, Michael 1307
Tisné, Antoine 1363
Titanic Recordings 694, 853
Titus, Alan 1350
To Bird with Love 327, 463
To Diz with Love 464
Toccata Francese 573
Tod und Verklärung 1226
Tokyo String Quartet 829
Tomasi, Henri 627, 982
Tomato Records 346, 347
Tomawa-Sintow, Anna 831
Tomlinson, John 1383
Tompkins, Ross 1142, 1143
Tonight Show Band 1142–1144
Tooley, Ron 377
Toomey, John 402
Torelli, Giuseppe 561
Tormé, Mel 1309–1311
Toronto Chamber Orchestra 1367
Tosca 975
Toth, Jerry 756
Toto 1312
Touch of Light 370
Toulon Days 926

Index

Toussaint, Jean 172
Toward an Unknown Region 1346
Towns, Efrem 349
Tozer, Geoffrey 764
Tragically Hip 1315
Tragicomedia 350, 983
Trauermusik 572
Travelers & Thieves 175
La Traviata 1355
Travis, Randy 1316, 1317
Treasure Island 139
Treestone 6
Triangular 931
Tribute 616
Tribute to Count Basie 535
Tricycle 418
Trio 83 159
Trio Jeepy 736
Trio l'Europa Galante 176
Trio Sonnerie 304, 1005
Trios for Baryton, Viola and Cello 560
Triplicate 578
Trittico Botticelliano 1023
Trois Nocturnes 339
Tromboncino, Bartolomeo 1031
Trombone Music 318, 1032–1034, 1050
Trompeten Consort Friedemann Immer 79, 89
Tropic Affair 212
Trumpet Music 27, 89, 166, 241, 250, 270, 273, 282, 379, 401–403, 408, 462–464, 532, 542, 561, 602, 738–744, 748, 796, 885, 909, 960, 982, 1141–1145, 1153, 1156, 1297, 1298, 1300, 1318–1322, 1363–1365
Trumpets in Stride 885
Trumpets No End 1153
Tuba Music 251
Tubb, Evelyn 805
Tucker, Mark 54
Tucker, Mickey 619
Tucker, Tanya 1323
Tuckwell, Barry 648
Tull, Dave 402
Tuncboyaci, Arto 347
Tunnel 419
Turangalîla-Symphonie 785
Turina, Joaquín 1049
Turner, Danny 104
Turner, Joe 109
Turning for Home 1020
Turre, Steve 23, 1149
Two by Four 626
Two of a Kind 568
Two on One 217
Tye, Christopher 1325
Tyner, McCoy 813, 1326–1328

UK Orchestra Limited 142
USSR Ministry of Culture Symphony Orchestra 1277
Uittenbosch, Anneke 33
Ulster Orchestra 111, 802
Unforgettable 280
Unforgettably Doc 1145
Union 1437
University of California Berkeley Chamber Chorus 399, 510, 516
Un-Led-Ed 353
Upchurch, Phil 1414
Upfront 1074
Upshaw, Dawn 83, 465, 544, 862
Uptown Recordings 411
Uptown Ruler 744
Utah Symphony Orchestra 154

Vaché, Warren 7, 1329
Vai, Steve 1330
Valdepeñas, Joaquin 830
Valente, Gary 1113
Valentin, Dave 1064, 1331
Valentini, Giuseppe 1349
Valois Recordings 5
Valsa da Dor 1361
Valse 1008, 1017, 1018
Valses Nobles et Sentimentales 1011, 1017
van Asperen, Bob 530
van Dam, José 336, 543, 1383
van der Kamp, Harry 55
van de Vate, Nancy 698
van Evera, Emily 869
Vangelis 180, 1332
Van Halen 1333
van Immerseel, Jos 838, 839, 843, 844
van Landeghem, Jan 909
van Ness, Jard 147, 721, 962
van Noordt, Anthoni 530
Van Zant, Johnny 1334
Varady, Julia 515
Varcoe, Stephen 54, 595
Variationen über das Motiv von Bach Liebesträume 678
Variations on a Theme of Chopin 998
Variations on a Theme of Corelli 998
Vasconcelos, Nana 752
Vaucher, François 674
Vaughan, Stevie Ray 1336
Vaughan Brothers 1335
Vaughan Williams, Ralph: Orchestral Vocal 595, 1340, 1341; Orchestral 1276, 1337, 1338, 1342–1348; Small Ensemble 1405; Vocal 903, 1339
Vazquez, Roland 287

Index

Veal, Reginald 285, 739, 741, 742, 744
Vegas, Carlos 1125
Vejvanovsky, Pavel Joseph 79
Veracini, Francesco Maria 1202
Verdi, Giuseppe 150, 684, 1350, 1355
Verklärte Nacht 649
Vermeer Quartet 125
Verve Recordings 529, 1402–1404, 1413
Vespers 999
Vichnievskaïa, Galina 873, 972
Victoria, Tomás 1356, 1357
Victory at Sea 1042
La Vida Breve 393
Videmus 1215
Vienna Philharmonic Orchestra 196, 215, 336, 366, 543, 833, 851, 1219, 1222, 1225, 1229
Vienna State Opera Choir *see* Konzertvereingung Wiener Staatsoperchor
Vierne, Louis 1358
Views from the Oldest House 1052
Vignoles, Roger 199, 357
Village Vangard 625, 659, 660
Villa-Lobos, Heitor 1359–1361
Vincent, Randy 113
Vinci, Gerry 1128
Vinson, Eddie "Cleanhead" 109, 1414
Vintage Year 1311
Viola Music 149, 199, 560, 574, 593, 850, 1070, 1194, 1207, 1362
Violin Highlights 6, 35, 68, 76, 87, 177, 245, 304, 305, 524, 613, 769–771, 776, 778, 781, 850, 861, 1024, 1085, 1096, 1215, 1288, 1371, 1375
Virgin Classics Recordings 32, 41, 245, 304, 352, 554, 613, 813, 903, 1005, 1261, 1340, 1369, 1371
Virgin Recordings 605, 883
Virtuoso Johann Strauss 1220
Vitry, Phillipe de 1366
Vivaldi, Antonio 52, 1198, 1202, 1313, 1367–1379
Vocalese 729
Volans, Kevin 1408
Vollenweider, Andreas 1381
von Essen, Eric 1062
Von Krufft, Nicholas 194
von Otter, Anne S. 56, 135, 834, 1230
von Stade, Frederica 945
von Suppé, Franz 186
Voyage 306

Wagner, Richard 684, 1380, 1382–1384
Waiting for Spring 144
Waiting in the Wings 640
Waldteufel, Emil 27

Walker, Sarah 136, 357, 1355
Wallace, Frank 24
Wallace, John 1297, 1365
Wallace, Matt 402
Waller, Fats 1385
Wallfisch, Peter 342
Wallfisch, Raphael 342, 635
Walrath, Jack 879
Walther, Johann Gottfried 1080
Walton, Cedar 809, 811, 1306, 1386
Walton, William 342, 1387–1391
Wand of Youth 371
Wang, Jian 956
War and Peace 972
Ward, Robert 1392
Warlock, Peter 1393
Warm Breeze 110
Warm Evenings 1329
Warner Brothers Recordings 348, 389, 417, 423, 425, 607, 609, 646, 686, 693, 705, 816, 817, 819, 959, 984, 1060, 1061, 1138, 1187–1189, 1316, 1317, 1333, 1439, 1440
Warnes, Jennifer 1394, 1395
Warning 276
Washer, Bill 236, 263
Washington, Freddie 646
Washington, Grover 274, 1396
Washington, Kenny 220, 222, 761, 792, 1299, 1400, 1427
Washington, Peter 172, 228, 532, 1197
Wasps 1338, 1348
Water Music 519–521
Watermark 384
Watkinson, Carolyn 497
Watts, Ernie 1135, 1141
Watts, Jeff 9, 645, 732, 734, 736, 737, 740, 743
Way It Is 591
Weaver of Dreams 483
Weber, Carl Maria 268, 684, 1050
Webern, Anton 203, 1090
Weckerlin, Jean-Baptiste 427
Weckl, Dave 298, 485, 893, 925
Weill, Kurt 1399
Weins, Edith 714
Weiss, Michael 1400
Welcher, Dan 12
Well-Tempered Clavier 73, 74
Welsh National Opera Chorus 281, 460, 975
Welsh National Orchestra 281, 460
Welt Music Recordings 872
We're Only in It for the Money/Lumpy Gravy 1444
Werner, Gregor Joseph 1318
Werner, Kenny 659–662, 695

Index

Wernick, Richard 1207
Wertico, Paul 788
Wess, Frank 1401
Wessman, Harri 408
Western Wynde Mass 1263
Westminster Cathedral Choir 920, 954, 1356
Weston, Randy 1402-1404
Westray, Ronald 1040
What I Do I Do with Me 1323
Wheeler, Kenny 577
When Lilacs Last in the Dooryard Bloom'd 575
Whigham, Jiggs 1407
Whirlwind 470
Whispers and Promises 646
White, Willard 754
Why I Like Coffie 879
Why Lady Why? 819
Why Patterns? 399
Widor, Charles Marie 907, 1038, 1072
Wiener Akademie 1370
Wiener Kammerorchester 825
Wiener Singverein 543
Wiesler, Manuela 628, 1067
Wiest, Steve 403
Wiggins, Phil 249
Wild, Earl 266, 680, 684, 765, 998
Wilde, David 1422
Wilkins, Jack 915
Wilkins, Rick 756
Wilkinson, Colm 1091, 1092
William Bennett and Friends 1359
William Tell 1059
Williams, Buddy 461
Williams, Buster 809, 811, 814, 1306
Williams, David 812
Williams, Hank, Jr 258, 1410
Williams, James 533, 1196, 1411
Williams, Janet 510
Williams, Joe 1412-1414
Williams, John 180-183, 186, 579
Williams, Mike 105
Williams, Robin 758
Williams, Tim 172
Williams, Todd 739, 741, 744, 1040
Williams, Tony 791, 977, 1415-1417
Willison, David 209, 372, 1393
Willson, Meredith 1418
Wilson, Dennis 106
Wilson, Glenn 138
Wilson, Nancy 1419-1421
Wilson, Scott 1119
Wilson, Thomas 1207, 1422
Wilson, Todd 359
Winard, Kevin 1037
Winbergh, Gösta 833

Winchester Cathedral Choir 691, 1325
Windham Hill Recordings 14-16, 310, 1063, 1095, 1445
Winds of Change 761
Windsock 1255
Winter, Bob 189
Winter, Paul 1424
Winter Pages 1053
Wise, Alan 400
Wispelwey, Pieter 70, 116
Witham, David 1204
Wolfe, Benjamin 284, 286
Wonder, Stevie 1425
Wooden Prince 103
Woods, Dave 1309
Woods, Phil 725, 1426-1429
Woods, Robert 1115
World Pacific Recordings 780
World Sinfonia 347
Wortman, Kurt 1095
Wright, Wayne 933
Württembergisches Kammerorchester Heilbronn 39

X, the Life and Times of Malcolm X 330
Xenakis, Iannis 1047, 1430

Yacoh, Yuqiujiro 1313
Yale Cellos 1212
Yamaha 23, 53, 107, 114, 153, 179, 237, 341, 413, 424, 447, 495, 512, 659, 664, 707, 734, 750, 788, 809, 887, 993, 1043, 1045, 1239, 1297, 1352, 1426, 1446
Yashino, Fujimaru 916
Yellow Jackets 1431-1435
Yes 1436, 1437
Young, John Bell 892
Young, Snooky 430, 535, 1144, 1401
Young, Thomas 330
Young Man 332
Yours and Mine 1260

ZZ Top 1439, 1440
Zádori, Mária 1378
Zappa, Frank 1441-1444
Die Zauberflöte 862-865
Zelenka, Jan Dismas 282
Zenlensky, Alexander 721
Zerer, Wolfgang 1296
Ziegler, Delores 57
Ziesak, Ruth 863
Zeitlin, Denny 1445
Zemlinsky, Alexander von 1446